T0270908

How a Ledger Became a Central Bank

Before the US Federal Reserve and the Bank of England, the Bank of Amsterdam ("Bank") was a dominant central bank with a global impact on money and credit. *How a Ledger Became a Central Bank* draws on extensive archival data and rich secondary literature to offer a new and detailed portrait of this historically significant institution. It describes how the Bank struggled to manage its money before hitting a modern solution: fiat money in combination with a repurchase facility and discretionary open market operations. It describes techniques the Bank used to monitor and stabilize its money stock, and how foreign sovereigns could exploit the liquidity of the Bank for state finance. Closing with a discussion of commonalities of the Bank of Amsterdam with later central banks, including the Federal Reserve, this book has generated a great deal of excitement among scholars of central banking and the role of money in the macroeconomy.

Stephen Quinn is Professor of Economics at Texas Christian University. He has published extensively on the origins of banking in London and Amsterdam, which has awarded him a visiting lectureship at the Bank of England and a *New York Times Magazine* Idea of the Year.

William Roberds is a Research Economist and Senior Advisor at the Federal Reserve Bank of Atlanta. He has been an economist with the Federal Reserve since 1984 and has published academic research in the areas of finance, monetary policy, payment systems, and central bank history.

STUDIES IN MACROECONOMIC HISTORY

Series Editor: Michael D. Bordo, Rutgers University

Editors:

Owen F. Humpage, *Federal Reserve Bank of Cleveland*
Christopher M. Meissner, *University of California, Davis*
Kris James Mitchener, *Santa Clara University*
David C. Wheelock, *Federal Reserve Bank of St. Louis*

The titles in this series investigate themes of interest to economists and economic historians in the rapidly developing field of macroeconomic history. The four areas covered include the application of monetary and finance theory, international economics, and quantitative methods to historical problems; the historical application of growth and development theory and theories of business fluctuations; the history of domestic and international monetary, financial, and other macroeconomic institutions; and the history of international monetary and financial systems. The series amalgamates the former Cambridge University Press series Studies in Monetary and Financial History and Studies in Quantitative Economic History.

Other Books in the Series:

Simon Hinrichsen, *When Nations Cannot Default: A History of War Reparations and Sovereign Debt* (2023)

Barry Eichengreen and Andreas Kakridis, *The Emergence of the Modern Central Bank and Global Cooperation: 1919–1939* (2023)

Alain Naef, *An Exchange Rate History of the United Kingdom: 1945–1992* (2021)

Barrie A. Wigmore, *The Financial Crisis of 2008: A History of US Financial Markets 2000–2012* (2021)

Max Harris, *Monetary War and Peace: London, Washington, Paris, and the Tripartite Agreement of 1936* (2021)

Kenneth D. Garbade, *After the Accord: A History of Federal Reserve Open Market Operations, the US Government Securities Market, and Treasury Debt Management from 1951 to 1979* (2020)

Harold James, *Making a Modern Central Bank: The Bank of England 1979–2003* (2020)

Claudio Borio, Stijn Claessens, Piet Clement, Robert N. McCauley, and Hyun Song Shin, Editors, *Promoting Global Monetary and Financial Stability: The Bank for International Settlements after Bretton Woods, 1973–2020* (2020)

Patrick Honohan, *Currency, Credit and Crisis: Central Banking in Ireland and Europe* (2019)

William A. Allen, *The Bank of England and the Government Debt: Operations in the Gilt-Edged Market, 1928–1972* (2019)

Eric Monnet, *Controlling Credit: Central Banking and the Planned Economy in Postwar France, 1948–1973* (2018)

Laurence M. Ball, *The Fed and Lehman Brothers: Setting the Record Straight on a Financial Disaster* (2018)

Rodney Edvinsson, Tor Jacobson, and Daniel Waldenström, Editors, *Sveriges Riksbank and the History of Central Banking* (2018)

Peter L. Rousseau and Paul Wachtel, Editors, *Financial Systems and Economic Growth: Credit, Crises, and the Regulation from the 19th Century to the Present* (2017)

Ernst Baltensperger and Peter Kugler, *Swiss Monetary History since the Early 19th Century* (2017)

Øyvind Eitrheim, Jan Tore Klovland, and Lars Fredrik Øksendal, *A Monetary History of Norway, 1816–2016* (2016)

Jan Fredrik Qvigstad, *On Central Banking* (2016)

Michael D. Bordo, Øyvind Eitrheim, Marc Flandreau, and Jan F. Qvigstad, Editors, *Central Banks at a Crossroads: What Can We Learn from History?* (2016)

Michael D. Bordo and Mark A. Wynne, Editors, *The Federal Reserve's Role in the Global Economy: A Historical Perspective* (2016)

Owen F. Humpage, Editor, *Current Federal Reserve Policy Under the Lens of Economic History: Essays to Commemorate the Federal Reserve System's Centennial* (2015)

Michael D. Bordo and William Roberds, Editors, *The Origins, History, and Future of the Federal Reserve: A Return to Jekyll Island* (2013)

Michael D. Bordo and Ronald MacDonald, Editors, *Credibility and the International Monetary Regime: A Historical Perspective* (2012)

Robert L. Hetzel, *The Great Recession: Market Failure or Policy Failure?* (2012)

Tobias Straumann, *Fixed Ideas of Money: Small States and Exchange Rate Regimes in Twentieth-Century Europe* (2010)

Forrest Capie, *The Bank of England: 1950s to 1979* (2010)

Aldo Musacchio, *Experiments in Financial Democracy: Corporate Governance and Financial Development in Brazil, 1882–1950* (2009)

Claudio Borio, Gianni Toniolo, and Piet Clement, Editors, *The Past and Future of Central Bank Cooperation* (2008)

Robert L. Hetzel, *The Monetary Policy of the Federal Reserve: A History* (2008)

Caroline Fohlin, *Finance Capitalism and Germany's Rise to Industrial Power* (2007)

John H. Wood, *A History of Central Banking in Great Britain and the United States* (2005)

Gianni Toniolo (with the assistance of Piet Clement), *Central Bank Cooperation at the Bank for International Settlements, 1930–1973* (2005)

Richard Burdekin and Pierre Siklos, Editors, *Deflation: Current and Historical Perspectives* (2004)

Pierre Siklos, *The Changing Face of Central Banking: Evolutionary Trends since World War II* (2002)

Michael D. Bordo and Roberto Cortés-Conde, Editors, *Transferring Wealth and Power from the Old to the New World: Monetary and Fiscal Institutions in the 17th through the 19th Centuries* (2001)

Howard Bodenhorn, *A History of Banking in Antebellum America: Financial Markets and Economic Development in an Era of Nation-Building* (2000)

Mark Harrison, Editor, *The Economics of World War II: Six Great Powers in International Comparison* (2000)

Angela Redish, *Bimetallism: An Economic and Historical Analysis* (2000)

Elmus Wicker, *Banking Panics of the Gilded Age* (2000)

Michael D. Bordo, *The Gold Standard and Related Regimes: Collected Essays* (1999)

Michele Fratianni and Franco Spinelli, *A Monetary History of Italy* (1997)

Mark Toma, *Competition and Monopoly in the Federal Reserve System, 1914–1951* (1997)

Barry Eichengreen, Editor, *Europe's Postwar Recovery* (1996)

Lawrence H. Officer, *Between the Dollar-Sterling Gold Points: Exchange Rates, Parity and Market Behavior* (1996)

Elmus Wicker, *The Banking Panics of the Great Depression* (1996)

Norio Tamaki, *Japanese Banking: A History, 1859–1959* (1995)

Barry Eichengreen, *Elusive Stability: Essays in the History of International Finance, 1919–1939* (1993)

Michael D. Bordo and Forrest Capie, Editors, *Monetary Regimes in Transition* (1993)

Larry Neal, *The Rise of Financial Capitalism: International Capital Markets in the Age of Reason* (1993)

S. N. Broadberry and N. F. R. Crafts, Editors, *Britain in the International Economy, 1870–1939* (1992)

Aurel Schubert, *The Credit-Anstalt Crisis of 1931* (1992)

Trevor J. O. Dick and John E. Floyd, *Canada and the Gold Standard: Balance of Payments Adjustment under Fixed Exchange Rates, 1871–1913* (1992)

Kenneth Mouré, *Managing the Franc Poincaré: Economic Understanding and Political Constraint in French Monetary Policy, 1928–1936* (1991)

David C. Wheelock, *The Strategy and Consistency of Federal Reserve Monetary Policy, 1924–1933* (1991)

How a Ledger Became a Central Bank

A Monetary History of the Bank of Amsterdam

STEPHEN QUINN
Texas Christian University

WILLIAM ROBERDS
Federal Reserve Bank of Atlanta

CAMBRIDGE
UNIVERSITY PRESS

CAMBRIDGE
UNIVERSITY PRESS

Shaftesbury Road, Cambridge CB2 8EA, United Kingdom

One Liberty Plaza, 20th Floor, New York, NY 10006, USA

477 Williamstown Road, Port Melbourne, VIC 3207, Australia

314–321, 3rd Floor, Plot 3, Splendor Forum, Jasola District Centre, New Delhi – 110025, India

103 Penang Road, #05-06/07, Visioncrest Commercial, Singapore 238467

Cambridge University Press is part of Cambridge University Press & Assessment, a department of the University of Cambridge.

We share the University's mission to contribute to society through the pursuit of education, learning and research at the highest international levels of excellence.

www.cambridge.org
Information on this title: www.cambridge.org/9781108484275

DOI: 10.1017/9781108594752

© Stephen Quinn and William Roberds 2024

First published 2024

A catalogue record for this publication is available from the British Library.

Library of Congress Cataloging-in-Publication Data
Names: Quinn, Stephen, 1966- author. | Roberds, William, author.
Title: How a ledger became a central bank : a Monetary history of the Bank of Amsterdam / Stephen Quinn, Texas Christian University, William Roberds, Federal Reserve Bank of Atlanta.
Description: Cambridge, United Kingdom ; New York, NY : Cambridge University Press, 2024. | Includes bibliographical references and index.
Identifiers: LCCN 2023030261 (print) | LCCN 2023030262 (ebook) | ISBN 9781108484275 (hardback) | ISBN 9781108706155 (paperback) | ISBN 9781108594752 (ebook)
Subjects: LCSH: Amsterdamse Wisselbank. | Banks and banking, Central–Netherlands–Amsterdam–History.
Classification: LCC HG3116 .Q56 2024 (print) | LCC HG3116 (ebook) | DDC 332.1/109492–dc23/eng/20230707
LC record available at https://lccn.loc.gov/2023030261
LC ebook record available at https://lccn.loc.gov/2023030262

ISBN 978-1-108-48427-5 Hardback
ISBN 978-1-108-70615-5 Paperback

For our parents

Contents

Figures

Tables

Acknowledgments

These acknowledgments will begin with an apology, borrowed from Andreades' (1909) history of the Bank of England: What follows is a book about a very Dutch institution, de Amsterdamsche Wisselbank (the Bank of Amsterdam), written by two foreigners and targeted mostly at foreigners. There are many subtleties of Dutch language, history, and culture that for us, as Americans, will forever remain remote. Dutch readers may find our take on the Wisselbank's history to be lacking in nuance if not inaccurate in places. Our hope is that the main messages of the narrative will be compelling enough for informed readers to forgive the inevitable omissions and mistakes.

This book is the culmination of a research project that began twenty-two years ago with a casual conversation between the two authors, at a conference in Colonial Williamsburg organized by the Federal Reserve Bank of Richmond. It has since morphed into an obsession that has tested the patience of our families, our employers, our colleagues, editors of journals where we submitted research papers, but especially our Dutch friends, who have always greeted our unenlightened inquiries with good humor and thoughtful responses. These include Joop Baneke, Ron Berndsen, Christiaan van Bochove, Pit Dehing, Oscar Gelderblom, Joost Jonker, Peter Koudijs, Lodewijk Petram, Menno Polak, Albert Scheffers, and Taco Tichelaar. Dutch treats have not been limited to generous explanations. The authors have enjoyed the hospitality of the Nederlandsch Economisch-Historisch Archief, the Universiteit Utrecht, and the Nederlandsche Bank, including multiple invitations to present seminars at these institutions. We also had the privilege of presenting our work at the Dutch–Belgian Finance and History Workshop. The Stadsarchief Amsterdam has graciously accommodated all requests for access to archival materials, including items that were in the process of restoration and not available to the general public. The staff there brought up many cumbersome, up to 1,000-page, ledgers on our behalf. The Internationaal Instituut voor Sociale Geschiedenis (IISG) provided us with an electronic copy of the Müntz (1769–70) manual. A special debt is owed to Harmen Snel, for help in sorting through the web of Prussian mint entrepreneurs' family relations in Amsterdam, and to Emile van Krefeld, who gave us a memorable tour of the canal house where Isaac de Pinto (likely) entertained Frederick the Great during the latter's fateful 1755 visit to the Dutch Republic. The Bridge Hotel became our home abroad.

We have had much help and encouragement from many other directions. The historical rigor of Chapters 7 and 8 has been improved by comments received at the meetings of the Caltech Early Modern Group. Parts of our research program have been presented at seminars at the Asian Development Bank, at the All-UC Conference on Central Banking in Historical Perspective, at the Fondazione Banco di Napoli, a conference organized by Barnard College, and at numerous universities, including George Mason University, the University of Alabama, the University of Leipzig, the University of North Dakota, Rutgers University, Sciences Po, Texas A&M University, Tokyo University, the University of Illinois, and the University of Texas. We have had many opportunities to convince modern central bankers that the Wisselbank might have some relevance for today. In particular we are grateful for invitations to present our work at the Bank of Canada, the Bank of Japan, conferences organized by the Deutsche Bundesbank and the Nederlandsche Bank, the European Central Bank, the Oesterreichische Nationalbank, and at various places within the Federal Reserve System (the Board of Governors and the Federal Reserve Banks of Atlanta, Chicago, Dallas, New York, and Richmond).

Among the many people who have provided us with helpful comments are Olivier Accominotti, Jeremy Atack, Ulrich Bindseil, Michael Bordo, Toni Braun, Ben Chabot, Bill Collins, Markus Denzel, Brennie Doyle, Roger Farmer, Marc Flandreau, Caroline Fohlin, Virginia France, Shelly Frank, Rod Garratt, Gary Gorton, Robert Hetzel, Anthony Hotson, Clemens Jobst, Stephen Kay, Elizabeth Klee, James Nason, Larry Neal, Nuno Palma, Angela Redish, Rob Reed, Hugh Rockoff, Jared Rubin, Charles Sawyer, Catherine Schenk, Carole Scott, Oz Shy, Peter Stella, Ellis Tallman, John Tammes, Francesca Trivellato, Dan Waggoner, Larry Wall, Kirsten Wandschneider, Warren Weber, and David Weiman. Anonymous referees have provided comments on this book as well as earlier research papers.

Charles Kahn provided us with detailed comments on the first draft of this book. The collective of Dan Bogart, Tracy Dennison, Mauricio

Drelichman, Philip Hoffman, Mallory Hope, Matteo Pompermaier, Jean-Laurent Rosenthal, and Thomas Sargent assayed a subsequent draft. François Velde backed up his many insightful comments with a fantastic dataset of price currents from Hamburg, Anthony Hotson shared his data on coin and bullion prices from Castaing's *Course of Exchange*, and Larry Neal shared his transcriptions of financial assets from the same source. Other people who have generously shared hand-collected data include Marc Flandreau, Clemens Jobst, Klemens Kaps, John McCusker, Pilar Nogues-Marco, Lodewijk Petram, and Albert Scheffers. Sally Burke copyedited our penultimate draft. Texas Christian University (TCU) and the Federal Reserve Bank of Atlanta (Atlanta Fed) generously funded numerous research trips. Jill Kendle and the other staff of the Interlibrary Loan Department of the Mary Couts Burnett Library at TCU have tracked down numerous publications. Similarly, the reference staff at the Atlanta Fed (Ernie Evangelista, Meredith Rector, Rob Sarwark, and Julia Schein) have cheerfully endured dozens of requests for obscure materials. For the past two years, Emory University has provided the second author with access to its libraries, which has been invaluable during a time when pandemic restrictions have limited access to other libraries. The reference staff at Baker Library of Harvard Business School, including Christine Riggle and Melissa Murphy, provided us with publication-quality images from the Müntz (1769–70) manual, including the drawing of the Ephraim smelter shown in Figure 8.10. It bears mention that the Müntz manual came to the Baker Library from the collection of the eminent German historian Paul Wallich, whose work we have relied on for Chapter 8.

The least glamorous but most essential aspect of this project has been the painstaking transcription of data from photographs of archival material. The ledgers and other materials in the Wisselbank archive are remarkable for their completeness and accuracy, but they do not come with user's manuals. A succession of research assistants (Michelle Sloan, Christina Hartlage, Pamela Frisbee, and Jeremy Land) have each endured a segment of our painful journey up the transcription learning curve. An equal amount of grim endurance was displayed by Florence Heybroek, who provided the second author with much-needed tutoring in the Dutch language.

Finishing this book invokes mixed emotions. After twenty years of work, we have arrived at a better understanding of an institution about which we originally planned to write perhaps one short paper. This work has left us with more questions than answers, and it is hard not to be overawed by the volume of unresearched material that remains in the Wisselbank archive. Our general feeling is remarkably close to that of Rhodes (1701, 57), who offered this description of the Wisselbank's location (the Town Hall):

Thô I have been in it five hundred times . . . I can safely say, I beheld it with as much Admiration, the last as the first time I saw it: my Eyes still meeting with new Objects of Wonder; nor could I make a description so exact of it, as to come near to what it really is.

Disclaimer

The views expressed in this book are those of the authors and do not necessarily represent the views of the Federal Reserve Bank of Atlanta or of the Federal Reserve System.

Similar yet Different?

During the Seven Years War, Frederick the Great of Prussia produced many coins that contained much less precious metal than they were supposed to have. The somewhat shady practice was called *debasement*, and such abuse had occurred as long as there had been desperate sovereigns minting coins.[1] The Seven Years War was an especially desperate time for Frederick, who spent much of the conflict expecting to be overwhelmed by the armies of three larger adversaries (Austria, France, and Russia) and their allies. Thanks in part to financial aid provided by debasement, however, Frederick was able to fend off repeated invasions and survive the war. Prussia emerged from the war as an improbable great power and would eventually unify most of Germany into a modern nation-state.[2]

Frederick's operation was one of the last great debasements as money was moving to paper notes and accounts. War finance would increasingly turn to the printing press, but Frederick's Prussia had no central bank, no paper currency, and underdeveloped private banks. To mint its debased coins, Prussia had only limited access to natural deposits of precious metal (some silver was mined in conquered Saxony) and no sovereign credit with which to borrow more metal. Where, then, did Frederick acquire the great quantities of credit and treasure needed to save Prussia? He found it in places that had what Prussia lacked, and the most abundant location for both metal and credit was Amsterdam.

Amsterdam was at that time a major conduit for gold and silver as it flowed from the New World, through Europe, and on to Asia. Amsterdam

---

[1] On the general phenomenon of debasement see Rolnick, Velde, and Weber (1996).
[2] The Seven Years War (1756–1763) was a multi-continent conflict involving many countries. Winston Churchill would later call it "the first world war." The impacts of the war on the Bank of Amsterdam are analyzed in later chapters.

was also a hub of credit with spokes that extended to northern Europe and much of the world beyond. To connect the flow of metal with the flow of credit, the City of Amsterdam operated a public bank, the Bank of Amsterdam (*Amsterdamsche Wisselbank* or simply "the Bank"), which flourished throughout much of the seventeenth and eighteenth centuries. The penultimate chapter of this book will describe how Frederick, and likely other desperate sovereigns, could utilize debts payable through the Bank to access metal flowing through the Bank. The Bank was well suited for these purposes because that was where the money was. At its high tide during the Seven Years War, around one quarter of New World silver production flowed through the Bank, and the Bank accounts backed by that silver were the most secure and liquid currency in Europe. Gillard (2004) terms the Bank's ledger money *le florin européen*, the Euro-florin, and private merchant banks made free use of Euro-florins to create an international system of credit. Engineering a successful debasement meant finding the right merchant with the right connections to Amsterdam.

Its evident power notwithstanding, the Bank was an enigma to contemporaries. This aura of mystery was not accidental. Accounting documents like balance sheets, income statements, and collateral inventories were kept rigorously shielded from public view.[3] Indeed, we will see in Chapter 5 that the Bank itself had difficulty knowing its true financial condition in real time. In the absence of public disclosures, wild rumors circulated. Writing in 1655, the Dutch poet Joost van den Vondel expressed one popular view when he claimed that the Bank had "received all of Peru" into its vaults (meaning this country's immense silver production; see Dehing 2012, 85). Not to be outdone, an English visitor to Amsterdam (Rhodes 1701, 67) guessed that the Bank vaults contained "an infinite number of Bags full of Money already Coin'd." The secretive Bank did little to discourage such flattering hyperbole. Later, more informed estimates of the quantity of precious metal held at the Bank (e.g., Melon 1754, 21; Steuart 1767a, 304; Smith 1981 [1776], 487) overshot the true amount by 50 percent or more.

---

[3] Reflecting the Bank's habit of secrecy, the cover illustration of this book is from an accounting manual and does not depict Bank employees. We can only guess at how well the Bank could keep its secrets among the close-knit Amsterdam financial community. Our conjecture is that the Bank's secrecy was motivated in part by a desire to promote its money as an opaque, "no-questions-asked" asset (cf. Chapter 3), despite a rather complex policy framework (Chapter 7). Some other contemporary public banks, for example, the Bank of Hamburg, pursued less complex policies and were more forthcoming about their financial condition.

The Bank of Amsterdam was liquidated at the close of the Napoleonic era (1820), but its storied activities have remained rather mysterious. This book seeks to illuminate these activities through a reconstruction based on original Bank records over the period from 1666 to 1792.[4] The reconstruction reveals both what the Bank did and what its customers did, with greatest accuracy over much of the eighteenth century (1711–1792), when surviving records are most complete. This analysis (see Chapter 6) shows that customer use of the Bank had large swings in intensity. The reconstructed data also show (see Chapter 7) that the Bank responded to those swings with offsetting actions of its own. Hence, while the Bank held large quantities of desirable gold and silver coins, it was not a simple deposit and withdrawal facility. In the reconstructed balance sheets, the Bank of Amsterdam appears as a central bank, perhaps the first central bank to actively and successfully manage its money stock over a long period.

1.1 Analogies

The thesis of this book is that the Bank of Amsterdam operated much as a modern type of central bank, arguably the first such institution.[5] In making this claim, we recognize that it is undoubtedly anachronistic and perhaps unfair to compare an eighteenth-century enigmatic municipal institution to today's transparent national or even super-national central banks. In the 1700s, worldly people knew of the Bank of Amsterdam, and select people used the Bank, but few understood it. Today, additional centuries of practical experience and academic inquiry have made central banking seem less alchemical than in eighteenth-century Amsterdam. Every country in the world has a central bank and every commercial bank has an account with the central bank. Central banks aspire for policy transparency and regularly publish statements of their financial condition. With some light, however, many aspects of the Bank look strikingly modern. And some people would argue that modern central banks retain a whiff of the Amsterdam alchemy.

---

[4] A limitation of our analysis is that, under currently available technology, transactions recorded in the Bank's archive must be hand transcribed, although machine digitization may become practical in the near future. For this book, about 172,000 ledger transactions were transcribed, or around 1 percent of the total available, from 40,000 photographs taken in the Bank's archives.

[5] At the time of the Bank of Amsterdam's founding, public banks had been operating in Mediterranean Europe for over two centuries. The novelty of the Bank was to combine certain features of earlier public banks with new touches to create an institution with recognizably modern aspects

Certain modernish aspects of the Bank bear special emphasis. To cite one example, at the Bank's founding in 1609, Bank accounts were convertible into silver and gold, but Chapter 5 will show how circumstances ended that convertibility around 1685. Similarly, the Federal Reserve at its founding in 1913 created accounts, called reserves, that were convertible into gold, and circumstances in 1933 put an end to that convertibility for domestic purposes. Such inconvertible money is now called fiat, and the Bank, like modern central banks, successfully offered it.

To give a second example, in recent decades, there has been a worldwide shift of large-value payment systems (used to settle interbank funds transfers) to *real-time gross settlement* (RTGS; see Bech and Hobijn 2018). RTGS systems, which allow for instantaneous transfer of central bank balances, are simply a modern version of the type of payment offered by the Bank of Amsterdam: payor-initiated balance transfers (now known as giro transfers) with no netting or automatic overdrafts (Bech and Garratt 2017).

To cite a third example, select central banks today enjoy an international demand for their fiat accounts. Foreigners with no obligation routinely choose to pay in US dollars, for example, and final settlement of those payments often entails a transfer of account balances at the Federal Reserve (Bank for International Settlements 2020). This settlement function supports a worldwide demand for the Fed dollar (often termed "exorbitant privilege"; see, e.g., Eichengreen 2012), much as a similar demand existed for Bank of Amsterdam money in the eighteenth century.

Unlike modern central banks, the Bank (with rare exceptions) did not issue circulating banknotes, but that distinction is losing relevance. Since the Global Financial Crisis of 2007–2008, for example, the size of reserve accounts at the Federal Reserve and other central banks has come to dwarf the stock of currency in circulation.[6] One reason for the increasing primacy of accounts is the declining use of banknotes as a means of payment in advanced economies.[7] Partly in response to this decline, central banks are considering and, in some cases, already issuing digital currencies. Central bank digital currencies (CBDCs) are essentially a new type of account offered to a wider cross-section of users, rather than the traditional central bank accounts only available to commercial banks and other select

---

[6] For the Federal Reserve, circulating cash now comprises only about 24 percent of total liabilities; pre-GFC this proportion was over 90 percent (*Financial Accounts of the United States*, Table L.109, accessed on August 25, 2022).

[7] Banknotes remain popular in some countries, however (Bagnall et al. 2016), and the use of banknotes as a store of value (i.e., for hoarding) has increased of late (Bech et al. 2018, 71–74).

counterparties (Bank for International Settlements 2021, 77–85). The Bank of Amsterdam's open-access policy of offering central bank accounts to any local merchant now seems less far-fetched than just a few years ago.

Large-scale open market purchases, known as "quantitative easing," are another reason for the relative decline of banknotes. Since the Global Financial Crisis, quantitative easing has dramatically increased the size of central bank balance sheets and account balances. While the scale is new, the technique is not. The early Fed learned to buy and sell "safe assets" (meaning US Treasury debt) in the 1920s (Garbade 2012), and Chapter 5 will explain how the seventeenth-century Bank of Amsterdam similarly learned to buy and sell precious metal. Over the centuries, the type of asset that people consider a *safe asset* (meaning one free from adverse selection; see Gorton 2017) has changed from select coins to select debt, but the buying and selling of safe assets remains the core activity of central banks.

In the early modern era, silver and gold coins were seen as safe in that they held value in most markets around the world, with the most ubiquitous trusted coin being the Spanish dollar (Irigoin 2020). The availability of such coins supported trade as the world economy expanded. Similarly, the rapid growth of the world economy since 1945 has generated an increasing demand for safe assets (Pozsar 2014; Gorton 2017). The international demand for the debt of developed economies, the United States in particular, has been interpreted as a manifestation of this safe-asset demand (Gourinchas, Rey, and Govillot 2017).

Yet another precocious aspect of the Bank of Amsterdam was the means by which it allowed safe assets to be converted to Bank money and vice versa. When customers sold coins to the Bank, they received ledger money (a credit to their Bank account) and a piece of paper called a *receipt*. The receipt was an option to repurchase the coins at a slightly higher price. To effect a repurchase, a customer needed both the receipt and the ledger money. Today, a similar conversion often occurs via *repurchase agreements*, also called repos. A repo is a contract to sell an asset (most often, government debt) and repurchase it at a slightly higher price. Chapter 5 will discuss how a combination of an initial coin sale to the Bank and later exercise of a redemption option often served as a de facto repurchase agreement.

Repurchase is relevant because today's repo markets are both immense and critical to the functioning of modern finance. As of this writing, there are over $4 trillion in outstanding US dollar-denominated repo contracts,[8] of which

---

[8] See the Federal Reserve's *Financial Accounts of the United States*, Table L.207, accessed on September 7, 2021.

more than $2 trillion is transacted each day (Baklanova et al., 2019), the great majority (roughly two-thirds) of these contracts being for US Treasury securities. A 2016 survey (Bank for International Settlements 2017, 5) estimated global repo positions in government bonds to be $8.8 trillion. A more recent estimate (International Capital Market Association 2021) puts the global size of repo in all asset categories at €15 trillion ($17.5 trillion).

Repo has also become both a focus and an important channel for central bank policy. In a crisis, a central bank's support for repo markets can be sudden and large as occurred in 2008 and 2020.[9] Chapter 7 will detail how the Bank also expanded the reach of its repurchase (receipt) facility in response to a financial crisis. In calmer times, modern central banks (the Fed and the European Central Bank (ECB) included) have come to integrate standing repo and reverse repo facilities into their policy frameworks. "Standing" means that the facility has pre-set terms available at the discretion of users, as was the case for the receipt facility of the Bank of Amsterdam. The policy frameworks of central banks such as the Fed and the ECB in effect offer both a floor (lowest rate) and ceiling (highest rate) for repo markets.[10] Modern central banks can offer both because they use repo to borrow and to lend. The Bank only used repurchase to lend, so it offered only a floor, and the implications of that difference will be explored in Chapter 6.

By virtue of the features described above (fiat money, giro settlement, exorbitant privilege, quantitative operations, repo facilities), the Bank of Amsterdam was able to operate much as a modern type of central bank. By "modern," we mean a system where repurchase supports safe assets (sovereign debt today, coins then), where those safe assets back fiat accounts, and where central banks manage the creation and destruction of fiat accounts to support repo liquidity. Walter Bagehot wrote, "Money will not manage itself" (1979 [1873], 10), and the Bank's approach to money management was to divide itself into two parts: passive and active. The passive part was a standing receipt (repurchase) facility that let customers decide when and how much to convert coins into or out of Bank money. The active part was operations wherein the Bank decided when and how much to trade in coins. The two parts shared the same Bank

---

[9] These disruptions are discussed in Chapter 9.

[10] The Fed's use of repos began as early as 1917, when the Fed used repos in US Treasury bonds to facilitate war finance (Garbade 2012, 193). After a long pause in the 1930s and 1940s, the Fed reinstated repos during the 1950s as a way to smooth short-run fluctuations in prices of Treasuries. The Fed's usage of repos was expanded in the 1960s to include repos in longer-term Treasuries, repos in agency securities (those of government-sponsored enterprises), and reverse repos (Garbade 2021, 152–66, 351–70).

money, and the Bank used that connection to direct its discretionary purchases (sales) to offset decreases (increases) in receipts. Through this management strategy, the Bank was able, in its successful years, to control the overall amount of its money.

Although the Bank's behavior was similar enough to be relevant to modern experience, it was different enough to reveal alternative possibilities. For example, the Bank created repo liquidity by issuing options to repurchase rather than entering into explicit repurchase agreements. In this way, claims to coin and Bank money were unbundled into two complementary assets, each providing a customized form of liquidity: ledger account balances for transactions within Amsterdam's credit market, and coin repurchases for transactions with other markets.

Another important difference was the terms under which repo financing was available. The Bank often left repo terms unchanged for long periods. The Fed and other modern central banks change repo rates when they adjust their policy stance, because modern central banks have macroeconomic mandates that translate into interest-rate adjustments to stimulate or cool the economy according to policy objectives. Standing facilities with inflexible terms could bring massive repo flows that might not align with macroeconomic goals. The Bank of Amsterdam did not have macroeconomic goals or even an explicit mandate, so it was free to focus on responding to repurchase activity.

1.2 Origins

The large and persistent demand for the Bank's fiat money is puzzling when one considers that during the early modern era, the concept of money was almost synonymous with coined precious metal.[11] The apparent paradox is resolved, however, by the fact that Bank money was intended to augment rather than displace the liquidity of the predominant metallic monies of the time. If we step back into the twenty-first century and view popular varieties of coins as *platforms* for connecting parties over time and space, then what the Bank offered was effectively a platform of platforms – a channel whereby Amsterdam merchants could exchange and

---

[11] The idea that money fundamentally consisted of precious metal coined by a sovereign had roots in Greek and Roman antiquity and persisted through medieval and early modern times (Ugolini 2017, 221–23; Fox, Velde, and Ernst 2016). In practice, there was often ambiguity as to whether the moneyness of a coin derived from its metallic backing or from its sanction by a sovereign, a theme that is explored in Chapter 3.

borrow against desirable safe assets at the lowest possible cost.[12] Such trading was facilitated by a unifying, hyper-liquid asset, which was provided by an abstract Bank money, one that could be predictably converted to safe assets, yet was not explicitly pegged to a single asset. The idea that fiat money could play such a pivotal role might not surprise many people in the modern world, but in 1750 this idea was unique to Amsterdam.

To make the Bank's system work, large quantities of precious metal were required, and much precious metal flowed through Amsterdam. Almost all of this flow originated in the New World, and in light of this fact, the most decisive event in the Bank's pre-history is undoubtedly the 1545 discovery of the Potosí silver lode in Peru (Lane 2019, 20–22).[13] Production from this one source soon trebled world silver output, and Potosí was followed by the discovery of other major silver and, later, gold deposits (Soetbeer 1876, 8; TePaske and Brown 2010, 56, 113). Elevated levels of New World mine production persisted throughout the early modern period and helped sustain new levels of global trade, as thousands of tons of silver and gold flowed from these mines to western Europe and thence on to Baltic, Mediterranean, and Asian markets (Barrett 1990; De Vries 2003; Irigoin 2018; Palma and Silva 2021).[14] Much of this precious metal would also remain in western Europe, where its circulation stimulated local trade (Palma 2019).

Historians have vigorously debated the impact of this Europe-centered flow of precious metal.[15] It has been pointed out that the direction of flow was not uniformly eastward, but contained many westward cross currents, such as the silver that was mined in Japan and then sent to China, or silver that was smuggled from Spain's American colonies to the Philippines (Flynn and Giráldez 2004). It has also been shown that despite the impressive quantities of metal flowing east, the offsetting westward flow of goods was, by modern standards, quantitatively small.[16] O'Rourke and

---

[12] A platform as defined by Choudary (2013) is a business entity that creates value by facilitating exchanges between two or more interdependent groups.

[13] A close second place would be China's fifteenth-century adoption of a de facto silver standard (Glahn 2016, 307–9), a policy change that ensured a large and growing global demand for New World silver.

[14] By the close of the eighteenth century, at least 70 percent of the world's silver stock and 40 percent of its gold had originated in New World mines (TePaske and Brown 2010, 67, 140; Irigoin 2018, 4).

[15] For a discussion of recent contributions to this debate, see De Zwart and Van Zanden (2018).

[16] De Vries (2003, 67) has calculated, for example, that the famous trade around the Cape of Good Hope accounted for (at its mid-eighteenth-century peak) about 50,000 tons of Asian goods transported to Europe each year, roughly the capacity of one modern

Williamson (2002) argued that the pace of early modern trade, while advanced over that of previous eras, was insufficient to ensure worldwide convergence in commodity prices and hence did not result in a true "hard" globalization.[17] On the other side, Palma and Silva (2021) estimated that New World precious metal combined with new routes to Asia increased trade between Europe and Asia by a factor of fourteen. According to their estimates, American precious metals were at least as important as the new routes for the observed trade pattern after 1500. Flynn and Giráldez (2002) noted that a hard globalization did occur for the two key monetary commodities, gold and silver, whose price ratio converged worldwide first in the seventeenth century, and after a period of disruption, again by the mid-eighteenth century.

We will offer no comment on this great debate, other than to observe that the eastward flow of precious metal helped keep European prices stable despite prodigious American mine production. The initial influx of New World silver set the stage for a sixteenth-century inflation in Europe – dubbed the "price revolution" by Hamilton (1934) – but as global trade expanded and Asia came to absorb the majority of the world's precious metal production (Barrett 1990), the trend in European prices (Dutch prices in particular) leveled out.[18] The offsetting forces of American production and Asian demand, in combination with global economic growth, allowed early modern Europe – including Amsterdam – ready access to desirable assets, packaged in the form of silver and gold *trade coins*, which were both abundant and reasonably stable in value. A trade coin had a high denomination, a high precious metal content, and an international network of users that favored it. The most ubiquitous trade coins came from Spanish Peru and Mexico and went by many names:

---

freighter. For this modest flow of Asian imports, Europe annually sent about 150 tons of silver (or its gold equivalent) in return.

[17] De Vries (2003) and others have pointed out that low volumes of trade between early modern Europe and Asia are in part attributable to the fact that much of this trade was restricted to monopolistic trading companies.

[18] In the Netherlands, these price trends come out as follows (Van Zanden, n.d.). Over the sixty years prior to the founding of the Bank in 1609, annual (nominal) inflation averaged 2 percent, in part due to increased silver imports but in part due to debasement of the coinage. Over the next fifty years, average inflation then fell to 0.9 percent, and over the following century, it fell to 0.1 percent. Because the silver content of Dutch money stabilized in the late seventeenth century, Dutch prices became stable in silver terms as well. This stability contrasts with the situation in Asia, where commodity prices expressed in silver terms increased steadily over the eighteenth century (Esteves and Nogues-Marco 2021).

reales de a ocho or *peso* in Spanish, "pieces of eight" or "Spanish dollars" in English, *piastres* in French, and *pilaren* or *mexicanen* in Dutch. By any name, it was "the most successful world money before the nineteenth century" (Irigoin 2020, 384).[19]

High-quality trade coins like the Spanish dollar offered Europe a better approximation to the modern idea of a safe asset than any type of government security then available. Safety, in turn, enhanced international trade. Popular "brand names" of trade coins served as essential platforms that could connect diverse groups of producers, consumers, and middlemen at long lags over great distance. The prevalence and near-global acceptability of early modern trade coins facilitated long-distance commerce that would have been challenging in previous eras (Irigoin 2018). The genius of Amsterdam was to find a way to increase the liquidity of these already highly liquid assets.

What initially drew much of the world's precious metal flow to Amsterdam was the economic dynamism of the Dutch Republic. This dynamism had its roots in the Republic's sixteenth- and seventeenth-century trade successes (see, e.g., Israel 1989; De Vries and Van der Woude 1997; Van Bochove 2008). Dutch merchants moved goods (and people) between the New World, the Baltic, the Mediterranean, western Europe, Asia, and Africa, giving rise to a steady stream of revenues from trade.[20] Trade activity pulled in precious metal from multiple directions, but especially from the world's principal supplier, Spain. Conflicts with Spain sometimes disrupted but ultimately could not halt the flow of precious metal into the Republic. Also contributing to the Republic's pull was the anti-mercantilist outlook of Amsterdam's governing class, who (atypically for this era) viewed precious metal imports as providing desirable opportunities for re-export.[21] Regulatory clampdowns on traffic in gold and silver were sporadic, ineffective, and usually short-lived. This laissez-faire attitude helped Amsterdam retain its status as a financial center well into the eighteenth century, even as the Republic's trade dominance faded.

---

[19] The production of dollars by mints in the Americas was highly private, with little oversight beyond a tax paid to the Spanish crown (Irigoin 2020, 390).

[20] The Republic's people-moving activities included transporting approximately half a million slaves from Africa to the New World (Postma 1990), and sending about 1 million Europeans to Asia (De Vries 2003).

[21] See van Dillen (1964a) on seventeenth- and eighteenth-century Amsterdam's attitude toward trade in precious metals. Local anti-mercantilist sentiment was grounded in profit motive rather than philosophical attachment.

Beyond metallic abundance, a second key factor behind the Bank's initial success was information technology, in the form of double-entry accounting. The origins of this technology are obscure, but its use expanded dramatically following the 1494 publication of the Venetian Luca Pacioli's *Summa de arithmetica*, which contained a helpful how-to chapter (Gleeson-White 2011). Pacioli's techniques could, of course, be used to record transfers of money, and by the mid-sixteenth century, certain merchants in the Southern Netherlands, known as cashiers (*kassiers*), were routinely keeping accounts that other merchants could use for payment (Aerts 2011). Cashiers had become commonplace in Amsterdam by 1609, when Amsterdam's governing council (*vroedschap*) tried to outlaw them and replace them with a more reliable City-owned bank – the Bank of Amsterdam (van Dillen 1934, 84). This was another idea borrowed from an Italian precedent, Venice's Banco della Piazza di Rialto, a public bank founded in 1585 to take over from failed private banks (Ugolini 2017, 39–45).[22] The basic business model of the cashiers, and the early Bank of Amsterdam, was simple: take in coins as deposits, record *giro* (book-entry, payor-initiated) payments on the ledgers, and pay out coins for withdrawals.

1.3 The Transformation

By the middle of the eighteenth century, the relationship between Bank of Amsterdam accounts and the other monetary platforms had transformed. Bank ledgers were now fiat money, yet a river of silver flowed through the Bank. One goal of this book is to explain that paradox. The main idea of our explanation is that the Bank of Amsterdam came to act as essentially two banks that shared one money. One bank held the trade coins under receipt that customers used as collateral for loans of Bank money. This bank attracted a prodigious flow of silver. The other was a pure fiat bank that adjusted the amount of Bank money through unsecured loans and stabilization operations. When the two banks supported each other, Bank money worked well. When they did not, it did not: an influx of collateral

---

[22] Ledger-money public banks were common in many Mediterranean commercial cities at this time, so this first step was not revolutionary. A 1606 resolution by Amsterdam's governing council mentions a bank in Seville, as well as the one in Venice, as models for an Amsterdam public bank (van Dillen 1925a, 5). Other Italian ledger-money public banks existed in Palermo, Gerona, Genoa, Milan, Rome (Van der Wee 1963, 367), and Naples (Costabile and Nappi 2018; Velde 2018). The function of these banks had commonalities with the earlier practices at certain trade fairs (Lyons, Piacenza, Castile) of settling debts in a stable money of account (Van der Wee 1993, 148–49).

could overwhelm the fiat bank, and a mismanaged fiat bank could provoke collateral flight.

Through this dual structure, the Bank orchestrated its suite of techniques. The Bank supplied a fiat ledger as a money used for the settlement of claims by the financial system. The Bank conducted open market operations as a tool to make substantial adjustments to the quantity of that fiat ledger money. The Bank offered customers repurchase agreements as a mechanism to support smooth flows between coins and fiat ledger money. In these respects, the Bank of Amsterdam flourished as a well-managed central bank.

The fiat side of the Bank, however, could also be used to channel funds to politically favored entities. In practice, the Bank lent large sums to the Dutch East India Company and routinely siphoned off profits to the City of Amsterdam. These activities made the fiat side a fractional reserve bank. Customers could not run on this portion because their accounts had no right of withdrawal, but markets could devalue Bank money. Such a devaluation happened in the 1780s when the Company borrowed heavily from the Bank but could not repay.

Overall, the fiat bank had a double-edged relationship with the receipt bank. Fiat open market operations helped counteract the swings in receipts, but excessive fiat exploitation undermined faith in the Bank's commitments to let customers repurchase coins under receipt. Lacking both private capital and explicit government support, the Bank was stable as long as it was popular, and was popular as long as it was stable. In truly extreme circumstances, it could be neither. Mismanagement of fiscal demands on the fiat portion of the Bank contributed to a general loss of confidence over the 1780s and to the Bank's ultimate collapse in 1795.

To build our case for the Bank's modernity, we first lay out all the key parts of the Bank's operations and how they fit together. Chapter 2 provides a snapshot of the monetary platforms in Amsterdam circa 1750, and Chapter 3 explains how the metallic side of the system was the foundation upon which paper monies could thrive. Chapter 4 describes the founding and early development of the bank as a response to the limitations of coinage in the 1600s. In Chapter 5, the story progresses into the eighteenth century as the maturing Bank reinvents its relationship with trade coins by adding a repo-like (receipt) standing facility for handling such coins. Chapter 6 ties these themes together to reveal the balance of passive policies that made receipts work well. Even then, the receipt bank was volatile, so Chapter 7 reveals how the Bank used open market operations to stabilize the overall level of Bank money, and shows how the Bank's policy approach was eventually overwhelmed by fiscal stress.

1.4 Relationship to the Historiography of the Bank

Compared to later central banks of similar pre-eminence (the Bank of England and the Federal Reserve), the Bank of Amsterdam remains an under-researched institution despite its wealth of archival material. Challenges to working with this material include its archaic language, its unfamiliar formats, and its sheer mass: the contents of the Bank's archive run to about 550 meters, most of this consisting of dense numerical data. The Bank's institutional setting may also seem alien to researchers more accustomed to the structures of modern central banking.

The Bank is nonetheless associated with a rich literature, beginning with contemporary descriptions such as Adam Smith's well-known "digression" on the subject of the Bank (Smith 1981 [1776], 479–88). Rather than attempt a full literature survey, our analysis will reference specific works at points where they relate to various aspects of the Bank. For more complete guides to the literature, we refer the reader to monographs by Gillard (2004) and Dehing (2012), which offer wide-ranging bibliographies.

A number of works require special mention. The researcher most closely identified with the history of the Bank is Johannes Gerard van Dillen (1883–1969). His monumental two-volume work, *Bronnen tot Geschiedenis der Wisselbanken* ("Sources for History of the Exchange Banks"; van Dillen 1925a,1925b), offers an accessible compilation of hundreds of archival sources relevant to the Bank, all transcribed in an easy-to-read modern typeface and currently available online. At more than 1,400 pages, the *Bronnen* give some hint of the complexity of the Bank and the vastness of its archive. Van Dillen also wrote introductory guides to the history of the Bank (van Dillen 1964b, 1964c, 1964d), which are based on original versions he published in the 1920s and which contain many data series. Van Dillen further compressed these guides into an English-language summary (van Dillen 1934). Finally, in a posthumously published volume (van Dillen 1970), van Dillen placed much of the Bank's history into the broader context of the economic history of the Dutch Republic. Our assessments of the Bank will at times depart from van Dillen's, but scholarly disagreement does not diminish our immense debt to his work.

The earliest systematic history of the Bank was written by Willem Cornelis Mees (Mees 1838). This was Mees' doctoral thesis, compiled under difficult conditions, since he was denied any access to the Bank's archives. Mees, who went on to become president of the Bank's successor institution, De Nederlandsche Bank, was a person of extraordinary capabilities. While Mees' work has subsequently been overshadowed by Van Dillen's, many of Mees' insightful characterizations of the Bank have, as noted by his biographer (Van de Laar 1978), retained their validity. We rely on these insights for our analysis.

More recently, a number of authors have sought to extend the scope and, with the help of modern information technology, the numerical reach of Van Dillen's work. Works in this vein include Dehing and 't Hart (1997), Gillard (2004), Dehing (2012), and numerous contributions to the 2009 volume prepared for the Bank's quadricentennial (Van Nieuwkerk 2009). This body of work, to which we are also greatly indebted, has helped to connect the traditional, largely narrative historiography of the Bank to more modern, more analytical approaches to financial history. In particular, we have relied heavily on Dehing's (2012) description of the emergence of the receipt system. Our previous research on the Bank has tried to build on the modern literature, with a primary focus on reconstruction of the Bank's master account. This book attempts to present a more complete, unified, and, it is hoped, accessible treatment of results presented in our earlier work.

In contrast with most of the historical literature, we take a consciously anachronistic approach. There are advantages and disadvantages: On the one hand, terms such as "platform," and "repo facility" were unknown during the time of the Bank, and obviously these terms cannot be taken as historically accurate descriptions of the Bank's structure and policies. On the other hand, both contemporary observers and historians of the Bank have at times struggled to understand aspects of its operations. Because these aspects have strong parallels in the modern world of money and finance, it may be at times useful to apply anachronistic terminology in order to advance our understanding. For example, the Bank's receipts for trade coins were, quite formally, claims that entitled their holder to repurchase a certain quantity of coins from the Bank at a fixed price, within a fixed time period. It would be difficult for anyone with a background in modern finance not to recognize these instruments as American call options on coin, even if the Bank had a different name for them ("receipts"). Once certain concepts are learned, they are hard to unlearn.

This study also takes anachronism the other way. The Bank's regime anticipated many of today's arrangements, by facilitating exchanges of safe but slightly illiquid assets through a system that enabled traders to take positions in different varieties of such assets, as dictated by their liquidity needs or speculative sentiment. This trading regime was made possible by the collective implicit agreement of Amsterdam merchants, remarkable for the time, that many of these trades would not be of safe assets against safe assets, but of safe assets for the Bank's fiat ledger money. The attraction of this regime is demonstrated by the fact that such arrangements continue to exist today. Frost, Shin, and Wierts (2020) go so far as to propose the Bank's ledger money as a model for certain types of digital currencies, "stablecoins" whose value is enhanced by arrangements that anchor them to traditional monetary assets.

With this focus on monetary architecture, this book is not structured as a traditional narrative history. The early chapters (2 and 3) start in 1750, during the third quarter of the Bank's existence, with a survey of the basics of money at that time: bullion, coins, bills, and banks. The middle chapters (4 and 5) jump back to 1600 and progress forward to the Bank's apogee. A purpose of these chronological chapters is to emphasize how messy the evolution of the Bank was. The ascendant design did not emerge quickly nor painlessly nor through penetrating foresight. Instead, it took the Bank nearly a century of dead ends, desperate fixes, bizarre turns, and unexpected successes to align coins and accounts with the political and economic realities of time and place. Only then do later Chapters (6 and 7) reveal how the mature form of the Bank thrived. With the full system explored, Chapter 8 broadens the perspective with the story of how Frederick's Prussia was able to exploit the liquidity within the Bank. Chapter 9 concludes by placing the Bank's techniques within the history of central banking.

Our book is also not intended as a comprehensive survey. Our focus is on monetary architecture, not on the Bank's relationship with the City of Amsterdam, the Dutch East India Company (VOC), or other important topics, although those relationships certainly form part of our story. Similarly, we do not catalog each crisis nor delve into the full variety of customers who used the Bank. The Bank's archives are vast, and we encourage others to pursue these worthy topics. Instead, this book focuses on the economics of coins and accounts. This approach acquires relevance through establishing similarities between then and now while highlighting differences. It is not meant to diminish the contributions of other researchers but to more firmly anchor the Bank's contribution to the history of money and finance. In doing so, we hope to inspire future generations to investigate the data contained in the remaining 99 percent of the Bank's ledgers.

A.1 Timelines

Table A1.1. *Key events in the history of the Bank*

1609: Bank is chartered by the City of Amsterdam
1638: Emergence of separate unit of account for Bank money
1659: Bank money (bank florin) given formal legal status with its own unit of account
1666: Start of continuous surviving ledgers
1672: France invades the Dutch Republic, run on the Bank
1683: Start of the receipt system and Bank's transition to fiat money
1694: Major reform of Dutch coinage
1763: Financial panic in Amsterdam
1772–1773: Another financial panic
1780–1783: Emergency loans to Dutch East India Company, run on the receipt system
1791: Partial recapitalization of the Bank
1795: Bank collapses in the wake of another French invasion
1820: Liquidation

Source: Authors.

Table A1.2. *Other relevant events in Dutch and European history*

1568: Netherlands revolts against Spanish rule, beginning the Eighty Years War with Spain
1579: Union of Utrecht, formation of the United Provinces, which become a republic in 1588
1609–1621: Twelve Years Truce between the Dutch Republic and Spain
1621–1648: Renewed war between the Republic and Spain (a phase of the Thirty Years War)
1672–1678: Franco-Dutch War, beginning with the Republic's "Year of Disaster" (1672)
1688–1689: Glorious Revolution, Dutch Stadholder Willem (William) III ascends the English throne
1694: Founding of the Bank of England
1701–1714: War of Spanish Succession
1716–1720: Rise and collapse of John Law's System in France
1740–1748: War of Austrian Succession
1756–1763: Seven Years War
1780–1784: Fourth Anglo-Dutch War
1795: France invades the Republic and replaces it with a client state (the Batavian Republic)
1813: Kingdom of the Netherlands established, replacing the Batavian Republic
1814: Founding of De Nederlandsche Bank (central bank of the Netherlands)

Source: Authors.

2

The World of the Bank

An eighteenth-century visitor to Amsterdam (the City) wishing to see its
Bank would have been directed to the Town Hall or *Stadhuis* (Figure 2.1),
an imposing neoclassical building located on the central square known as
the Dam.[1] The Dam was originally built as a structure to regulate the flow
of the Amstel River through the City. Visitors to the Town Hall must have
been impressed – as are tourists today – by the scale of its exterior,
79 meters wide by 55 meters high, and by its opulent reception room,
the *Burgerzaal*, with 25-meter ceilings and marble floors inlaid with maps
of the earth and heavens. A visitor to the Town Hall would not have left
with an underestimate of Amsterdam's commercial ambitions.

The heavily guarded Bank was located on one side of this prominent
building and the significance of this location was apparent to any resident
or visitor. In addition to the Town Hall, the Dam was bordered by two
other notable public structures. These were the Weigh House (seen at left
in Figure 2.1), which was used for goods offloaded at nearby docks, and the
Exchange (Figure 2.2), which housed merchants' markets for goods and
financial assets. This physical setting is a tempting metaphor for the Bank's
function of verifying and regulating the stream of precious metal flowing
through Amsterdam, to the benefit of the denizens of the Exchange.

To continue setting the scene, this chapter will sketch the monetary,
financial, and political environment in Amsterdam in the mid-eighteenth
century – the high tide of the Bank. Historians have traditionally portrayed
this period as an era of economic decline for Amsterdam and the Dutch

---

[1] The Town Hall was built in the 1650s to replace a burned-out medieval structure
(Goossens 2009, 59–60; Dehing 2012, 82–88). In the nineteenth century, the Town Hall
was repurposed as a palace of the Royal House of the Netherlands, a function it continues
to serve today.

Figure 2.1. Amsterdam's Weigh House, Dam, and Town Hall, circa 1743
Source: Jan Gaspar Philips 1743–1744, courtesy of the Rijksmuseum
Note: The entrance to the Bank was on the south (opposite) side of the Town Hall.

Republic, but more recent research indicates that the Republic's economy may have instead continued at a high level (Israel 1989, 399–415; De Vries and van der Woude 1997, 681–83; van Zanden and van Leeuwen 2012). For certain sectors, banking and finance included, the latter half of the eighteenth century was even a time of "second bloom" marked by episodes of prosperity (Van Dillen 1970, 558–91). The activity recorded in the Bank's ledgers at mid-century is consistent with this characterization and reveals a vibrant financial sector supported by a sophisticated central bank.

How exactly did the Bank fit into Amsterdam's world of money and finance? This chapter will lay out the many ways the Bank was distinct from the other parts of Amsterdam's monetary system. These distinctions created room for financial markets to connect the Bank to the rest. Sometimes the Bank managed those markets, sometimes the reverse. Understanding how each of those markets worked is a research goal of this book. Pulling them together into a system is another goal. The Bank was central to only part of that system, so discovering how the Bank managed its role within the rest of the system is a third goal. Assessing how the political superstructure constrained the Bank and the system is yet another goal. Also, as these elements of the system were interlocking,

Figure 2.2. Amsterdam's Exchange, circa 1662.
Source: Pieter Hendricksz Schut 1662–1668, courtesy of the Rijksmuseum
Note: Merchants of the same type were to be found within assigned areas of the Exchange.

so too are the goals. We begin the analysis by first mapping Amsterdam's monetary system in terms of form and function at a point in time. This map will orient detailed stories of coins in Chapter 3, of receipts in Chapter 6, of stabilization operations in Chapter 7, and of monetary manipulations in Chapter 8. The map also shows the endpoint of the Bank's origin story in Chapter 4 and its transition to the eighteenth century in Chapter 5.

2.1 Political Location

It was natural for the Bank to reside in the Town Hall, because it was a municipal agency, owned and at all times controlled by the City of Amsterdam. Given the Bank's broader relevance to the Dutch Republic, Europe, and the world, municipal ownership may seem an odd arrangement, but there were two reasons for this. The first was that during the era of the Bank, municipal rather than national public banks were the norm (Roberds and Velde 2016a). Public banks in commercial cities were seen as conducive to sound local money, and such institutions thrived in places such as Genoa, Hamburg, and Venice.[2] Within the Dutch Republic, the cities of Delft, Middelburg, and Rotterdam, in addition to Amsterdam, each operated a chartered public bank. Larger sovereign states at this time were often more interested in seigniorage than in sound money, and this preference was seen as incompatible with the operation of public banks.[3] The nationally chartered Bank of England, founded in 1694, offered an exception to this rule, although at the time it was so closely identified with the London financial markets, it was often called "the Bank of London" (Clapham 1945a, 107). Other early attempts at national public banks had led to either mixed results (in Sweden; see Heckscher 1934) or disastrous bankruptcy (in France; see Velde 2003).

A second reason the Bank existed as a municipal rather than a national institution was that decentralized governance was a characteristic feature of the Dutch Republic ("Republic"). The Republic (formally known as the Republic of the Seven United Netherlands or the United Provinces) existed (roughly) from 1579 (the signing of the Union of Utrecht, an alliance of provinces in revolt against Spain) until 1795 (when the Republic was invaded by France and converted to a client state).[4] The Republic was basically a provincial confederation with a weak central governing body: the States General (or the Estates General or *Staten Generaal*). The Republic had no monarch, although for much of its history it had hereditary leaders (Stadholders or *Stadhouders*) with limited executive powers.[5]

---

[2] Reliance on municipal banks in part reflected the general pattern of trade finance, which at this time was more of an intercity than an international phenomenon (Jobst and Nogues-Marco 2013).

[3] Summarizing the accepted wisdom of the time, Frederick the Great's financial counselor stated in 1765 that "a ledger-money bank is not allowed under a monarchy because it makes most coin payments unnecessary and therefore reduces the income from seigniorage" (Niebuhr 1854, 183).

[4] The United Provinces first tried establishing themselves as a protectorate under the English crown, but in 1588 rejected this arrangement in favor of a republican government (Israel 1995, 219–30).

[5] Before the Revolt against Spain, the Stadholders were provincial-level representatives of the Spanish monarchy. This function became obsolete after the Revolt, but the positions of the Stadholders were nonetheless retained, except during certain intervals ("Stadholderless periods") when the offices went vacant. Different provinces could have different Stadholders, but from 1747, all provinces had the same Stadholder, which led to more power being associated with that position. Technically speaking, the Republic's executive

Decentralized governance was a hallmark of the Republic throughout its existence, although the largest province (Holland) and the commercial capital (Amsterdam) exerted disproportionate influence over policy decisions.

As a municipal agency, the policy decisions of the Bank were taken by a hierarchy of City officials ('t Hart 2009). Major policy decisions, such as the authorization of credit lines to the Dutch East India Company, were set by the governing council of the City (the *vroedschap*). More routine guidance was given by the City's executive council of four burgomasters (*burgemeesters*). Down one level of bureaucracy, short-term decisions and supervision of employees were delegated to a six-member board of commissioners (*commissarissen*), who were appointed by the vroedschap for one-year terms. An analysis of Bank commissioner biographies by 't Hart (2009) shows that during the eighteenth century, commissioners tended to be somewhat younger members (in their thirties or early forties) of well-connected political or mercantile families. Almost all of these were adherents of the Republic's dominant religion, the Dutch Reformed Church. The Bank's credibility with Amsterdam's financial markets was usually bolstered by its management's connections to the City's governing class.

2.2 Monetary Location

Eighteenth-century Amsterdam was well known as a globally significant entrepôt for precious metal assets of all types. Less visible but quantitatively larger than the metal flows were various forms of paper money entering, leaving, and turning over within the City: bills of exchange, private ledger-money (cashier ledgers and notes), and, at the heart of Amsterdam's monetary system, Bank money.

The Bank's money existed only as entries in its ledgers, as was common for early modern public banks.[6] As discussed in Chapter 1, however, a distinctive feature of eighteenth-century Bank money was that it was, according to modern concepts, fiat money. More precisely, people with

power resided in an organ of the States General, known as the Council of State (*Raad van State*), which consulted with the Stadholders (Israel 1995, 300–6; Fritschy 2017, 39–40).

[6] In the seventeenth century, the Bank engaged in some minor, largely unsuccessful attempts to issue banknote–like liabilities. These are discussed in Chapter 5. More generally, the Bank operated for too long for all behavior to conform to absolutes. We often acknowledge this through modifiers or counterexamples, and it is best to assume that the remaining generalizations have exceptions either unstated or undiscovered.

funds in a Bank account, but without a coin receipt that had been issued by the Bank (discussed below), could not withdraw their account balance as coins. The term "fiat money" was not in common use during the eighteenth century, but people understood the irredeemable nature of Bank funds. To give one example, James Steuart (1767b, 76), in his description of the Bank, stated that "[t]he bank of Amsterdam pays none in either gold or silver coin, or bullion; consequently it cannot be said, that the florin Banco is attached to the metals."

Bank account holders were parties who dealt in bills of exchange, which were the dominant instrument of international credit. These parties were primarily wealthy merchants but also chartered corporations and governmental entities such as the City Treasury. Reflecting the high status of its clientele, payments through the Bank were usually made for large sums. A typical Bank transaction amount of 2,500 florins would have been in the order of 2,500 times the average daily wage in Amsterdam during this era, or more than 5,000 times the daily wage of a worker in contemporary central Europe or China (van Zanden 1999; Allen et al. 2011). The average Bank account balance in 1750 was for about 8,000 florins (Dehing 2012, 143). In January 1750, the Bank had 2,134 customer accounts as compared to Amsterdam's total population of about 200,000.[7] While in principle the Bank was open to any merchant in Amsterdam, in practice the Bank functioned as an institution serving the wealthiest tier of the City's population.[8]

Payment in bank occurred when an account holder ordered the clerks to transfer funds to another account. This was a giro system in which the payor pushed funds to the payee; that is, a transfer occurred when the clerks debited the payor's account and credited the payee's account. Such transfers had a special legal status (discussed below) that made Bank money into a uniquely powerful medium of exchange. In an era of hand calculation, it was no small job to keep track of these transfers, sometimes running to over 100,000 transactions per year. Inevitably, some errors crept in, as did occasional frauds. Key to the operation of the Bank were its bookkeepers as well as its auditors ("counter-bookkeepers"), whose job it was to ensure the accuracy of the Bank's financial records. Later chapters

---

[7] Data on account holders are from the Amsterdam City Archive (ACA) 5077/1167. Amsterdam population is from Israel (1995, 1007).

[8] Literally, the individuals who dealt with the Bank comprised 1–2 percent of Amsterdam's population. Assuming an average family size of four people, the Bank's clientele comprised the top 5–10 percent.

will discuss the methodology the Bank employed to keep discrepancies to a tolerable level.

The vast majority of payments were made between customer accounts, but sometimes the Bank itself was payee or payor in a transaction, thereby creating new balances or destroying old balances, as metal flowed in or out of the Bank's vault. Those actions used a master account called the coin room (*specie kamer*). As managing its money stock was how the Bank conducted monetary policy, the master account is the research focus of this book. While the Bank had many employees, only two types had the authority to create balances with the master account from inflows of silver and gold: receivers and the assayer.[9] The job of the Bank's receivers (*ontvangers*) was to record coins sold to the Bank through the receipt facility, as discussed below. This activity entailed little discretion, and the results were routinely transferred to the Bank's master account.

The other official empowered to influence the master account was the assayer (*essaijeur*), who managed many of the Bank's idiosyncratic activities. As the title suggests, the assayer was tasked with ensuring that any coins or ingots entering the Bank were of requisite weight and quality, so a metallurgical background was necessary for this job. The responsibility of the assayer was more than that of a mere technician however, but on occasion closer to that of a modern-day head of central bank trading operations. The assayer would sometimes buy and sell coins and precious metals for their own account, but such transactions were clearly undertaken in order to implement policy when subsequently moved to the Bank's master account. This mingling of personal and business accounts was not unusual for the time. Unlike the receivers, the assayer at times ran large and persistent open positions in their Bank account, positions that were eventually transferred to the Bank. Or the assayer would sometimes conduct trades directly on behalf of the master account.

The Bank's relationship with its assayer was thus rather loose (by the standards of later central banks) and entailed a high degree of moral hazard. It was as if a modern central bank hired a primary dealer to trade on the bank's behalf. How the Bank attempted to align the assayer's incentives is in general unknown, but a 1782 directive to the Bank's commissioners is suggestive (Mees 1838, 327–28). The directive specified that the assayer should receive 10 percent of the Bank's gain from purchases and subsequent profitable resale of metallic assets.

---

[9] For a full organization chart of the Bank, see Dehing (2012, 102).

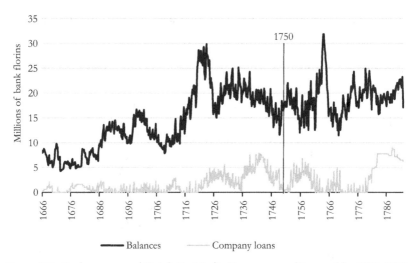

Figure 2.3. Bank money and Dutch East India Company credit, monthly, 1666–1792
Source: Authors' calculations

The activities of the receivers and the assayer created much of the aggregate stock of Bank money. To investigate this money creation, we encoded 172,000 extant master account transactions starting in 1666, when the Bank's accounts began to survive with regularity. Figure 2.3 gives the level of bank florins at the start of each month from February 1666 to January 1792.[10] The master account also included loans to the Amsterdam Chamber of the Dutch East India Company, or just "Company," and those levels are also displayed. Almost all of the remainder was created through flows of gold and silver, which is why so much of this book focuses on precious metals and their relationship to Bank money. Most transactions using Bank money did not involve coins, but most transactions that created or destroyed Bank money did.

The overall stock of Bank money is comparable to modern base money aggregates (stocks of central bank money, often denoted M_0), with several provisos. Unlike some modern central banks, the Bank imposed no reserve or minimum balance requirements and it never paid interest to its customers; a merchant's only motive for keeping a balance at the Bank would

---

[10] For readability, the series in Figure 2.3 and most figures in this book are presented from the start of each month. February was the first full month of each fiscal year, because the Bank closed for about two weeks each January to inventory assets and liabilities that were then reconciled into a balance sheet. These balance sheets were reproduced in van Dillen (1925b, 701–807). The Bank also shut each July but only to inventory balances.

have been to use this balance for transactions. Also, the Bank generally did not issue circulating notes, which constitute a large part of the monetary base for modern central banks. In the mid-eighteenth century, the stock of Bank money tended to fluctuate between 18 and 20 million florins, about 7–8 percent of Dutch GDP.[11]

Descriptions of the eighteenth-century Dutch Republic often refer to its money as "the Dutch guilder." Guilder was, however, an ambiguous term, covering at least three different concepts. Bank money was denominated in a distinct unit of account called the *bankgulden*, which can be translated as "bank guilder" or "bank florin." Most other money in Amsterdam was denominated in another unit of account, *courantgulden*, translatable as the "current guilder" or the "current florin."[12] The symbol for both units of account was a script *f*. A separate unit of account for public-bank money was not a phenomenon unique to Amsterdam (for example, a similar distinction existed in Hamburg), but this separation enhanced the status of Bank money as a medium of exchange and store of value.

Both current and bank guilders were subdivided into smaller nominal units called stivers (*stuivers*, each equal to 1/20th of a florin) and pennies (*penningen*, each equal to 1/16th of a stiver or 1/320th of a florin), so an account entry in the Bank's books and most outside ledgers showed up as a triple of florins: stivers: pennies.[13] In the hope of minimizing confusion, throughout this book we will call bankgulden "florins" and courantgulden "guilders" (see Table 2.1). Yet a third type of guilder was the guilder coin, described later in this chapter.

Coins and bullion were valued in guilders when outside the Bank but in florins when inside. Bills of exchange were represented in guilders when made payable outside the Bank and in florins if payable inside. Most financial assets, however, were always in guilders because they had no direct interaction with the Bank. For example, cashiers' (private deposit banks') accounts were in guilders. So were the debt instruments of various

---

[11] This percentage assumes an annual GDP of 259 million bank florins, based on national income estimates for the Dutch Republic given in De Vries and van der Woude (1997, 702).

[12] The current guilder was also known as the *casgulden* or "cash guilder," a term we will avoid using in this book.

[13] To add to the complexity, there existed at this time a parallel unit of account known as the Flemish pound (*vlaamse pond*), which was used in the Dutch Republic as well as Flanders and other parts of the Southern Netherlands. A Flemish pound was equal to 6 Dutch guilders and was subdivided into 20 *schellingen*, which were in turn subdivided into *12 grooten*. Notations in Flemish pounds show up in many sources, but we will not use them in this book.

Table 2.1. *Nomenclature for types of guilders*

Dutch name	English names	Monetary function	Our preferred term
bankgulden	bank florin, bank guilder, florin banco	unit of account for Bank money	(bank) florin
courantgulden	current florin, current guilder	unit of account for money outside the Bank	(current) guilder
gulden (munt)	guilder (coin)	a coin with a face value of one current guilder	gulden

Source: Authors

Dutch provinces (van Bochove 2013), English government debt (when traded in Amsterdam), and stocks of various corporations (van Dillen 1931; Petram 2011).[14]

2.3 Conceptual Location

These distinctive features resulted in the separation, but not isolation, of Bank money from the other parts of the Amsterdam monetary system. This separation could be confusing to outsiders. In a 1753 banking manual, for example, Nicholas Magens was careful to warn English readers that "in the Bank of England, the Gold, Silver, and Credit runs promiscuously, but in Amsterdam they are Separate Things" (1753, 36).

To visualize the system around 1750, Figure 2.4 offers our conceptual arrangement: the "map." To sort the system into basic hows and whys, the monetary map placed Bank money in a space with two dimensions. On the horizontal, precious metals were the base form of money, and paper was the supplemental form that worked to reduce the use of coins. On the vertical, local methods of payment often differed from international methods. Local money was called current money (*courantgeld*) because, whether metal or paper, it was denominated in current guilders. Bank money was paper that mostly supported international payments, even

---

[14] The most heavily traded stocks in Amsterdam, according to van Dillen, were those of the Dutch East and West India Companies, the English East India and South Sea Companies, and the Bank of England. See Neal (1990) for the integration of Amsterdam and London stock markets. Investors could also trade stock futures contracts via brokers. For stocks in high demand, brokers offered options on futures. Prices of all these instruments were quoted in current guilders.

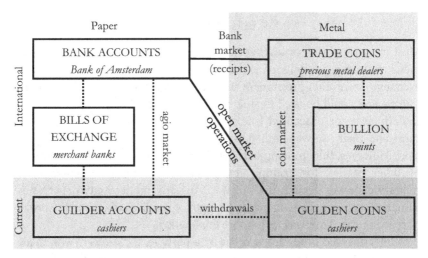

Figure 2.4. Map of monetary assets in Amsterdam, circa 1750
Source: Authors.

though Bank money never left the ledgers in the Town Hall. The schematic then located other major forms of payment: coins, bullion, bills of exchange, and cashier accounts. Each quadrant had a dominant form with an associated intermediary who helped make it work. In modern argot, each was a platform. Other activities at other scales and in other locations had other arrangements beyond the scope of this book. For example, Lucassen (2014) has assessed the availability of the Republic's smallest coins for use by day laborers, and Felten (2022) has investigated the monetary arrangements of farmers in Gelderland and in the sprawling estates of the Orange-Nassau family. In contrast, this book focuses on large payments made in Amsterdam between the economic elite who used the Bank, and in that situation accounts and big coins were the relevant monies.

Connecting the monies were markets, represented by lines in Figure 2.4. As a result, the map assigned Bank accounts four different lines of engagement with the outside platforms, and each will be reviewed in the following sections of this chapter. The interactions we reconstructed from the Bank's ledgers were shown as solid lines, and they will be the primary focus of this book in later chapters. The map also emphasizes that Amsterdam's system had markets that did not directly involve the Bank. They too were important as relevant alternatives. When taken as a whole, the map delineates what Bank money was central to (bills) from what was central to Bank money (trade coins) from what indirectly connected them (current money).

2.4 Bills of Exchange

Most money entering or leaving Amsterdam came or went not as precious metal, but as paper bills of exchange (or "bills," *wisselbrieven*). Bills of exchange were the preeminent financial instrument of early modern Europe and could be used for many purposes, including remote payment, trade finance, or unsecured lending. Bills were typically written for large sums and their use was limited almost exclusively to merchants (*kooplieden*). However, bills moving between merchants could be used indirectly by other parties, for example, by governments transferring funds for military expenses during times of war. An early modern city's success as a financial center depended on the strength of its bill market, and the broad purpose of the Bank was to support this market.

A bill consisted of a written order by a party A, the *drawer* (who made out the bill), to party B, the *drawee*, to pay a sum to C, the *payee* or beneficiary, at a certain time and place.[15] Upon presentment of the bill, B would indicate his willingness to pay by signing or *accepting* the bill, in which case it became a binding obligation on B (now called the *acceptor*) to pay C at the specified time. Or the drawee could refuse to pay the bill drawn on him, a formal act known as a *protest*, which in Amsterdam required a notary and two witnesses to have legal force.[16] Protesting a bill did not erase an obligation to repay an existing debt. Bills were customarily written or "drawn" in one city and made payable in another. These could be different cities within the same country (within the Dutch Republic, in the case of Amsterdam), but the more important types of bills were those that connected major commercial cities in different countries; hence the map represents bills as international instruments. Bills were typically specified to be payable at *sight* (upon receipt) or at a standard term known as *usance*, which varied by location.

Merchants during this era cultivated relationships with merchants in other places, known as "friends" or "relations," who could be called upon

---

[15] Here we employ (with some reluctance) modern legal terminology for parties A, B, and C. For contemporary terminology and examples of how bills were used, see Neal (1990, 5–9). Dutch terms for bill transactions are given in the Glossary.

[16] Our main source for bill market practice is Le Moine de L'Espine and Le Long (1763, 141), a later edition of a merchants' manual first published in 1694. At least by the time of this edition, bills originating within the Dutch Republic could sometimes be returned to the drawer in lieu of a protest. This informal procedure was not possible for the more important foreign bills. Records of bills protested to notaries have been preserved in the Amsterdam City Archive.

to accept bills drawn on them, up to a mutually agreed limit. A merchant's friends were often (but not exclusively) firms with which the merchant had an ongoing trading relationship. Merchants wanting to send funds to a certain city, but not having a friend there, could purchase a bill drawn by another merchant who did. Bills of exchange drawn on Amsterdam merchants were *negotiable*, meaning that their use fell under strict rules enforced by law and custom. Among other things, negotiability meant that anyone endorsing a bill over to another party became liable for it, and the assurance provided by joint liability facilitated the circulation of bills as a type of money. It is not clear, however, how common it was for bills of ordinary Amsterdam merchants to circulate, as opposed to bills of banks and other financial specialists (De Jong-Keesing 1939, 65). Someone who ended up with a bill at its maturity, perhaps the original beneficiary or perhaps someone who obtained the bill via endorsement, was known as the bill's *holder*.

Formal settlement of a bill in Bank money occurred via an order from the acceptor to the Bank's clerks to transfer funds to the holder of the bill. To facilitate settlement, bills were commonly lodged with the Bank's clerks before they came due. A book-entry transfer then served as legal discharge of the acceptor's liability, and holders were advised to carefully verify the transfer of funds before returning a canceled bill to its acceptor (Le Moine de L'Espine and Le Long 1763, 206, 211–12). Because this was the legal and customary way to settle Bank-money bills, any Amsterdam merchant who regularly dealt in such bills needed an account at the Bank. To quote Adam Smith: "Every Merchant, in consequence of this regulation, was obliged to keep an account with the bank in order to pay his foreign bills of exchange, which necessarily occasioned a certain demand for bank money" (1981 [1776], 481).

The Bank's ledger entries usually do not record the purpose of a transaction, but most of these were undoubtedly transactions relating to bills, recording either the settlement of a bill at maturity or the purchase of another merchant's bill with Bank funds (called "discounting," since such purchases were usually for less than the face value of the bill). Indeed, the original purpose of the Bank was to expedite the settlement of commercial debts such as bills.[17] At its founding, the City granted the Bank a monopoly

---

[17] The negotiable bill of exchange was an up-and-coming financial instrument in Amsterdam at the time of the Bank's founding in 1609, eventually displacing an earlier form of commercial debt known as the letter obligatory. Bills of exchange were originally introduced into the Netherlands by Italian merchants and negotiable bills became used in

for settlement of all bills in sufficiently large amounts (600 florins, later reduced to 300), but this monopoly proved impossible to fully enforce. In practice, bills drawn on Amsterdam merchants had to specify whether they were payable through the Bank. If they were, then they were customarily settled through a giro transfer that was recorded in the Bank's ledgers.[18] Or if a Bank customer used his balance at the Bank to purchase a bill drawn or held by another Bank customer, this transaction also shows up in the Bank's ledgers. In the map, these types of transactions are represented as the line running between bills of exchange and Bank accounts.

A complication of Amsterdam's bill market during this period was that it was also possible for merchants to draw and settle bills in current money, meaning money outside the Bank. Price currents (financial reporting sheets) in foreign cities sometimes list two sets of prices for bills drawn on Amsterdam: current-money bills and Bank-money bills. How current-money bills were actually settled remains something of a mystery. In principle, these obligations could be discharged by transfer of coin or by a giro transfer on the books of a private intermediary such as a cashier. De Jong-Keesing (1939, 80–81) describes a third mode of settlement, which was transfer of a deposit receipt issued by a cashier.[19] Amsterdam's cashiers would gather daily to net settle or "clear" mutual obligations arising from exchange of deposit receipts (Mees 1838, 250; Jonker 1996, 175). Unfortunately, no systematic records remain of this clearing process, making it hard to determine the size of the current-money segment of the bill market. Transactions in the current-money bill market are also mapped as a line running from the bills-of-exchange box to the guilder accounts.

Bills could serve simply as payment instruments, a way of moving money from one city to another, but bills could also have a credit function. In a classic use, a merchant *A* in one city would ship goods to a friend *B* in

---

Antwerp from the late sixteenth century (Van der Wee 1963, 340–52). Negotiable bills were popularized in seventeenth-century Amsterdam by immigrants from the Southern Netherlands (Heyvaert 1975, 94, 120–21).

[18] See Justine (1707, 335–36) and Le Moine de L'Espine and Le Long (1763, 204–5). Bills drawn in Bank money could also be settled outside the Bank, in current money, by mutual consent of the bill holder and the acceptor as to the appropriate adjustment in value. We suspect that this alternative was sufficiently cumbersome that it was infrequently used.

[19] Cashiers (proto-deposit bankers) were introduced in Chapter 1 and are discussed in more detail in Section 2.6.

another city, who would then sell the goods on commission. Merchant *A* could tap the liquidity to be generated by these sales by drawing bills on *B*, subject to mutually agreeable terms.[20] In such cases, any advance credit granted by *B* to *A* would have been implicitly collateralized by the goods that were shipped.[21] The two hypothetical merchants could add liquidity to such a bill by finding a reputable third party in a location with a deep bill market, such as Amsterdam, to be the acceptor (Santarosa 2015, 697). To give one example, Postlethwayt (1774, 684) described purchases in St. Petersburg by London merchants as typically occurring via bills drawn on Amsterdam counterparties. Market depth in Amsterdam allowed an accepted bill (bearing a sufficiently reputable signature) to be sold at a discount to investors, and such discounting created a money market that funded merchant *A* before payment by the acceptor on merchant *B*'s behalf.[22]

Bills could be written without any implied bond to collateral, however, which meant that they could be used to generate credit without a connection to any underlying real transaction. For example, a merchant *A* could accept a bill drawn by a friend *B* with the expectation that *A* could then draw a bill on *B* that would cover the value of the original bill plus a premium that incorporated an implicit interest rate. Again, liquidity could be enhanced by drawing and redrawing bills (*wissel en herwissel*) through reputable Amsterdam merchants. The related and notorious practice of bill-kiting (*wisselruiterij*) consisted of indefinite cycles of drawing and redrawing, often among a small group who were simply gambling on better circumstances.[23] There was, however, no exact dividing line between legitimate bill finance and bill-kiting.

From a modern perspective, bills of exchange were neither pure credit nor pure money, but a mixture of both.[24] A twenty-first-century economist

[20] Wilson (1941, 11) suggests that credit granted by *B* under such circumstances would have been limited to a portion, say, three quarters, of the anticipated value of the goods shipped. In return, *B* would receive interest on any advance credit as well as a commission on the amount of the sale. In an earlier form of this arrangement, *A* would draw bills not on the commission agent *B* but on the party who purchased the goods from *B*.

[21] Collateralization was implicit because bills could not be formally bound to collateral.

[22] The acceptor would, of course, arrange to be repaid for this service, for example, via a bill drawn on the London purchaser.

[23] See, for example, De Vries and Van der Woude (1997, 154). Bill-kiting is our term. Contemporary, more colorful English-language terms for this practice included "raising money by circulation" (Smith 1981 [1776], 310) and "swiveling" (Kosmetatos 2018, 110–13).

[24] According to a definition proposed by Dang, Gorton, and Holmström (2019) and Gorton (2020), debt became money-like when it was short-term, information-insensitive, and backed by other debt. Bills that circulated by endorsement obviously met this definition.

transported back to eighteenth-century Amsterdam would be frustrated in an attempt to construct M_1, M_2, and similar monetary aggregates. Because deposit banking and banknote issue were underdeveloped in Amsterdam, these concepts would have had little meaning. Perhaps a more relevant monetary aggregate would have been the mass of outstanding bills (call this B) either (1) drawn on Amsterdam merchants or (2) drawn on merchants in other locations and sold in the Amsterdam market. No official statistics were ever compiled on B, but the archives of the Bank contain an almost photographic record of the Bank-money component of Amsterdam's bill market. Due to data challenges, we must defer a comprehensive investigation of this market to future research. Using statistics compiled by Dehing (2012), however, it is possible to make an informed guess of its size.

Dehing (2012, 82) shows that the annual number of transactions through the Bank peaked during the 1760s at about 160,000. A typical eighteenth-century bill transaction was for about 2,500 bank florins (Dehing 2012, 140), suggesting a maximum annual payment flow through the Bank of about 400 million bank florins.[25] Assuming these payments were (1) all transactions involving bills and (2) these bills had on average a month to run before settlement, this flow of payments would imply a figure for B of about 33 million (=400 million/12) bank florins. If the stock of current-money bills was (conservatively) half as large as Bank-money bills, then B at its peak would amount to at least 50 million bank florins, or 19 percent of contemporaneous Dutch GDP. The ratio of M_1 to GDP in the United States today is about 18 percent, so even this cautious estimate suggests a high degree of financial development. More generous assumptions would imply a larger size for the Amsterdam bill market. For example, assuming a two-month average maturity for bills and a current-money bill market equal in size to the Bank-money bill market brings the total size of the Amsterdam market to 130 million (=2*400/6) florins. A roughly contemporary (1780) estimate puts the size of this market at about 190 million bank florins (Jonker 1996, 105), which may be near the upper range of reasonable figures.

All major European commercial cities had markets for bills of exchange at this time, but there are reasons to believe that Amsterdam's market was

---

Kahn and Roberds (2007) noted that a bill of exchange could meet this definition even when it did not circulate. More specifically, if the drawee B owed a prior debt to the drawer A, then by drawing a bill on B, A was in effect using the bill to transfer A's claim on B to the beneficiary C.

[25] Of which 11 million, on average, would be through the master account.

the densest of these, despite intense competition from cities such as London, Paris, and Hamburg. Researchers who have analyzed the frequency of eighteenth-century bill price quotations in European cities (Flandreau et al. 2009a; Dehing 2012) have concluded that bills were more likely to be drawn on Amsterdam than anywhere else. Gillard (2004, 261) argues that the success of the Amsterdam bill market derived in part from what economists would term a network effect: merchants in other cities believed that the density of the Amsterdam market, combined with its lack of capital controls, would protect them from idiosyncratic movements in precious metal prices and exchange rates. In addition, Amsterdam's wide range of market connections could allow them to redirect funds obtained there to elsewhere in Europe, at a low cost. Payment, borrowing, or lending through Amsterdam was thought to be cheap, reliable, and convenient. Such beliefs tended to be self-reinforcing, or in plainer language, success bred success.

The Bank of Amsterdam was functionally a central bank, in that its money was central to Amsterdam's core financial market, the bill market. Bank money was a vehicle currency, in that foreign borrowers relied on bills payable at the Bank and maintained access to Bank money through Amsterdam intermediaries, especially merchant banks. The records of this activity have survived for most years of the eighteenth century and comprise a vast amount of information, well beyond our ability to reconstruct. Instead, we focus on how the Bank interacted with the rest of the Amsterdam system.

2.5 Merchant Banks

In this mix of trade credit, discounting, and rollover lending, there was no sharp separation of banking and commerce. Any Amsterdam merchant with sufficient standing could draw a bill, accept a bill, or buy and sell a bill (the last as long as they could find a willing buyer). Yet, over time, there arose distinct types of financial specialists within the Amsterdam market, and the Exchange recognized the sorting of merchants into these types and others. To facilitate trading, merchant groups were assigned a specific area within the interior of the Exchange, which was an open rectangular courtyard surrounded by a colonnade of 46 columns (Figure 2.2). The columns demarcated areas ("arcades") that were allocated to different merchants according to type.[26] Table 2.2 compares three types of

---

[26] The allocation of the arcades is described in Le Moine de L'Espine and Le Long (1763, 49) and illustrated in Petram (2009, 76). Much business, especially money changing, was also conducted just outside the Exchange.

Table 2.2. *Select types of merchants in Amsterdam, circa 1750*

	Approximate number	Specializations
Merchant banks	10	Commission trading, acceptance credit, proprietary trading, sovereign lending
Precious metal dealers	30+	Trading and brokerage of precious metal assets
Cashiers	60	Brokers in the agio (spot) market for Bank money; deposit banking

Sources: van Dillen (1925a, 381–82, 1403–29); Jonker (1996, 235).

merchants that receive attention in this chapter because of their conspicuous presence in the Bank's master account. The Bank's ledgers did not record merchants by type, and these must be inferred from other sources (e.g., Van Dillen 1925a, 1403–29).

The dominant players in Amsterdam's bill market were the merchant banks (*banquiers*), which we will call "banks" (lowercase *b*). Whereas a typical merchant's account at the Bank had one or two transactions a week and a balance of several thousand florins, a top merchant bank's account might record a balance of hundreds of thousands of florins and contain dozens of transactions each week.

The merchant banks' business was often based on family connections. Many banks had family origins in other countries and an extensive network of international contacts.[27] Banks accepted and drew bills from merchant relations all over Europe, and the complexity of a larger bank's account at the Bank (measured in numbers of transactions and counterparties) often rivals or even exceeds that of the Bank's master account. It should be emphasized that the merchant banks did not see themselves as competitors of the Bank, since they occupied distinct niches in the marketplace. This was in part because the concept of a bank in mid-eighteenth-century Amsterdam, as epitomized by its great merchant banks, was quite different from that of deposit banks as then existed in England and as exist in most countries today.[28]

---

[27] Famous examples of Amsterdam banks with foreign roots include Cazenove (France), Clifford (England), Deutz (Germany), Hogguer (France), Horneca (Switzerland), and Hope (Scotland).

[28] According to Clapham (1945a, Chapter 4), few London firms specialized in English deposit banking before 1750, and it then developed rapidly nationwide.

Amsterdam's banks were also merchants, and they dealt extensively in goods as well as finance.[29] Accordingly, assets held by these banks included goods as well as bills and other financial claims. On the liability side of the balance sheet, these banks did not rely on deposits but sought out other channels of funding, notably the Amsterdam bill market. Any bill that bore the signature of a major merchant bank (as drawer, acceptor, or endorser) found ready buyers in the Amsterdam market. Funding via the bill market was seen as a normal way of running a banking business, rather than deposit-taking. The 1763 partnership contract of Hope & Compagnie, one of the largest Amsterdam banks of its day, made this preference explicit with the warning, "... that this firm shall deal exclusively in matters of commerce and commissions, and shall not trade in moneys of deposit or the like" (De Jong-Keesing 1939, 69). This funding preference was evidently not limited to Hope. In Le Moine de L'Espine and Le Long (1763, 50), Amsterdam's banks are generically defined as "great banks [which deal] in bills of exchange" (*groote banquiers in wissel*).

Despite merchant banks' aversion to deposits, their voluminous transaction records show that they did not lack in funding. No charter or other official sanction was required to become a bank, but other merchants only applied the esteemed title of banquier to firms that had demonstrated the requisite financial muscle over long periods of time. At any given moment, there were maybe ten firms in Amsterdam that indisputably qualified as banks, but many more that aspired to be known as such.

A defining activity of merchant banks was placing loans from Amsterdam creditors to foreign sovereigns (Van Dillen 1970, 456–57; Buist 1974; Riley 1980). Sovereign lending was pioneered during the seventeenth and early eighteenth centuries by high-profile firms such as Deutz, Pels, Muilman en Meulenaar, Horneca en Hogguer, and Hope (De Vries and Van der Woude 1997, 140). By the mid-eighteenth century, however, the sovereign lending business had flattened out somewhat and was largely restricted to two borrowers: Britain and Austria (Riley 1980, 119–36). The annual amount of new foreign sovereign debt floated in Amsterdam at mid-century was only about 4 million guilders, small in comparison with its bill market (De Vries and Van der Woude 1997, 120). During the latter half of the eighteenth century, however, demand for sovereign loans (and hence the services of Amsterdam banks) expanded rapidly, increasing Amsterdam creditors' holdings of foreign sovereign

---

[29] Reflecting this real-side activity, an alternative designation for the merchant banks was *handelshuizen* ("trading firms"; see Jonker 1996, 188).

debt from 200 million guilders in 1763 to 350 million by 1780 (Riley 1980, 221). Perhaps the most enduring achievement of the Amsterdam banks would occur later in the century, when a group of them, headed by the Van Staphorst firm, floated loans that refinanced the United States' shaky war debt (Veru 2018, 2021a, b).

The elite merchant banks formed the core of Amsterdam's financial system (Carlos and Neal 2011, 28). Bills drawn on and accepted by the most reputable banks enjoyed special status (i.e., favorable prices and unquestioned liquidity) in the Amsterdam bill market, and by virtue of this status, banks were large suppliers of "acceptance credit," a form of bill finance in which foreign merchants drew bills on Amsterdam merchants, with repayment occurring through bills drawn in the opposite direction.[30] The liquidity of these merchant banks was in turn largely channeled through a single institution, the Bank of Amsterdam, on whose books the bills were traded and settled. The volume of Bank money used by the merchant banks in the bill market was usually much larger than their participation in the other linkages, but merchant banks took full advantage of the Bank receivers' receipt window (described below) to accommodate their own and their customers' needs. Hence, Amsterdam's banks were a major channel through which one form of paper money (bills) was exchanged for metallic assets (especially trade coins), with Bank money serving as the intermediate asset in many such exchanges. In short, merchant banks were all over the map.

Another noteworthy point about Amsterdam's merchant banks is that they were, as compared with deposit banks of later eras, institutions of indeterminate financial "polarity" (Howell 2020, 50). That is, the banks could supply large amounts of liquidity to other participants in Amsterdam's bill markets, but it would be a mistake to think of them as net liquidity providers under all circumstances. Because these banks faced no regulatory constraints on their own trading activity, "polarity reversals" could occur in which the banks could pull liquidity from the Amsterdam market in order to support their own trades. Chapter 8 will provide evidence of a reversal during the Seven Years War, when the banks as a group relied heavily on the Amsterdam bill market in order to fund their

---

[30] See, for example, Büsch (1797, 121) and De Jong-Keesing (1939, 71). The market for acceptance credit was sufficiently competitive that the fees charged by banks for acceptance were surprisingly low, with one-third percent (0.33%) being typical. The availability of such cheap "credit insurance" enhanced the attractiveness of Bank money as a vehicle currency. A disadvantage of this arrangement was that acceptance credit could be withdrawn suddenly in crisis situations, as famously occurred in 1763 (Chapter 7).

large purchases of trade coins, most likely to supply the needs of warring countries.

2.6 Cashiers

Merchant banks were not the only financial intermediaries operating in eighteenth-century Amsterdam. Another important category of intermediaries were the cashiers, who offered paper-based accounts denominated in current guilders. Jonker and Gelderblom (2018) have shown how Dutch commerce made prolific use of ledger balances for payments, of which cashiers were the most specialized in offering accounts that circulated as a medium of exchange. To do so, cashiers also took deposits in local coins, represented by the silver *gulden* coin worth one current guilder. The gulden was the name for a traditional coin in the Netherlands that had disappeared from circulation during the sixteenth century, but which had persisted as the Dutch Republic's unit of account (Korthals Altes 2001, 33–47). A new gulden coin was then reintroduced by Dutch mints starting in 1681 (Polak 1998a, 197–98) and became more prevalent in the eighteenth century. We will refer to the gulden coin by its Dutch name to avoid confusion with the current-money unit of account, the current guilder (cf. Table 2.1).

A deposit and withdrawal relationship with a cashier connected local coins and current-guilder accounts, so cashiers spanned the bottom half of Figure 2.4. The monetary map also splits coins used in international transactions from those used in local transactions. Large coins dominated foreign trade and small coins dominated retail trade, but the line between these types of coins was not always distinct. For simplicity, we will take one current guilder as the boundary between small-value and large-value coins.[31] Various types of small-value coins (*kleingeld*) were used for local transactions, typically coins with some silver content but below one guilder in nominal value (*schellingen*, *dubbeltjes*, and *stuivers*), sometimes referred to collectively as *payement* (Lucassen 2014, 111–21). At the bottom of the monetary prestige scale was the humble *duit*, a copper coin with a nominal value of two pennies or 1/160th of a current guilder.

As noted in Chapter 1, the original business of the cashiers was limited to payments, that is, book-entry settlement in lieu of transfers of coin (Van

---

[31] For an authoritative introduction to the coinage of the Dutch Republic, the reader is referred to Van der Beek, Brzic, and Pol (2009). Our classification of the Republic's coins follows theirs (p. 47).

Velden 1933, 48–50; Heyvaert 1975, 100–5). In the early seventeenth century, widespread complaints about the cashiers caused Amsterdam's governing council to repeatedly attempt to ban them outright (in 1604, 1608, 1609, and 1619) and to displace their business through creation of the Bank (Van Dillen 1925a, 1, 12, 23–25, 45–46). These efforts at eradication were not successful. The services of the cashiers proved too convenient to forgo and they were again given legal status in 1621 (Van Dillen 1925a, 47–49). The business model of the cashiers then expanded toward fractional reserve banking along the lines of the better-known early London goldsmiths.[32] On the liability side of their balance sheet, eighteenth-century cashiers issued deposit receipts or *kwitanties*, demandable obligations that resembled the London goldsmiths' notes (De Jong-Keesing 1939, 80; Jonker 1996, 174–75). On the asset side, the cashiers had become heavily involved in direct lending by the mid-eighteenth century (De Jong-Keesing 1939, 80–84).

Cashiers connected to the Bank in two ways. The first was account-for-account swaps of Bank money for current money, labeled the *agio market* on the map, that cashiers conducted each morning outside the Bank. Persons other than cashiers could participate in this market, but the cashiers were active as brokers. Cashier accounts and Bank accounts were thoroughly separate, so a typical trade in the agio market was for one side to transfer current guilder accounts and the other side to transfer bank florin accounts. Neither transfer created or destroyed either type of account money. Instead, they swapped ownership. The market measured prices of this domestic exchange as the ratio of the two units of account: current guilders per bank florin. For most of the eighteenth century, the ratio favored Bank money, so florins enjoyed a premium. As Dutch book-keeping was derived from Italian accountancy, a premium was often called an agio, and people reported this local rate as the agio of the Bank (a term also applied to monies of other public banks).

At mid-century, a normal range for the agio was between 4 and 5 percent. Bank money was consequently seen as a reasonably stable store of value. Because it did not pay interest, however, and because it had a unique role in the Amsterdam bill market, Bank money tended not to sit idle in customers' accounts. Subsequent disruptive events would cause the agio to fall below this range for extended periods. Figure 2.5 plots monthly agio premia from 1711 to 1793, the period for which the Bank's records are most complete.

---

[32] On the London goldsmith-bankers, see Quinn (1997) and Temin and Voth (2013).

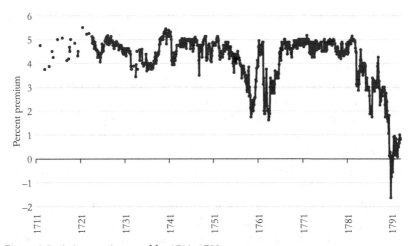

Figure 2.5. Agio premia, monthly, 1711–1793
Sources: Gillard (2004) and Schneider, Schwarzer, and Schnelzer (1991).

The other cashier-dominated connection involved the occasional trade of local coins for Bank accounts. These operations were initiated by the Bank as a discretionary policy to stabilize the quantity of Bank money (Quinn and Roberds 2019).[33] The map represents this as a diagonal line labeled open market operations. When the Bank purchased gulden coins with Bank money or the reverse, cashiers were the frequent counterparty because they traded in both types of money. Cashiers kept accounts at the Bank to be able to take either side of the agio trade, and cashiers held gulden local coins to satisfy withdrawals. These operations let the Bank manipulate the current side of the monetary system without directly interacting with the current guilder accounts offered by cashiers. In effect, the Bank engaged in domestic exchange interventions, as will be detailed in Chapter 7.

As many as 61 firms operated in mid-eighteenth-century Amsterdam as cashiers (Jonker 1996, 235). These appear to have been much smaller firms than the merchant banks, judging from tax records (Gelderblom, Jonker, and Kool 2016, 1180) and cashiers' names that can be matched to specific Bank accounts.[34] Despite their lesser individual size, the cashiers in

---

[33] It is unknown whether these transactions occurred privately or in the daily open market for Bank money. A 1782 directive required that all trades by the Bank's assayer remain secret, which we suspect was the usual practice (Mees 1838, 327–28). Technical details of these transactions are deferred until Chapter 7.

[34] Unlike Amsterdam's precious metal dealers (discussed below), there were a few (if any) Jewish cashiers (De Jong-Keesing 1939, 83).

aggregate formed a substantial deposit-based, current-money banking system that operated in parallel to the Bank-money system that was dominated by the merchant banks.[35] Compared with the deposit banks that were developing in contemporary London, however, Amsterdam's cashiers operated at a relatively informal level. Specialized rules governing creditors' recourse with kwitanties, for example, were not published until 1776 (Van Dillen 1925a, 424–25).[36] The slow development of deposit banking in Amsterdam was likely more attributable to the success of the traditional alternative – merchant banking in combination with the services offered by the Bank – than financial backwardness (Gelderblom, Jonker, and Kool 2016). With the decline of the Bank at the close of the eighteenth century, the cashiers grew to occupy a more prominent position in the Republic's financial system (Jonker 1996, 233–47).

The roles of banks and cashiers in eighteenth-century Amsterdam offer a notable contrast to the present-day situation in the United States. Especially since the 2008 financial crisis, there has been much discussion of "shadow banks" in the US-dollar financial system (Pozsar et al. 2010). Modern shadow banks have been defined as institutions that functionally resemble banks but (1) lack bank charters and so cannot take deposits and are thus entirely market-funded and (2) have no public-sector credit guarantees. Shadow banks nonetheless have created liabilities that, under normal conditions, are seen as safe and liquid enough to substitute for bank deposits. Loss of confidence in these pseudo-deposits played a prominent role in the 2007–2008 financial crisis.

In eighteenth-century Amsterdam, the status of market-funded and deposit-funded institutions was reversed. The more respectable institutions were the market-funded merchant banks, which were also the institutions most connected to the Bank. Playing second fiddle were the deposit-taking cashiers, who could interact with the Bank, but preferred to do much of their business away from the Bank and its tight restrictions on eligible collateral (generally, only trade coins qualified for Bank credit at the receipt window). The distinction between mainstream (merchant) banking and lesser (cashier) banking was underlined by the existence of dual units of

---

[35] Knowledge of the cashiers' operations has been limited by the lack of any surviving set of books. Some indirect evidence on the cashiers' activity was provided by Dehing (2012, 138–39). Dehing identified 55 cashiers that had active Bank accounts in 1726. The total turnover in their Bank accounts, 30 million florins for that year, was about equal to that of the merchant banks.

[36] We conjecture that these formal rules were a response to distress experienced by cashiers during financial crises in 1763 and 1772–1773.

account, merchant banks dominating transactions in the former (bank florins) and cashiers the latter (current guilders). Mainstream banks lacked state guarantees, but strove to be seen as above the market disruptions that could buffet smaller players such as the cashiers. As occurred in 2008, however, the walls separating mainstream banks and lesser banks did not always hold. The Crisis of 1763, discussed in Chapter 7, was an event where failure of one merchant bank provoked widespread runs on the cashiers, which in turn exerted pressure on even the most respected merchant banks in Amsterdam.

Both merchant banks and cashiers used the Bank of Amsterdam, but their relationships were different. The Bank was central to the international bills of exchange used to fund the merchant banks. The Bank was not central to the current money system used to fund cashiers, and it was the cashiers who maintained the agio market that connected current and Bank money. The Bank only occasionally intervened in current money with open market operations that constituted monetary policy of the large-scale, operational style. What remains to survey is international trade coins, the type of money central to the Bank and thus a focus of this book.

2.7 Trade Coins and Precious Metal Dealers

Trade coins dominated the last quadrant of the monetary map. Many types of coins were present in the eighteenth-century Republic and in large numbers. De Vries and Van der Woude (1997, 90) put the Republic's total stock of coined money at 200 million guilders by the end of the century, equal to about 73 percent of its annual GDP. Coins present in Amsterdam included both Dutch coins and foreign coins of gold and silver. Oftentimes the Bank's vaults held more foreign than domestic coins. Foreign coins tended to be large-value trade coins used for international transactions (*negotiepenningen* or *handelspenningen*), and people could utilize precious metal dealers to move between them and domestic coins. Some types of large-value Dutch coins functioned mainly as trade coins and others functioned mainly as local coins (*standpenningen*). The economic distinction between trade coins and local coins is the focus of Chapter 3.

The direct connection between Bank money and trade coins was a standing facility we call the *receipt window*. With this facility, a merchant could sell eligible (Dutch and foreign) trade coins to a Bank receiver at a fixed price, receiving in turn credit on their Bank account and a receipt (*recepis*). The receipt was a negotiable American call option (a purchase option) on the sold coin, entitling its holder to repurchase that coin within six months at a slight premium over the sale price (¼ percent for most silver coins). The option could be rolled over at the same cost. A merchant wishing to redeem Bank money for a certain type of large coin could either redeem their own receipt or purchase a receipt from another merchant (van Dillen 1934, 102–3). Small-value coins were not eligible for use at the receipt window.[37]

We will cover the origins of the receipt window in Chapter 5, and we will delve into the challenge of making it work in Chapter 6, but receipts had several features that merit mention here. The Bank viewed credit granted through the receipt window as extremely well secured, so well secured that it did not even consider it as credit, even though the fee for redeeming a receipt often functioned as an interest rate on Bank money (if the receipt was eventually redeemed, as most were). If a receipt expired without being exercised, however, the Bank simply kept the "fallen" coin and sold it off when conditions were right. This degree of comfort allowed the Bank to offer uniform, low interest rates (i.e., receipt redemption fees) at the receipt window to all customers, with some rare exceptions, a feature that contributed to the receipt window's popularity as a funding channel. Also, the Bank only rarely varied redemption fees in response to market conditions, another feature that increased the predictability of merchants' funding costs and bolstered the Bank's popularity.

The monetary map also reveals an alternative way to exchange trade coins for Bank money. This took three steps that could be combined: trade foreign coins for domestic coins, deposit the domestic coins with a cashier, and have the cashier sell your account balance to someone for their Bank balance. The process relied on (1) a price set in the market for coins and (2) a price set in the agio market, the daily spot market held outside the Town Hall. Spot trades in the second market could be executed either directly or through cashiers, who served as brokers in this market. Trading of coins (in addition to cashiers' balances) in this market was normally for small-value coins, although large-value trade coins could also be exchanged at a premium (Le Moine de L'Espine and Le Long 1763, 187). These transactions occurred outside the Bank and created a relevant alternative that constrained Bank policies governing the receipt window.

Merchants we will designate as *precious metal dealers* mediated these various ways to trade between coins, and between coins and accounts. These dealers were firms with family roots in Germany or eastern Europe,

---

[37] The term "small" here is relative, meaning less than one guilder in value. In today's money, a gulden (one-guilder) coin would approximate a €200 note.

were invariably Jewish, and in contemporary sources are often referred to simply as *hoogduytsche Joden* or German Jews.[38] Like the cashiers, Amsterdam's precious metal dealers were smaller-scale firms than the merchant banks and were not involved in sovereign lending. Nor did they offer proto-deposit banking services, as did the cashiers. Entries in the Bank's master account and other sources suggested that during the mid-eighteenth century, about 25 to 30 of these firms were active in Amsterdam.[39] Lacking the same easy access to bill market funding as the merchant banks, the precious metals dealers' business was focused on trading and arbitrage of various types of gold and silver, coined and uncoined. These firms' trading activity is reflected in their frequent sales of trade coins at the receipt window, and equally in their frequent repurchase. The precious metal dealers served as intermediaries for other merchants and were also important suppliers of metals to the Dutch mints, an activity we will return to in later chapters. Again returning to the map, the precious metal dealers played an instrumental role in every connective market that involved gold and silver.

The receipt facility was how the Bank conducted its routine, daily monetary policy. Chapter 5 visits how this facility came to be, and Chapter 6 reveals how the Bank's choice of terms and conditions dramatically affected customers' use of the window. The underlying factor driving these developments was the universal recognition of trade coins as safe assets, and that function of trade coins will be addressed in Chapter 3. To explore the last major way the Bank created money, we now turn to lending.

2.8 The Dutch East India Company

The monetary map and preceding sections focused on merchants who made the money markets work: merchant banks, cashiers, and

---

[38] This group was described, for example, in Le Moine de L'Espine and Le Long (1763, 49, 59) or van Dillen (1970, 452). Van Dillen described another group of Jewish firms in Amsterdam of at least equal economic importance, most with family roots in Portugal. This group served as brokers in bills of exchange and other financial claims, and showed up less frequently in the Bank's master account. Brokerage and precious metal dealing were among the limited number of occupations open to Jewish residents of eighteenth-century Amsterdam.

[39] The total number of precious metal dealers was uncertain. Dehing (2012, 383) counts 49 German Jewish account holders at the Bank in 1726. By 1749, however, only 26 Amsterdam merchants with German Jewish family names are listed on a petition concerning coinage (van Dillen 1925a, 381–82).

moneychangers. These merchants also used most of the types of money. The same was true for the Bank's largest customer: the Dutch East India Company (units of the *Vereenigde Oostindische Compagnie*, often known by its initials *VOC*), a limited-liability, nationally chartered company. The Bank also serviced a second chartered company, the West India Company (*Westindische Compagnie* or *WIC*), but the East India Company had by far the greater impact on the operations of the Bank. This was in part because the Bank from its earliest days extended credit to the East India Company (van Dillen 1934, 94). Such lending was an apparent departure from the Bank's original mission, but it was nonetheless repeatedly sanctioned by the City's governing council (van Dillen 1970, 449). The Bank was reluctant to extend credit to the less successful West India Company (van Dillen 1970, 168).[40]

The Dutch East India Company (VOC), founded in 1602, enjoyed a legal monopoly on the Dutch Republic's trade with Asia. Its scale of operation was remarkable for the time. Over the course of the seventeenth and eighteenth centuries, the VOC dispatched approximately 4,700 ships and 1 million people to Asia (Bruijn, Gaastra, and Schöffer 1987, 143). In the 1750s, the VOC was sending about 23 ships and 8,000 personnel eastward each year, and it employed some 36,000 people worldwide (DeVries 2003, 57, 72). The organization of such a large, geographically dispersed enterprise was necessarily decentralized. Top-level management decisions were made by a board of directors, known as the Seventeen Gentlemen (*Heren Zeventien*). Each year the directors decided, based on a request from the Governor General (the highest official stationed in Asia), what goods would be imported to various Dutch cities and what goods would be shipped out to exchange for Asian goods (Gaastra 1983, 462–63). Implementation of the directors' master plan, however, was delegated to the VOC's semi-autonomous divisions or "chambers" based in six Dutch cities: Amsterdam, Middelburg, Enkhuizen, Delft, Hoorn, and Rotterdam (Gaastra 1983, 448). The Amsterdam Chamber was by far the largest player among these, and for shorthand, we will often refer to the Amsterdam Chamber of the VOC simply as the Company. Each chamber had an active account at the Bank, and the complexity (as measured in

---

[40] In the eighteenth century, the West India Company's principal line of business was delivering slaves from Africa to the New World, many of them to Spanish colonies (Postma 1990). This activity brought the WIC into direct competition with state-sponsored traders based in other European countries and private slave traders. The East India Company's trade with Asia was logistically more challenging and thus more secure from competition.

transactions and counterparties) of the Amsterdam Chamber's account rivals that of the Bank's master account.

The overall character of the Company's relationship with the Bank was one of symbiosis occasionally straying into parasitism. The Bank helped the Company acquire the enormous amounts of precious metal necessary for its trade with Asia, and loans to the Company provided the Bank with a steady stream of rich earnings. These were profitable activities but not without risk.

The VOC's business model relied on ready access to large amounts of hard assets – gold and silver in both trade coin and bar form, often supplemented with copper coin – because European goods were not in demand in Asia. The basic mix of metallic assets chosen for each year's voyages was determined by the Seventeen Gentlemen, with leeway allowed to the individual chambers. Records compiled by Gaastra (1976, 1983) and Bruijn, Gaastra, and Schöffer (1987, 187, 223–45) show an upshift in the VOC's precious metal demand after about 1685, which was attributed to Japan curtailing its silver exports. In earlier decades, the VOC had been able to rely on Japan as its principal source of precious metal to purchase goods from other places in Asia.[41] Afterward, it relied increasingly on Europe and especially on Amsterdam. During the 1750s, the VOC sent about 6 million guilders in metallic assets around the Cape of Good Hope each year, equivalent in value to 58 tons of silver (De Vries 2003, 76). Most (about 85 percent) of this material was destined for India (De Zwart and van Zanden 2018, 155). One measure of the stress placed on the VOC by this cash flow was its tolerance of insider chicanery as a secondary means of transporting silver to Asia. During this time period, silver transport via unofficial channels (mostly, smuggling by VOC ships' crews) amounted to about 2.3 million guilders or 22 tons of silver annually (Gaastra 1976, 259; Lucassen and Van Rossum 2016; this activity is discussed in Chapter 3). Other ongoing sources of cash drain on the VOC included the outfitting of trading fleets, as well as payment of wages to crews and dividends to stockholders.

The Bank helped maintain the liquidity of the Dutch East India Company (and its silver-smuggling employees) in several ways. Pol (1985) documented that the VOC often purchased coins held at the

---

[41] The VOC's other within-Asia sources of silver were Persia and the Philippines (Gaastra 1983, 466–67; De Vries 2003, 76). Early eighteenth-century political developments shut off supply from these countries as well as Japan, leaving Amsterdam as the VOC's main source of silver.

Bank for its supply of hard money. Favored types of coin included Spanish dollars, Dutch gold coins, and Dutch *ducatons* (also called *zilveren rijders*), silver trade coins that were also heavily used for smuggling. In addition, the Bank often directly sold trade coins on its own account to various chambers of the VOC (Pol 1985, 181–85). Finally, when prices were right, various parties would withdraw coins from the Bank and melt them into specialized ingots for use by the VOC.[42] All of these activities tended to place the Bank and its customers into competition with the Dutch mints as purchasers of precious metal and as VOC suppliers. This sometimes led to complaints by the mint masters that the Bank and the Company were overbidding the metal prices, thereby undermining the Republic's monetary standards (see, e.g., Van Dillen 1925a, 359–60).

A more profitable, but ultimately more destructive channel of Bank support for the VOC took the form of direct loans to the Amsterdam Chamber. The Bank granted the first such loan in 1615 and the loans continued up until the Bank's downfall in 1795, with occasional pauses (Van Dillen 1934, 110–15). Much of this lending nominally took the form of anticipation loans (*anticipatiepenningen*), advances granted by the Bank against the expected sales of Company goods in transit from Asia. In practice, one anticipation loan would often be granted by the Bank just as another was paid off, effectively giving the Company a standing credit balance at the Bank, one that could be increased or paid down, largely at the Company's discretion (Van Dillen 1970, 449). At the mid-eighteenth-century, Company debt carried an interest rate of 3 percent and payment of this interest was an important source of income for the Bank (Van Dillen 1934, 110–12).[43]

Lending large sums to a globally extended mega-firm was an inherently risky line of business. The Bank seems to have done very little to actively manage this risk, such as accumulate reserves against possible loan losses or significantly adjusting the interest rates charged to the Company. Instead, the Bank's comfort with a steady source of income led Bank managers to accept a status quo of high exposure to the Company (Uittenbogaard 2009). This exposure expanded sharply during the

---

[42] For much of its trade in Asia, the VOC used standardized silver ingots, whose weight and fineness were matched to the specifications of Indian and Thai mints (Pol 1985, 73). Some of the VOC's trade ingots were cast by the Bank, others by Bank assayers for their own account, and yet others by Dutch provincial mint masters, again trading for their own account (Pol 1985, 104).

[43] Before 1751, the rate was occasionally adjusted within the range of 2.5–3.5 percent (Van Dillen 1925a, 950).

Fourth Anglo-Dutch War, with disastrous consequences for the Bank. Later chapters will explore these and other aspects of the relationship between the Bank and the Company.

2.9 Fiscal Aspects of the Bank

To operate as a central bank, the Bank needed political support, and the quid pro quo for that support was fiscal exploitation. Although the Bank was not conceived as a debt management agency, it was subjected to fiscal pressure from its earliest days. Subsequent chapters will note that the City's fiscal exploitation of the Bank took two forms, in addition to the lending to the Amsterdam Chamber of the VOC that was described earlier. The first and more routine form of exploitation was the City's annual skimming of Bank profits. A second and more insidious form of exploitation nominally took the form of loans granted to the City, which only rarely were followed by repayment of either principal or interest. Instead, the loan balances were written off on a gradual schedule that preserved the nominal solvency of the Bank. Our more realistic view is to recognize such loans as immediate and permanent subtractions from the Bank's equity.

Why was the Bank exploited in this way? The relevant records are incomplete, but available evidence indicates that the City of Amsterdam was not under acute fiscal pressure in the mid-eighteenth century. This was to some extent a reflection of the Republic's fiscal structure, which delegated tax burdens primarily to the provincial rather than to the municipal level (Fritschy 2003). At mid-century, the City's annual interest expense was about 300,000 guilders, an amount easily covered by tax revenue (Fritschy 2003, 81). The City's fiscal exploitation of the Bank continued nonetheless, perhaps as a politically expedient means of extracting revenue in a high-tax environment. Given the close connections of the Bank's management to the Amsterdam patriciate, however, it is unlikely that the Bank's fiscal exploitation would have continued without their consent.

Modern macroeconomists (e.g., Bassetto and Sargent 2020 or Buiter 2021) might even be tempted to argue that the Bank's exploitation by the City and the Company was only a matter of bookkeeping, since a true accounting would unify the balance sheets of the fiscal authority (the City), its government-sponsored enterprise (the Company), and its central bank (the Bank).[44]

---

[44] Perhaps one of the few contemporary thinkers to have understood the unity of fiscal accounting was John Law (Murphy 1997; Velde 2003; Neal 2012). However, Law was unable to convert his prescient vision into a viable monetary and fiscal system.

Practical unity, however, would have required explicit acknowledgment of responsibility by the City for the financial condition of the Bank. During the Crisis of 1790, angry Bank customers presented a petition to the effect that such a City guarantee had always been implicit in the Bank's charter (Van Dillen 1925a, 449–54). While City leaders agreed with the petitioners in principle, their subsequent attempt at bailing out the insolvent Bank was belated and partial.

2.10 Conclusion

Eighteenth-century visitors to Amsterdam's Town Hall may have been surprised to learn that this monumental building, the Bank included, rests on a seemingly precarious foundation. To erect a 22,000-square-meter sandstone structure on the fluid soil bordering the Amstel River, engineers first had to drive over 13,000 wooden piles into the earth beneath. The Town Hall, the Bank included, was thus not so much anchored into the underlying ground as it was balanced above it. Amsterdammers themselves were not bothered by this building technique, which was common to many structures throughout the city, their (often slightly tilted) houses included. Wooden piles were widely used in construction throughout the Republic, not in the least as a component of the dikes that provided protection against floods.

The mid-eighteenth-century Bank's financial condition embodied this same tension between solidity and fragility. Outwardly, the Bank was wildly popular, the liquidity available through its receipt facility attracting and dispensing trade coins to and from diverse locations, and in record quantities. Atop this pool of metallic liquidity was a dense bill market, whose credit-creating capability extended over much of Europe. Market insiders, including chartered corporations, banks, precious metal dealers, and cashiers, transacted in and arbitraged across various types of monetary assets: bills of exchange, bullion, trade coins, gulden, cashiers' receipts, and, above all, Bank money.

The great buzz of metal and paper around the Bank masked an inward vulnerability, however. At the end of the day, the Bank was a lightly capitalized fiat money issuer chartered by a single municipality in a small country with a weak central government. Within Amsterdam, the Bank enjoyed firm political support though from a narrow, if politically dominant clientele, but interests aligned with this clientele (the City Treasury and the Amsterdam Chamber of the Dutch East India Company) subjected the Bank to routine and at times excessive exploitation, without providing guarantees in return. Since the Bank's financial condition was not public information, the only binding limit on such exploitation was that it would not put the Bank into obvious financial distress, that is, put the Bank into a situation that would require an immediate capital injection from the City. Later chapters will show how the Bank was able to manage away from this vulnerability, in the sense that capital injections were avoided until late in the Bank's existence (1791). The downside of this vulnerability, however, was that the Bank's policy choices were sharply constrained in crisis situations.

During the eighteenth century, many coastal areas of the Republic were invaded by a mollusk, the *paalwurm*, which attacked and gradually hollowed out the wooden piles that were exposed to the sea (De Vries and Van der Woude 1997, 22). Residents in these areas were left with little choice but to replace these piles at enormous expense. In what follows, we will argue that a similar if less obvious hollowing out was occurring at the Bank, with the role of the paalwurm played by prominent local interests. Efforts at shoring up this vital piece of financial infrastructure did not come until they were too little and much too late.

A.2 The Fiscal and Monetary Policies of the Dutch Republic

Readers familiar with the history of the Bank of England may ask why the Bank of Amsterdam did not assume a more active role in managing the debt of the Dutch Republic. This appendix attempts to shed some light on that issue by providing a brief overview of the fiscal and monetary policies of the Republic and how these related to the Bank.

The most remarkable attribute of the Dutch Republic may be that it survived for over two centuries, despite its loose political organization and the active hostility of larger countries. While it is a gospel of American history that states with weak central governments are fragile constructs (the United States of America under the Articles of Confederation cited as the canonical example), the seventeenth-century Republic contradicted this principle by repeatedly getting the best of larger adversaries. Full independence from Spain was achieved in 1648 and a major invasion by France was repelled in 1672.[45] A successful takeover of the British throne was implemented in 1688.[46]

---

[45] 't Hart (2014) attributed these victories in part to a high degree of professionalism in the Republic's military, which itself was revolutionary for the time.

[46] This last event was known as the Glorious Revolution, and in classic accounts (e.g., Macauley 1848) is presented as the Stadholder of several Dutch provinces, Willem

The Republic enjoyed at least two key advantages in such conflicts: a natural endowment of waterlogged terrain that was resistant to invasion, and an acquired advantage of a robust fiscal capacity that allowed the Republic to outlast its often bogged-down (fiscally as well as physically) enemies. The Republic's fiscal policy, though evidently effective, was complex due to its decentralized character.[47] In keeping with the political structure of the Republic, most of its public debt was issued by individual provinces and the dominant province Holland bore a disproportionate share of the fiscal burden. High taxes were a fact of life, although 't Hart (2014) notes that much of the Republic's military expenditure occurred within its own territory, with the resulting economic stimulus helping to offset its cost. The bill for ongoing warfare against larger countries was nonetheless substantial, and by the early eighteenth century, the Republic's per capita tax burden was easily double that of even its richest rival, Britain (Fritschy 2017, 270).

By the mid-eighteenth century, the accumulated cost of various wars pushed Holland's debt to 300 million guilders or twice the province's annual GDP (Fritschy 2017, 165). This debt load could only be sustained through a combination of imaginative marketing and the Republic's immense pool of accumulated savings, which combined to keep interest rates low (Gelderblom and Jonker 2011). This was nonetheless a barely sustainable debt burden and one with negative consequences. Following the end of the costly War of Spanish Succession in 1714, the Republic attempted to limit its fiscal commitments by withdrawing from European politics. In the 1740s, however, it was pulled back into the political theater by the War of Austrian Succession, leading to a surge in military expenditures and to forced reductions of interest (i.e., partial default) on Holland's debt (Fritschy 2017, 158), as well as to the imposition of a one-time, Republic-wide wealth tax (the "Liberal Gift" of 1747; see Liesker and Fritschy 2004, 104). In 1748, dissatisfaction with increasing taxation led to riots against tax farmers, threatening the Republic with civil disorder (De Vries and Van der Woude 1997, 123). By mid-century, Holland's debt

---

(William) III, graciously accepting an invitation from English dissidents to take over the British throne. Modern scholarship (Israel and Parker 1991) has emphasized that Willem acted on this invitation by showing up with a well-funded invasion force, double the size of the better-known Spanish Armada.

[47] Literature on the fiscal history of the Republic has included DeVries and Van der Woude (1997, 91–129), Fritschy and Van der Voort (1997), 't Hart (1997), Gelderblom and Jonker (2011), and the recent monograph by Fritschy (2017).

had ballooned to 350 million guilders (Fritschy 2017, 165) and carried a hefty annual interest expense of 14.5 million guilders (Fritschy 2003, 77).

In this environment of fiscal duress, it is notable that little provincial debt found its way onto the books of the Bank, which remained firmly in the grip of the City. At the mid-eighteenth century, Holland's loan balance comprised less than 2 percent of Bank assets, and this balance was not a major source of income or risk exposure to the Bank. With so much government debt being issued, it is also significant that the Dutch Republic did not develop a centralized secondary market for the debt, as occurred in contemporary Britain. Reasons for this divergence are laid out in van Bochove (2013). Diffusion of political power discouraged the formation of a centralized market. Debt tended to be issued and redeemed at the provincial or even local level. Creditors were dispersed throughout the Republic rather than concentrated in Amsterdam, and much of the public debt was issued as short-term bills that were either rolled over or simply held to maturity rather than traded in secondary markets. The overall level of satisfaction with this system was sufficiently high that there was little impetus for the creation of an entity to manage government debt at a national level.

The Republic also took a decentralized approach to monetary policy. Coinage standards were set in mint ordinances enacted by the States General, but actual production of coin was delegated to mints owned by the provinces (Polak 1998a).[48] In particular, for reasons of political jealousy, no mint was located in Amsterdam. The two closest provincial mints to the Bank were in the cities of Utrecht (owned by the Province of Utrecht) and Dordrecht (owned by the Province of Holland). The latter attempted to open a branch office in Amsterdam, which was soon shut down by the States General (Van Dillen 1925a, 382). Typical for the time, these mints were run as entrepreneurial, revenue-producing operations, with negative implications for coin quality. A national supervisory body, the General Mint Masters (*Generaalmeesters van de Munt*), monitored the mints and reported its findings to the States General, but in practice, the General Mint Masters could not exercise perfect control. Decentralization of responsibility for coin quality inevitably led to conflicts among the Bank and its Amsterdam clientele, the provincial mints, and the General Mint Masters. Chapter 4 will explore these conflicts of interest and their consequences for the Bank.

---

[48] Municipal mints had operated in earlier times, but these were closed at the end of the seventeenth century (van Dillen 1970, 445).

Of course, the Republic's decentralized approach to monetary policy could not alter the de facto concentration of money and credit flows through Amsterdam. As noted previously, however, bills drawn on Amsterdam counterparties from within the Republic were often current-money rather than Bank-money bills. In this sense, the Bank did not play the role of a national central bank for the Dutch Republic.

3

Coins in Eighteenth-Century Amsterdam

To explain how coins worked in the eighteenth-century Dutch Republic, the Scottish economist James Steuart (1767a, 78) observed,

It is very true that what must appear an inextricable perplexity to a stranger, is really none at all to the Dutch.

We today are among the strangers, for the Republic certainly had an idiosyncratic monetary system. Its popular gold coin had no official price. Silver coins had assigned prices, but those prices were often ignored. It was, however, the world within which the Bank operated. To extricate some coherence, this chapter describes the coinage system as the union of two distinct but related sub-systems: trade coins and local coins.[1] Trade coins traveled the world and passed at their market prices. Local coins stayed home and circulated at their assigned prices.[2] Bullion formed a background system because all coins were created from it and could be melted back. All this comprised the metal side of the monetary map in Figure 2.4. The preceding chapter introduced these assets: Bank money, bills of exchange, trade coins, local coins, current-guilder ledger balances, and bullion. This chapter focuses on the three metallic forms and how they link to each other. Most of the Bank's monetary policies discussed in Chapters 5 through 7 were interactions of its ledger money with these forms of metallic money.

To distinguish between bullion and coins, this chapter takes a functional approach focused on how people used coins to deal with information

---

[1] The situation in eighteenth-century Amsterdam could be viewed as what Velde, Weber, and Wright (1999, 303–4) term a "by-weight equilibrium." In the context of their model, local coins in Amsterdam functioned as "light coins" and trade coins functioned as "heavy coins."

[2] Fantacci (2008, 67–71) described a similar sorting by usage in Renaissance Florence.

problems. Bullion was an important store of value but required expertise to trade. Turning bullion into coins solved some of these problems by *reducing* access to information. At first glance, it seemed obvious that people viewed coins as safe precisely because they knew what was in the coins. Upon further reflection, such clarity would be problematic, because actual contents varied and people would be motivated to investigate (Gorton 2017, 551). Such discoverability was what impeded bullion from passing with the highly desirable quality of "no questions asked." This chapter argues that opacity reduced questions about the relevant variation between individual coins. It helped the Bank to proceed as if coins were uniform and complemented the perception of homogeneity promoted by governments and mints.

The Dutch Republic supplied a variety of coin brands and usually assigned each a price. How people responded to those official prices distinguished trade coins from local coins.[3] In retail transactions, people used assigned prices because local commerce benefitted most from coins maintaining stable prices within a jurisdiction. In wholesale transactions, people ignored the assigned prices because international trade benefitted most from coins maintaining a stable value between jurisdictions.[4] An innovation of the Bank was to offer a space wherein trade coins had a stable price. The Bank could do this because the bank florin was a distinct unit of account. Within the Bank's network, trade coins had retail convenience in high-value increments.

Economists have described how local coins functioned as circulation by tale and how trade coins functioned as circulation by weight, puzzling: "Why would coins circulate by tale?" (Rolnick, Velde, and Weber 1996, 790). The question combined the quantum of metal (tale if by the coin, weight if by gram) with the mode of its pricing (tale if by ordinance, weight if by market). The Dutch answer parsed the question. Successful coins were usually transacted by tale even if they were described as circulating by weight. Instead, how coins were priced depended on usage. The result was that coins played the role of safe assets in the Dutch system comparable in some respects to the roles of paper currency (local coins) and government securities (trade coins) in today's world. In principle, a coin could perform

---

[3] This distinction can be seen as an example of the nominalism (local coins) versus metalism (trade coins) perspectives with a long legal history. See Fox, Velde, and Ernst (2016).

[4] The model of Velde, Weber, and Wright (1999, 293, 297) concorded with this outcome by incorporating an assumption that international trade required coins to circulate at prices reflecting their intrinsic metallic content.

in either role, and in the seventeenth century, coins were often asked to do both. The complications that ensued form the gist of the Bank's origin story addressed in the next chapter. In the eighteenth century, however, people used most types of coins in only one of these two ways. Coins bifurcated into distinct transactional platforms with each focused on a specialized role, and it worked rather well. The Dutch produced many trade coins for export and kept the quality and price of local coins stable. This dual coinage system gave rise to a "mirror-image" dual monetary system (as shown in the top row and bottom row of Figure 2.4), within which the high-tide Bank operated and which strangers found inscrutable.

3.1 Safe Assets Then and Now

Gorton (2017, 548) defined safe assets as those that are "relatively immune to the costly production of private information about their value." Safe assets ordinarily trade with no questions asked and hence may take on a (quasi-) monetary role. Gorton cited fiat money, insured bank deposits, and government debt as leading examples of safe assets today. In modern economies, the perception of safety has been promoted by transparency: publicly available information has reduced incentives for private discovery. Government debt is auctioned and subsequent trading is dense. Central banks have gone to great lengths to explain the policies that govern their creation of fiat money. Bank deposits have been backed by explicit governmental guarantees. For certain developed countries, the perceived convenience (safety and liquidity) of those countries' monies and debts has allowed them to trade at higher prices than fundamental factors and economic models would predict.[5] Market participants expect that such assets can trade at premium prices, in part because everyone agrees that they can.

Modern safe assets are also easily valued. Residents of present-day Amsterdam can purchase a €5 coffee drink with five €1 coins, a €5 note, or a €10 note with the expectation of receiving €5 in change. Alternatively, they can buy the same beverage with their bank account (via a debit card) and expect to pay the same price. Their bank can exchange euro coins and banknotes one-for-one for credit in its account with De Nederlandsche Bank (the Dutch central bank, a member of the Eurosystem). The same commercial bank can easily convert government securities to euros by

---

[5] The existence of a convenience premium on US Treasury debt, for example, was documented in studies such as Krishnamurthy and Vissing-Jorgenson (2012) or Jiang et al. (2019).

borrowing against them at De Nederlandsche Bank at a fixed policy interest rate. The prices in all these exchanges are so predictable that these assets are seen as inextricably bound to the unit of account. A coin euro is a banknote euro is a bank-account euro.

In the early modern era, the production, dissemination, and valuation of safe assets was less straightforward. The human cost of these activities was also high. Great quantities of gold and silver ore were extracted in unimaginably squalid conditions, through intense utilization of (mostly low-) wage labor, forced labor, and outright slave labor.[6] Mass exploitation of human resources did not stop once ore had been mined: the popular refining process of amalgamation required workers to wallow in pools of crushed ore mixed with mercury, to cite one example. To cite another, the majority of sailors on the specie-laden ships of the Dutch East India Company would never return to the Republic (De Vries 2003, 72).

The end result of this chain of misery was a worldwide distribution of coins that were seen as safe assets, albeit ones of high opacity over relevant margins. Opaque means that it was difficult to discover a coin's precise content. This shared ambiguity simplified the use of coins, because people often treated them as possessing what they *should* have and not what they *did* have. This helped nations promote coins as a trusted, homogeneous product. Popular coins could trade at prices above their legally assigned value and above what many people felt was justified by fundamental factors, which in this era meant fine metal content (Kuroda 2008a, 13). The phenomena of opacity and the associated convenience premia applied locally, aided by legal restrictions. For trade coins, these premia could project across borders through the medium of international brands, often to the consternation of contemporary observers. Johann Philipp Graumann, for example, who served as Brunswick's and later Prussia's mint master, lamented the elevated value that Baltic merchants attached to the Dutch *rijksdaalder*:[7]

We have seen their price holding at eight percent above their value in Dutch current money, and four percent above their value in the money of the Bank of Hamburg. ... [T]he Dutch really have an eight percent advantage [in the Baltic trade], and your lordships see why.

(Graumann 1749, 14)

---

[6] On early modern methods of ore extraction and refining, see Brown (2012).
[7] This passage refers to a coin with the official name of *zilveren dukaat* (Polak 1998b, 72). This coin was commonly called the rijksdaalder in the Netherlands and the Albertusthaler in Germany.

Table 3.1. *Common trade coins in Amsterdam, circa 1750*

Name at the Bank	Translation	Place of origin	Name at origin
SILVER			
Ducatons	Silver ducats	Dutch Republic	Zilveren rijders
Rijksdaalders	Imperial dollars	Dutch Republic	Zilveren dukaten
Staten drieguldens	Republic three guilders	Dutch Republic	Staten drieguldens
Pilaren	Pillar pieces of eight	Peru	Reales de a ocho
Mexicanen	Mexican pieces of eight	Mexico	Reales de a ocho
Franse kronen	French crowns	France	Ecus
Englische kronen	English crowns	England	Crowns
GOLD			
Dukaten	Gold ducats	Dutch Republic	Goude dukaten
Crusaden	Coins with a cross	Portugal	Cruzados
Franse pistolen	French gold coins	France	Louis d'ors
Spanse pistolen	Spanish gold coins	Spain	Escudos
Guinees	Guineas	England	Guineas

Source: Authors' assessment, based on examination of the Bank's records.
Note: The spelling of coins' names varies in the original sources. For consistency, we employ modern Dutch spelling for ducats (singular *dukaat* and plural *dukaten*).

More succinct but no less wistful was James Steuart's (1767a, 59) commentary on French gold coins:

Louis d'ors, . . . pass current, almost everywhere, for more than their intrinsic value.

Both writers recognized, however, that it was pointless to melt down such apparently overvalued coins, for to do so was to destroy the premia that they carried.

This chapter references various kinds of trade coins that were present in eighteenth-century Amsterdam, and Table 3.1 lists the coins most commonly encountered. All enjoyed a network of international recognition and trust that made them acceptable for deposit at the Bank. Most European states offered a mint that would turn bullion into coins, and there were many such states. Germany alone had 61 (Cuhaj 2010, 266). Few mints, however, had the international network of trust needed to support their brand. Making high-quality coins was the easy part.

Getting foreigners to think of those coins as trade coins was the hard part, and it was the network that made coins into safe assets.

Chapter 8 will offer an illustration of this point. Beginning in 1750, Prussia tried to displace Dutch and French trade coins from Baltic markets and to elevate its own coins to the status of premium-bearing trade coins. Prussia's method of attack was to mint lots of coin from silver purchased on credit abroad, with the idea that a large supply of coins would automatically create its own demand. Since Prussia lacked the necessary financial networks to sustain such a demand, this strategy was unsuccessful. True trade coins could not be created by numbers alone.

3.2 Bullion: The Not Quite Safe Asset

During the early modern era, gold and silver were seen as a robust store of value because people could take precious metal almost anywhere and have a mint turn it into local coins. For example, half of the silver sent by the Dutch East India Company to Asia in the 1740s was bullion to be minted in Bengal and Siam.[8] As a result, a string of bullion markets circumnavigated the world, and precious metal flowed to locations that valued it most. This global market, however, had frictions. Most localities had controls on exports, so much of the trade was in defiance of legal restrictions. Also, bullion was a high-value commodity, so its loss was expensive and protection was necessary.

Another practical difficulty was that bullion could have a "lemons problem" similar to that famously described by Akerlof (1970) for used cars. A persistent problem with the resale of cars has been that a seller often knows if a car is bad (a lemon) when a buyer does not. Worse, the seller can also have an incentive to misrepresent the quality of the car. Likewise, gold and silver could contain less precious metal than advertised. Ignorance was costly. This worry made bullion information sensitive, meaning the benefits of discovering bullion's content could exceed the costs (Dang, Gorton, and Holmström 2019).

A related complication was that investigating bullion content was also costly (Gandal and Sussman 1997, 444). In a process called assay, someone had to assess the weight and the fineness of metal. Measurement of mass required scales and a set of incremental weights purchased from specialized manufacturers (Aerts and Cauwenberghe 1987, 58). The equipment

---

[8] For an accounting of VOC precious metal shipments, see Pol (1985, 73) and Bruijn, Gaastra, and Schöffer (1987, 240).

also required routine calibration. Measuring fineness was even more difficult. One common verification technology was a touchstone on which
people rubbed a coin on a slate and compared the color to a set of rubbings
made by metal of a known quality (Redish 2000, 22–24). The process was
similar to matching color samples at a paint store, and the process could be
made less discretionary by applying increasingly stronger acidic washes to
see at what level a rubbing dissolved. A touchstone, when handled by an
expert, could achieve an error margin of 2–4 percent (Gandal and Sussman
1997, 444). To gain a more precise measure of fineness was even more
expensive in equipment and effort. Separating gold or silver from metals
like copper or lead required dissolution of a sample in nitric acid to remove
impurities (Aerts and Van Cauwenberghe 1987, 24). The alternative was to
smelt metal with added lead and then cook off the lead (together with any
copper in the coin), using a process called cupellation, or more poetically,
"trial by fire." The processes were not just about equipment: "the essayer's
craft required a very high technical skill" (Aerts and Van Cauwenberghe
1987, 18). For example, one family kept records of assays going back two
generations and "a collection of recipes for manipulating metals and acids"
(Felten 2022, 114).

High costs meant buyers had to develop expertise, or hire trusted
experts, or remain vulnerable. The result, in Amsterdam as elsewhere,
was a bullion market dominated by insiders. As noted in Chapter 2, only
about 100 merchants were easily identifiable in Bank records as monetary
specialists (banks, precious metal dealers, or cashiers), as compared with
2,000 account holders at the Bank. The insularity of the Amsterdam
bullion market could also be seen from the Bank's own activity. From
1656 to 1753, the City required specialists who pulled metal into wire for
the jewelry trade (*draadtrekkers*) to acquire their silver as ingots (*lingotten*)
from the Bank (Dehing 2012, 96).[9] Others could as well, but we know that
for the last seven of those years (1747–1753) the Bank sold ingots to only
26 different customers. Three-quarters of those transactions were to just
three customers.[10]

Bullion was thus a store of value, but it was not a universally traded, "no
questions asked" asset. Information mattered. To trade in bullion required

---

[9] It was unlikely that these "local" ingots were produced for export by the Dutch East India
Company. First, the Bank did not produce ingots of the fineness (0.986) most desired by
the VOC (Bruijn, Gaastra, and Schöffer 1987, 223). Second, the Bank's production
volume was far less than the Company's needs.

[10] Being Molière en Company (known cashiers), Weduwe Christiaan Benning en Soonen,
and Phillipus van der Nolk.

knowledge of an ingot's weight and fineness, the current market price, and how to adjust for variation in fineness from the market standard. For its purchases in India, the Company tried to minimize such problems by shipping silver ingots of highly uniform weight (eight marks) and of fineness matched to local needs: 98.6 percent fine for silver to be minted into Bengal rupees and 94.2 percent for silver minted into Thai ticals (Pol 1985, 73).[11] The use of standardized ingots limited disputes with local mint masters over assay values (Pol 1989, 51). These ingots were coin-like in the sense that they were reliably standardized, but unlike coins, they were always assayed and used for essentially one transaction, that is, delivery to an Asian mint.

3.3 Trade Coins

Coins were a more general, yet still partial solution to bullion's information problem. In this section, we use the Bank's records to demonstrate that coins were a technology that increased the costs of assay by shrinking and standardizing the unit of metal. At a small scale, the costs of assay exceeded the benefits. This reversal helped people accept imprecision and treat individual coins as homogeneous when, physically speaking, they were not. Mints aided this conceptual leap by promulgating brands around which homogeneity could coalesce. Success brought a norm: the measurement of weight and fineness was skipped or approximated. Such norms turned metal disks into safe assets and were common in small volumes and where legal obligations applied. These will be the local coins explored later in this chapter.

What was uncommon was a trade coin that could extend such a norm over scale and distance. Large-value payments involved hundreds or thousands of coins, and to not ask questions relied increasingly on brand because the relative costs of assay decreased as the number of coins increased. Brands were a result of network economies: more users made a brand more valuable. To gain an international network, a brand had to appeal to people without reliance on the legal obligations of its home jurisdiction. Exploring how brands like Spanish dollars and Dutch dukaten won network market share is beyond the scope of this book. Instead, this section focuses on the consequences of that success. To show the power of trade coin norms for the Bank, this section first visits an uncommon

---

[11] In contrast, the Bank did not supply ingots of a uniform weight.

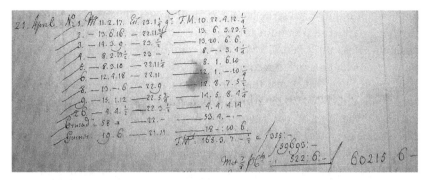

Figure 3.1. Bank acquisition of gold on April 21, 1718
Source: ACA 5077/1420, folio 5.

transaction wherein the Bank simultaneously purchased *both* bullion and trade coins. It shows how opaque an individual coin was and how that homogeneity scaled even in a world of transactions by weight. The second example jumps to a common transaction wherein the Bank embraced the full norm of trade coins and exemplifies how the Bank interacted with the world of silver and gold.

We have details of how metal was measured because the Bank employed an assayer to handle incoming gold and silver, and some records of these activities remain in bullion inventory books covering the years 1718–1731 (ACA 5077/1420 and ACA 5077/1421).[12] As noted in Chapter 2, assayers traded gold and silver on behalf of the Bank and periodically transferred their positions to the Bank's master account. The image in Figure 3.1 is the record of an assayer moving nine gold bars, a sack of Portuguese gold *crusaden* (*cruzados*), and a sack of English gold guineas into the Bank on April 21, 1718. The first set of columns listed the mark weight (*M.*) of each item.[13] The next pair of columns was the fineness, recorded as essay (*Ess*), a variant spelling of assay.[14] The final set of columns was the weight in pure gold, called fine marks (*F.M.*).[15] The summation at the bottom was the

---

[12] ACA stands for Amsterdam City Archive; 5077 is the particular collection, and 1420/1421 are the relevant items.

[13] A mark was a unit of weight equal to one half of a pound. A mark was also 8 ounces, and each ounce contained 20 esterlins. The metric equivalent of a Dutch mark is 246.084 grams (Polak 1998b, 64; Scheffers 2013b, 375).

[14] A mark of pure gold was measured as 24 karats, and each karat was 12 grains. As a result, the fineness of gold was reported as the weight in fine gold per mark of raw (*bruto*) gold bullion (Scheffers 2013b, 374–75).

[15] Although the fine mark weight was formidably precise, it was not a direct observation. Instead, each entry was the multiplication of the fineness level by the observed weight.

total weight in fine marks, the baseline valuation of gold at 355 bank florins per fine mark, the premium for this transaction of ⅞ percent, and the resulting total value of 60,215 bank florins and 6 stivers.[16] The Bank's silver transactions had a similar accounting process.

Examples like this reveal that the Bank measured the fineness of gold bars by increments of 1/1152 or 0.09 percent.[17] In other folios, the Bank measured the fineness of silver bars by increments of 1/576 or 0.17 percent.[18] Silver was less valuable by volume than gold, and the larger increment followed, because greater precision was not worth the effort.[19] The middle columns of Figure 3.1 gave the fineness of each gold bar separately and in descending order. The Bank did not record if these levels of fineness were given by suppliers or derived by the assayer, but either way spoke to the precision applied to each bar within the market.

In contrast, the coins had a generalized fineness. All the crusaden were valued at 22 karats (91.6 percent) fine. All the guineas were 21 karats, 11 grains (91.3 percent) fine. This was because people could not ascertain the fineness of an individual coin over a relevant range. The most precise technologies then available, being acid baths or trial by fire, required destruction of a coin, and the gentler touchstone technique delivered far less precision than the 0.4 percent tolerance of most large Dutch coins (Polak 1998a, 67–75). For an individual coin, fineness was highly opaque, and people had to generalize. As the coins grew in number, the generalization had to hold for a trade coin to work. As safe assets, the actual fineness of the coins was secondary to whether people would test them.[20] The vast

---

The resulting number was no more accurate than the weight and the fineness used as inputs. In other words, fine mark was an accounting construct: a fiction that allowed the content of each line to be summed into the aggregate at the bottom. This example illustrates how accounting precision could substitute for physical precision.

[16] In this transaction, the Bank applied the same gold price to bars and coins of varying fineness. This was dissimilar to the adjustments the Bank used when selling silver ingots. We do not know why, but this simplified pricing was also used when this gold was sold to Andries Pels en Zonen on April 8, 1719 at 355 bank florins per fine mark plus 2⅛ percent (ACA 5077/1420, folio 5). The purchase and sale cleared the Bank a profit of 1¼ percent.

[17] That is, the Bank recorded gold fineness by the ¼ grain, as seen for bar number 1 in Figure 3.1.

[18] That is, the Bank recorded silver fineness by the ½ grain (ACA 5077/1421, folio 11) with fine (pure) silver being 288 grains.

[19] In Figure 3.1, gold was purchased at 358.1 bank florins per fine mark. That same month, silver was purchased at 23.6 florins per fine mark (ACA 5077/1420, folios 3, 5). The gold value was divided by 320 and silver by 32.

[20] Similarly, the safe asset status of private bank money turned on whether anyone involved would test it through redemption and not the actual collateral of a bank.

majority of trade coins moved through the Bank with no assay, and if the Bank rarely tested, then Amsterdammers could reasonably expect that few others would. The Bank's acceptance of coins shown in Table 3.1 might have been an important signal that the Bank was not asking questions.[21] A widespread expectation could emerge that few people were actually testing these types of coins, and a safe asset, as defined by Gorton (2017, 548), was precisely one that mitigates the fear of being taken advantage of by others who might know more.

But the Bank and other specialists could pay the cost and test a random sample of coins. This was how masters assayed output at mints, and it was also likely how the Bank determined that the English guineas in Figure 3.1 were slightly under the 22 karats the coins were supposed to possess (Cuhaj 2010, 696). The circumstances were that only three weeks earlier the Bank had paid for an assay, and the Bank had not received any guineas over the previous four years.[22] Whether the adjusted fineness came from an internal test or a market determination, the transaction still proceeded as if all the guineas in that sack were the same. If a coin could not retain this norm of homogeneity, then it would lose its premium or even suffer demonetization. The Bank did at all times have the right to refuse coins its assayer judged to be substandard.[23]

An individual coin was also opaque in weight. The Bank measured the weight of gold in increments of 1/320th of a mark or 0.77 grams.[24] For comparison, a single US dollar bill weighs one gram.[25] This increment translated into a small margin of error in comparison to the total mass of a bar. For example, the fourth bar weighed 2,057.1 grams, so the increment was 0.04 percent (4 basis points) of that bar's total weight. Other folios record silver bullion in increments of 1/32 of a mark (7.7 grams). This same weight increment was also used for decades when the Bank produced and sold silver ingots. Silver had a less precise increment because it had less value by weight.

---

[21] The nineteenth-century Bank of England used bill discounting to signal debtor quality (Flandreau and Ugolini 2012; Sissoko 2016).

[22] The Bank paid Anthony Grill 6.3 current guilders for assay on March 28, 1718 (ACA 5077/1283, folio 32). This was in addition to his salary of 750 guilders. The record did not specify the coins tested, but it was the only explicit assay expense that year.

[23] Deficient Dutch coins were cut in half and returned to the mint where they were produced, as occurred in 1758 with a batch of substandard *rijksdaalders* from the Utrecht mint (van Dillen 1925a, 390–407).

[24] In Figure 3.1, that increment was the ½ at the end of bar number 4's weight of 8 marks, 2 ounces, and 17.5 esterlins.

[25] www.moneyfactory.gov/resources/faqs.html, retrieved January 15, 2020.

These increments of weight created large margins of error if applied to individual coins (see Table 3.1). The gold dukaat was the dominant Dutch trade coin, and gold's weight increment created an error range of 22 percent of that coin's weight.[26] Similarly, an increment of silver created an error range of 23 percent.[27] Far more precision was required to discern if an individual coin was within its assigned range.

Such precision did exist. Someone wanting to know if an individual coin was light could purchase a special box of weights (*muntgewichtdoos*). The box contained a weight equal to the ordinance weight for each coin type and a set of scales for weighing mass of a few grams, that is, of single coins (Aerts and Van Cauwenberghe 1987, 58–59). To additionally measure how light a coin was, one also needed a set of very light weights (Felten 2022, 150). To enhance the credibility of such measurements, moneychangers and goldsmiths were to have their equipment regularly tested and adjusted by a sworn "calibration master" (*ijkmeester*, Scheffers 2013a, 108). Such precision was specialized, expensive, slow, and fraught with potential abuse.

The Bank, however, rarely transacted in only a few coins. In Figure 3.1, the crusaden and guineas had collective weights greater than the weight of individual bars. When aggregated, coins overcame opacity, since a sack of coins could be weighed at a cost similar to a bar of bullion. To record an accurate weight for a sack of trade coins, however, was rare. Far more common in the same bullion book were sacks of coins of uniform weight. For example, the Bank purchased 84 sacks of the French louis d'or gold coins in 1719. Each sack was listed individually, yet they all reportedly weighed exactly 50 marks (ACA 5077/1420, folios 9–11). The Bank might have checked if each sack was of approximate weight, but the Bank did not record the actual weight. Instead, a sack of coins (we know not the number of individual coins,[28] yet more opacity) was given a norm weight even when testing was not prohibitively expensive. As with fineness, people extrapolated a norm from individual coins to sacks.

---

[26] A gold *dukaat* coin weighed 3.52 grams (Polak 1998b, 67).

[27] Assumed a silver ducaton coin that weighed 32.78 grams (Polak 1998b, 74).

[28] In a separate account, the Bank handled coins it called *nieuwe sware France pistolen* (ACA 5077/1364, folio 77). Their weight was 12.12 grams per coin, slightly less than the 12.24 grams per coin of the 1716 French mint ordinance for the *louis d'or noailles* coins. If these were the 1719 coins in sacks of 50 marks, then each sack had 1,015.2 coins, and the fineness of 21 karat, 7.5 grains (90.1 percent) was noticeably less than the ordinance 22 karat (91.17 percent).

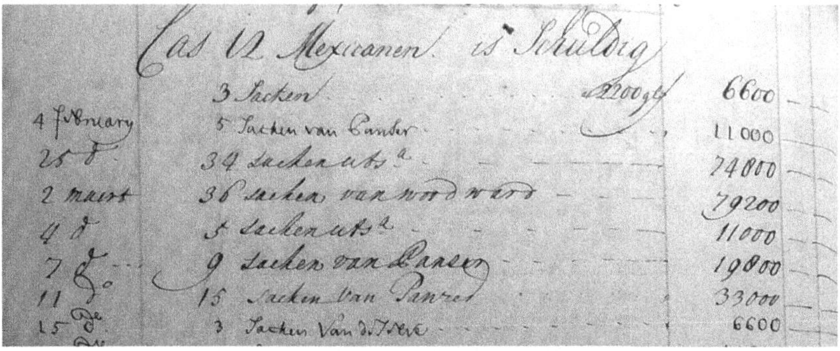

Cas 12 Mexicanen is Schuldig

	3 Sacken à 2200 gl	6600
4 february	5 Sacken van Panser	11000
25 d°	34 Sacken uts	74800
2 maert	36 Sacken van woodwert	79200
4 d°	5 Sacken uts	11000
7 d°	9 Sacken van Panser	19800
11 d°	15 Sacken van Panser	33000
15 d°	3 Sacken Van d. Werd	6600

Figure 3.2. Deposits of Mexican dollars, 1718
Source: ACA 5077/1362, folio 33.

A norm of homogeneity that people shared over scale and distance is our functional definition of a trade coin, and a second example shows its power at the Bank. Figure 3.2 is an account of the inflows of Mexican dollars in February and early March 1718. The left column recorded dates, the middle was the number of sacks by receiver (either Panser or Woodward), and the right was the value of those sacks at 2,200 bank florins each. The folio noted neither weight nor fineness. Every sack was identical even though they were of similar value to the bullion in Figure 3.1. If questions were asked, then no answers were recorded. Chapter 6 will show how tons of silver flowed into the Bank each year in this way. The same sacks flowed out through receipt redemptions. Everyone tacitly acquiesced, and perhaps appreciated, that they were part of a network of mutual ignorance built on a trusted brand. As a result, trade coins (metal) enjoyed the same uniformity as bank florins (paper).

3.4 The Business of Trade Coins

The foregoing examples illustrate why trade coins could carry a premium relative to bars of the same assay.[29] With weight and fineness accepted as standardized instead of measured, such a premium included the value of saved transaction costs relative to bullion, as reflected in the coin's markup above the market price of the precious metal it contained. If the price of bullion were to increase, then so would the coin's market value, so as to

[29] This stylized fact accorded with the conclusion of Velde, Weber, and Wright (1999, 306): "as long as coins circulate, they have value as media of exchange in addition to their intrinsic value as commodities."

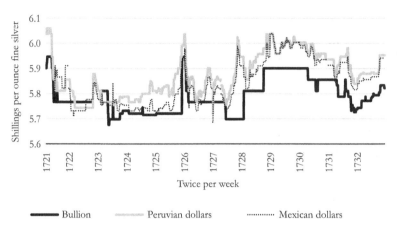

Figure 3.3. Premia on Spanish dollars in London, 1721–1732
Sources: Hotson (2017, 79).
Notes: Bullion is adjusted for being 0.925 fine (Hotson 2017, 197). Mexican dollars are adjusted at their official fineness of 0.9305 fine up to 1728 and 0.9166 fine thereafter (Irigoin 2018, 13, 15). Peruvian dollars are adjusted at 0.925 fine up to 1728 based on internal Bank assessment (1724 cashbook, 5077/1368, folio 99).

maintain the premium. The premium also incorporated location-specific factors such as network connections, market depth, and seasonality.[30]

We cannot plot these premia for eighteenth-century Amsterdam outside the Bank, because the Dutch financial press did not systematically report them. The City granted the brokers guild of the Amsterdam Exchange a monopoly over the publication of prices for everything traded therein (McCusker and Gravesteijn 1979, 44). Foreign coins were the purview of traders in gold and silver, coined and uncoined. We do not know why the press did not list these prices, but London's commercial press was not controlled by its exchange, and it did routinely report the price of Spanish dollars on a twice-weekly basis (Hotson 2017, 76, 79).

To illustrate the coin-premium phenomenon, we focus on London in the decade after the South Sea Bubble of 1720. Figure 3.3 reports the prices of silver bullion, Peruvian dollars, and Mexican dollars, with an adjustment for fineness. For the years 1721 through 1732, dollars had an average premium over bullion of just over 1 percent. The decade also suggested how trade coins could offer economic value. During the first two years after the crisis, changes in the price of silver were infrequent, suggesting limited trading. Then, in 1723, high-frequency (by eighteenth-century standards)

[30] Kuroda (2008b, 18) called these "currency circuits."

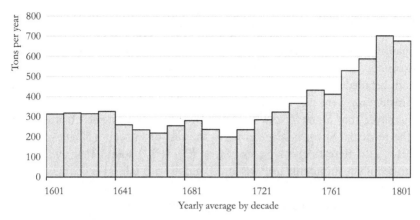

Figure 3.4. New World silver production by decade, 1601–1610 to 1801–1810
Source: TePaske and Brown (2010, 113).

trade began in Spanish dollars while bullion remained thinly traded. Only in 1732 does the bullion trade also catch gear. For the rest of the century (not shown), the coin premium shrinks, and all three prices move together in active trading. It seems that the London silver market relied on Spanish dollars during those years of recovery, and even when the bullion market was deep and robust, silver dollars remained an active substitute. For less developed markets, dollars had much to contribute.

The existence of convenience premia for popular trade coins created a strong incentive to transform precious metal into such coins. For silver trade coins, the dominant supplier was the Spanish empire. Figure 3.4 shows TePaske and Brown's (2010, 113) estimates of average annual American silver production by decade. A large portion of that silver arrived in Europe already minted into dollar coins.[31] Much of the remaining portion was coined at Spanish mints or processed by mints in other European countries, including the Dutch Republic.

Due to a lull in Peruvian output, American silver production started the eighteenth century with a slow decade of 200 tons of fine silver per year. This flow then gradually increased as new sources of silver came into production,

---

[31] The questions of how much silver and gold were mined in the New World, what proportion of this was minted in colonial mints, how much was sent to Europe, and how much arrived via official versus unofficial channels have all been subjects of intense scholarly investigation; see TePaske and Brown (2010, 305–15) for a discussion. A lesson of this literature was that the figures in Figure 3.4 cannot be taken as precise according to modern standards, but rather as indicative of trends in the amount of silver made available to Europe through American production.

especially in Mexico. From about 1720 forward, this development was echoed in the Bank's vault inventories, which recorded large numbers of Spanish coins. The increased availability of silver trade coins was the great exogenous factor behind the Bank's high-water era introduced in Chapter 2 and detailed in Chapter 6. The paths by which these coins reached Amsterdam were not recorded in the Bank's archive, but "a majority of the silver that arrived from Spanish America was smuggled from Cadiz [the principal Spanish silver port] to the rest of Europe" (Nogues-Marco 2011, 2). Interestingly, Nogués-Marco (2011, 17) found that syndicates funded illicit shipments to Paris and London with bills of exchange drawn on Amsterdam. Chapter 8 will detail a similar process by which Prussia acquired large amounts of silver via Amsterdam's bill markets.

Some of the Spanish silver became raw material for the Dutch and French mints. The popularity of the latter countries' trade coins in certain markets created incentives for this rebranding (melting and reminting) of already-popular Spanish trade coins. For the Dutch, rijksdaalders circulated as a preferred medium of exchange in many Baltic markets, creating opportunities for profitable export of coins there. Also lucrative was the export of silver ducatons to Asia, much of this occurring through smuggling by Dutch East India Company employees. The ducaton's ordinance value in the Dutch Republic was 3.15 guilders, but its market value was higher at the VOC's Asian headquarters, where the VOC would purchase ducatons with "checks" (*assignaties*) payable in the Netherlands at 4 percent interest (Pol 1985, 90–96). The VOC's Asian purchase price rose as high as 4.875 guilders in 1737 (Lucassen and Van Rossum 2016, 108). Attempts to limit this trade, including the minting of more easily traceable VOC-imprint ducatons, were unsuccessful. Ducatons were smuggled in great numbers.

Figure 3.5 gives the annualized total of known production of all silver coins by the mints of the Dutch Republic from 1680 to 1794.[32] While Figure 3.4 already showed that the amount of silver leaving the Americas climbed during the eighteenth century, Dutch silver coin production did not. Instead, Dutch production had peaks and valleys. Dutch production was 13 percent of New World output in the 1730s but only 7 percent the next decade.[33] Within Dutch production, however, trade coin production was far more stable than local coin production. To see this, Figure 3.5 disaggregates output into three parts. The figure defines trade coins as all coins having an

---

[32] These series do not extrapolate the occasional missing production information, see Lucassen (2014, 112).

[33] Those ratios were 43.5 tons over 324.1 and 25.9 over 367.

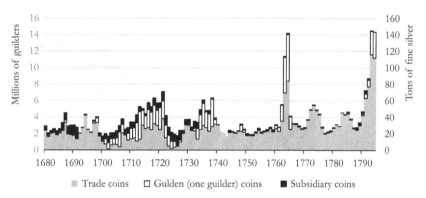

Figure 3.5. Annual Dutch silver coin production, 1680–1794
Source: Stapel (2016).
Note: For ease of display, the right-hand axis adopts a ratio of 100 guilders per kilo. Gulden coins as the reference would deliver a ratio of 103:1.

ordinance value larger than a current guilder, and the Bank came to accept all these coins for receipt deposits. Trade coins comprised 72 percent of Dutch mint production. The remainder was gulden (one-guilder) coins and even smaller coins that we label subsidiary coins, that is, small change. Trade coin production was far more consistent than the sporadic production of the coins that dominated the supply of local coins. The reason seems to be that trade coins most always delivered a mark-up premium. Local coins had a different premium structure, detailed in the next section, that often did not provide much incentive for production.

The Dutch East India Company was a major consumer of trade coins and the Bank had the capacity to accommodate them. For example, during the decade 1741–1750, the Company ordered 38.3 million guilders worth of silver be sent to Asia, of which 50 percent was to be bullion, 40 percent a mixture of Mexican dollars and Dutch ducatons, and the remainder small change (Bruijn, Gaastra, and Schöffer 1987, 240). Bank records did not follow coins after they left, but large amounts of these coins flowed through the Bank, as will be shown in Chapter 6. For now, Table 3.2 gives the vault inventory of the Bank in January 1746. We divided the inventory into coins held under receipt and those the Bank owned outright. Again, being under receipt meant that customers had sold them to the Bank with the option of subsequent repurchase (see Chapter 2).[34] Most coins parked at the Bank in

---

[34] If customers did not redeem or roll over receipts, then the coins became owned outright by the Bank, and the 1746 inventory has some mexicanen and pilaren in that column.

Table 3.2. *Silver and gold held by the Bank on January 16, 1746, in millions of bank florins*

		Under receipt	Owned outright	Totals
	Mexicanen	2.2	0.7	
	Ducatons	1.3	0.3	
	Staten drieguldens	1.8		
SILVER TRADE COINS	Pilaren	1.1	0.2	
	Rijksdaalders	0.7		
	Franse kronen	0.5		
	Englische kronen	0.2		
	Sub-totals	7.8	1.2	9.0
	Guldens		3.2	
OTHER SILVER	Miscellaneous		0.2	
	Sub-totals		3.4	3.4
	Crusaden	0.1		
GOLD	Dukaten	0.1	2.8	
	Sub-totals	0.2	2.8	3.0
	Totals	8.0	7.4	15.4

Source: ACA 5077/1387, folio 1.

this manner were either still in the form of Spanish dollars (mexicanen from Mexico and pilaren from Peru) or had been reminted into Dutch coins (ducatons, rijksdaalders, and staten drieguldens). French and English coins participated at lower levels. The Mexican dollars and Dutch ducatons in the Bank at that moment could have supplied 22 percent of the total trade coins the Company wanted shipped that decade. The other coins under receipt, if melted, could have supplied a similar portion of required bullion. The Company cast its own ingots for export and for this purpose preferred to melt and refine Spanish dollars like the pilaren (Pol 1985, 102–4).

Table 3.2 shows that the Bank also interacted with two other parts of the Dutch coinage system: gold coins and local coins. In 1746, people held few gold receipts, and most gold was owned outright by the Bank. These gold coins had fallen into the Bank in earlier years and the Bank would

The coins had fallen (became *vervallen*) into the Bank in 1743. Eventually, the Bank sold these coins.

eventually sell them. The final section of this chapter will review gold coins, and Chapter 6 will address why customers abandoned so much gold at the Bank. The last component in Table 3.2 is current money in the form of gulden coins. The Bank had intentionally purchased these coins, and Chapter 7 will explain how and why. For now, our focus turns to how these local coins functioned, as it was different than trade coins.

3.5 Local Coins

If trade coins had flexible prices, then local coins used assigned prices called par, and the change in how coins were priced derived from a change in the relative costs and benefits. For large-value transactions among sophisticated merchants and bankers, the costs of discovering a coin's market price were negligible relative to the benefits of adjusting for conditions in Amsterdam relative to the wider world. Also, the community of merchants trading in Spanish dollars and the like self-selected into the need to be trade-coin savvy. At the other extreme, the trade-off reversed. The coins used for retail transactions between locals did not have a premium abroad, the amount of metal was small, and the inconvenience of haggling was greater relative to the size of the transaction. Also, common people could reasonably expect that others in their locality, like moneychangers or cashiers, knew much more.[35] A norm of not questioning the value of coins in small transactions was convenient and protective.

Such par pricing was particularly helpful for circulating media of exchange, that is, currency. Today, a two-euro coin is worth exactly €2 and is expected to continue to be worth €2. Today, users neither know nor care about these coins' metallic content, and that disconnect makes them "token" money, in contrast to "commodity" money (Sargent 2019). The Dutch story was less binary, more of a continuum. In Amsterdam, many foreign coins were unfamiliar and traded like bullion. Select foreign and domestic trade coins, however, successfully used brand recognition to represent commodity content, and those brands carried premia in Amsterdam because they carried premia in distant markets. Local coins were brands with a different type of premium in the form of par pricing, and that premium was local.

---

[35] Adverse selection has been a feature of theoretical models seeking to explain debasement, clipping, and Gresham's Law. See, for example, Velde, Weber, and Wright (1999), Bignon and Dutu (2017), and Bajaj (2020).

For the Dutch, the first step was the promulgation of ordinances that assigned a price to each type of coin, that is, a "legal tender value." The public and official nature of the ordinances could coordinate endogenous price convergence. If convergence was successful, then people would use the assigned price because the coins needed to unify around some price, and it was easy to do so around the government standard, like driving on the left or the right side of the road today. In application, the Republic offered an ordinance value for each type of its silver coins. In the Dutch story, however, this coordinating price was ignored for trade coins. That was also a common story across late-medieval Europe (Rolnick, Velde and Weber 1996, 800–1).

In contrast, ordinance prices often held for local coins. When they did, a coin's price became independent of the value of the precious metal it contained. To calculate the implications, people used a concept called the *mint equivalent*.[36] The mint equivalent took the number of coins needed to contain one fine mark and translated it into a monetary value. For example, 25.3 gulden coins contained one mark of pure silver (Polak 1998b, 76). At one current guilder per gulden coin, the mint equivalent was $25.3 \frac{\text{coins}}{\text{fine mark}} \times 1 \frac{\text{guilders}}{\text{coin}} = 25.3 \frac{\text{guilders}}{\text{fine mark}}$. The mint equivalent let people compare the assigned value of a local coin to the bullion it contained. For example, if the market price of silver bullion was 24.8 guilders, then the gulden had a premium of 25.3 − 24.8 = 0.5 guilders, or 2 percent of its mint equivalent. The top half of Figure 3.6 gives this example along the dimension of the price of silver.

The monetary premium offered an incentive for people to bring silver to a mint to create local coins. It also opened space for a mint to charge customers for the production of those coins. Deducting the mint's cost of production (called brassage) and profit (called seigniorage) from the mint equivalent leaves the *mint price*, the price paid by the mint for precious metal to be coined. For gulden coins, ordinances put the mint price at 25.1 current guilders per fine mark (Polak 1998b, 76). This is drawn in the bottom half of Figure 3.6. It meant the mint was to charge customers 4 stivers (0.2 guilders), and it left customers gaining 6 stivers (0.3 guilders). For local coins, this was how mints attracted business and made a profit.[37]

---

[36] Modern Dutch, especially the technical literature, applies the identical term *muntequivalent* for mint equivalent. The traditional term is *muntvoet* ("foot of a coin"), which may also refer to a coinage standard, that is, a set of mint equivalents and other technical specifications as applied to a group of coins.

[37] The actual production of coins was rarely as clean a process as this discussion suggests. Mints could bid up the price of precious metal beyond a coin's legal mint price and also

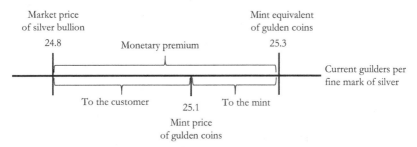

Figure 3.6. Monetary premium of gulden coins
Source: Authors' adaptation of Sargent and Velde (2002, 344).

Figure 3.6 also lets us see why changes in the price of silver have dramatic consequences for the production of local coins. As the price of silver increases (slides from left to right), the premium decreases. When that rising price of silver exceeds the mint price, customers lose their incentive to bring silver to the mint. That was why production of local coins was so sporadic, as can be seen in Figure 3.5. This feast or famine was driven by changes in the price of silver bullion (Redish 1990; Sargent and Velde 2002). If the price of silver keeps rising, it would eventually exceed the mint equivalent, and the premium will turn negative, as the silver in the coin becomes worth more than par. This occurred repeatedly in the seventeenth century and will be examined in the next chapter. For most of the eighteenth century, however, silver prices were low enough to avoid this problem.

The local coinage story was most pronounced for small coins. These coins had the most opacity, the least international recognition, and had the most to gain by passing at par. They also had high production costs that ordinances offset with high mint equivalents.[38] In effect, small coins were quasi-token with less silver by volume and by price than larger coins. To contain this token-like system, the amount of small coins payees were obliged to accept was limited. In circulation, local coins also suffered wear that made them even lighter and culling that removed heavier coins. Steuart (1767a) concluded that local coins came in "two sorts of silver currency in Holland; that which is bagged up, and weighty; and that which is not, and light" (96).

dilute the coin's precious metal content, effectively raising its mint equivalent. The consequences of such behavior and the policies meant to control it are discussed in the next chapter.

[38] On the many problems of producing small change, see Sargent and Velde (2002).

Table 3.3. *Ordinance prices and mint equivalents of large Dutch silver coins, circa 1750*

	Ordinance value in current guilders	
	per coin	per fine mark
Ducaton	3.15	25.1
Staten driegulden	3.00	25.2
Rijksdaalder	2.50	24.9
Gulden	1.00	25.3

Source: Polak (1998b, 73–76).

Guldens were the frontier between local and trade coins, and another aspect of legal tender suggested why. When substantial obligations like taxes or a contract had to be settled in current money, ordinance prices pertained when people could not agree on a coin's value. This has been called a latent role (Lagos and Zhang 2020). This role was not very relevant for small coins because they had limited application in larger transactions. This situation was not relevant for spot trades because the alternative was no deal. It was relevant for the settlement of obligations with larger coins. For example, bills of exchange settled outside the Bank in coin were "generally paid" (Steuart 1767a, 92) with 60 percent good silver (*grof geld*), 30 percent schellingen (0.3 guilders each), and 10 percent dubbeltjes (0.1 guilders each). Table 3.3 lists the prices assigned by ordinances to the four largest Dutch silver coins, that is, good silver. The table also reports the mint equivalent of each coin, and the mint equivalents were not the same. If payors had to choose silver coins from this list, then they had an incentive to select guldens, because those coins delivered more guilders per unit of silver than the others.

Settlement became another reason to associate gulden coins with their assigned price, and that association especially applied to cashiers, the proto-banks that supplied paper-based payments convertible into coins on demand. In terms of silver content, the best coins a customer could compel a cashier to pay out were guldens at their assigned price. Having the highest mint equivalent among large coins made guldens the latent unit for settlement of the various credit arrangements common to retail commerce (Jonker and Gelderblom 2018). The par interoperability between gulden coins and cashier accounts connected the metal and paper forms of current money in the monetary map (see Figure 2.4).

The gulden eventually became synonymous with the current guilder unit of account, and that was also by design. The guilder unit of account originated in 1521 with the minting of gold guldens whose value was fixed at 20 silver stivers, a ratio that seriously undervalued gold relative to silver (Korthals Altes 2001, 31). Gold guldens soon disappeared, but the associated unit of account endured.[39] In 1671, the General Masters of the Mint began to pressure the provinces to produce a new coin that would tangibly bind a quantity of precious metal to the Republic's unit of account, under the theory that doing so would reduce incentives to circulate debased coins (Van Dillen 1970, 442). It was not until ten years later that the Province of Holland responded with production of a one-guilder silver coin, the gulden (Polak 1998a, 198). One side of the coin had the stamp "I G" for one guilder, that is, a face value. Finally, in 1694, a new mint ordinance recognized the gulden as a valid coin for the entire Republic (Polak 1998a, 201). The silver content of the current guilder was stable at 25.3 guilders per fine mark, even though not that many gulden coins were actually minted.[40]

Finally, when local coins were aggregated into sacks for large-value payments, they still behaved like current money. The common wholesale unit for guldens was the sack of 600 coins priced at par, with the caveat of rejection if a sack was more than 3 ounces light of ordinance (Steuart 1767a, 93). The Bank purchased and sold these sacks through open market operations examined in Chapter 7. The City took these sacks when collecting seigniorage from the Bank. Throughout, sacks of guldens remained at par.

3.6 Gold Coins

Gold coins let us review how precious metal worked through the three functional platforms: bullion, trade coins, and local coins. The big difference between the metals was that gold flows were more episodic than silver. For gold bullion, the shock is the opening of flows from Brazil at the beginning of the eighteenth century. Figure 3.7 gives the average yearly production of gold in the New World by decade. From 1710 to 1730, gold production jumped by a magnitude and maintained a high level for the rest of the century, as Brazilian gold sources became augmented by significant

---

[39] Monetary history provides many examples of coins that became obsolete in circulation but then continued as a unit of account. Cipolla (1956) and Sargent and Velde (2002) label such coins "ghost monies."

[40] The silver gulden coin was introduced in 1681. By 1740, the cumulative known production of guldens was 52 million guilders, less than 1 million per year on average.

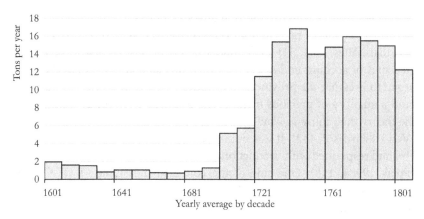

Figure 3.7. New World gold production by decade, 1601–1610 to 1801–1810
Source: TePaske and Brown (2010, 56).

finds in Spanish colonies. The previous century averaged 11.7 tons of gold per decade, but after 1730, the decadal average was 149.7 tons. Gold production on all other continents was at this time about 100 tons per decade (Soetbeer 1876, 8), so the expansion of American production was transformative for the world's gold markets.

Much of this gold translated into demand for new trade coins, and this can be seen from the Bank's eighteenth-century vault inventories, which at one time or another recorded Portuguese, Spanish, French, English, and Dutch coins (Table 3.1). For the Dutch mints in particular, gold trade coins became a big business. The gold dukaat was the Republic's most popular coin and was widely used for trade with the Baltic, the Levant, and Asia (Van Dillen 1964a, 261). Figure 3.8 shows that from 1720 to 1790, these gold coins were regularly produced and that some years had dramatic surges. For many of those years, production of gold dukaten well exceeded the value of all silver coins produced in the Dutch Republic (see Figure 3.5). It was also a substantial share of New World production. For example, gold dukaten were 20 percent of American gold production in the 1730s and 50 percent of it in the 1740s.[41] This pattern was a change from the last quarter of the seventeenth century, which saw minimal gold coin production in the Republic.

Despite its great popularity abroad, the gold dukaat coin played relatively little role in the Republic's domestic monetary system. The dukaat's intended specialization as a trade coin was reinforced by the fact that,

---

[41] The ratios were 3.1 tons over 15.4 tons and 8.3 over 16.6.

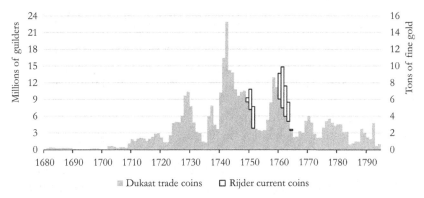

Figure 3.8. Annual Dutch gold coin production, 1680–1794
Source: Stapel (2016).
Note: For ease of display, the right-hand axis adopts a ratio of 1,500 guilders per kilo fine. Rijder coins as the reference would deliver a ratio of 1,522:1.

unlike other Dutch coins, it had no domestic ordinance value within the eighteenth-century Republic (Polak 1998a, 203), making it awkward to use for local payments. It was also a controversial coin elsewhere, in part due to its lack of milling, meaning that dukaten encountered in circulation were often clipped. Steuart (1767a, 85) noted that any amount of circulation automatically reduced the value of a dukaat by ¼ percent in his estimate. In 1749, formal protests over the poor quality of the dukaten were lodged by Prussian diplomats in Amsterdam and the Hague, but these were met with a spirited denial that problems existed on the production side (Schrötter 1908, 62). This profession of innocence notwithstanding, Dutch mints soon thereafter began milling all coins as a deterrent to clipping. Substandard dukaten were then declared to be *billon* within the Republic, that is, were explicitly demonetized for local payments (Van Dillen 1925a, 382, 408).

A more fundamental problem with the dukaten, however, was that many of them were simply not produced at the Republic's standards for weight and fineness (Graumann 1762, 128; Van Dillen 1970, 593). Dutch mints competing for gold deliveries paid their suppliers "commissions" (*provisie*) above the dukaat's legal mint price, most likely in the form of additional "light" coins destined for export markets. By 1749, mints' commissions had reached the level of 7/8 percent for gold dukaten in particular, in excess of the legal profit margins (*marge*) and quality allowances (*remedie*) specified by the Republic's mint ordinances (Van Dillen 1964a, 263; Polak 1998b, 67). The States General cracked down on this practice in August 1749, by outlawing mint commissions (Van Dillen 1964a, 262) but soon had to suspend this ban (in February 1751) following a collapse in the mints' business (Van Dillen 1925a, 387). Protests about the dukaten continued to be lodged by Dutch merchants, Polish merchants, and Amsterdam's governing council, to little avail (Van Dillen 1925a, 407–8, 413). Despite such widespread complaints, the near-universal acceptance of dukaten in Germany, the Baltic, and eastern Europe made their prohibition in these areas an unenforceable policy option (Schrötter 1908, 63).

Although dukaten were evidently targeted at foreign markets, by the 1740s so many had been minted that increasing numbers found their way back to the Republic, where their valuation proved troublesome and their presence was seen as contributing to a shortage of silver coins (Van Dillen 1964a, 262; Van Dillen 1970, 593). Even within the Republic, dukaten were intended to be valued by their metallic content, but often circulated at an informal tale value of 5.25 guilders. Merchants in the know, however, commonly adjusted this value to reflect market gold prices; writing in 1761, Steuart (1767a, 85) put the merchants' discounted value of a top-quality dukaat at 5.23125 guilders.[42] Variation in quality made dukaten even more difficult to use for local transactions and often unacceptable in the eyes of the Bank's assayer. In the end, the dukaat remained chiefly a trade coin.

Perhaps in response to these problems, the Province of Holland introduced a current gold coin for domestic use in 1749. To do so, Holland resurrected an old type of coin called the gold *rijder*, which was last produced a century earlier at an ordinance value of 12.6 guilders per coin (Polak 1998a, 68). The coin was revived at the same size and fineness but with a value increased to 14 current guilders per coin (Scheffers 2013b, 376). The higher value produced a competitive gold-to-silver ratio of 14.8 to 1, yet the high denomination was not well suited for retail.[43] Figure 3.8 shows that the up-valued rijders were only produced in two spurts (1749–1751 and 1760–1764) when gold prices were particularly low (Posthumus 1946, 183).[44] Clearly, public demand was limited, and Steuart (1767a, 82) mentions that only the state could call on a mint to produce rijders. If so, then even the state rarely wanted to produce them.

---

[42] Graumann (1762, 129) lists a range of market values for the dukaat of 5.25 to 5.4 guilders.
[43] Calculated as (26.75 rijder coins per fine mark gold)*(14 guilders each)/(25.3 gulden coins per fine mark silver).
[44] Total known production was 29.4 million current guilders.

The Bank did buy and sell gold rijders as current money along with the more usual silver gulden coins.[45]

3.7 Conclusion

If James Steuart found the Dutch Republic's coinage system perplexing, then a modern observer can be forgiven for finding it chaotic and alien. In our comfortable world of abundant and easily valued safe assets, it is hard to imagine an economy where the nation's renowned coins were exported, well-worn coins circulated, and the central bank dealt primarily in foreign coins. Part of the confusion was that coins behaved differently by type. Smaller coins tended to circulate at the prices assigned to them by the Republic. Larger coins did not. They routinely passed at higher prices than assigned, and those prices moved with the underlying prices of silver and gold.

This distinction aligned with usage. Small coins were used for retail payments and stayed within their local unit of account and jurisdiction. Large coins were used for wholesale payments that often moved across borders, and select large coins gained sufficient international reputation to become trade coins. That international dimension added more confusion, as it meant much of the Republic's coinage system was foreign. The Dutch did produce and export successful trade coins like the gold dukaat and the silver ducaton, but trade coins from France, Portugal, and especially Spanish America flowed into the Republic. Foreign coins formed a large share of trade coins but were not a large part of the current money.

The Bank's receipt window turned on this division. The Bank accepted trade coins, foreign and domestic. It did not accept local coins. The result was the connections in the monetary map in Figure 2.4. The dominant connection between Bank money and coinage was through trade coins under receipt. At the same time, the Bank distanced itself from local coins, the everyday money most people used. The Bank sometimes chose to buy or sell local coins, but only when and how it wanted to. The rest of the time, people with current money bought Bank money from cashiers in the agio market outside the Bank. All this made the Bank and its unit of account the mirror image of the cashiers and their unit of account. Cashier accounts were in current guilders that had a stable price relationship with guldens and

---

[45] Because of incomplete records in the 1750s, the first extant direct observation of the gold rijder at 14 current guilders in the Bank occurred in 1761 (ACA 5077/1387, folio 44). That value holds constant at the Bank through the last extant cashbook of 1792.

Table 3.4. *Shifts in how the Bank related to coins*

Chapter	Year	Bank and current units of account	Customer access coins through	Dominant type of coins at the Bank
4	1609	Same	Withdrawal	Domestic
4	1659	Different	Withdrawal	Domestic
5	1683	Different	Repurchase	Domestic
6	1725	Different	Repurchase	Foreign

Source: Authors.

a variable one with trade coins. Bank accounts were in bank florins that had a stable price relationship with trade coins (if one had a receipt) and a variable one with guldens. Connecting markets unified the two systems, and the whole could adapt, because the price of trade coins and the agio (price of Bank money) could rise and fall. The result was two spheres of safe assets (local coins at cashiers and trade coins at the Bank) that orbited each other like binary stars.

Almost none of this was how things were supposed to work when the Bank was founded. In 1609, there was to be only one way to price coins, only one unit of account, and only one Bank to make it all work. This original plan had the advantage of simplicity and the disadvantage of not working very well. The next three chapters tell the story of how the Republic, the City, and the Bank stumbled into the system described in these initial chapters. In the seventeenth century, upheavals in the coinage system were shocks to what was central to the Bank. For example, none of the large Dutch silver coins that the Bank accepted in 1750 even existed in 1609. These new coins altered the monetary environment and pushed the Bank to evolve.

Table 3.4 summarizes the three key shifts that are the focus of the next set of chapters. Each shift appeared as a minor, pragmatic adaptation in the Bank's business model, but their cumulative impact was transformative. At its beginning, the Bank took in the same coins at the same prices as the rest of the Dutch economy. By 1659, Bank money had emerged as a distinct unit of account that still relied on domestic coins. In 1683, a receipt (i.e., repurchase) system began to replace traditional withdrawal, and Bank money became fiat. Finally, foreign coins came to displace domestic coins in the 1720s. The eventual result was the popular, if perplexing, system of coins and Bank described in these first three chapters.

4

First Steps, 1609–1659

Here we pause for a moment and acknowledge our anachronistic perspective. With the hindsight afforded by four additional centuries of monetary history, it was not surprising that a public bank in a major commercial center such as Amsterdam would evolve into a central bank. The concept of a "central bank," however, was an idea popularized by early-twentieth-century economists to describe the public or semi-public institutions that had come to dominate money and finance. And even if the founders of the Bank had been familiar with this alien concept, it is doubtful they would have applied it to the early Bank. Instead, the Bank was founded as a conceptually straightforward solution to a rather complex problem. Advanced features of the Bank, such as the bank florin (the distinct unit of account for Bank money) and the agio market (the daily spot market for Bank money) only developed as the Bank struggled with the daunting practicalities of its assigned task.

The problem was coins. In 1600, the Dutch Republic was a small, rapidly growing open economy inundated with a "startling" variety of foreign coins (Dehing and 't Hart 1997, 39). To promote the orderly use of coins and the production of its own coins, the Dutch Republic promulgated rules to harmonize domestic coins of gold and silver with the plethora of foreign coins in circulation. In practice, however, the system was a confusion of goals and implementations. One problem was that the Republic expected trade coins to behave like local coins, that is, to circulate at par (see Chapter 3). As a result, either production volumes were low or coins circulated above par or both. Another problem was that the Republic lacked the political unity to get its constituent provinces to maintain standards of quality. As a result, coinage regulations sought an ambitious combination of outcomes that lost, or never had, alignment with actual usage.

Table 4.1. *Timeline of the emergence of the bank florin*

1606	Republic-wide mint ordinance designated the rijksdaalder as the lead silver coin.
1609	Founding of the Bank of Amsterdam.
1622	Invading coins from Southern Netherlands (patagons) prescribed at 2.35 guilders.
1638	Patagons raised by toleration to 2.5 guilders, yet the Bank accepted patagons at 2.4 guilders, creating a domestic exchange rate.
1659	Republic introduced new rijksdaalder and ducaton coins and recognized the bank florin as a unit of account distinct from the current guilder.

Source: See text.
Note: Here, a toleration (*tolerantie*) refers to a putatively temporary change in the legal value of a coin.

Such a misalignment prompted the City of Amsterdam to create the Bank in 1609. Three years earlier, the Republic had promulgated a new mint ordinance, and soon provincial mints and their customers were skirting the directives. The City created the Bank to implement the Republic's rules when others did not. Also, the Bank was to supply a paper substitute for those coins. Unlike in some cities before it, Amsterdam's municipal bank was not seeking space for credit facilities. Instead, Amsterdam desired a network of payments, centered on the Bank, in which monetary standards would be maintained. Coins and their rules were to be central to the Bank.

This initial and rather narrow vision for the Bank could not be sustained, because the Republic kept changing the rules. This chapter and the next will mention many of them, and Table 4.1 lists the critical ones. The rules were altered because the system repeatedly failed to deliver the prices, quantities, and qualities of coins that the Republic desired. In response, political will would eventually coalesce into a regulatory realignment that typically did not fix the underlying problems, and the cycle continued. It was not until the end of the seventeenth century that the system described in Chapter 3 emerged: a system based on the separation of trade from local coins and the control of provincial mints.

In the meantime, each new regulation created a dilemma for the City: it either required the Bank to join the new system or honor commitments under the old regulation and remain in the past. Instead of choosing one or the other, the City slowly gave the Bank a more elastic relationship with both. For example, during the Bank's first decade, coins from the Southern Netherlands invaded the Republic. The foreign coins displaced native coins and eventually forced the Republic to recognize the uninvited guests in 1622. To keep economically viable in this hostile environment, the Bank abandoned some of its original standards, including a one-to-one correspondence between Bank money and current money. Then, in 1659, the Republic replaced the intruders and reasserted control over its own money. The Bank kept the old unit of account even as the domestic system moved on.

By 1660, the Bank was neither the ghost of its 1609 structure nor a mirror of the current. Instead, the Bank came to blend the old unit of account with the new media of exchange to create a distinct transactions platform. This outcome was stable and popular and a half-way point between the original design and the high-tide Bank of the next century. The Republic's struggle to make its coins into safe assets both created demand for substitute assets and undermined the supply of substitutes. The imperfections of this monetary environment created space for technologies like the Bank, cashiers, and bills of exchange: technologies that helped people avoid coins. At the same time, those paper substitutes relied for credibility on a latent convertibility back into coins. Buffeted by a series of monetary shocks, the City made awkward accommodations to forces beyond its control. Through these adjustments, the City invented a form of Bank money with an elastic relationship to coins expressed through the agio market. The deep and stable agio was the end of the Bank's beginning. The beginning of the beginning was the Republic's coinage policies.

4.1 Debasement

To promote monetary stability, the Republic assigned values to Dutch coins that would bind when people might not agree on valuation, such as for paying taxes or settling debts. The Republic also prescribed values to some foreign coins to align them with domestic money. The result was a set of coins that authorities wanted to function as local coins but markets often treated as trade coins. For policymakers, the local coinage system had at least three goals: that the coins function as money at an assigned value (par medium of exchange), that the coins hold that value (store of value), and that people pay mints to produce these coins (seigniorage). In the years just before the Bank, the system struggled to meet any of these goals.

The Republic's struggles with coinage were hardly unique. Directed forms of monetary degradation were endemic virtually everywhere in early modern Europe. Redish (2000, 61–62) cataloged the four most common techniques of monetary manipulation, all applied with the goal of enhancing seigniorage.[1] The first technique was just to reduce the weight of coins as they were produced at the mint while assigning the same nominal value to the now lighter coin. A second, marginally subtler method was to hold a coin's weight constant while reducing its fine content. A third method did not rely on physical modification of the coin but instead "cried up" (assigned a higher nominal value to) an existing coin. A fourth method was to introduce a new coin with a higher nominal value per unit of fine content, yet close enough in weight and appearance to substitute for an existing coin.

All four types of monetary degradation were present in the early Dutch Republic, as were repeated attempts to limit their effects through restrictive mint ordinances. The Bank's narrative begins in 1606, when the Republic promulgated an overhaul of Dutch coin standards that assigned values to its two largest silver coins: 1.9 guilders to the *leeuwendaalder* and 2.35 to the new Dutch rijksdaalder (Nederlandschen rijksdaalder) (Scheffers 2013a, 26). Table 4.2 gives the ordinance values assigned at that time for both coins.

The ordinance values did not stick, because the market valued the coins for more. In 1606, the spot market put rijksdaalders at a 2 percent premium over ordinance (Van Dillen 1964d, 343). Leeuwendaalders were similarly elevated. This impaired their function as current money. People could pay with the coins at par and take the 2 percent loss. Or people could sell the coins to moneychangers for a fee (1.25 percent was the allowed maximum) and hope the resulting small change (if enough could be found) captured the remaining purchasing power.[2] Or people could negotiate a spot value as occurred with trade coins (see Chapter 3). The mismatch also discouraged people from bringing silver to the mints because the local premium was negative.

One way to solve the mismatch was by increasing (crying up) the official price of the coins, but, as Redish (2000) pointed out, this amounted to a backdoor debasement. An adverse consequence would be that creditors would be repaid with fewer coins than originally contracted. The Republic

---

[1] A fact emphasized by Redish (2000), Sargent and Velde (2002), and others is that these manipulations were sometimes applied for relatively benign purposes, for example, to counter the effects of coin clipping or to ensure sufficient availability of coins of different denominations. These benign explanations for coin manipulation do not apply to the early history of the Dutch Republic.

[2] Small coins were impractical or disallowed for large transactions (see Chapter 3). Also, gold dukaten at this time had an even higher premium of 2.6 percent, so they were no solution (Van Dillen 1964d, 343).

Table 4.2. *Ordinance specifications in 1606*

		Rijksdaalder	Leeuwendaalder
A	Guilders per coin	2.35	1.90
B	Coins per mark	8.48	8.89
C	Fineness as share	0.89	0.75
D = (A*B)/C	Mint equivalent in guilders per fine mark	22.50	22.52
E	Seigniorage in guilders per fine mark	−0.05	−0.05
F	Brassage in guilders per fine mark	−0.30	−0.25
G = D + E + F	Mint price in guilders per fine mark	22.15	22.22
Maximum allowable percent deviation (remedy) in weight		0.30	0.45
Maximum allowable percent deviation (remedy) in fineness		0.20	0.35

Source: Polak (1998b, 70–71, 170–71).
Note: A remedy (remedie) refers to the maximum permissible variation in weight or fineness of a coin as it leaves the mint.

cried up anyway and raised rijksdaalders to 2.4 guilders in 1608 and leeuwendaalders to 2.0 in 1615 (Polak 1998b, 70–71).[3]

Another, more brute-force fix would have been to reduce the silver content per coin, but the Republic's ordinances expressly forbade that. Table 4.2 lists ordinance specifications for weight and fineness. For rijksdaalders, these qualitative regulations began with a sheet of silver that was to be 10 pennies and 15 grains fine (88.5 percent pure). Each mark (half pound) of that sheet was to be cut into 8.48 disks that were each hammered between molds to create a coin. These specifications could be pulled together into a single number called the mint equivalent (Chapter 3): the guilders per mark of fine silver in that type of coin. Regulations also specified how much a mint operator was to deduct for operational costs (*brassage*) and for seigniorage (*sleischat*). Seigniorage was the profit to be given to the mint's controlling political authority. Subtracting seigniorage and brassage from the mint equivalent left the mint price: the guilder value

---

[3] The 1608 increase was temporary and called a tolerance. The price of 2.4 guilders was made permanent in 1610.

of coins to be returned to customers per mark of pure silver brought to the mint. Table 4.2 gives these specifications. The elements were carefully balanced across the two coins to produce similar mint equivalents. The mint prices were slightly different because allowable fees were lower for the leeuwendaalder. Overall, the two schedules struck a remarkable balance given the differences in weight, fineness, and denomination.

Dutch mints, however, did not follow these content goals. Coins naturally varied, so ordinances also specified acceptable deviations in weight and in fineness, and these additional regulations are reported in the last two rows of Table 4.2. For example, a mint master faced penalties if rijksdaalder coins were more than 0.3 percent (30 basis points) lighter in weight than ordinance. As a result, mints had incentives to err toward a weight and a fineness below ordinance but just above the remedy. Mints would try to "tickle" the tolerance because the mint got to keep the metal not returned to customers (Gandal and Sussman 1997). Often, the manipulation did not stop at tickling.

The outcome could have been different if customers had favored full-bodied coins, presuming that they had sufficient market power to assert that preference. It seems that customers did have market power. Most mint business began when customers chose to bring silver or gold to a mint, and supply was competitive, at least between the eight provinces, and a few cities, with the authority to operate a mint (Dehing and 't Hart 1997, 39).[4] The central republican government (States General) had limited authority and no mint of its own. The Republic, however, did send General Masters of the Mint to inspect production: they assayed output samples, calculated fines for violations of tolerances, and reported the results to each mint's political authority. If provinces wanted to maintain standards, the masters supplied the information (Polak 1998a, 137). The problem was that neither customers nor provinces seemed to prefer following the ordinances. Indeed, they favored debasement.

To understand this situation, it is instructive to consider the production of rijksdaalders and leeuwendaalders by four provincial mints in 1606 and 1607.[5] The rijksdaalders from these mints were lighter than ordinance by a

---

[4] These were not competitive private mints as envisioned by White (1984, 704–5) and investigated by Selgin (2008). White (2022) found that private mints did build successful brands based on high-quality coins during nineteenth-century American gold rushes.

[5] Utrecht's production run extended into early 1608, so its output was prorated on a daily basis. Also, this analysis excluded mints in the provinces of West Friesland and Gelderland because their production runs included rijksdaalders and leeuwendaalders under old and then new prices that we could not disentangle.

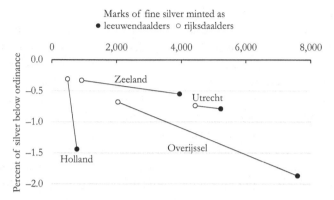

Figure 4.1. Output by provincial mint, 1606 and 1607
Source: Derived from Polak (1998b, 103, 123, 130, 150, 205, 212, 215, 223).

quantity-weighted average of 0.65 percent. The leeuwendaalders were light by 1.23 percent. This was not a massive debasement. Rather, it was a systemic inability to maintain standards. Also, it was not that massive quantities were flowing into mints: just the opposite. Mints were competing for a modest demand.

But would not customers have preferred mints that delivered full-bodied coins (Rolnick, Velde, and Weber 1996)?[6] Based on Table 4.2, that would have meant preferring rijksdaalders over leeuwendaalders and preferring mints that supplied heavier coins over those that supplied lighter coins. Actual behavior was the opposite. To see this, Figure 4.1 plots the quantity and quality of coins produced by four provincial mints in 1606 and 1607. Rijksdaalders are empty circles, leeuwendaalders are solid circles, and the lines connect output from the same mint. The horizontal axis measures marks of fine silver coined. The vertical axis is the percent below ordinance reported by Republic investigators: this combines under-weight and under-fine.[7]

---

[6] Referring to the discussion of Chapter 3, preference for full-bodied coins may have been higher for coins likely to be used as trade coins. Dutch silver coins of this era could serve both functions, which appears to have contributed to a preference for slightly debased coins.

[7] Samples of coins were randomly collected from each mint, boxed up, and examined in a formal procedure (*de opening van de muntbus*) similar to England's "Trial of the Pyx," both procedures likely deriving from a common Italian precedent (Polak 1998a, 109–11). The sampled coins were weighed and a few melted. Penalties were levied if coins were found to be underweight or lacking sufficient fine content. This procedure served as a check by the General Mint Masters on the activities of the mints, but also as a check by the mint owners (provinces and municipalities) on the behavior of their mint masters.

For each mint, leeuwendaalder production exceeded rijksdaalder production despite the leeuwendaalder having the greater deviation from ordinance. Even comparing only rijksdaalders, going from least production (Holland) to most (Utrecht) brought an increase in debasement. Leeuwendaalders would have been the same except Holland produced the least, despite aggressive debasement. The only two runs that the Republic investigators did not penalize were Holland's rijksdaalders and Zeeland's leeuwendaalders.[8] If customers were trying to avoid debasement, then they were systematically unsuccessful. The reality apparent in Figure 4.1, and in the results from the General Mint Masters' investigations for years to come and in numerous complaints, was that people with silver sought out mints that debased coins (Dehing and 't Hart 1997, 40; Polak 1998b, 205–24).

How did debasement reward such customers? We do not know exactly, but the simplest answer is that the mints kicked back some of the light coins to attract business (Velde, Weber, and Wright 1999, 308). A mint could offer customers more coins if each coin contained less silver. If the monetary valuation of the debased coins held at par, then customers gained purchasing power. In effect, the customers were offered a mint price above ordinance. By the mid-eighteenth century, such kickbacks ("commissions") had become so rampant that the States General felt it necessary to outlaw them (Van Dillen 1964a, 263). Amsterdam merchants then protested that commissions were a necessary part of the coinage business and that these had been routinely paid out by the mints since about 1670 (Van Dillen 1925a, 383). We suspect that commissions were not unknown before then.

Did debasement create a surplus to kick back? It certainly did for the provinces. Consider the extreme example of Overijssel in 1606–7. Leeuwendaalder production delivered over three times the seigniorage of rijksdaalder production. If the province also collected the fees assessed by the Republic, then the ratio of revenues was over 12 to 1. Table 4.3 gives a breakdown of revenues net what the mints were supposed to return to customers (that is, the ordinance mint price). Debasements likely were also profitable for the mint masters. The extra volume made the mint's total revenue much larger, but the penalties did undermine revenues on the margin. Isolating mint masters' profit margins required something we do not know: the composition of a mint's cost structure. The simplest

---

[8] Zeeland's rijksdaalders were penalized because their fineness was just beyond tolerance. In contrast, their weight was slightly above ordinance, so their total deviation was modest.

Table 4.3. *Estimated net revenues in guilders, 1606 and 1607*

Province of Overijssel	Rijksdaalders	Leeuwendaalders
Seigniorage	102.1	380.2
Fines assessed	81.4	2,170.4
Total	183.5	2,550.6
Overijssel Mint		
Brassage	612.6	1,901.0
Silver not returned	312.4	3,199.4
Fines assessed	−81.4	−2,170.4
Total	843.6	2,930.0
Total per mark	0.413	0.385

Source: Derived from Polak (1998b).

assumption, however, was that mint masters were not debasing coins to lose profits.

All this raises the larger question: how did the customers, mints, and provinces find someone to take the debased coins? One answer was that some people did not much care. When people used coins as current money, their purchasing power did not depend on the content of that coin. The lost silver did not change the par value. Indeed, moneychangers and cashiers culled out heavier coins that circulated alongside lighter coins of the same type (Dutu 2004). As lighter coins remained in circulation, they set the expectations of quality for the payments network. As modern token coins demonstrate every day, content does not matter if users acquiesce.

Another answer was that discrimination was not worth the effort. This would have been coins acting as a safe asset, and the effect was aided by the output of each mint looking similar (Gorton 2017). To see an example, Figure 4.2 presents images of 1606 leeuwendaalders from three different mints: Holland, Utrecht, and Overijssel. The coins declared their mint of origin in the writing around the edge. Otherwise, they have only minor stylistic differences. The design of rijksdaalder coins was similar. While the design did not deny the source of each coin, it clearly encouraged people to see the various mints as producing the same type of coin.[9] Homogeneity helped people combine these coins into a shared expectation of what was a

---

[9] White (2022, 18) concluded: "Coins in the Netherlands case lacked distinguishing brand names as a matter of government policy."

Holland   Utrecht   Overijssel

Figure 4.2. Leeuwendaalders from 1606
Source: Nationale Numismatische Collectie (NNC) Database.

leeuwendaalder even if none left the mint at ordinance standards. Also, for large-value transactions, coins were combined into sacks of 200 that were assigned a standard weight if the actual weight was close enough (see Chapter 3).

The result was that none of the ordinance elements in Table 4.2 bound tightly. Prescribed values struggled to apply in local circulation and encouraged debasement when they did. Ironically, debasement helped to offset the valuation mismatch by increasing the effective mint equivalent of silver coins. Subsequent wear and shaving added to that effect. While all this might have muddled along, it was not how the Republic envisioned its coinage system working. The Republic wanted stable values, busy mints, and sound coins, of which it was achieving none.

4.2 The Fed That Wasn't

When the mint ordinances did not work as planned, the Republic's merchants paid the price. Their dissatisfaction trickled upward to the Republic's capital, The Hague, and in early 1606, the General Mint Masters addressed this dissatisfaction with a classic policy response: extensive interviews with the aggrieved parties, followed by an insightful report that was completely ignored by everyone involved.[10] The Mint Masters' policy proposal echoed some aspects of the 1911 Aldrich Plan for the

---

[10] Because the Republic did not have a centralized structure, the Hague was not a capital in the conventional sense but more of an administrative center. The Republic's diffuse political structure made it difficult to implement nationwide measures such as the one recommended by the General Mint Masters.

founding of a central bank in the United States (Lowenstein 2015, 113). In a decentralized polity such as the United Provinces, much as in the early-twentieth-century United States, there could be no thought of creating a single national public banking institution. Instead the Mint Masters proposed a sort of proto-Federal Reserve System, consisting of public banks to be located in "all cities engaged in commerce," as well as in lesser cities with commercial aspirations (Van Dillen 1925a, 5–7). The Mint Masters thought that the public banks, although locally controlled, could be relied upon to uphold the mint ordinances more steadfastly than private parties, thereby ensuring Republic-wide uniformity of coinage. This proposal, however innovative and reasonable, seems to have died the same type of quiet death as did the Aldrich Plan.[11]

Dissatisfaction ran especially hot in Amsterdam. Amsterdam did not have a mint, and Holland's provincial mint was away in Dordrecht. Mints in West Friesland and Utrecht were more conveniently situated, and their debased coins easily migrated into the city. Also, Amsterdam was a center of international trade that relied on credit (obligations, cashier deposits, and bills of exchange) to reduce the use of coins. Merchant creditors were particularly vulnerable to mild debasement because ordinances obliged them to accept repayment in light coins at official values or go to the trouble of disputing such payments in court. Whether local law would recognize such a claim was unclear as the issue was in dispute within civil law (Fox 2016).

Admittedly, the amount of loss was more nettlesome than debilitating, but it did work against Amsterdam's business model.[12] In 1600, the Low Countries were in the midst of the Eighty Years War (the Republic's revolt against Spain), and concern for foreigners in most places was low, if not at a nadir. Amsterdam was an exception (Gelderblom 2013). By the standards of the era, Amsterdam was tolerant, law abiding, and open for business. The Twelve Years Truce with Spain, which began in 1609, offered new opportunities for trade. To attract foreign business, Amsterdam tried to treat all merchants fairly. Compromised coinage was not fair.

Frustration was manifested through intermediaries such as moneychangers (*wisselaars*). Moneychangers during this era operated

---

[11] Eventually, public banks would be independently established in Amsterdam, Delft, Middelburg, and Rotterdam. Lack of coordination between these banks meant that they never functioned as a coherent national network.

[12] The contemporary term for the common practice of picking out the better-quality coins, *bicqueteren*, reflects the merchants' view of the coinage situation. A rough translation is "nibbling, as if by young goats."

under official charters granted by the City and had to swear to uphold the mint ordinances. In June 1606, five Amsterdam moneychangers refused to swear: they pointed out that the legal valuations of the coins were too low, and that they would rather trade the coins freely in the market, as other people were doing, than follow the oath and be forced out of business (Van Dillen 1964d, 342–43).

The Republic created this situation by demanding that moneychangers help with two policy goals: get metal to Dutch mints and stabilize values at ordinance. To advance both, the Republic obliged moneychangers to buy foreign coins at ordinance but not to sell foreign coins. Instead, they were to send foreign silver to Dutch mints for re-coining. Putting the two restrictions together, moneychangers were to acquire foreign silver at ordinance, use the silver to purchase coins from Dutch mints, and then supply the new coins at ordinance. In 1606, that meant moneychangers purchased Spanish dollars at 22.73 guilders per fine mark and sold Dutch rijksdaalders at 22.5.[13] The trade made for a loss in silver of 1 percent. Moneychangers were permitted a 1.25 percent fee, so they could deny customers arbitrage gains, but the moneychangers still had to pay to get the dollars reminted. After deducting minting costs, a moneychanger was at a 1.3 percent loss converting Spanish dollars into Dutch rijksdaalders.[14] For a moneychanger, following the rules was a losing game.

If moneychangers were victims, then cashiers were accessories. According to the Amsterdam governing council, unscrupulous cashiers would

allow for fraudulent activity, especially the removal of heavy gold and silver coins, and their transport to prohibited and other Mints, in order to be converted into new (light) coins, which are then circulated within the community (Van Dillen 1964d, 344).

Even if cashiers were not feeding silver into the debasement process, they were natural users because cashiers could easily cull out heavy coins and unload light coins on depositors. As noted earlier (cf. Chapters 1 and 2),

---

[13] A Spanish dollar was 0.93055 fine, 17 engels and 25 azen weight, and 2 guilders and 7 stivers in value (Placaet ende ordonnantie 1606). The mint equivalent was $\left(\frac{2.35 \text{ guilders}}{1 \text{ dollar}}\right) * \left(\frac{1 \text{ dollar}}{17.78 \text{ engels}}\right) * \left(\frac{160 \text{ engels}}{1 \text{ mark}}\right) * \left(\frac{1 \text{ mark}}{0.9305 \text{ fine marks}}\right) = 22.73 \frac{\text{guilders}}{\text{finemark}}$.

[14] The loss was 22.15 + 0.28–22.73 = –0.3 guilders per fine mark, and that loss as a share of the initial Spanish dollars was 0.3/22.73 = 0.013, where 22.15 was the mint price for rijksdaalders, 0.28 was a 1.25 percent fee when selling rijksdaalders at their mint equivalent (0.0125*22.5 = 0.28), and 22.73 was the Spanish dollar mint equivalent. When the rijksdaalder value was raised in 1608, the moneychangers converted Spanish dollars into rijksdaalders at a small profit of 0.66 percent (66 basis points).

resentment of these practices led to multiple efforts by Amsterdam's governing council to suppress this problem by simply outlawing cashiers (Van Dillen 1925a, 1, 12, 23–25, 45–46).[15]

In the end, all these attempts were unsuccessful, because too many merchants found the cashiers too useful. The merchants' codependency on the cashiers was recorded, for example, in a 1608 petition by a group of prominent Amsterdam merchants, pleading for reinstatement of the banned cashiers and pinning the blame for any abuses on other parties (moneychangers in particular):

> The importance of the cashiers is that certain merchants who are involved in wholesale trade simply cannot do without their services; it is therefore very necessary that some means be found by which these merchants may retain the advantages of cashiers, while at same time guarding against the difficulties caused by the moneychangers (Van Dillen 1925a, 16).

To cut the Gordian knot, Amsterdam decided not to wait for a Republic-wide solution. In 1609, the City created the Bank to act as both a money-changer *and* a cashier. As noted earlier, chartered municipal banks were already operating in many Mediterranean cities, so the founding of the Bank did not represent a departure from established practice. Nor did the Bank appear as a direct challenge to the monetary sovereignty of the States General. Instead, the Bank was presented as a technocratic means to ensure the smooth functioning of payments stemming from Amsterdam's expanding commerce. Its founding circumstances were thus less like those of later nationally chartered central banks and perhaps more comparable to "infrastructure"-type institutions such as the New York Clearing House (founded in 1854; see Gorton and Tallman 2018, 14).

The Bank's moneychanger–cashier combination had been prohibited for private enterprises because money changing expanded the opportunities for cashiers to hold back heavy coins (Mees 1838, 25). The Bank as a cashier would avoid this problem because the City mandated that its Bank abide by the mint ordinances. The plan relied on the credibility of the City to assure merchants that the public Bank would release only coins of

---

[15] Another, equally controversial method for avoiding the need to pay in coin was for a debtor to assign a debt in their possession, such as a letter obligatory, to their creditor. Because such debts often contained bearer clauses, these sometimes functioned as proto-banknotes (Heyvaert 1975, 104). Ultimately, however, these debts would be discharged by payment in coin, often of questionable quality, except in cases where a circulating debt found its way to the original debtor. How such debt was valued in the marketplace has remained a subject for investigation. The 1608 City ordinance outlawing cashiers also prohibited payment by assignment (Van Dillen 1925a, 12).

ordinance quality at ordinance values. The goal was for account holders to not worry about debasement or market prices.

The scheme sought to solve problems that neither cashiers nor money-changers would and to do so simultaneously. As a cashier, the Bank was to accept whatever trade coins people presented and to do so at ordinance. The 1606 ordinance assigned a value to 40 types of gold trade coins (not counting doubles, halves, and quarters) and 15 types of silver trade coins (*Placaet ende ordonnantie* 1606). As a moneychanger, the Bank was obliged to pay out Dutch coins for every balance (subject to redemption fees). Dutch mints supplied two types of gold coins (dukaat and rijder) and two types of large silver coins (rijksdaalder and leeuwendaalder).[16] The Bank had to pay Dutch mints to create its own required reserves.

Conceptually, the set of coins acceptable for deposits was larger than, but also contained, the set for withdrawals. Each coin type could have a different mint equivalent, so the Bank was exposed to arbitrage: people might deposit high-mint-equivalent coins and withdraw low-mint-equivalent coins. The Bank reduced this by handing out the highest mint-equivalent coin within the set of withdrawal coins. Another solution was withdrawal fees.

The first two inventories of the Bank provide a glimpse into this situation. Table 4.4 summarizes the metallic holdings of the Bank in 1610 and 1611. After one year of operation, the Bank's gold was mostly in Hungarian and Portuguese coins. It had no Dutch gold. A year later, half the foreign coins disappear while Dutch gold dukaten appeared at a level similar to the previous year's foreign gold. These circumstances worked with the story that depositors brought gold coins to the Bank and then the Bank had them reminted. In contrast, the Bank already held large quantities of rijksdaalders in 1610. The level of rijksdaalders, however, falls by 65 percent in 1611, and that agreed with Dutch silver coins being used for withdrawals. The Bank also held bullion that was available to be turned into Dutch coins. Sadly, no additional metallic inventories are extant until 1711, so this peek into foreign coins rolling in and Dutch coins rolling out is all we get at this early stage of the Bank's story.

The inventories used to construct Table 4.4 do not include withdrawal fees, but some adjustments were already present. The Bank booked rijks-daalders with a premium of ½ percent over ordinance and gold dukaten at

---

[16] The Bank might also have had a half-guilder coin (*tienstuiverpenning*) that was introduced in Holland in 1606 (Polak 1998b, 72).

Table 4.4. *Metallic inventory of the early Bank, in guilders*

Category	Metal	Name	1610	1611
Coins by tale	Gold	Dukaten	0.0	272,652.5
	Gold	Rijders	0.0	13,117.5
	Gold	Others (foreign)	260,872.4	121,162.2
	Silver	Rijksdaalders	413,563.0	144,875.0
	Silver	Leeuwendaalders	68,640.0	56,160.0
	Silver	Others (foreign)	30,352.5	176,436.0
Coins by weight	Gold		58,351.6	179,097.3
	Silver		0.0	15,143.0
	Unclear		17,489.4	0.0
Bullion by weight	Gold		51,372.1	107,833.4
	Silver		12,858.4	19,003.3
	Unclear		11,641.5	209,307.0
Held by receiver	Unclear		0.0	88,888.7
Total			925,140.8	1,403,675.9

Source: Van Dillen (1925b, 880–83).
Note: The current guilder and bank florin were not yet separate units of account.

an extra 2 percent; this meant that the Bank did not wait until withdrawal to add this premium.[17] The implication was that the Bank offered a premium to depositors of Dutch coins. If so, then the Bank was not strictly following ordinance pricing. To be viable as a moneychanger, the Bank needed withdrawal fees or adjusted prices to prevent arbitrage.

Withdrawal fees might have been necessary for the Bank as a money-changer, but the fees undermined the Bank as a cashier. For example, if someone deposited coins, used the balances to make a payment, got paid by others to reload the account, and relinquished the balances to withdraw the original coins, then the fee was effectively the price paid to borrow balances. If coins-to-balances-to-coins took a month, then the 1.25 percent fee compounded to an annualized interest rate of over 16 percent. The fee made the Bank an expensive cashier for short-term coin parking.

Instead, this high effective rate encouraged the recycling of Bank balances to keep coins in the Bank and thus stretch out the deposit. A market in avoidance emerged as dealers in Bank money (in reality often a cashier, since these were again legalized in 1621) undercut the Bank's withdrawal

---

[17] This was underscored by a 1611 entry of light (*lichte*) gold *dukaten* that did not get a premium.

Table 4.5. *Dealers in Bank money*

	Debtor		Creditor	Dealer
	Assets	Liabilities	Assets	Assets
Start	100 coins	100 bill	100 bill	100 balances
Dealer sells Bank money with −0.25	−99.75 coins +100 balances			+99.75 coins −100 balances
Bill settles in Bank money	−100 balances	−100 bill	+100 balances −100 bill	
Dealer buys Bank money with +1.00			+99 coins −100 balances	−99 coins +100 balances
End	0.25 coins		99 coins	100 balances 0.75 coins
Alternative result via deposit and withdrawal	Assets	Liabilities	Assets 98.75 coins	Assets 100 balances

Source: Authors' example.

fee and overcut the Bank's deposit fee. Dealers could arrange this because they were not moneychangers and did not need a high fee to prevent arbitrage. Table 4.5 walks us through a conceptual example. Time moved from top to bottom and participants from left to right. To begin, the debtor had coins (assets) that will soon be used to pay off a bill of exchange (liability). The creditor was owed for the bill that would be settled in Bank money. The dealer had an inventory of balances at the Bank. Finally, the Bank (not shown) had the deposited coins as an asset, had the dealer's balances as a liability, and charged a 1.25 percent withdrawal fee.

Instead of depositing coins in the Bank, the debtor sold coins to the dealer for balances at a slightly better price ($0.25 > 0$) than offered by the Bank. Next, the debtor transferred the balances to the creditor to settle the bill. Finally, the dealer sold the creditor coins at a slightly lower price than the Bank offered ($1 < 1.25$). Everyone gained relative to a cycle of deposit and withdrawal because the Bank's fee was redistributed among them. In this example, 0.25 went to the debtor, 0.75 went to the dealer, and the creditor saved 0.25. The result was a secondary market that moved balances within the Bank and moved coins outside. At the same time, the option to withdraw coins kept bid-ask spreads less than the Bank's fees and pressured dealers to sell coins of a similar quality. Based on the many complaints regarding cashiers and the questionable quality of circulating coins, this pressure might have been valuable.

Still, building a successful municipal bank based on the combination of moneychanger and cashier must have seemed doubtful. At the time, other cashiers and moneychangers were portrayed (disapprovingly) as finding success by not following the rules. The legitimate route was available but less profitable. The same likely applied to the Bank, so the City bolstered the Bank with financial coercion targeting its rivals. The City banned other cashiers. The City banned other moneychangers. The City banned payment by assignment of debts. The City required merchants to settle bills of exchange at the Bank.

The suppressions of cashiers and moneychangers failed because the Bank did not satisfy either role well enough. It was too easy for illicit moneychangers to operate, as they had been doing before the founding of the Bank. Following the chartering of the Bank in 1609, it took the City longer (until 1620) to relent on cashiers, but, again, merchants pleaded need. One convenience supplied by cashiers was an account that could be spent to acquire Bank money through the agio market. In effect, a cashier account replaced coins in Table 4.5, so no coins had to move inside or outside the Bank.[18]

The coercion that perhaps endured longest was the requirement that bills of exchange (especially the more critical bills emanating from outside the Republic) settle at the Bank, because merchants mostly went along with it. The requirement compelled most large merchants to have an account, and that outcome supported what made the Bank potentially helpful. All large merchants had access to high-quality coins through the Bank or through dealers. Merchants might usually choose dealers, but the option to use the Bank helped keep dealers honest. As mentioned in Chapter 2, however, a substantial bill market eventually evolved in current money and settled outside the Bank. Even with bills, the Bank had competition.

Overall, the intitial design of the Bank made for an expensive cashier and an uncompetitive moneychanger, but at least it could maintain standards for customers who sufficiently valued that service. Unfortunately, even that success was compromised when the standards outside the Bank changed.

4.3 Displacement

It was Redish's fourth channel of debasement, coin substitution, that would upset the Dutch system and push the Bank to evolve. The debasement

---

[18] Dehing (2012, 121–22) found that cashiers dominated the agio market by 1648.

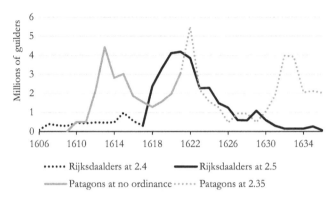

Figure 4.3. Annual production of rival coins, 1606–36
Source: Stapel (2016).

impulse came from the Southern Netherlands, whose provinces were
related in language and culture to the northern provinces that formed
the Dutch Republic. The south, however, was ruled by the Spanish
Habsburgs, who were striving to reconquer the Republic. The start of the
Twelve Years Truce in 1609 did not erase the hostility between the
Habsburgs and the Republic, and in fact, this interlude of military peace
was marked by strident monetary warfare.

In 1610, mints in the Habsburg provinces unleashed an assault in the
form of a new silver coin called the *patagon*, being Dutch for the Spanish
patacón, meaning large coin. The coin was part of the family of dollar coins
created by various parts of the Holy Roman Empire.[19] The coin's key
feature was being slightly smaller than the Republic's rijksdaalder; it was
to weigh 3.2 percent less and be 1.4 percent less fine, and it also suffered
additional debasement by Flemish mints (Van Cauwenberghe and Metz
1954, 131–32). The intention was that people in the north might treat
patagons and rijksdaalders as substitutes. In this, the patagon would prove
so successful that it eventually displaced the rijksdaalder as current money
in the Dutch Republic. The invader's triumph made the Bank's original
commitments untenable, and the City responded by beginning the disengagement of Bank money from current money.

To see the initial surge of patagons, Figure 4.3 plots the known production of patagons and rijksdaalders. By 1618, the cumulative production of
patagons was 18 million guilders. That is over twice the cumulative

[19] The patagon was also called the cruisdaalder (cross-dollar) because one side had a
Habsburg cross.

rijksdaalder production going back to that coin's introduction in 1606. Many of the coins migrated north, and as early as 1612 the patagon was common in Amsterdam (Van Dillen 1964d, 335). The patagon had less mismatch between par and content because it contained less silver. This asymmetry helped patagons satisfy the demand for current money as rijksdaalders were repurposed as trade coins. People could also use patagons as trade coins, but they had no advantage in international trade. Indeed, the rijksdaalder was popular in the Baltic trade (North 1989, 60), and the Republic was always happy to export its trade coins to foreign markets (Van Dillen 1964a, 250–51).

The wrinkle, however, was that the patagon was assigned a value of 2.4 guilders in the south but not in the north (Cauwenberghe and Metz 1984, 131). Initially, the patagon had no legal status in the Republic. This meant that displacement relied on people in the Republic choosing to use the patagon at its southern par. Already in 1613, the Province of Holland was complaining about "counterfeit Burgundian silver dollars at [2.4 guilders]" (Nederlantsche munt-boek 1645, 104). The patagon was not a counterfeit in a strict sense, but it did rely on people overlooking differences. Why exactly people initially accepted patagons as a substitute for rijksdaalders remains underdeveloped.[20] We can speculate that as the patagon achieved some market share, a feedback loop began. The supply of patagons into the local coin stock made it easier for cashiers and moneychangers to cull rijksdaalders from circulation. In turn, fewer rijksdaalders in the remaining monetary stock tilted the balance of local expectations toward patagons and that strengthened network expectations and rewarded the minting of yet more patagons. The momentum must have been powerful, because in 1618 the mints of the Spanish Netherlands began producing an even larger silver coin called the ducaton. Ducatons were 3 guilders each in the south and had no legal standing in the Republic. Moreover, the coin had no northern cousin to displace, yet it also found acceptance in the north at a valuation anchored by its ordinance relationship with the patagon. Apparently, the invaders brought their ordinance schedule with them.

Figure 4.3 also shows the response. In 1619, the Republic again cried up the value of the rijksdaalder to 2.5 guilders per coin. Rijksdaalder production surged as its local function was again relevant. Put differently, the incentive to cull was replaced by an incentive to mint because par was

---

[20] We can offer the possibility that having a legal value in the southern provinces was enough to suggest an anchor, and that anchor was adopted because it approximately matched the silver content of the coins.

realigned. When the Republic boosted the value of the rijksdaalder, the Bank's depositors, like other creditors, suffered a 4 percent loss in silver content should they withdraw those coins (Mees 1838, 57–58).[21] The Bank and its customers discovered the political risk of not being in control of the rules. Apparently, the Republic also learned to avoid such dislocations, as the value of the rijksdaalder and the leeuwendaalder were not changed again.[22]

Within a couple of years, however, local valuation of the patagon followed to 2.5 and local displacement of rijksdaalders reengaged. In effect, northerners again adopted the invader into the native coin's denomination. The production of patagons again surged (Figure 4.3), and that coincided with the end of the Twelve Years Truce between Spain and the Republic. Ironically, the Spanish crown was displeased with this development, in the sense that patagons used for military expenditures in the Low Countries tended to inject monetary stimulus into the Republic's economy (Israel 1982, 34–35). A royal advisor, Pedro Alvares Pereira, even argued that land war against the Dutch was futile, "because the money Your Majesty spends on it all ends up in their hands" (Israel 1982, 67).

The Republic was also displeased, and it switched tactics in 1622. Instead of crying up the rijksdaalder yet again (Holland had preemptively done so in 1621 but relented), the Republic added its enemy's coins (patagons) to the ordinance list at 2.35 guilders per coin. This new strategy was to compel a separation in values, and maybe people would stop treating patagons the way ordinances wanted them to treat rijksdaalders. At ordinance, the patagon's mint equivalent would now be 6 percent less than the rijksdaalder. The new rule applied to the Bank, and the Bank followed the rules, and few customers wanted to deposit patagons at that low price. Outside the Bank, however, the new policy did not succeed in changing behavior. Indeed, it was largely ignored. The patagon continued to circulate at 2.5, the par value of the rijksdaalder, and the rijksdaalder circulated as a trade coin above that amount (Korthals Altes 2001, 104). "We therefore find that after 1622, for several years, the premium of the

---

[21] The leeuwendaalder was similarly cried up in 1615 from 1.9 to 2.0 guilders. Usually, the Bank did not have to follow temporary increases called tolerances, but the 1619 ordinance explicitly compelled the Bank, and debt settlement in general, to abide by the new values of gold dukaten, rijksdaalders, and Spanish dollars (Nederlantsche munt-boek 1645, 112).

[22] Both coins were still at these values in the first extant cashbook in 1711 (ACA 5077/1355, folio 1).

bank money, being equal to the premium of the rijksdaalder, was 4.5 to 5 per cent" (Mees 1838, 58).

In October 1638, the Republic accepted monetary defeat and acknowledged the patagon at 2.5 guilders (Van Dillen 1964d, 357). The Republic was not happy about it. The status was provisional and came with a stern warning to not import any more (Nederlantsche munt-boek 1645, 198, 201, 206). That provisional status, however, did not apply to the Bank (Nederlantsche munt-boek 1645, 198). As a result, customers would take a silver loss of 1 percent (before fees) to deposit patagons at 2.35 and then withdraw rijksdaalders at 2.5. The Bank would starve for deposits.

The next month, November 1638, the City's governing council intervened. It allowed the Bank to lend to its customers for four months if these customers surrendered southern coins as collateral (Van Dillen 1925a, 80). In this way, the Bank finessed the ordinance by taking possession of patagons at 2.4 guilders instead of ownership at the required 2.35. This veneer was thin. If customers did not repay the loan, then the coins fell into the Bank's outright ownership: functionally a deposit.

The result was yet more frustration. The City's governing council complained that self-seeking people withdrew rijksdaalders from the Bank, not to finance trade, but to send it to the Southern Netherlands to be minted into new invaders (Van Dillen 1925a, 80–81). The Bank discovered that when a patagon deposit price was too low, it discouraged inflows, but if it was too high, then it encouraged arbitrage. Two years later, the City Council clarified that southern ducatons and patagons were "good bank money" (Van Dillen 1925a, 80). This implied that the Bank was given authority to deliver out the southern coins for withdrawal. If so, it would have broken the arbitrage loop by matching patagons in with patagons out. We do not know for sure because no metal accounts survive for this era.[23]

Tension between the Republic and the City continued. Republic ordinances in 1645, 1647, 1652, and 1653 restated that the Bank was to follow the asymmetry of taking in patagons at 2.35 and not let them out (Van Dillen 1925a, 91, footnote 2). The City ignored them and instead discussed and experimented with how the Bank would actually handle patagons (Dehing 2012, 114). The last arrangement came in 1656. The City told the Bank to accept patagons at 2.4 and ducatons at 3 by receipt that charged 1/8 percent when leaving the Bank (Van Dillen 1925a, 112–13).

---

[23] Dehing (2012, 146) ascribed a rush of deposits in 1645 to the Bank having then moved to both taking in and delivering out patagons.

This arrangement was very similar to the receipt system that would be adopted in 1683.

As a result of the patagon odyssey, Bank money developed an agio, or premium, of 4–5 percent.[24] Before 1638, this was because Bank money represented a claim on superior collateral, rijksdaalders instead of patagons. After 1638, the agio was because the Bank measured patagons and ducatons using different prices than the rest of the economy. Bank money had become a distinct unit of account.[25] From this time forward, we apply a convention of calling the Bank's unit of account "florins" and the current-money unit of account "guilders," recognizing that, in reality, the terms florin and guilder were used interchangeably.[26] As noted earlier, we refer to the units of account in English (i.e., florin and guilder) and domestic coins in Dutch (e.g., rijksdaalder and leeuwendaalder). We do this for clarity and to reinforce that the Bank florin was distinct from the current guilder and that both units of account were distinct from coins.

4.4 Replacement

A more durable peace between the Republic and Spain was achieved by the 1648 Treaty of Münster, which ended the Eighty Years War and acknowledged the Republic's sovereignty. This treaty marked a historic concession by Spain to a rebellious territory, but from a monetary perspective, a more significant concession had already been granted the year before. This took the form of an agreement proposed by Spain and presented to the States General on August 1, 1647, under which Amsterdam would become a recognized staple market for Spanish silver from the New World. The catch was that the Republic would have to allow imported Spanish silver to be reexported to the Southern Netherlands, which remained under Habsburg control. The States General assented to this deal with the

---

[24] Note that altering the level of the agio did not change how dealers made the agio market work in Table 4.5.

[25] The preeminent historian of the Bank (Van Dillen 1964d, 359–60) rejected the idea of early-seventeenth-century Bank money as a separate type of money. The term "Bank money," in Van Dillen's view, at this time chiefly referred to the higher-quality type of coins that were held in the Bank's vault. Van de Laar (1978, 43), writing after a career in banking, disagreed with Van Dillen's characterization and argued that the great popularity of the Bank among Amsterdam's practical-minded merchants, the Bank's high withdrawal fees notwithstanding, was proof that these people saw Bank money as a unique and desirable asset.

[26] Indeed, up until the adoption of the euro, the currency symbol employed for the Dutch guilder was the cursive f for florin.

reservation that one-third of the silver imports would go to Dutch mints, "the remaining two thirds being freely available for export to hostile or neutral nations" (Van Dillen 1925a, 96–98.) Objections from some provinces (Gelderland, Groningen, and Utrecht) that the free flow of silver "would empower our common enemy" were swept aside in general anticipation of expanding business prospects.

Van Dillen (1970, 29–32) characterized this somewhat stunning agreement as little more than a formal recognition of the facts on the ground. By the mid-seventeenth century, Amsterdam was on its way to becoming the financial capital of northern Europe. Any Spanish coins flowing in that direction, for example, to pay for Baltic or Asian trade goods, or even to pay Spanish armies, tended to pass through Amsterdam. Traditional routes between Spain and the Southern Netherlands had been disrupted by the Thirty Years War. The appeal of London as an alternative entrepôt for Spanish silver diminished following a 1640 decision by the English king, Charles I, to confiscate all silver at the English mint.[27] Spain had increasingly used Amsterdam to route silver to the Southern Netherlands, in order to fund its military campaigns against France. For its part, the Republic realized that more silver would be attracted to its ports if it could be reexported with few restrictions. Although quantitative data for this period are lacking, the deal seems to have worked. By July 1648, Spanish pieces of eight were sufficiently abundant in Amsterdam that the City found it necessary to outlaw their use as current money, an action that had to be repeated in 1651 and again in 1674 (Van Dillen 1925a, 99, 103–4, 177–78). Much of the imported Spanish silver then left Amsterdam as bullion, without export restrictions (Van Dillen 1963a, 251). This anti-mercantilist policy, a rarity for its time, deepened Amsterdam's markets for precious metal assets.

The influx of Spanish silver set the stage for yet another coinage reform. The Southern Netherlands' role as a provider of the north's local coins ended in 1659, when the Republic and its provinces agreed to introduce two new coins: the silver dukaat (*zilveren dukaat*) and the silver rijder (*zilveren rijder*).[28] It seems policymakers wanted to displace the southern invaders but not otherwise disrupt the system. To that end, the two new

---

[27] At the time, England had been offered the same deal on Spanish silver (one third domestic coinage, two-thirds free for export) as later enjoyed by the Republic (Pepys [1666] 1902, 447). The king's seizure of silver was temporary, but its chilling effect persisted.

[28] The 1659 reform attempted to channel business to the Republic's mints by prohibiting the export of precious metal, apparently in violation of the 1647 agreement with Spain.

Table 4.6. *The silver coins of 1659*

Name at the Bank	Rijksdaalder	Ducaton
Name at ordinance	Zilveren dukaat	Zilveren rijder
Ordinance value in current guilders	2.50	3.15
Ordinance value in bank florins	2.40	3.00
Implied agio in percent	4.17	5.00
Mint equivalent in current guilders per fine mark	24.93	25.13

Source: Polak (1998b, 73–74).

coins were designed to replace the invaders by being of a similar size yet containing less silver. Sometimes history does repeat. As testimony to how entrenched these current money concepts were, people called the new silver rijders after the Flemish ducatons they replaced, and people called the new silver dukaten after rijksdaalders because that was what people called patagons because patagons had earlier displaced the rijksdaalders of the 1606 ordinance. Even the Bank called silver rijders by ducatons and silver dukaten by rijksdaalders.[29]

The new coins kept the quirky dual price structure, as shown in Table 4.6. The new rijksdaalder (officially the silver dukaat) was assigned an ordinance value of 2.4 bank florins and 2.5 current guilders. The new ducaton (officially a silver rijder) was assigned a value of 3 bank florins and 3.15 current guilders. At this juncture, the Republic had the opportunity to recalibrate the values of Bank money to equal current money but chose not to, effectively ceding some monetary sovereignty to the Bank. The long-run consequence was that the Bank took another step of disengagement from current money.

The distinct units of account created room to arbitrage differences in ordinance valuations. People could deposit the new rijksdaalders worth 2.5 current guilders each at 2.4 bank florins each for a ratio of 1.0417 or an implicit agio of 4.17 percent. This agio was implicit because deposits were a primary market: they created and destroyed Bank money. The explicit agio was a secondary market that rearranged who owned Bank money through the intermediation of cashiers (see Table 4.5). The implicit agio of the ducaton was 5 percent. Depositing rijksdaalders and withdrawing ducatons

---

The States General soon (in 1660) rescinded this prohibition, however, following intense lobbying by Amsterdam merchants (Van Dillen 1964a, 252–53).

[29] Following the 1659 reform, the original Nederlandsche rijksdaalder became known as the *bankrijksdaalder*.

gained a person 0.8 percent more current guilders. The Bank now had a new reason to charge withdrawal fees: to prevent agio arbitrage.[30]

4.5 Agio Anchor

The combination of implicit agios and attendant fees created an anchor for the market agio. When people sold Bank money through the resale market via dealers, the price was measured as the agio, or premium, derived from the ratio of current guilders over bank florins. When 104 current guilders bought 100 bank florins, the ratio was 1.04, and the agio was 4 percent. When the market agio drifted away, the implicit agios worked to drag it back. For example, if the market agio floated above 4.17 percent, then people gained more bank florins by depositing their coins than by selling the coins to dealers. The greater the difference, the greater the incentive. When people responded to the high agio with deposits, the stock of Bank money increased and the stock of current money decreased. These adjustments, other things equal, pushed the agio downward. In this way, the implicit agio set a threshold for a specie-flow adjustment whereby a flow of specie into the Bank pulled the market agio back to its anchor. The larger ducatons could also play this role, but their implicit agio was 5 percent, so the market agio had to climb substantially higher.

But primary and secondary markets were not the same. The regular agio market engaged everyone with bank florins to sell with everyone looking to buy the same, and many of them had cashier accounts. The implicit agio was only for people with specific coins seeking bank florins. The ability of rijksdaalders to flow into the Bank and push down the agio was limited by whether there were rijksdaalders about, whether depositing them brought a higher value than exporting them, and whether enough rijksdaalders would be deposited to move the overall agio market. The implicit agio was not an iron chain that decisively contained the larger market. Instead, it was an elastic band that pulled more strongly with distance, but it still might not pull enough to offset destabilizing pressures.

Figure 4.4 presents these forces in a supply and demand schematic. Supply was people with Bank money seeking current money. Demand was people with current money seeking Bank money. Dealers made the

---

[30] To prevent silver arbitrage, the Bank had already set the price of the two coins in bank florins so that their interchange delivered no additional silver content. The mint equivalent in bank florins was 23.936 for rijksdaalders and 23.935 for ducatons (Polak 1998b, 73–74).

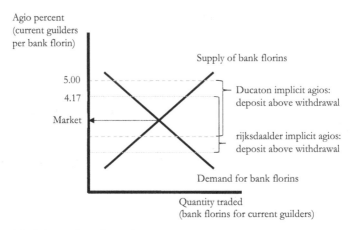

Figure 4.4. Agio market schematic
Source: see text.

trade easy, and a market clearing agio developed. The implicit agios for the rijksdaalder and the ducaton created upper thresholds above which deposit incentives increased. Sufficient deposits would increase the supply of bank florins and pull the agio down. A reversed story played out when the agio got low. People could withdraw coins instead of selling bank florins. The implicit agio at withdrawal would be the deposit agio less fees, but now, other things being equal, customers would rather withdraw ducatons than rijksdaalders. If we assume a 1.25 percent fee, then the lower thresholds are 3.75 for the ducaton and 2.92 for the rijksdaalder.

The implicit agios produced relevant thresholds. Figure 4.5 plots market agios from January 1663 to January 1683. The implicit agios for the ducaton and rijksdaalder form the deposit and withdrawal thresholds, and the withdrawal values assume a 1.25 percent fee. Observed agios stay within the outer thresholds (ducaton deposits and rijksdaalder withdrawals) except for 1666 and 1672. The 1666 observations are as low as 2.5. In contrast, the agios of June through August 1672 drop to around negative 2.5 (not shown) because a surprise assault on the Dutch Republic by the French and their allies triggered a run on the Bank. The run subsided and the agio recovered when it became clear that the Republic would not be conquered. Figure 4.5 shows how the implicit agios anchored the market. The relationship between bank florins and current guilders was an agio that varied (mostly) between 3 and 5 percent.

After decades of monetary tumult, Bank money traded in a stable range, and the Bank was again taking in and offering out Dutch coins of stable

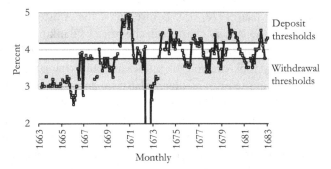

Figure 4.5. Agio with silver thresholds, 1663–83
Sources: for agios see McCusker (1978, 47) and ACA 234/290–95; for thresholds see Table 4.6 for deposits and an assumed 1.25 percent fee for withdrawals.

quality. These coins were not the original coins of 1609, and the Bank used a different price than the rest of the Dutch economy. Stability between the platforms of Bank money and coins was maintained by fees, reducing the set of deposit coins with high mint equivalents in bank florins, and setting bank values to equalize the mint equivalents in bank florins of withdrawal coins. Stability between Bank money and current money was now measured by the market agio, and that price was mostly corralled by implicit agios. The agio continued to be the measure of bank florin price stability for the next century.

4.6 Conclusion

The City of Amsterdam created the Bank in 1609 to bring coins into compliance with the Republic's ordinances. The City's Bank would reliably convert account balances into high-quality coins. This conceptually straightforward but practically challenging assignment became hopeless when the Republic changed to a lesser standard, yet expected the Bank to continue its original mission. To save it, the City gave the Bank a first push toward becoming a central bank, awarding it the monetary independence that attached Bank money to a distinct unit of account. This distinctiveness was reinforced by the emergence of a secondary market. When the Republic reformulated its coinage system yet again, the Bank got to switch to the new standard and keep its own unit of account. The Bank had adapted, survived, and become a recognized part of the Republic's monetary system.

The Bank's new status was marked by a noteworthy psychological milestone (Van de Laar 1978, 53). Before 1659, the Amsterdam market viewed changes in the agio as changes in the price of Bank money relative to silver, as expressed in the fine content of various coins. After 1659, Bank money increasingly took the role of numeraire, and changes to the agio were seen as shifts in the price of silver relative to an invariant bank florin.

What these developments did not do was to allow the Bank to escape from the Republic's coinage system. With the 1659 restoration of domestic silver coins, the Republic once again set the Bank to supporting a bimetallic coinage system of different denominations. The variety of coins and metals continued to force the Bank to charge substantial fees to prevent arbitrage. Even then, the Republic could, and would, again change that system. As the first half century repeatedly demonstrated, eventually the Bank would get caught between protecting its depositors and the Republic's quest for a stable local coinage system. The next chapter recounts how the Bank finally solved this dilemma by letting go of any formal connection to current money.

5

Emergence of the Receipt System, 1660–1710

The two previous chapters surveyed the complexities and woes of coins, because coinage problems became Bank problems. Paper money, however, had its own challenges. Bills could be lost, forged, or protested. Accounts could be abused by overdraft and identity theft. More perilous was malfeasance by the people who supplied accounts, and, in 1673, the Bank faced such a crisis in a most public setting. On Saturday, May 13, Rutgert Vlieck was flogged and beheaded on the Dam square in front of the Bank, after he had recited a lengthy lamentation for his misdeeds. See Figure 5.1 for one pamphlet's rendition. Vlieck had been a bookkeeper for the Bank, and he had used that position to fraudulently create accounts and remove coins (Dehing 2012, 103–7). The scale of the fraud was never fully reconstructed but was estimated at least several hundred thousand florins. Worse for the City, Vlieck's crimes had become public knowledge, and the execution only confirmed the Bank's inability to control its ledger and inventory. The sensational beheading of Vlieck could not relieve the Bank of its own guilt.

After years of rumination, the City responded in 1683 with reformation. Additional clerks were hired to better watch the watchers. At the same time, the City revived the receipt experiment from the 1650s and applied it to the silver ducaton. This occurred as the ducaton was already drifting from local to trade coin usage. Unlike similar situations in earlier decades (see Chapter 4), this disengagement of the Bank from current money became permanent, seemingly because the experiment with the receipt system went so well. The Bank accepted a new way to operate.

The impact of these changes can be measured more precisely than in the previous era, because the first continuous run of surviving Bank ledgers began in 1666. The creation and destruction of Bank money was preserved in the ledger folios that track the Bank's master account. Interpretation of these money stock changes can be challenging, because the surviving runs

Een Beklagh-Liedt van Rutgert Vlieck , **Boeck-**
houder in de Banck van Leeningh op het Stadt-huys tot Amsterdam/ van
wegen syn groote dieverp die hy aldaer in gepleeght heeft/ waer over al syn
goederen syn verkocht / en hy op den 13. May 1673. met den Swaerde is
gejusticeert/ en het lichaem begraven. Stemme : Bel Yris.

Figure 5.1. The execution of Rutgert Vlieck
Source: Anonymous pamphlet 1673, courtesy of Rijksmuseum.

of the Bank's cashbooks, which track the Bank's metallic assets, do not begin until 1711. However, the patterns of transactions on the liability side of the Bank (the ledgers) were consistent enough to allow for some reconstructions of the asset side for select years.

An essential component of the Bank's transformation was something potentially even more sensational than Vlieck's execution: a changeover to a fiat-money regime. Nor was this deep policy shift proclaimed on the Dam square or any other public place. Soon after initiating its new accounting procedures and new receipt facility, the Bank simply (and quietly) removed customers' traditional rights of deposit and withdrawal; that is, the Bank imposed new restrictions on the convertibility of accounts and coins. Receipts became the sole channel through which customers could determine the timing and quantity of coin flows into and out of the Bank.

Monetary history has recorded many restrictions of convertibility, but these were often conspicuous measures adopted in response to war or economic crisis.[1] The Bank's removal of deposit and withdrawal was unusual in that it had neither an obvious external impulse nor a formal authorization. There was no record of a policy change, nor was there any evidence of customer outrage. This chapter proposes that the City did not pronounce this change, and customers did not agitate against it, because it was part of a larger initiative to improve the functionality of Bank money.

The end of withdrawal was not an explicit part of the 1683 resolution. Our contention is that a combination of intentional changes instead allowed for the quiet extinction of traditional withdrawal. Receipts gave customers a better way to remove coins and tightening the ledgers justified the change without additional promulgations or debate. Acquiescence was aided by the popularity of the new arrangement. To summarize by proverb, nothing succeeds like success.

The end of withdrawal was only the first of a series of lasting consequences. In the decades to follow, the Bank extended receipts to additional coins. This process came to offer receipts to foreign trade coins but not to domestic local coins. Again, this evolution occurred as implementation decisions within the Bank rather than formal directives from the City. As a result, the Bank quietly disengaged from the current money system as it created new ways to engage with the international system. The monetary map (see Figure 2.4) emerged.

Similarly, we find it unlikely that policymakers in 1683 intended to create a fiat-money central bank, even if this is what actually resulted. Functionally, the Bank became fragmented into two parts: a narrow receipt bank and a fractional reserve fiat bank.[2] Those parts shared a common monetary liability. We doubt the City intended to create a new way to back Bank money, because the consequences were too radical to not stir up controversy. Even today, the full extent of the monetary revolution that occurred in late-seventeenth-century Amsterdam is only gradually becoming apparent, hence, this book and the growing scholarly literature on the

---

[1] Two famous instances being the Bank of England's Napoleonic-era restriction of convertibility beginning in 1797 (Clapham 1945a, 272; O'Brien and Palma 2020, 390) and the collapse of the international gold standard starting in 1931, which ended convertibility in most countries (Eichengreen and Flandreau 1997, 20).

[2] This was a de facto division of the Bank rather than a de jure division, as occurred with the Bank of England following the passage of the Bank Charter Act of 1844 (a.k.a. Peel's Act). This division is explored further in Chapter 7. Chapter 9 compares the divided post-1683 Bank with the post-1844 Bank of England.

Bank. From the perspective of the time, the changes seemed incremental, technical, and effective. The City also slowly reconciled itself to new principles of exploitation: coins owned outright could be taken, but coins under receipt were sacrosanct.

5.1 Yet Another New Local Coinage System

The 1659 investiture of the rijksdaalder and ducaton coins re-established that Republic silver coins would anchor the domestic monetary system, and the same legislation recognized the Bank's ledgers as a distinct unit of account within that system.[3] However, the new regime still sought to attain an incompatible combination of goals: the production of high-quality coins at stable prices, minted from two precious metals, in diverse denominations, by rival provincial mints that the Republic could not control. After a dozen years, the system of local coinage (yet again) started to degrade.

In 1672, the Province of Friesland reasserted its right to produce an old silver coin called the *florijn* with 11 percent less silver than the original (Polak 1998b, 78). In 1676, Zeeland joined in by creating a new *daalder* coin that was also much lighter than the ducaton (Polak 1998b, 83). These provinces were already abusing the production of small coins, but now they were moving up the hierarchy to coins worth 1.4 and 1.5 guilders, respectively. This would be the fourth daalder the Bank had to contend with, the previous ones being the 1606 Nederlandschen rijksdaalder, the Flemish cruisdaalder (a.k.a. the patagon), and the 1659 rijksdaalder (a.k.a. the zilveren dukaat).

The Province of Holland and the City of Amsterdam complained and asserted that such coins were not acceptable as current money. Perhaps having learned a lesson from the patagon invasion (see Chapter 4), Holland did not rely on prohibitions alone. In 1681, the province introduced its own new local coins: the gulden with a one-guilder face value and the *driegulden* with a three-guilder face value. The gulden would fend off the domestic invaders. The driegulden would replace the ducaton for local payments as few people were minting ducatons anymore (Van Dillen 1925a, 194–95). Ducatons were becoming trade coins as described in Chapter 3. Some of the other provinces adopted the driegulden coin at this time but kept on producing their mid-sized daalders and florijnen.

---

[3] The formal names for these coins were the *zilveren dukaat* for the *rijksdaalder* and *zilveren rijder* for the *ducaton*. See Chapter 4.

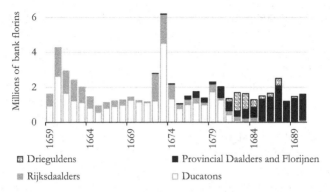

Figure 5.2. Production of large Dutch silver coins, yearly, 1659–1690
Source: Stapel (2016).

Figure 5.2 tracks the drama by reporting the known production of two sets of silver coins. The first set is ducatons and rijksdaalders. Production favored the ducaton over the rijksdaalder until around 1680 when production of both stalled. The push by some provinces into the new types of larger silver coins (larger defined here as greater than one guilder) is shown in Figure 5.2 by driegulden production and the combination of daalder and florijn production. Production of this new local system was displacing the old by 1683. Drieguldens had a brief surge at that time, but it was provincial daalders and florijnen that dominated production for the rest of the decade.

So, in addition to fraud, the City was pressured to act because the Bank again faced a dilemma: follow the new standard or defend the old. The Republic would not set an ordinance on the gulden system until 1694; until then ordinances would have had the Bank using ducatons. In the earlier era, when the patagons were the new local coins, the City had experimented with deposit by receipt for the invader coins. Reimplementation of that approach would have had the Bank accept the new drieguldens by receipt and keep the old ducatons for traditional deposit and withdrawal.

The newest twist was that Amsterdam's home province of Holland was promulgating the new gulden standard, whereby the unit of account was bound to coins (the gulden and driegulden) with fixed nominal values. Should the City have accepted the new provincial standard? It could have. Assuming the Bank retained its distinct unit of account, it could have taken in drieguldens at 2.85 bank florins per coin to prevent silver arbitrage with the older ducatons.[4]

---

[4] That value was what the City assigned the driegulden at the Bank in 1683 (Van Dillen 1925b, 202).

At that price, the coin's implicit agio would be 5.26 percent compared to the ducaton's 5 percent, so an agio spread for arbitrage would have been modest.[5] The agio gap relative to the rijksdaalder would have been a substantial 1.13 percent, but rijksdaalder deposits were a vanishing threat. In 1672, Zeeland had cried up the rijksdaalder to 2.55 current guilders per coin to try to keep them relevant as current money. None of the other provinces followed, but Zeeland's standard was enough to reset valuations nationwide, so the coin's implicit agio was 6.25 percent.[6] At that price, rijksdaalders were very expensive to deposit, so all the Bank had to do was not hand out rijksdaalders to keep that problem under control.

Did the Bank then switch to the new standard like it had in 1659? No. Did the Bank cling to the old standard? No. Instead, the City revived the receipt approach with yet another tweak. Both ducatons and drieguldens would be eligible for receipts. The innovation was to introduce the receipt mechanism to the ducaton, a coin the Bank also paid out for withdrawals. The consequences, both intended and unintended, fill the rest of this chapter. Of those, the immediate and expected consequence was a reduction in fees. To appreciate the power of this change, the next two sections lay out how high fees choked deposits and how low fees via receipts opened the throttle.

5.2 Deposits

High fees made it expensive to use deposit and withdrawal to move between coins and Bank money. As a result, withdrawals were rare and deposits rarer. The Bank's master account for 1666 recorded that silver and gold inflows created 1.5 million bank florins, precious metal outflows destroyed 2.1 million, and transfers reassigned 182.9 million.[7] Bank accounts had an annual velocity of 22, while bank metal had a velocity of 0.5.[8] The Bank was busy as a payment platform but moribund as a coin dealer. More charitably, the Bank was as a latent participant in the

---

[5] The ratio of the driegulden being $3/2.85 = 1.0526$ and of the ducaton being $3.15/3 = 1.05$.

[6] The 1659 ratio of the rijksdaalder being $2.5/2.4 = 1.0417$ and the Zeeland valuation being $2.55/2.4 = 1.0625$.

[7] Total debit volume (i.e., transfers of funds by Bank customers) was 185.0 million (Dehing 2012, 163), and 2.1 million of that was in exchange for metal held by the Bank. The Dutch East India Company did not repay any of its debt to the Bank in 1666, so Company repayments do not enter into calculations for that year.

[8] The calculations being $182.9/8.4 = 21.77$ and $(1.5 + 2.1)/7.5 = 0.48$, with the denominators being the Bank's stock of accounts and precious metal, respectively, at the start of 1666.

system of current money, and that potential was occasionally expressed as withdrawals but rarely as deposits.

A knock-on effect of the high withdrawal fees was to deepen the secondary (agio) market for Bank money, which allowed merchants to bypass the Bank's high withdrawal fees (see Chapter 4). The agio market, that is, the swap of Bank money for current money, was a portion of the overall transfer volume recorded in the Bank's ledgers. To maintain a liquid agio market, however, required that the Bank maintain a sufficient stock of Bank money, even as a lack of deposits exerted downward pressure on this money stock.

A lack of deposits also eroded the credibility that the Bank needed to support loans. As early as 1615, the Bank had become a lender to the Dutch East India Company and to the City itself (Van Dillen 1934, 94–95). Such lending violated the original scheme of a fully backed or narrow bank, but it did help two important local institutions. The Company repaid the advances with interest and so was a source of income. The City, however, usually chose not to pay interest to its own Bank.[9] Instead, the City repaid its debts by allowing the Bank to retain earnings. The City would gradually write off its debt while simultaneously reducing the corresponding equity of the Bank.

These developments increasingly pushed the Bank in the direction of partial metallic backing. At the start of 1666, 10 percent of the Bank's balances did not have metallic backing. That share increased to 26 percent by the start of 1669. To restore the ratio of metallic assets, the Bank employed what may at the time have seemed like a purely technical fix: large-scale purchases of silver or gold. In addition, the Bank did not just passively allow its metallic assets to simply be withdrawn but also actively engaged in open market sales.

To see how the Bank actually operated over this time period, it was necessary to separate the Bank's metal inflows into those initiated by customers (deposits) from those initiated by the Bank (purchases). Records of the creation of bank florins have survived, but the records detailing the corresponding movement of the metal involved have not. Some filtering process must therefore be applied to distinguish purchases from deposits. Fortunately, the Bank made the distinction through its own procedures. Deposits arrived through receivers.[10] As described in

---

[9] Originally the City paid 3 percent interest on these loans, but by 1650, it had ceased paying interest (Van Dillen 1925a, 972).

[10] From 1666 through 1682, 80 percent of the bank florins entering through receivers were for whole values. The primary exception was the rijksdaalder at 2.4 per coin; so looking at

Table 5.1. *Balance-sheet and account effects of a coin deposit*

	Balance-sheet effects		Non-balance-sheet effects			
	Assets	Liabilities				
		Customer account	Receiver account		Master account	
	debit	credit	debit	credit	debit	credit
August 14, 1666	+600	+600	+600			
January 26, 1667				+600	+600	

Source: ACA 5077/63, folio 1052.

Figure 5.3. Select deposits (debits) to the Receiver Isbrant Rodenburch
Source: 1666 Great Ledger. ACA 5077/63, folio 1052.

Chapter 2, receivers would take in ordinance-compliant coins and create Bank money with their own account. Figure 5.3 shows the debit side of the account of the receiver Isbrant Rodenburch in August 1666. Rodenburch started with a balance of 84,667.55 florins because he had received 104,063.85 during the first half of the year but had transferred only 19,396.3 to the master account. Most of that balance would not be fully moved over until the end of the fiscal year in January 1667. The figure also includes two deposits. The receiver created 600 in new balances for the Widow of Gerard Martens (folio 77) and 1,000 for Andries van Dalen (folio 124). The entries do not specify what coins were received.

Table 5.1 puts the first deposit transaction of Figure 5.3 into the framework of the Bank's balance sheet and system of accounts. The deposited coins and the new balances, being credits to the customer's account, each increased their respective sides of the balance sheet by 600. The debit to the receiver's account, however, did not. Similarly, when the debit was moved

receiver inflows that did end with change finds 34 percent had the set of rijksdaalder multiples: being 0.2, 0.4, 0.6, and 0.8. Another 23 percent ended conveniently at 0.5. Overall, less than 10 percent of receiver deposits included other values.

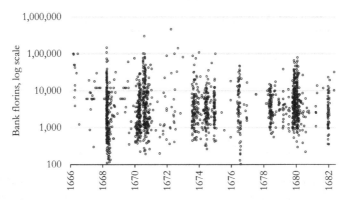

Figure 5.4. Bank purchases, each transaction, 1666–1682
Source: Authors' calculations.
Note: Blank verticals in 1673 and 1677 are half-years of missing ledgers.

to the master account in January, the transfer did not alter the balance sheet. These entries tallied the creation of Bank money and were the types that Vlieck would compromise.

In contrast, purchases of bullion or non-standard coins entered the Bank by way of its assayer: either through the assayer's Bank account or directly into the Bank's master account. In this way, the Bank segregated the responsibilities of employees handling standardized deposits from the employees handling idiosyncratic purchases. This distinction revealed that the Bank occasionally engaged in large purchase operations. Figure 5.4 plots each purchase from 1666 to 1682. The scale is logarithmic for easier visualization. The vertical streaks are periods of a few months wherein the Bank purchased large amounts of metal. In modern central banking parlance, these were open market operations. The other periods had only sporadic purchase activity. The purchase operations were nonetheless critical to maintaining the Bank's balance sheet, because total purchases were twice total deposits over this era. A reasonable conjecture is that bursts of purchase activity marked the arrival of fleets bringing silver to Amsterdam. For example, four months before the 1668 purchases, a treasure fleet from the New World had arrived in Spain (Morineau 1985, 233), and almost all such inflows of precious metal eventually left Spain (Chen et al. 2021).

To see that deposits were insufficient relative to withdrawals, it is necessary to also filter outflows. Outflows were recorded in the Bank's master account (i.e., subtractions from the stock of Bank money) and were not separated into withdrawals of coin or open market sales. The Bank

Table 5.2. *Metal flows, 1666–1669*

		Transactions	Bank florins
Inflows	Deposits	526	1,876,249.53
	Purchases	384	3,074,541.80
	Total inflows	910	4,950,791.33
Outflows	Ingot sales	668	708,499.20
	Bankrijksdaalder sales	475	3,281,390.00
	Leeuwendaalder sales	40	114,400.00
	East India Company withdrawals	15	1,617,448.05
	Other withdrawals	196	1,657,287.08
	Total outflows	1,394	7,379,024.33

Source: Authors.

mingled sales and withdrawals, presumably because all metallic assets leaving the Bank had already been accepted and assessed by someone, so there was no need for separate channels. This mingling makes it difficult to distinguish sales from withdrawals. Luckily, one informative set of credit books survived from this era that included activities involving metal.[11]

From 1666 through 1669, these books tallied the Bank's production of silver ingots, and we used those totals to confirm an identification of ingot sales.[12] Similarly, the books revealed how the Bank conducted coin sales. For example, in the early months of 1668, the Bank deputized receivers to sell trade coins, and those accounts show that *bankrijksdaalders* sold in sacks of 200 coins at a premium of ¾ percent.[13] The experiment of using receivers as sales agents was short-lived, but it demonstrated a regularity in how the Bank sold coins directly from the master account. With these insights, we sorted metal outflows into ingot sales, coin sales, and withdrawals. An appendix to this chapter shares examples of this filtering process. Some of the large withdrawals were labeled as going to the Company or its cashiers, so we added that delineation (cf. Dehing 2012, 158–160). Table 5.2 lists the results.

The table finds that total inflows lagged total outflows by 40 percent. Large withdrawals by the Company and others created much of that gap, but regular sales of trade coins by the Bank were also much larger than deposits. The Bank had minted such coins a decade earlier and likely

---

[11] These books were called balance books (ACA 5077/1311–1314).
[12] Knowing the price per mark and the weight increments of ingots lets us match individual sales.
[13] *Bankrijksdaalders* being the Bank's name in this era for the *Nederlandschen rijksdaalders* of 1609. See Chapter 4.

retained a stockpile that was now being sold.[14] To restore the overall level, the Bank purchased metal, and two-thirds of that came in the four months of April through July 1668. The Bank would initiate more purchase operations in early and late 1670 as per Figure 5.4.

The Bank was thus managing persistent shortfalls of precious metal inventory. Demand for trade coins from the Bank, especially by the Company, exceeded what people were willing to deposit. To maintain its balance sheet, the Bank responded with occasional but large purchases. Fees stabilized the Bank by preventing inter-coin arbitrage, but the consequence was that few customers wanted to park silver in the Bank.

5.3 Receipts

Receipts were an opportunity to improve the deposit situation because merchants found alternative solutions lacking. Silver abounded as it flowed from the New World through Amsterdam. Separately, Bank money circulated at a high velocity to settle bills of exchange and to support the agio market. What Amsterdam lacked was an ultrareliable way to move between the two monies. To acquire an affordable short-term borrowing rate, merchants had to use coins as collateral, but none of the private contractual solutions guaranteed the collateral would work as intended. In 1673 and again in 1677, a former Bank bookkeeper named Johannes Phoonsen argued that the Bank was uniquely positioned to improve this situation with an arrangement offering credibility and low fees (Van Dillen 1921). To reduce fees, however, the Bank had to find an alternative way to prevent inter-coin arbitrage of the type described in Chapter 4. Phoonsen's proposal was to revive receipts.

To understand the appeal of Phoonsen's proposal, consider a hypothetical Amsterdam merchant who needed a short-term loan. The merchant had a ship soon to sail and had drawn and discounted a bill of exchange to pay for provisions and a cargo of ducaton coins. That bill had come due and needed to be settled in Bank money. The friction was that the merchant expected an infusion of Bank money before departure (perhaps from the sale of previous imports or other assets) but did not have it yet. Hence, the need for a loan to cover near-term operating expenses while funding was arranged. Such short-term loans were, and have remained, the foundation of money markets.

The merchant would like to use the coins as collateral to secure a favorable short-term loan rate but needed assurance that the coins would

---

[14] See balance books starting in 1653, ACA 5077/1298.

Table 5.3. *Money market options circa 1680*

Option	Disadvantages
1. Deposit coins and later withdraw them from the Bank.	The Bank's deposit and withdrawal facility was reliable but not that cheap; an arbitrage-blocking withdrawal fee of 1 percent or more was to be expected.
2. Sell the coins on the agio market and later repurchase them.	The agio market was cheap but volatile. Selling and then repurchasing the ducatons needed for the voyage was another risk as their availability could change.
3. Draw a bill on a friend in another city and sell the bill on the Amsterdam market.	The bill market was expensive. Bills of exchange were unsecured; interest rates ran around 4 percent and these could vary short term. Bills also had counterparty risk. If the bill was protested (not accepted by the drawee), then the merchant faced demand for immediate repayment.
4. Borrow from another Amsterdam merchant, pledging the coins as collateral.	Pledging coins as collateral could lower short-term rates but it took time for a creditor to liquidate the collateral and recover the pledged amount in case of default.[15]

Source: Quinn, Roberds, and Kahn (2020, 4–5).
Note: Table shows financing options available to a merchant in possession of ducatons needed for a later voyage.

be free to ship when the loan was repaid. Unfortunately, none of the existing money market options combined affordable rates with reliable near-term release of collateral. Table 5.3 lists some of the available options

---

[15] Similarly, a debtor might face delays in reclaiming collateral if a secured creditor went bankrupt. Dutch law did not allow for what modern repo finance calls a "safe harbor" (Gorton and Metrick 2010), a creditor's right to immediate control of collateral. Contemporary Dutch bankruptcy procedures were complex, but are summarized by De Jong-Keesing (1939, 124–127) for the infamous case of Gebroeders de Neufville (see Chapter 7). Bankruptcies were handled by a municipal agency, the Chamber of Bankrupt Estates (*Desolate Boedelkamer*), which imposed a stay on the bankrupt's assets. Secured creditors were given accelerated repayment through liquidation of collateral, but repayment delays could occur. The unsecured creditors could then either collectively negotiate with the bankrupt for a discharge against partial repayment or wait 33 years for judicial resolution.

and their deficiencies. To be fair, these options were rather good by early modern standards, but the money market could not deliver an asset that was cheap and safe.

Phoonsen argued that receipts were a better arrangement. Receipts worked like an option that the Bank could credibly guarantee, because its assets were exempt from attachment by outside parties.[16] The option granted a customer the right to repurchase the same type of coins within a half-year at the original price plus a small fee (Phoonsen: "interest"). The Bank created the receipt when a customer delivered coins for Bank money. The option only applied to the type of coin originally delivered. If the option expired, then the Bank took immediate and uncontested ownership of the "fallen" coins. The customer could also roll over ("prolong") the option period by paying the fee. To quote the proposal:

> It should be allowed for everyone to pledge coins [to the Bank] ... at an interest of no more than one-half percent for a period of six months. This under the condition that these coins may be again removed from the Bank within six months or prolonged upon payment of interest; but after this interval has passed, the coins should become the absolute property of the Bank .... (Van Dillen 1921, 96)

Phoonsen recognized that through this arrangement, the Bank could function as a superior type of secured creditor, one that could afford to charge very low interest rates. The superiority resulted from the fact that the Bank had not granted credit in a technical sense, but only engaged in a coin purchase from a customer while granting the customer an ironclad right to repurchase an equivalent coin at a fixed price. Mees (1838, 138–39) argued that this was a privileged contract that contemporary Dutch law would not have allowed between two private parties. In addition, such privileged financing through the Bank did not inhibit other channels of finance. In particular, Bank customers could still finance themselves through the bill market when this was more advantageous.

The receipt system was to prove transformative, but it had a rather quiet beginning. In January 1683, the City ordered the Bank to offer receipts on ducaton and driegulden coins, with no other coins mentioned in the decree (Van Dillen 1925a, 202–3). Both coins were assigned a fee rate of 1/8 percent per half-year. No receipts from this era are extant (Dehing 2012, 331), but we can infer how they were issued and processed from the more

---

[16] Exemption from attachment was granted in the Bank's original 1609 charter (Van Dillen 1925a, 20–21) and affirmed by the States of Holland in 1670 (Van Dillen 1925a, 147–148).

complete accounts that begin in 1711. A receiver would take in the coins, credit the customer's account, and issue a receipt for the same value. At repurchase, the customer paid back the principal with account money and paid the redemption fee off ledger, most likely with smaller-value coins. Prolongation fees were also paid off ledger.

From the Bank's perspective, receipts gave customers an incentive to sort themselves into non-arbitrage sets. If customers deposited and withdrew ducatons, then they got a low fee. If they deposited rijksdaalders and withdrew ducatons, then they got a high fee. Customers proved they deposited ducatons by retaining the receipt. No receipt meant high fees, so customers had an incentive to keep and use receipts.

Also, because the arrangement was not a loan, the Bank avoided the legal complications that impaired secured loans in Table 5.3. If the option expired, then the Bank automatically gained unencumbered possession of the coins. The Bank did not have to deal with legal proceedings to gain title. The Bank's internal accounting system treated the coins as belonging to the Bank until repurchased by a customer. The encumbrance assigned by the receipt does not show up in the Bank's balance sheet (except occasionally the Bank would note if it owned coins outright). From the customer's perspective, the Bank was a uniquely reliable counterparty. If our hypothetical merchant now sold ducatons to the Bank, the merchant was assured of access to bank florins now and of getting back the coins when the Bank money was repaid. In more modern terminology, the Bank had provided the merchant both liquidity and a low-cost hedge against fluctuations in the value of the ducatons.[17]

Such hedging was almost certainly not the only use of receipts. People less interested in hedging and more interested in turning a quick trading profit, for example, could sell their receipts to people who wanted to carry a long position in trade coins. For the latter group, the receipts offered easy leverage, because they conferred control over trade coins at a small fraction of their value. Transactions in receipts typically occurred off the Bank's books, but the resulting long positions can be detected if the purchased

---

[17] In a similar vein, the need to hedge against fluctuations in collateral value is one motivating factor behind the modern use of repurchase agreements (Gottardi, Maurin, and Monnet 2019). The next chapter offers more comparisons the receipt facility with modern repo.

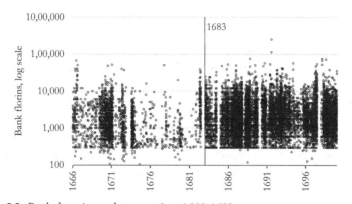

Figure 5.5. Bank deposits, each transaction, 1666–1699.
Source: Authors' calculations.
Note: Blank verticals in 1673, 1677, 1682, 1684, and 1697 are half-years of missing ledgers.

receipts were subsequently rolled over.[18] Chapter 8 will show examples of this type of trading.

The receipts' combination of credibility and low fees soon proved popular. Figure 5.5 plots each deposit into the Bank from 1666 through 1699. The receipts' impact on receiver inflow intensity was dramatic, as annual deposit rates after 1683 increased fivefold. There were doubtless external factors at work in this upsurge. Japan had restricted silver exports beginning in 1668 (De Zwart and Van Zanden 2018, 234), bolstering the Company's demand for silver supplied through Amsterdam, and 1685 saw an inflow of flight capital from France following the revocation of the Edict of Nantes (Gillard 2004, 179). What clearly changed was that much more silver was now moving into the Bank.

The receipt facility was popular because it let customers borrow Bank money cheaply, while still retaining control of their coins. A customer could park ducatons at the bank and pay only a ¼ percent fee per year (⅛ percent rolled over once). That customer could also use the resulting Bank money until the coins were repurchased. One use was to pay a bill due like that of our hypothetical merchant. Another was to buy a bill of exchange due on Amsterdam. The bill would pay back in Bank money and pay relatively well because the borrower did not have coins to use as collateral (see option 3 in Table 5.3). In this way, the surge in deposits deepened the

---

[18] See sample receipt in the appendix to this chapter. The bearer nature of receipts meant that a transfer of Bank money was not needed to purchase a receipt, and for this reason very few such purchases are recorded in the Bank's ledgers.

Amsterdam discount market by increasing the supply of funding. The Bank of Amsterdam did not directly engage in the bill market, as would the Bank of England starting a few decades later, but it did supply liquidity to the market. Another use was to sell the Bank money for current money to pay taxes, purchase Dutch East India Company shares, or whatever else the domestic Dutch economy offered or demanded. In this way, the surge in deposits deepened the agio market.

The coin side of a receipt also had some flexibility. For the Bank, the point of a receipt was to match coins in with coins out. It did not matter if the person depositing the coins was the same as the person who withdrew the coins, so receipts contained an (implicit) bearer clause allowing them to be freely transferred, over the counter. A customer could either retain the receipt or find someone to buy it. Transfer made a receipt a convenient way to sell coins, because people did not have to move the actual coins and the purchaser knew and trusted where and how to retrieve the coins at a modest fee. In this way, the Bank became a more active part of the coin market.

It was, however, the combination of flexibilities that made receipts so popular with people who had choices as to where to put their coins. Prussia's mint master Johann Philipp Graumann, a fervent admirer of the receipt system, put it this way:

How advantageous this lending [facility] must be for the merchant community, can be seen from the fact that with this facility, the merchant can put into motion and utilize all the [trade coins] that accrue to him. Otherwise he would have to allow the same foreign coins to sit unused, and at going [bill] interest rates lose more money than he would pay for borrowing [at the receipt window]. By this means the money is effectively doubled, or twice put at the disposal of commerce, since the merchant can make use of practically all of the capital that he has placed in the bank. In addition, he remains master of this money, and by repayment of the sum advanced, is authorized to either withdraw it himself, or sell it to others. (Graumann 1762, 137)

Graumann was writing in the mid-eighteenth century and, by then, people were describing receipts as secured loans against all kinds of trade coins, when technically they were not. As an option contract, a receipt conferred no obligation to repurchase the coins, and the Bank owned the coins until repurchase. If the receipt were a secured loan, however, customers would be under an obligation to repay, and the coins would be collateral controlled by the borrowers until default. Our point is not that customers felt an obligation to redeem receipts. They did not. Rather, customers came to think of the coins as their own, as if collateral for a loan.

The shift was subtle and telling, and it has remained similarly pervasive in modern repurchase finance and in central banking practice (Gorton and Metrick 2010; Garbade 2021). In a modern repurchase agreement, one side (the cash lender, which can be a central bank) would purchase a security from the other (the cash borrower) with a commitment to resell the security to the cash borrower at a specified price on a specified date. In its repo transactions, a modern central bank would not list the purchased bond as an asset even though it holds the bond. Instead, the cash borrower does. Today, everyone (the cash lender, regulators, external auditors, etc.) treats the agreement "as if" it were a loan and the bond were collateral.[20] Similarly, merchants could sell their coins to the Bank, obtaining Bank money in return, and yet still consider the coins as theirs as described by Graumann. This duality created a powerful type of safe asset because both the lender and the borrower proceeded as if they controlled the asset.[21]

5.4 The End of Withdrawal

The adoption of receipts also brought the end of traditional withdrawal and a transition of Bank money to a de facto fiat money. Before discussing this development, it may be worthwhile to define terms. Traditional definitions of the term "fiat money," as, for example, given in the *Oxford English Dictionary*, imply a degree of coercion from a government "fiat" of legal tender at a nominal value greater than intrinsic or promissory value. In the case of the Bank, there was no identifiable fiat, as in an announcement that people were now compelled to use the Bank's ledger money, which was already in wide use for bill transactions. Instead, the right to withdraw Bank balances in coin was quietly taken away, and the Bank became unobliged to convert balances into coins without a receipt. Monetary historians have searched the Bank's archives for documentation

---

[20] Unless the cash borrower goes bankrupt. Then the collateral can be seized and liquidated by the cash lender (Gorton and Metrick 2010).

[21] The dual nature of coins under receipt was already noted by Mees (1838, 133). Van de Laar (1978, 68–69), however, criticized Mees' discussion of duality, noting that collateral cannot be simultaneously controlled by two parties. While Van der Laar is technically correct, we would argue from the example of modern repo finance that the "as if" view of duality proposed by Graumann and Mees was a functionally valid one. This situation was in principle not so different from the situation with deposit banking, whereby a depositor of a coin and a new borrower from the bank may both view the bank's coin reserve as belonging to them.

of this seismic shift, yet have found none: "For that great change no ordinance nor any precise date can be assigned" (Van Dillen 1934, 101). Nor have historians, even after generations of searching, uncovered documentation of why this shift occurred. The contention of this chapter is that a detailed examination of the receipt system and its accounting can fill a void in the literature, by offering coherent explanations of when, why, and how the Bank of Amsterdam came to offer irredeemable money, "as if" by fiat.

We argue that the reintroduction of receipts in 1683 was necessary, but likely insufficient, for the transition. By offering receipts for ducatons, customers now had two ways to acquire the same coins from the Bank: redeem a receipt at a low fee or claim traditional withdrawal at a high fee. Customers chose receipts, so the end of withdrawal took away an option that few people used. In this way, receipts were necessary to prevent upset. Receipts, however, did not require the end of withdrawal, and the two, albeit in a slightly different form, had coexisted in the 1650s. More importantly, the change took away a latent option that customers might want to exercise in the future. Receipts made the change easier but did not justify the change.

What did benefit from the end of withdrawal was the other big change of 1683: the enhancement of internal supervision. Phoonsen had argued for receipts, but he had also argued for a tightening of accounting processes to better prevent fraud. In the 1660s and 1670s, the Bank bookkeeper Rutgert Vlieck stole coins worth at least 300,000 bank florins, wiping out about five years of Bank profits (Willemsen 2009, 86; Dehing 2012, 103). Discovery of the fraud brought great embarrassment to the Bank, embarrassment that was only slightly diminished by Vlieck's public execution (see Figure 5.1). To shore up the Bank's credibility, a thorough overhaul of its bookkeeping was needed. Vlieck's massive fraud thus led to accounting reforms that would prove advantageous both for the Bank and for future generations of researchers.[22] Our contention is that the end of withdrawal supported that process through the simplification of the Bank's internal structure of information.

The goal in 1683 was to suppress theft and mistakes, and the most frequent opportunity for miscreation of Bank money was for a bookkeeper to credit one account but not debit an offsetting account. To get an overall measure of this problem, the Bank had to compare the actual change in the

---

[22] Another benefit of the accounting reforms of the 1680s was the reduction in overdrafted (negative-balance) accounts (Dehing 2012, 141).

amount of Bank money with the expected change under double entry. For the Bank to know the expected change, the ledger system had a master account that would, ideally, be the only account that created or destroyed Bank balances. If net creation in the master account matched the actual change in balances, then no one was creating credits without debits. The Bank performed this balancing exercise each January and July.

Unfortunately, tracing an overall discrepancy to an individual transaction was a daunting problem. Wayward credits got lost in the crowd of giro transactions. Worse, Vlieck had been in charge of balance-sheet reconciliation.[23] He used that authority to manipulate the summation process such that no discrepancy would appear at that time (Dehing 2012, 104). Eventually mismatches surfaced, but no one could pinpoint when and where they had occurred. The Bank repeatedly wrote off the unreconciled discrepancies in its accounts (Dehing 2012, 93). To deal with this, the City expanded the set of bookkeepers. The number of salaried personnel increased from 15 in the mid-seventeenth-century Bank to 26 by the mid-eighteenth-century (Dehing 2012, 101).

Some earlier experiments with receipts had actually worked to increase the scope for fraud. Beginning in 1656, the Bank issued negotiable receipts against ducatons, patagons, and apparently other types of coins. These receipts were not the post-1683, option-like instruments, but instead resembled cashiers' kwitanties, that is, banknote-like claims to deposited coin, which could be used for payments to merchants without a Bank account (Dehing 2012, 93).[24] Circulation of these receipts outside the Bank increased the possibilities for fraud, especially when some did not even specify the type of coin. Receipts could be, and were, made for fictitious or substandard coin, deposited by fictitious customers.[25]

The Bank's experiment with banknote-like receipts had been ended in 1674, after it was discovered that receipts had been issued against substandard Russian coins, resulting in another large loss to the Bank (Dehing 2012, 321). All transfers of Bank money were henceforth to take place only on the Bank's ledgers: no more experiments with circulating notes. The

---

[23] Readers of a certain age will note a parallel with the case of Nick Leeson, the rogue futures trader who brought down Barings in 1995. Leeson was authorized by Barings to settle his own trades and so was able to conceal his losses.

[24] These notes were issued at roughly the same time as notes issued by the *Stockholms Banco* (Wetterberg 2009, 33–42), which are sometimes described as the first public banknotes in early modern Europe. Both the Amsterdam and Stockholm notes were, however, preceded by public banknotes issued in Naples (Costabile and Nappi 2018; Velde 2018).

[25] Vlieck's pseudonym on some of these fake receipts, "Dirck Hoola," did raise suspicions.

1683 receipts would be options that required Bank money to redeem. Merchants needing to transact in Bank money, but without a Bank account, were allowed to designate a Bank customer to send and receive payments for them (Van Dillen 1925a, 176–77). Anonymity was sacrificed to gain control.

Vlieck had also exposed another threat. He had used bogus receipts and other techniques to fake documentation of metal inflows (Dehing 2012, 104). This fraud was insidious because it did not appear as a mismatch in the ledgers as Vlieck had debited the master account. To detect this, the Bank had to compare changes in the ledgers to changes in the actual stock of gold and silver. This happened each January when the Bank composed its balance sheet. The process was arduous.[26] Again, when the Bank did find a discrepancy, it was at a loss as to where the misstep occurred. Once metal entered the vault, it joined the inventory, and its provenance was lost. Vlieck's behavior was analogous to a retail till being short at the end of the day, but the time frame was a year. And Vlieck was not the only criminal. As late as 1686, the Bank was discovering that coins were missing without a trace (Dehing 2012, 96).

Receipts helped with internal control by adding a third source of useful information. Receipts encoded the name of the original depositor, the relevant type of coin, and the date that the coin entered the Bank. The specification of date and coin was a necessary aspect of the contract, but, as a bearer instrument, the depositor's name was not. Its inclusion, however, was easy and assisted in the tracking down of discrepancies because, unlike accounts and coins, a controller could verify the provenance of receipts, as receipts retained origin-specific information.[27] When coins legitimately entered the Bank under receipt, three records – (1) the coins delivered into the vault, (2) the balances created in the ledger, and (3) the receipt given to the customer – agreed to create a triple redundancy. An investigator had much more information with which to track down a discrepancy.

And now we come to the benefit of the ending of withdrawals. Triple redundancy was not available through traditional withdrawals. To tighten the overall structure, receipts had to become the *only* way customers could initiate the removal of coin. Admittedly, Vlieck had falsified the earlier type

---

[26] In 1686, the new Bank commissioner Adriaan van Loon was "not pleased with the transfer documents" (Dehing 2012, 145) given to him by the outgoing administration, so he conducted his own inventory of the vault. It took him six weeks.

[27] Additional staff were also needed to handle the receipt system (Dehing 2012, 101–102).

of receipt, so they were no guarantee, but many of the surviving documents used to reconstruct Vlieck's behavior were receipts. In contrast, the Bank struggled to trace which accounts ended up with falsely created balances.

Internal control was also a reason to end traditional deposits. From its beginnings, the Bank had accepted a wide variety of coins based on the Republic's ordinances (see Chapter 4). In 1683, however, receipts only applied to two coins. With the end of non-receipt deposits, coins like the rijksdaalder, the bankrijksdaalder, and the leeuwendaalder could no longer be brought to the Bank at a time and volume determined by customers. This greatly reduced the set of possible receiver transactions that had to be monitored. As long as even a few people were using a traditional pathway, forensic accounting still had to consider the possibility. If finding a discrepancy was like solving a Sudoku puzzle, then ending the possibility of a deposit-withdrawal category was like removing an entire column and row from the puzzle. The benefit was systemic simplification, and it was a powerful way for the Bank to become more internally aware. Simplicity of structure reduced accounting accidents and increased incentives to reduce mistakes. By the middle of the eighteenth century, the Bank's internal processes involved only a few types of transactions, and most of those had only one standardized form. Simplicity was crucial as the volume of creation and destruction grew.[28]

Another example of simplification was the apparent cessation of small change through receivers. For example, from 1666 through 1682, a deposit of exactly 500 bank florins was relatively common, being 3.7 percent of all receiver transactions. There was no combination of ducatons (3 each) or rijksdaalders (2.4 each) that summed to 500. It seemed 500 was a convenient number that customers acquired through a combination of large and small coins.[29] After the adoption of receipts and *only* receipts, that transaction value disappeared. To see this, Figure 5.6 plots the number of deposits of exactly 500 florins before and after 1683. The end came quickly, and that speed agreed with the contention that the end of traditional deposit and withdrawal was part of the implementation of accounting changes.

Figure 5.6 also shows the sudden increase in receipt-based inflows. To see that, the figure plots the number of deposits of 600 bank florins, a

---

[28] The authors can attest to the importance of simplicity when reconstructing the Bank's balance sheet for years missing cashbooks in the 1720s as compared to the more streamlined 1750s.

[29] Other possibilities were *bankrijksdaalders* or *leeuwendaalders*, but the Bank was busy selling those coins, as noted in Table 5.2.

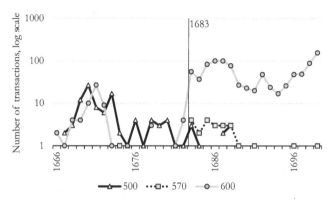

Figure 5.6. Annual deposits by select amounts of bank florins, 1666–1699
Source: Authors' calculations.

sum that before and after 1683 was the commonly used sack of 200 ducaton coins. The number of these potential sacks jumped an order of magnitude in 1683 (the scale is logarithmic to improve visualization). It shows how the values of legitimate deposits became much more standardized. Deposits and withdrawals had to conform with the new system or look suspicious. The figure also plots observations of 570 bank florins that could have been similar sacks of 200 drieguldens. That value began to appear regularly in 1683 but only for a few years and never near the rate of ducatons. It suggested that the modest demand for driegulden receipts faded by 1690, and that was also about the time (1694) when the Republic, but *not* the Bank, adopted the gulden standard.

Another indicator of timing was the agio market. Recall from Chapter 4 that the agio anchor after 1659 was well explained by the implicit agios and fee structure of the ducaton and rijksdaalder. The new receipt system did not include rijksdaalders, so that coin lost the ability to anchor the agio. At the same time, the elimination of inter-coin arbitrage removed a powerful incentive to pull the market agio to within the nexus of implicit agios. To see this, Figure 5.7 plots the agio from 1663 through 1699. The discontinuity in March 1685 was sharp. The agio seemed to re-anchor around the ducaton's implicit agio of 5 percent, but clearly the market agio is no longer trading within the ducaton's narrowed fee rate. The driegulden's implicit agio was 5.3 percent, so it may have been contributing. Again, the change seems to happen shortly after receipts and accounting reforms were introduced.

The rapidity with which the Bank ended traditional deposit and withdrawal made the change contemporaneous with receipts and tightened accounting. A related circumstance was the lack of outrage when the Bank effectively turned about 8 million receipt-less bank florins into fiat money.

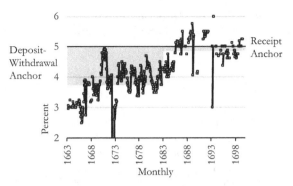

Figure 5.7. Percent agio with ducaton anchors, monthly, 1663–1699
Sources: McCusker (1978, 47) and ACA 234/290–95.
Note: The fee structure is a gray area of 1.25 percent before receipts and 0.125 percent after. The 1692–1693 wiggle in the agio resulted from the revaluation of two debased coins, the schelling and the florijn (Mees 1838, 113–14).

What justification would have brought acquiescence from relevant parties (who, recall, were from the top tier of Amsterdam's merchant class) without a known public ordinance or recorded debate? The simplest answer was the same justification that was already motivating reorganization: that the credibility of the Bank as a supplier of ledger money required trust in the accounting. "This Vlieck fraud showed that an accumulation of deliberate forgeries left deep financial scars for a long time and put confidence in the bank at risk" (Dehing 2012, 96). Limiting customers to receipts offered a way for the Bank to reduce such accounting risks while simultaneously lowering customer costs, a classic case of a win-win.

5.5 Expansion

The end of withdrawal, in turn, accelerated the evolution of the Bank by easing the expansion of the receipt facility into additional types of coins. Again, inter-coin arbitrage occurred when customers could sell coins to the Bank at a higher price (relative to silver content or to the agio) than the coins they purchased from the Bank. Replacing deposits with receipts did not solve this problem because abandoning a receipt was functionally equivalent to a deposit. From the start, the Bank had used large fees and control over the types of outflowing coins to reduce these incentives (see Chapter 4). In contrast, ending withdrawal eliminated the threat entirely, and receipts could be extended to new coin types without fear of internal arbitrage. Those differences in value would now be expressed in the market price of receipts relative to each other.

Table 5.4. *Bank balance sheet, 1711, in bank florins*

Metal			7,856,682
	Owned Outright	6,108,828	
	DUCATONS	2,083,031	
	LEEUWENDAALDERS	2,112,800	
	FRANCE LOUISEN	1,276,207	
	BANKDAALDERS	406,800	
	Small coins in sacks	145,995	
	BANKRIJKSDAALDERS	43,500	
	Silver bullion	32,977	
	Miscellaneous	7,519	
	Under a Receiver Receipt	1,049,454	
	DUCATONS	603,574	
	PILAREN	257,400	
	MEXICANEN	107,800	
	RIJKSDAALDERS	65,280	
	CRUSADEN	15,400	
	Under an Assayer Receipt	698,400	
	ZEEUWSE RIJKSDAALDERS	396,480	
	Gold bullion	300,000	
	Silver bullion	1,920	
Credit			3,002,824
	City of Amsterdam	1,475,560	
	Dutch East India Company (Amsterdam)	1,300,000	
	Province of Holland	227,264	
Total Assets			10,859,506
Balances		10,206,425	
Equity		653,081	
Total Liabilities and Equity			10,859,506

Sources: Van Dillen (1925b, 765), ACA 5077/1355, and authors' calculations.
Note: Names of trade coins (i.e., individual coins valued at more than one guilder) are in all capitals.

To gauge the impact of the end of convertibility and the expansion of the types of coin under receipt, let us glance ahead to the first complete set of surviving records of the new system. The first extant cashbook from 1711 shows that the receipt facility had expanded to include many new coins. Table 5.4 gives the Bank's balance sheet on January 28, 1711.[30]

---

[30] The year 1711 was not, however, typical. The country was in the depths of the War of Spanish Succession, and overall Bank activity was rather low.

We use information from the cashbook to subdivide metal assets into three categories: metal owned outright by the Bank, metal under a receipt created by a receiver, and metal under a receipt created by the assayer.[31] Per 1683, ducatons were under a receipt created by a receiver. By 1711, other coins that had come to be accepted by receivers were Dutch rijksdaalders, crusaden from Portugal, and Spanish dollars in the forms of pilaren from Peru and mexicanen from Mexico. The assayer receipts covered metal not accepted by receivers such as bullion and *Zeeuwse rijksdaalders* from the Province of Zeeland. The receipt system had expanded beyond the domain of domestic coins and beyond the narrowly prescribed role of the receivers.

The expansion of coins under receipt also modified the process. Receivers only accepted the new trade coins by the sack. For example, rijksdaalders came and went in increments of 200 coins per sack. Exchange by the sack was common for trade coins because people did not question the quality of individual coins or even the precise weight of a sack (see Chapter 3). It was a convenient fiction that helped make a sack of trade coins a safe asset. The foreign coins followed a similar system based on weight. Every sack of Spanish dollars was valued as if each weighed exactly 100 marks. When the Bank let receivers issue receipts for a type of trade coin, a sack of that type of coin became the increment of transaction, and its quality was assumed to be the same as all other sacks. The Bank treated it as a safe asset, and that likely helped customers do the same.

Another change regarded fees. The new bookkeeping for receipts collected fees in balances instead of in small coins. This moved a routine flow of payments from coins to paper, a move that mostly eliminated the circulation of small coins within the Bank. The fees (i.e., the implicit interest rates) also changed. For silver, the new rate was ¼ percent every half year, in line with Phoonsen's proposal (for ducatons, the rate was still ⅛ percent). For gold, the rate would be ½ percent.

To see these changes in action, Figure 5.8 shows the outflow side of the cashbook for mexicanen in 1712. Here, on April 5, one sack was repurchased by the Gebroeders da Rocha for 2,200 bank florins plus a ¼ percent fee of 5.5 florins. In the second line, Isaac and Salomon Abas paid 11 bank florins to prolong a receipt for 2 sacks of mexicanen for 6 months. Notice that the page recorded both metal and fees. When summed and compared

---

[31] The Bank also owned outright a diverse collection of coins that included *leeuwendaalders* and *bankrijksdaalders* (a.k.a. *Nederlandschen rijksdaalders*) from the Bank's early decades (see Chapter 4) and *bankdaalders*, likely being Zeeland provincial daalders from the 1680s as per Figure 5.2 (Van Dillen 1925b, 883; Polak 1998b, 83).

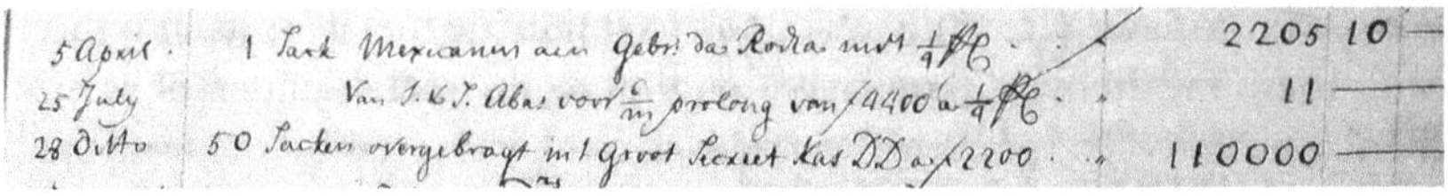

Figure 5.8. Select Spanish dollar outflows in 1712
Source: 1712 cashbook, ACA 5077/1356, folio 24.

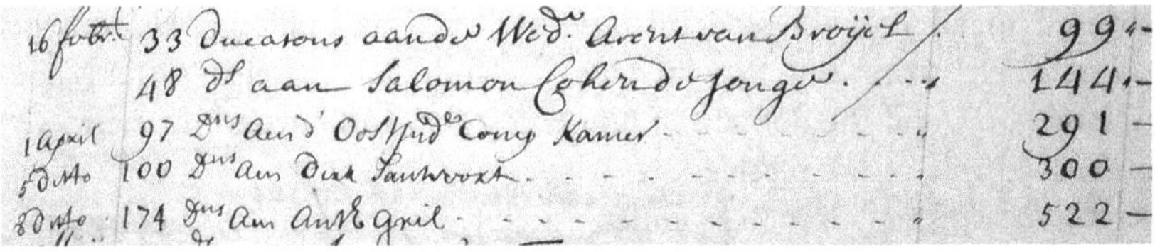

Figure 5.9. Select ducaton outflows in 1712
Source: 1712 cashbook, ACA 5077/1356, folio 38.

to the inflow side, the Bank knew how many sacks of mexicanen it had in this box, how many bank florins of this type of coin should have been created and destroyed in the master account, and how many of the destroyed bank florins were for coins leaving the bank versus for fees that the Bank needed to book as profit. We would add that the third line was the Bank transferring 50 sacks to long-term storage in box DD of the large vault chamber (*groot secreet*). This reemphasized that the sacks were fungible. Sacks from a specific delivery into the Bank were not held as unique collateral to be returned at the redemption of that receipt.

As with the end of deposit and withdrawal, we have no formal authorization for the expansion of receipts; however, the exacting nature of the new system left evidence. For example, redemption of a sack of Spanish dollars cost exactly 2205.5 bank florins (see Figure 5.8). Starting in 1666, the first appearance in the master account of that debit was August 1701 (curiously, quite close to the outbreak of the War of Spanish Succession, which would cut off Amsterdam's supply of dollars). Similarly, redemption of a rijksdaalder sack was 481.2 bank florins and that first appeared in May 1700. Their multiples also start to appear at that time, so we place the implementation of the new receiver-based receipt system at around 1700.

The cashbooks also let us see how the earlier 1683 system likely worked and ended. Figure 5.9 shows the redemption side for a ducaton account in the 1712 cashbook. Notice that transactions were measured by coins instead of sacks. Also, fees were not included. In the eighteenth century, the ducaton was the only coin for which the Bank did this, and that

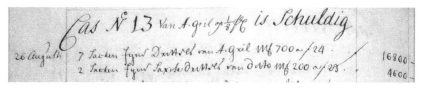

Figure 5.10. Select German drittel inflows in 1712
Source: 1712 cashbook, ACA 5077/1356, folio 23.

distinction was fading. In 1723, the Bank moved ducatons to sacks only and to fees by ledger balances.[32]

The new receipt system did not include local coins like the gulden coin. Also, driegulden receipts of 1683 were gone from the Bank by 1711. Driegulden coins do not reappear until 1721 and then under the new system.[33] This was despite the Republic's formal adoption of the gulden system as the domestic standard in 1694. The Bank no longer offered standing facilities to support local coins. In the years from 1683 to 1711, the Bank had escaped its founding mission. Its emerging purpose was to support the liquidity of trade coins.

All this was not to say that around 1700 the Bank just realized and implemented a superior approach to receipts. For the period around 1711, the volume of coins under receipt by receiver was rather modest (see Table 5.3). Instead, the two decades after 1683 seemed an era of experimentation from which the new system emerged. The clearest evidence was the other major category of new receipts, those created by the assayer. Receipts for metal through the assayer were heterogeneous. Categories of collateral came and went. Rates varied. It seemed that the assayer had authority to create bespoke receipts for collateral not accepted by receivers. The assayer had always handled transactions in bullion and non-standard coins. In other eras, these transactions were purchases and sales, meaning the Bank owned the metal outright. In 1711, however, a substantial amount of the assayer's business was now conducted by receipt instead (see Table 5.3).

To see the differences in accounting, Figure 5.10 shares the start of a page from the 1712 cashbook for deliveries of silver coins (*fyne drittels*) from Germany. The coins were put into box 13, and the account was labeled for Anthony Gril (or Grill), the assayer for the Bank. The coins

---

[32] The coin did retain its distinctive ⅛ percent rate for the duration of the Bank, perhaps in support of its specialized use for smuggling by Company employees. Note in Figure 5.9 that the Company withdrew 97 ducatons.

[33] Except for the fee rate that remained ⅛ percent until 1765.

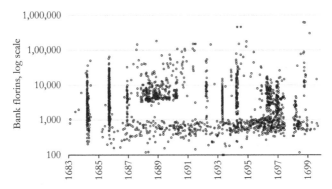

Figure 5.11. Purchases and assayer receipts, each transaction, 1683–1699
Source: Authors' reconstruction.
Note: Blank verticals in 1684 and 1697 are half-years of missing ledgers.

were in sacks weighing 100 marks as was typical of foreign silver coins, yet these coins did not enter through a receiver. The eventual prolongations and withdrawals of these coins were also handled by the assayer. The assayer was running his own receipt facility for himself or for customers that worked through him. We do not know how much autonomy the assayer had to set terms like price and rate, but they did differ from receiver receipts. The rate here is ⅛ percent instead of the ¼ percent that receivers offered on foreign silver. Also, the coins were 24 and 23 bank florins per mark (24.2 and 24.3 per fine mark), while Spanish dollars were 22 (23.6).[34]

To see when assayer receipts might have begun, Figure 5.11 plots all the metal inflows that bypassed receivers from 1685 to 1699. With no cash-books, we cannot say which was a purchase and which was an assayer receipt, but a change in pattern was evident. The massive purchase operations of the pre-receipt era receded but did not disappear. Also, a more consistent dispersion of transactions emerged. We suspect many of these were the expansion of assayer receipts. The assayer, on behalf of the Bank, began to engage the coin and bullion markets in a new way: the assayer could negotiate a receipt if the collateral was good but did not fit the standing receipt window.

The simplest reason for all the new receipts was Phoonsen's argument: customers wanted to turn collateral into Bank money with confidence that

---

[34] The Saxon (*saxise*) drittels were 11 pennies and 9 grains fine (0.948), and the other drittels were from Lunenburg and were 11 pennies and 22 grains (0.993): ACA 5077/ 1357, folio 27.

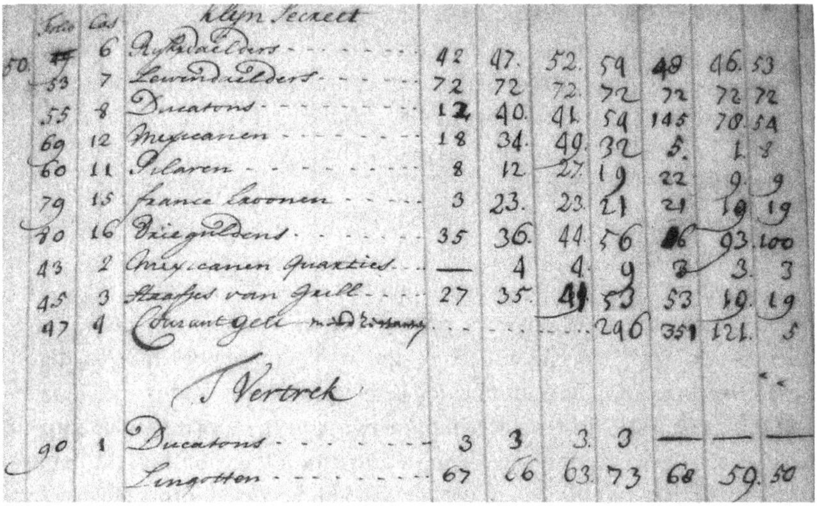

Folio	Cas	Klyn Secreet							
50	6	Rijksdaalders	42	47	52	59	49	46	53
53	7	Leeuwendaalders	72	72	72	72	72	72	72
55	8	Ducatons	12	40	41	54	145	70	54
69	12	Mexicanen	18	34	49	32	5	1	8
60	11	Pilaren	8	12	27	19	22	9	9
79	15	france Croonen	3	23	23	21	21	19	19
80	16	Drieguldens	35	36	44	56	86	93	100
43	2	Mexicanen Quarties	—	4	4	9	3	3	3
45	3	Staafjes van Gull	27	35	41	53	53	19	19
47	4	Courant geld [illegible]				296	351	121	5
		't Vertrek							
90	1	Ducatons	3	3	3	3	—	—	—
		Lingotten	67	66	63	73	68	59	50

Figure 5.12. Weekly inventories by coin in sacks, 1726
Source: ACA 5077/1422, August 9 to September 13, 1726.
Note: Units for lingotten are ingots.

the transaction could be unwound at a low cost. With the elimination of traditional withdrawal, the assayer could try the technique on new coins, and, if successful, the Bank could establish a standing facility with receivers under the new system.

The assayer experiment was transitory. For the Bank (and modern scholars), it was complicated and not particularly profitable. In the era of extant cashbooks, assayer receipts peaked at 20 percent of the Bank's coins in 1713 and quickly declined after 1720. The apparatus vanished around 1734. We do not know why the Bank moved away from assayer receipts, but the shift did coincide with the rise in volume of receiver receipts for Spanish dollars.

To summarize how receipts transformed the asset and information structure of the Bank, we jump ahead a few years, to the last page of an inventory book that ran from 1720 to 1726.[35] The image in Figure 5.12 is a table reporting the location in the cashbook (*folio*) and the location in the vault (*cas*) of each type of coin in which the Bank was transacting from August 9 to September 13, 1726.[36] Most of the rows were standard trade

[35] This is the only extant copy of this type of inventory.

[36] More precisely, the small vault chamber (*klyn secreet*) and the transit room (*het vertrek*) were the parts of the vault that interacted with the world outside the Bank. The inventory

coins held by the Bank under receipt through receivers: rijksdaalders, ducatons, Spanish dollars from Mexico (mexicanen) and Peru (pilaren), French crowns (*france kroonen*), and drieguldens. Experiments were there too with sacks of Spanish dollars in pieces (*quarties*) and staves (*staafjes*) of silver under receipt with the assayer.[37] The operations were there with leeuwendaalders waiting to be sold and with local coins (courantgeld) purchased during the inventory period. The last row was ingots (lingotten) of silver that the Bank produced for sale to the local wire trade.

The columns to the right gave the number of sacks held each Friday. The result was a concise seven-week perspective on levels by asset type. Such information gave commissioners of the Bank an opportunity to digest timely information. The number of asset classes was less than a dozen, and the use of sacks instead of bank florins kept the numbers small enough to fit a few weeks on one page. The reformation of accounting, the expansion of receipts, and the end of withdrawals had evolved into a new system that was popular with customers over a variety of assets while remaining manageable for the Bank. While likely not the intention of the City in 1683, this streamlined system would prove the foundation for the Bank's high tide in the eighteenth century.

5.6 Political Economy

Another set of consequences also seem more emergent than intentional. The changes of 1683 reshaped the political economy of the Bank. For example, the Bank was tested in 1672 when the French and their allies nearly overran the Republic. Customers redeemed 46 percent of Bank money in two months.[38] The Bank covered the run and gained lasting credibility for having done so. Adam Smith noted a century later that "In 1672, when the French king was at Utrecht, the bank of Amsterdam paid so readily as left no doubt of the fidelity with which it had observed its engagements" (Smith 1981 [1776], 486). In the 1650s, the Bank became an active part of the City's balance sheet. The City began to take substantial sums of coins from the Bank, and the City authorized regular lending to the Company, that is, the Amsterdam Chamber of the VOC. Figure 5.13

---

levels were a net position of coins entering and leaving the Bank and coins being moved back to and up from long-term storage.

[37] These staves match the type of silver bars exported by the VOC (Pol 1985, 104).

[38] Metal outflows in June and July were 3,295,553 bank florins (Quinn and Roberds 2010, 77; Dehing 2012, 440). Total balances at fiscal year start were 7,210,433 bank florins (Van Dillen 1925b, 963).

Figure 5.13. Equity less City loans, annually, 1610–1792
Source: Van Dillen (1925b, 701–95).

reports the Bank's equity less loans to the City.[39] In the 1650s, the City
borrowed all the accumulated equity and then some. The threat of a run
added some discipline to this creation of fractional reserves, and the City
allowed the Bank to rebuild this net position in the 1660s and 1670s. It was
positioned to survive the run in 1672 with a small, negative net equity.

The changes of 1683 rebalanced this constraint. On one side, coins under
receipt were harder for the City to take from the Bank than coins owned
outright. Receipts had claims to a specific type of collateral instead of the
general claims under traditional withdrawal. The City likely had the authority to abrogate receipt contracts, but the damage to credibility (already
damaged by fraud episodes) would have been substantial. On the other side,
ending the withdrawal option made it easier for the City to take coins that
the Bank did own outright, as customers no longer had any claim to those
coins. Similarly, loans to the Company could not add to the maximum size
of a redemption run. As a result, the marginal constraint on taking and
lending lessened. Starting in 1684, the City aggressively exploited the Bank
(see Figure 5.13). At its lowest in 1699, the City's negative position was, in
absolute value, a 12 percent hole in the balance sheet. The situation
recovered before a large dip around 1750 and a lesser dip in 1772. The great
drop in 1789 was the City taking annuities owed by the Province of Holland
from the Bank in exchange for City debt, and the recovery in 1792 was the
City using a recapitalization addressed in Chapter 7 to write down municipal loans. Overall, the Bank had a negative net equity in 73 percent of years
after 1683 and the average size was negative 4 percent of the balance sheet.

[39] Here, "equity" refers to assets at book value less liabilities.

Part of the story was that the redemption threat shifted from all Bank money to only Bank money encumbered by a receipt, and the credibility of the Bank split into two components: the receipt and the account. Smith noted this bifurcation (Smith 1981 [1776], 486). For receipts, the question that determined credibility became whether customers expected the City to leave alone coins under receipt. We know that after 1711, the City scrupulously respected coins under receipt. In the years between 1683 and 1711, the Bank had such a large inventory of coins owned outright that the will to violate the receipt contract was likely never tested. Customers had good reasons to view receipts as more credible than rights of withdrawal. Receipts without traditional withdrawal was an unusual approach to the collective action problem of bank runs. Other times and places would deal with the threat of ruinous runs with temporary suspensions of all convertibility (see Chapter 9). In contrast, the Bank of Amsterdam stumbled into the permanent suspension of convertibility for a portion of Bank money and the resale of convertibility for the other portion. There is no known evidence of contemporaries arguing in favor of fiat money, much less using it as a way to prevent a bank run.

For monetary balances, the credibility question shifted from redemption to something very modern. Did customers expect that the City would keep the value of Bank money stable? This was a question regarding fiat money that unpacks along multiple dimensions. Does a central bank whose money was irredeemable have sufficient tools to stabilize the value of its money? If doable, will the bank's political authority choose stabilization? These questions, in their early modern form, will become the focus of our story in the chapters to come, but they were likely unintended in 1683.

Finally, the collection of new policies had the Bank develop more independence. From its founding, the Bank had operated under and in support of Republic ordinances. After 1683, Republic ordinances were no longer binding. The Republic set current guilder values and the Bank set bank florin values. Similarly, the Bank started setting policies without any known City directives. The City was still appointing commissioners each year to run the Bank, but the end of traditional deposit and withdrawal, the expansion of receipts, the list of acceptable coins for receivers, and the prices of those coins appeared to be internal implementation decisions.

5.7 Conclusion

In 1683, the combination of reintroducing receipts and reforming accountancy triggered an era of rapid evolution for the Bank. Traditional deposit and withdrawal were ended. With that the Bank could open itself to a variety of coins without fear of arbitrage. The Bank's assayer experimented with receipts for all sorts of coins and bullion. The Bank ceased all standing relationships with local coins while offering new receipt windows for select foreign trade coins. Relative to the Bank's original concept, many strands of its business model had changed. The early Bank struggled to supply money that was a substitute for local coins. The new Bank stopped trying. The old Bank was shunned by trade coins. The new Bank learned to supply a combination of money and receipts that complemented trade coins. Instead of giving up coins for money, customers saw themselves gaining accounts while retaining their coins. People began to park their trade coins in the Bank. A stable fiat money attracted safe assets.

The evolutionary path was a narrow one. The Bank might have chosen not to engage in extensive open market operations and then contracted to the point of irrelevance. It might have chosen to continue to issue banknote-like receipts, with unpredictable results. It might have kept segregated accounts by type of collateral, with ducaton deposits that produced ducaton-linked accounts and driegulden deposits that produced driegulden-linked accounts.[40] Instead, receipts left ledger balances identical and general, preserving the depth of the bill market (debt-to-Bank money) and the agio market (Bank money-to-current money). Most of these policy decisions were internal to the Bank. The transformed Bank was likely not the intention of the City, but the result must not have been unwelcome. In the process of pleasing customers, the new Bank increased its capacity to be exploited. The City could take more and the East India Company could borrow more.

In 1711, the structures of the new Bank were mostly in place, but realization of the full potential awaited. The mass of the Bank's assets were still domestic ducatons, and most of those were owned outright by the Bank. Customers could bring in Spanish dollars for receipt, but not many did during the worst years of the War of Spanish Succession. The wings were still drying on this new species of central bank. The next chapter tells how the Bank learned to manage its new form, gain lift from trade coins, and sustain flight.

---

[40] The segregated-accounts approach was used earlier by Genoa's public banking institution, the *Casa di San Giorgio*, which discouraged arbitrage by fragmenting the stock of public bank money into separate accounts for different types of coin (Roberds and Velde 2016a, 327–28).

A.5 Additional Details of Receipts and Master Account Credits

Text of a receipt (Mees 1838, 135).

<Date>.

<Customer's name> *has brought in 1000 ducatons,* <valued at> *at 60 stivers* < 3 bank florins> *each, with the condition that he* < or the bearer> *shall be obliged to withdraw the same within six months' time, upon payment to the Bank of 1/8 percent, or that otherwise, upon expiration of the aforementioned time period, these shall be understood to have fallen to the Bank at the same price.*

Sample of Master Account Credits

Table 5.5 is an excerpt from the credit side of the master account (specie kamer) in the Bank's ledger. It includes seven transactions from September 28 to October 4, 1668. It has been selected because it exemplifies the sorting used to create Table 5.2. It reproduces the seven transactions and adds the filter results for each transaction.

The first, fourth, and fifth transactions were sales of bankrijksdaalder coins. Each sack of 200 coins was sold at 503.75 florins, being the traditional Bank price of 500 per sack (2.5 per coin) plus a premium of ¾ percent. We identified this coin and this price because receivers were selling those coins at that price at that time. The process was recorded in the 1668 balance book (ACA 5077/1313). For example, from April into September, the receiver Huybert Keift was given 459 sacks of bankrijks-daalders worth 229,500 bank florins. From June into September, he sold all of them at 503.75 florins per sack. He also sold 22½ sacks of leeuwendaalders at 410 florins each, being 400 florins per sack (2 per coin) at a premium of 2.5 percent.

The second transaction was a loan repayment by the Amsterdam Chamber of the VOC for 400,000 florins. It settled advances of 200,000 each on August 24 and September 13. The payment included 1,088.5 in interest at 4 percent. This repayment was listed in the 1668 balance book (ACA 5077/1313).

The last two transactions were sales of silver ingots. At this time, all silver ingots created and sold by the Bank were 11 pennies, 17 grains fine (0.976) and were sold at 23.8 bank florins per mark. These attributes were also noted in the 1668 balance book, but the book did not list each ingot sold. It only listed total ingots and total florins. To filter individual ingot

Table 5.5. *Explanations of master account transactions, credit side, 1668*

Date	Name	Folio	Florins: stivers	Explanation
28 September	Gerard Martens Wed.	124	3,022:10	sale of 6 sacks of bankrijksdaalders priced at 500 florins each plus 0.75 percent premium
28 September	VOC Amsterdam	1132	401,088:10	loan repayment of 400,000 in principal plus 1,088.5 in interest
1 October	Gerard Martens Wed.	1115	5,000:00	general withdrawal
1 October	Andries van Dalen	124	1,511:05	sale of 3 sacks of bankrijksdaalders priced at 500 florins each plus 0.75 percent premium
2 October	Jaquin Tidry	390	1,813:10	sale of 4 sacks of bankrijksdaalders priced at 500 florins each plus 0.75 percent premium
4 October	Jan van de Koort	680	830:00	sale of 1 silver ingot: weight 34 marks, 7 ounces; priced at 23.8 florins per mark of 0.976 fine
4 October	Marcus Muyssaert	713	818:20	sale of 1 silver ingot: weight 34 marks, 3 ounces; priced at 23.8 florins per mark of 0.976 fine

Sources: ACA 5077/67, folio 1010. Authors' calculations.
Note: 20 stivers made one florin, and 8 ounces made one mark.

transactions, we used patterns from inventories from extant cashbooks starting in 1711. The weight of an ingot was usually between 30 and 40 marks, and the increment of weight measurement was ¼ of an ounce. With the price per mark known, the florin value of each potential ingot weight was calculated, and individual master account transactions were compared. The sixth transaction was a match for the weight 34 marks, 7 ounces; and the last transaction was a match for the weight 34 marks, 3 ounces. The number and value of identified ingots were checked against the totals reported in the 1668 balance book.

The third entry we categorized as a general withdrawal. It was not explained by a known loan repayment, coin sale, or ingot sale. It was likely some combination of the standard silver coins (ducatons at 3 each and rijksdaalders at 2.4 each) with some small change to create a round number. We do not know if customers paid withdrawal fees in bank balances or small change.

Metal in Motion: The Mechanics of Receipts

With receipts, precious metal flowing into the Bank rarely stayed there long. An unusually transparent example is illustrative.

On Wednesday, January 15, 1727, the precious metal dealer Alexander Samuel Keyser sold six sacks of gold coins to the receiver Hector van Hertogveld.[1] The coins were Dutch dukaten (ducats) at 5 bank florins each in sacks of 1,000 coins. No evidence of assay was recorded (see Chapter 3). Each sack was worth 20 years of wages for a day laborer and weighed 3.5 kilograms or the weight of a typical newborn baby.[2] As a receiver, Hertogveld created Bank money when he debited his own account by 30,000 florins and credited Keyser's account by the same amount.[3] The receiver also gave Keyser a receipt for the coins. Two days later, the sacks had been moved into a chest (*goude kas 2*) in the vault where they joined other sacks of the same type. Over in the ledgers, Hertogveld's account was reimbursed for the coins by the clerks who managed the master account (specie kamer). The master account was the centralized record of changes in the amount of Bank money. The process of accepting trade coins, creating Bank money, and issuing a receipt was complete.

---

[1] Coin information was recorded in a cashbook (ACA 5077/1369, 85). In 1727, Keyser also dealt in receipts for Dutch (ducatons, rijksdaalders, and staten drieguldens), Spanish (mexicanen and pilaren), and French (louisen) silver coins, along with Portuguese (crusaden) gold coins (ACA 5077/1369, 49, 57, 61, 66, 79, 80, and 86). Keyser also purchased a sack of old Dutch silver leeuwendaalders (ACA 5077/1369, 53).

[2] Each coin was supposed to weigh 3.52 grams (Polak 1998b, 67), and the calculation assumed a wage of one guilder per day, an agio of 5 percent, and 260 work days per year. The same value (30,000) in Spanish dollars weighed 56 kilograms.

[3] Hertogveld created balances in that his account was allowed to be negative and he initiated the payment (ACA 5077/273, 1735).

Five months later, on June 16, the receipt was used to repurchase three sacks from the chest, but not by Keyser.[4] Keyser had sold the receipt to the merchant bank partnership of Andries Pels & Zonen, and Pels used it, plus a payment to the master account, to reclaim the coins.[5] This payment destroyed 15,075 florins, 15,000 for the coins and 75 for the ½ percent fee. Alternatively, Pels could have paid just the fee to extend the option period for another six months, that is, from July 15 to January 15, 1728. Normally the Bank left no record of how an individual receipt was resolved, but at this time the Bank made (and retained!) a supplementary reconstruction of receipts for these gold coins, and that exercise explicitly connected Keyser's receipt to Pels' redemption (see ACA 5077/1464). This example illustrates how receipts were redeemed, coins were repurchased, and Bank money was undone.

The Bank reconnected Keyser to Pels to ascertain which receipts did *not* have such a conclusion, and Keyser's receipt was chosen as this example because no one paid to redeem or extend its other half. Instead, the option to repurchase the remaining three sacks expired, that is, the sacks "fell to the Bank." The regular system of accounts did not track this, and that was not a problem as such expirations were unusual. The late 1720s, however, were an intense period when many gold receipts were abandoned, and the Bank scrambled to learn how many sacks of gold coins were no longer encumbered by a receipt, that is, were now fallen (*vervallen*) to the Bank. With that knowledge, the Bank was free to, and eventually did, sell such sacks at market prices. This was what happened when receipts expired.

This chapter aggregates such receipt transactions into a systemic perspective of how the receipt facility worked. Often, receipts were created and redeemed in large volumes. This was the outcome the Bank seemed to favor. Sometimes receipts were not redeemed, and sometimes people avoided creating receipts. These outcomes were less welcomed. Keyser and Pels were an example of how a receipt could succeed and how it might not. To see both more generally, this chapter contrasts the experiences of silver and gold. For each metal, we reconstructed the flows that brought in coins and created receipts like Keyser did, and separately we did the same when people like Pels used receipts to repurchase coins. With these data series, we show the overall flow of silver and gold coins under receipt through the Bank from 1711 to 1792. At this grand scale, we discover that

---

[4] Receipts were divisible down to the individual sack, but we lack a precise description of how that was done (Dehing 2012, 100).
[5] The reconstruction did not record the sale price of the receipt or any other people who might have been in its chain of possession.

receipts for the two metals behaved differently. The creation of gold receipts often swung from a trickle to a flood as redemptions shifted from routine to sporadic. Keyser's receipt lived at such an inflection point, hence its split destiny. In contrast, silver receipts were routinely created in large quantities and were consistently redeemed.

To explain why silver had a more reliable receipt facility than gold did, this chapter builds from the fact that the Bank let customers make their own decisions regarding receipts. Keyser decided to bring in coins. Keyser and Pels decided to trade the receipt. Pels decided to redeem the receipt. We also assume that dealers like Keyser and banks like Pels were focused on the profitability of these actions, and profits, at a minimum, depended on the price the Bank offered for coins relative to the prices offered elsewhere.[6] The differential between prices inside and outside the Bank defined an implicit discount (in modern terminology, a "haircut") on the value of collateral flowing through the receipt facility. The price the Bank assigned to trade coins became yet another design feature and potential policy tool.

Even before receipts, a high Bank price encouraged inflows, and a low Bank price encouraged outflows. What changed with receipts was the concurrent elimination of a right of conversion attached to Bank money on its own (see Chapter 5). People like Keyser could still bring in acceptable coins in any quantity they desired, but people like Pels could not remove coins without balances *and* receipts. As a result, a high Bank price (essentially, a low or even negative haircut) set off receipt inflows similar to the pre-receipt era (see Chapter 4). In contrast, a low Bank price (a high haircut) could produce a pattern of roughly matching creation and redemption that was mediated by the resale of receipts. The low and stable interest rate on credit through the receipt facility (¼ percent interest or less on silver coins, ½ percent on gold coins) helped attract collateral to the facility, even if it endured a low Bank price, that is, a stiff haircut.[7]

For customers like Keyser and Pels to judge high or low required an alternative price, and that was created by the larger system of markets in

---

[6] The example is illustrative of the trading strategies of the precious metal dealers and merchant banks. A dealer like Keyser would have had the connections to bring gold into the Bank, which could then be put under receipt and used to fund additional trades. A merchant bank such as Pels could have easily funded its gold purchase via the bill market.

[7] To reiterate: haircuts in modern repurchase agreements are stated as discounts from market prices of collateral used for repo. The Bank, by contrast, did not set haircuts per se but rather set a (usually) submarket purchase price for trade coins. The resulting implicit haircut of a coin under receipt was the difference between its market price and its Bank price, the latter changing only infrequently. The consequences of setting haircuts in this fashion are explored in this chapter.

Amsterdam that connected trade coins, current money, and Bank money. This system was sketched in Chapter 2. People could exchange trade coins for bank florins directly with the Bank or indirectly through cashiers and the agio market. This integrated system formed the environment in which the receipt system flourished or failed. Not everyone in Amsterdam was savvy about these markets, but dealers and banks were (see Chapter 2).

With a detailed reconstruction of receipt transactions, we find that for silver trade coins, the Bank set a low price relative to market and did not adjust it; haircuts were positive and substantial. Most outside price changes altered the degree of incentives but not the direction. Customers responded with vigorous if fluctuating in-and-out flows of silver coins. Few receipts were abandoned. An important adaptation was when customers shifted the bulk of silver receipts from domestic to foreign coins after 1720. Spanish dollars under receipt became the dominant way the Bank held trade coins.

For gold coins, we find that the Bank set a price nearer that of the outside market. Fluctuations in market price could shift gold receipts from positive haircuts, when gold behaved like silver, to negative haircuts, when people like Keyser dumped gold at the Bank, and people like Pels did not redeem receipts. Sometimes the Bank even responded by altering the Bank price of gold coins. These policy choices, combined with the Bank's higher interest rate (redemption fee) on gold receipts, resulted in bursts of receipt activity but also intermittent periods of doldrums or even abandonment of gold under receipt.

Sometimes receipts worked well (silver), sometimes they did not (gold), and Bank policies explained much of the difference. These differences led to divergent roles within the Bank. Silver coins under receipt became the dominant way the Bank held trade coins. The receipt facility became a major channel for Spanish dollars, and the redemption of receipt options became reliable enough to approximate loans in a manner similar to modern repurchase agreements. The success of silver receipts was the foundation of the Bank's overall success. In contrast, gold under receipt did not become a reliable presence for the Bank. Gold's less favorable interest rate and high Bank price made their receipt values precarious and usage volatile. Sometimes, market conditions pushed the Bank into the role of a gold dealer, a role that caused the Bank evident discomfort.

6.1 Transformations: 1711–1736

The introduction of the receipt facility in 1683 started an era of growth in the level of Bank money that was slowed by the War of Spanish Succession

(Quinn and Roberds 2014; see also Figure 2.3). Growth in Bank money resumed with peace in 1714, and it came by way of receipts. The contribution of receipts after 1711 can be seen because of the survival of cashbooks. While account ledgers organized transactions by customer, cashbooks organized transactions by types of coin. Chapter 5 used the 1711 cashbook to see how far the receipt system had developed from its beginnings in 1683. This chapter uses the transactions in that and subsequent cashbooks to see how customers utilized the system. For example, Figure 6.1 plots the monthly level of precious metal in the Bank for 25 years starting in 1711. We used the cashbook information to subdivide metallic assets into those owned outright by the Bank, those held under (general) receipt through a receiver, and those held under (specialized) receipt through the assayer. Sorting account transactions into these categories, and others that will follow, necessitated considerable forensic accounting. A description of some of these processes is offered in an appendix to this chapter.

The story in Figure 6.1 starts during the last years of the War of Spanish Succession, when receipt activity was minimal. At that time, most coins were owned outright by the Bank. The end of withdrawal rights around 1685 had caused the Bank to own about 8 million florins in coin, and the Bank still owned 6 million in 1711. The subsequent growth in Bank money, however, came from receipts (shaded gray in the figure). By 1736, the Bank had 22 million florins in metal, but only 3 million were owned outright. Receipts switched from an ancillary to the primary way the Bank held trade coins. And those receipts were via the receiver. The assayer system of bespoke receipts faded after 1720 and ended in 1735.

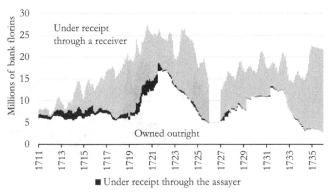

Figure 6.1. Precious metal in the Bank, monthly, 1711–1735
Source: Authors' calculations.
Note: 1726 is missing.

The decline of owned outright was another consequence of the end of withdrawal rights discussed in Chapter 5. The Bank was careful to retain all coins under receipt, and receipts were the only way customers could initiate redemptions, so the Bank no longer needed additional coins as a precaution against runs. The success of receipts also meant that the Bank did not need to own large quantities of unencumbered coins to support the overall level of Bank money. The Bank could sell off the coins that it had purchased or that customers abandoned without risk of illiquidity. By 1736, the Bank had sold off 90 percent of the silver ducatons it owned in 1711. How the Bank turned this freedom into a policy tool will be developed in the next chapter. For the moment, we note that the success of the receipt facility gained the Bank some freedom to make these sales.

During this transformative era, the Bank did have surges of coins owned outright, but they were transitory and undesired. The coins were gold and were abandoned because the receipt system for gold was unstable, as per the example of Keyser and Pels. Later sections of this chapter will show that the Bank did not seek out these coins and that the Bank let go of these unwanted peaks through the sale of gold coins, by the end of 1735, only 1 percent of the Bank's metal was gold. The rise of receipts was the rise of silver receipts.

The transformation of the Bank into a warehouse of silver under receipt had yet another aspect. The silver that customers brought into the Bank shifted from being mostly domestic coins (ducatons and rijksdaalders) to mostly Spanish dollars. Figure 6.2 shows the value of silver coins under receipt over this transitional period and splits them into domestic or foreign origin. Domestic silver coins under receipt reached 6 million florins

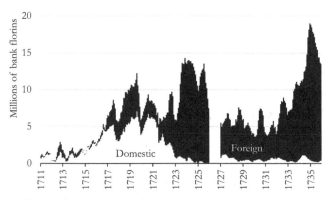

Figure 6.2. Silver under receipt, monthly, 1711–1735
Source: Authors' calculations.
Note: 1726 is missing.

by the start of 1721, while foreign silver was 2.2 million. Over the next four years, that relationship reversed. By the start of 1725, over 9 million florins in dollars from Mexico were at the Bank under receipt. Domestic silver was down to a quarter million. That shift coincided with the growth in silver production in the New World (Chapter 3). The Bank "dollarized," and foreign silver would dominate silver receipts for the rest of the century.

6.2 Flows under Receipt

With receipts, most of these coins were in motion. To visualize this, we have also constructed a measure of flow. Figure 6.3 reports the total annual flow of silver under general receipts, that is, through receivers, into the Bank (shown as positive numbers) and out of the Bank (negative numbers), measured in bank florins and in metric tons. Net flows for a year are total inflows minus total outflows and are shaded gray. Net inflows are positive if sales at the receipt facility exceed repurchases, and net outflows are negative if the reverse. Years with net inflows were slightly more numerous and averaged 2.5 million bank florins (25 tons), while net outflows averaged –2.7 million (–27 tons). A given year could see substantial swings in the level of Bank money when January-to-January balance sheets were compared.

The remaining inflows had offsetting outflows, and both are shown in black. These flows did not alter the level of Bank money on an annual basis, but they were large. On average, 4.7 million bank florins (47 tons) moved each way each year. These were deposits redeemed within the same year

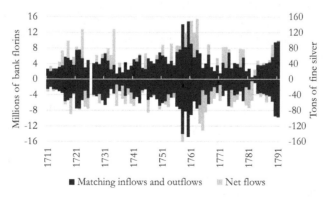

Figure 6.3. Annual flows of silver under general receipt, 1711–1791
Source: Authors' calculations.
Notes: 1726 is missing. Years are fiscal and start late January. The right-hand scale approximates the value of 1 metric ton of pure silver as 100,000 bank florins.

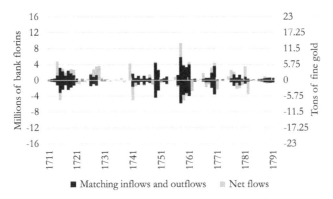

Figure 6.4. Annual flows of gold under general receipt, 1711–1791
Source: Authors' calculations.
Notes: Years are fiscal and start late January. The right-hand scale approximates the value of 1 metric ton of pure gold as 1,437,500 bank florins.

and new deposits offset by the redemption of receipts from a previous year. While we could not track each sack of coins through the Bank, this more generalized measure does illustrate a point. Silver under receipt at the Bank was a river. Many more tons moved through the Bank each year than only entered or only left.

The same did not apply to gold. Figure 6.4 reports the annual through-put and net flows for gold under receipt using receivers. The florin scale is the same as on silver's chart to communicate how much smaller was gold's receipt volume in Bank money. The florin value of gold throughput averaged one-fifth that of silver. Gold receipts were also abandoned at a much higher rate than silver receipts, and gold occasionally suffered multi-year periods of negligible receipt business. Gold flows were intermittent, more of an arroyo than a river.

To globalize the perspective, both metal flows could be viewed as branches of the mighty streams emanating from Brazil, Mexico, and Peru. Figure 6.5 presents the ratio of each metal flowing into the Bank in tons per year (the top half of each flow figure using the right-hand axis) over the annual New World production of the same metal (cf. Figures 3.5 and 3.8). For silver, flows into the Bank averaged 16 percent of contemporaneous New World production. Most years were below that average because a few years around 1720 and 1760 were well above. At the other extreme, inflows fell to near zero in 1782 during the bitter dislocations of the Fourth Anglo-Dutch War. Those extremes and how the Bank responded will receive attention in the next chapter. For now, it should

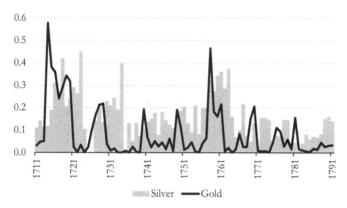

Figure 6.5. Annual ratio of metal deposited at the Bank over-produced in the New World
Source: TePaske and Brown (2010, 56, 113) and authors' calculations.
Note: For silver, 1726 is missing.

be stressed that the remaining three-quarters of years shown in Figure 6.5 had customers put silver into the Bank at rates equal to 5–25 percent of contemporaneous New World production. The production series was stable within each decade, so most of the variation derived from changes in Bank inflows.

Did New World silver flow directly from Spain to the Bank? Likely it did sometimes. As circumstantial evidence, Figure 6.6 plots the arrival of silver into Spain from the New World in 1749 (Morineau 1985, 385–86). Note that the Spanish scale is 20 times the Bank's scale. That year, a treasure fleet arrived in June and July with 654 tons of silver, and most all of the arriving silver eventually left Spain (Chen et al. 2021).[8] Then, over August and September, silver inflows at the Bank combined to 28 tons, or about 4 percent of the recent fleet deliveries. We, of course, do not know if the coins into the Bank were the same as those recently unloaded in Spain. Also, the rest of 1749 had silver inflows into the Bank, and the ratio for the year was 8 percent, a number in line with Figure 6.5.[9]

---

[8] The calculation assumed that 85 percent of the 31 million dollars of treasure was silver (based on Morineau 1985, 475) and that the silver dollars were 0.917 fine and weighed 37.07 grams each.

$$(31 \text{ million dollars}) * \left(\frac{.85 \text{ silver dollars}}{1 \text{ silver equivalent dollars}} \right) * \left(\frac{27.07 \text{ grams}}{1 \text{ silver dollar}} \right) *$$
$$\left(\frac{0.917 \text{ fine grams}}{1 \text{ gram}} \right) * \left(\frac{1 \text{ fine ton}}{1,000,000 \text{ fine grams}} \right) = 654 \text{ fine tons.}$$

[9] Being 62 tons into the Bank over 751 tons into Spain.

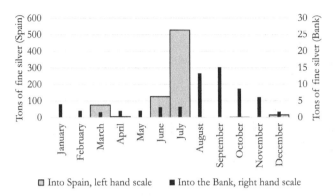

Figure 6.6. Flows of silver in 1749
Sources: Morineau (1985, 385–86); authors' calculations.

The year 1749 offered an example of how a newly arrived treasure fleet might quickly become receipt inflows, but 1749 was atypical. Other years had longer delays or no apparent response at all. Still other years had Bank surges without any recent New World arrivals. As a result, annual silver into Spain had a modest correlation coefficient of +0.25 with silver entering the Bank.[10] Overall, the two flows move together, but with limited synchronization. A likely reason for the loose pattern was that a large stock of silver separated Spain and Amsterdam. For example, Palma and Silva (2021, 11) estimated the total stock of precious metal in Europe in 1750 to be approximately 120,000 tons silver equivalent, a number many times larger than either flow. By itself, Spain's monetary stock at that time was about 4,600 tons (Chen et al. 2021). Dollars fresh off the boat had many places to go, such as mints to become yet newer coins (see Chapter 3). Silver took a circuitous route to the Bank, and Palma (2022, 1610–11) estimated that it took years for newly arrived silver to promote real economic growth.

As gold receipt inflows were more erratic than silver, so too was gold's share of New World production in Figure 6.5. Sometimes, gold's share rivaled and even exceeded that of silver. Despite such bursts of activity, however, people often did not send gold through the Bank. That avoidance was despite the exuberant production of dukaten at Dutch mints (cf. Chapter 3). Overall, gold's ratio averaged half of silver's ratio because the lows were very low.

This quantitative evidence on receipt flows has revealed a set of contrasting facts for two metals under the same receipt system. While both

[10] Calculated for the years 1711–1780.

series had variation, silver throughput remained substantial, while gold throughput often disappeared. Silver had reliable redemptions, while gold had spurts of abandonment. While there were idiosyncratic differences between markets for silver and gold trade coins, the remainder of this chapter argues that some of the differences can be explained by differences in Bank policy. For receipt flows, the Bank set the price of silver right and the price of gold wrong. To see how, we consider flows from the perspective of the Bank's customers.

6.3 Economics of Receipts

Why did people find both deposits and redemptions of silver attractive? Why did people sometimes find either deposits or redemptions of gold unattractive? We do not know on a case-by-case basis, so we apply a more general framework that seems to fit: the Bank usually offered a better deal than the alternatives for silver receipts and not so much for gold.

The deal that receivers offered for trade coins was Bank money and a receipt, and some details of this offer were relevant to assess alternatives. The Bank converted coins into balances at a posted ratio we call the Bank price. For silver foreign coins over most of the eighteenth century, the Bank price was 22 bank florins per mark in sacks of 100 marks. The Bank applied this price to coins ranging in fineness from 93.05 percent for traditional Spanish dollars to 91.66 percent for French *écus* and post-1728 dollars (Irigoin 2018, 13, 15; Velde 2003, 26).[11] For all of these coins, the Bank used sacks worth 2,200 bank florins each. Each sack did not weigh exactly 100 marks, but the Bank and its customers carried on as if they did (see Chapter 3). This fiction made the sacks interchangeable within each type of coin and that made the large volumes of flow convenient to administer (see Chapter 5). The receipt was the option to repurchase the same number of sacks of the same type of coin within 6 months at the Bank price plus a ¼ percent redemption fee for most silver coins. The option could be extended by increments of 6 months by paying just the fee each time. The specificity of coin type prevented inter-coin arbitrage, a problem in the previous century (see Chapter 4). Recall that a receipt was

---

[11] For some periods, select types of finer silver coins were accepted at a higher price. Coins of lesser fineness were not accepted for receipt until the Spanish dollar was reduced to 90.27 percent in 1772, and with that the Bank adjusted down the price of new dollars at 21.5 florins per mark (Irigoin 2018, 16). An exception to the exception was the deposit of 14,000 marks of *Hamburger ryxdaalders* at 21 bank florins per mark in January 1773 (ACA 5077/1400, folio 46).

transferable by the bearer, so the option could be sold over the counter, with no Bank involvement.

For gold, the receipt fee was ½ percent. Otherwise the rules were the same. The most common unit of gold under receipt was seen in Keyser's receipt: the sack of 1,000 Dutch dukaten at the Bank's preferred price of 5 florins per coin.[12] That number was the last official price set to that coin in the previous century, and it seemed the Bank sought to keep the price at this traditional par value. Five florins also carried on in the bullion market. The ordinance fineness of a Dutch gold dukaat was very high for a coin at 98.6 percent, so people also thought of it as a form of bullion (Polak 1998b, 67). Seventy-one full-weight dukaten (those produced at ordinance, which not all were) contained one mark of fine gold, so 71*5 = 355 became the standard for bullion pricing. To recall an example from Chapter 3, the Bank reported the price of a fine mark of gold bullion as 355 bank florins with a premium of 7/8 percent. The same applied outside the Bank. To cite an example, the *Groninger Courant* told readers on October 27, 1750, that the price of gold bars was a premium of 4.375–4.5 percent over 355 current guilders.[13] This use as a bullion benchmark was distinct from the price at which the coins actually circulated and was part of a relevant legacy effect, as the Bank strove to keep this par price.

The receipt window offered these Bank prices for silver and gold coins, so what were the alternatives? Instead of selling to the Bank, customers like Keyser could sell trade coins to other people, like Pels, at a mutually agreeable price. If such an outside or secondary price was below the Bank price, then Keyser might not be interested, as the Bank offered a better deal. Indeed, arbitrageurs could purchase coins at that low price and then deposit them at the Bank for the higher price. Coins would rush in and create Bank money and receipts. The resulting receipts, however, would have little value as it would be unprofitable to repurchase the coins. Customers might even abandon receipts by not paying the prolongation fee after 6 months, as per the introductory example. Such a situation would correspond with large inflows, few redemptions, and much abandonment. That scenario often comported with gold's behavior. It did not for silver.

In contrast, if the outside price was above the Bank price, then a seller like Keyser would be interested, but trading outside the Bank also meant

---

[12] For guineas (*guinees*), cruzados (crusaden), and other gold coins of similar fineness, the unit was a sack of 22 marks at 310 bank florins per mark.

[13] *Opregte Groninger Courant*. Groningen, 1750/10/27, p. 1. Accessed on Delpher on May 23, 2021, http://resolver.kb.nl/resolve?urn=ddd:010410588:mpeg21:p001.

the seller got no receipt. The attractiveness to the sell-side depended on the forgone receipt versus the gain in price. In Chapter 5, we presented a hypothetical merchant who had trade coins, wanted bank florins, yet did not want to relinquish control over the trade coins. These hedging-oriented merchants were the natural customer base of the Bank, as they valued both the Bank money and the receipt. Such risk-averse customers might be rather insensitive to outside prices over relevant ranges.

Other people were monetary specialists like Keyser and Pels. As a dealer, Keyser could sell coins and not need the surety of repurchase. He could maximize immediate gains. Sellers like Keyser would form the supply side of an outside market. A bank like Pels would be on the demand side, but why pay Keyser a higher price than that offered by the Bank? Because Pels did not have a receipt. Here was where the lack of withdrawal rights created an asymmetry. Keyser could deposit unlimited coins at the Bank price, but Pels did not have a similarly unfettered conversion of accounts back into coins. When people lacked receipts yet wanted their Bank money turned into coins, they had to bid up coin prices outside the Bank. The end of withdrawal rights created a demand for coin flow outside the Bank.

As the introductory example showed, what pulled that flow back into the Bank was that Pels could buy a receipt from Keyser. If the receipt price plus the redemption fee were less than the outside mark up, then trading with Keyser through the Bank was a better deal for Pels. Receipts offered a bank like Pels the additional attraction of leverage, allowing speculative long positions to be built at low cost. Because the receipt resale value went to the seller, receipt sales also increased incentives for Keyser to move flow into the Bank. The result was that the sequence of coin deposit, receipt sale, and coin repurchase replaced much of what would otherwise have occurred outside the Bank. We have found no evidence of a deep outside market for trade coins in bank florins; Le Moine de L'Espine and Le Long (1763, 187) described such exchanges as exceptional. These trades were not illegal and did happen, but the volume needed to support brokers, dealers, and price listings does not seem to have emerged. Instead, that secondary market moved from coins to their receipts.

Figure 6.7 puts the resale process into a supply and demand schematic. Supply was created by people like Keyser with trade coins who wanted Bank money and were fine with selling their receipt to the highest bidder. They were part of the inflows in Figures 6.3 and 6.4 when they sold coins to the Bank. Demand was created by people like Pels with Bank accounts who wanted trade coins and were willing to buy receipts to do it. They were outflows when they redeemed receipts and purchased coins from the Bank.

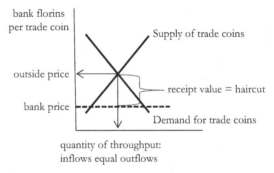

Figure 6.7. Primary Bank market with resale of receipts
Source: see text.

The intersection of the two schedules was the market clearing price outside the Bank. It cleared the market because inflows equaled outflows. The dashed horizontal line was the Bank price, and it was set below the outside price. At the Bank price, demand for redemptions exceeded supply. As buyers bid up the price of receipts, more supply was induced to go through the Bank as the sale of receipts supplemented the Bank price for sellers. Conceptually, the process stabilized where the price of a receipt matched the difference in prices. The receipt resale market built on the receipt facility to mimic a secondary coin market outside the Bank. This allowed the Bank to offer a stable Bank price for trade coins and yet retain the price flexibility needed to stabilize flows.

Actual situations were more complicated. Receipts had redemption fees, brokers charged fees also, and dealers had bid-ask spreads. Moreover, receipts had an option value beyond their immediate redemption because circumstances in the near future could change. People could prolong options, so the speculative future could be extended, and the available quantity of receipts could build over time. While receipt values were not solely determined by present redemption value, they were directly related (Dehing 2012, 115). The simplification presented here provided intuition of how receipt resales brought in people who would otherwise not have moved coins through the Bank. Conceptually, it was a market that supplemented the people who only wanted to borrow Bank money. In reality, the two blurred as people decided during the option period whether to redeem, sell, prolong, or abandon their receipts.

When it worked, the process relied on the easy resale of receipts, and the Bank assisted that too. When people created receipts, the Bank acted as a trusted counterparty and did not charge a fee. When people sold receipts to others, the Bank allowed the new party to displace the old, again without a fee. In effect, the contract replaced the seller of the receipt with the buyer, so only a single receipt contract remained. This is analogous to the modern practice of a central counterparty in a financial market replacing (or "novating") a chain of trading commitments with a single netted commitment.[14] Without such an arrangement, buyers and sellers would have to layer a second contract on top of the initial contract when the receipt was sold, as can occur in certain modern over-the-counter markets. The de facto novation promoted resale liquidity by keeping the Bank and the receipt holder as the only counterparties. While sellers and buyers set receipt prices and arranged payments, the Bank interposed itself to make sure that transfer of the repurchase option remained simple and clean.

The easy resale of receipts helped people to mimic market pricing despite the Bank having set an inflexible Bank price, but it only worked when the outside price was above the Bank price and the receipt facility had an implicit haircut. The result helped explain the large throughput of silver. Moreover, the persistent nature of the receipt market encouraged specialists and foreign investors (through their relations in Amsterdam) to participate. Intermediaries such as the precious metal dealers connected buyers with sellers of receipts, and foreign flows added volume. Such people might not commit to the Amsterdam market if it flickered in and out of existence.

6.4 Comparisons with Modern Repos

For silver coins, the predominance of receipt options being executed through redemption or rollover increased the similarity of receipts to modern repurchase agreements. In a modern repo, a collateral seller is expected to repurchase the collateral and the collateral haircut adds an incentive to do so. For the receipt facility, the gap between the market value of silver coins and their Bank price created a haircut, and persistence of that gap made execution of the repurchase option into a reliable expectation. Modern repos are often viewed functionally as loans (carrying an obligation to repay by executing a repurchase) instead of options (no

---

[14] Formally, receipts were structured as a repurchase right exercisable by the customer who brought in the coin, or "by the bearer," and were traded over the counter, outside the Bank, for current money (with very rare exceptions). When someone showed up at the Bank with a receipt they wanted to redeem, the Bank's obligation to resell did not depend on how many hands the receipt had been through.

obligation to execute). The redemption or prolongation of silver receipts at the Bank became so consistent that they functioned like loans, despite the structuring of receipts as options. The deepening of the receipt market supported the throughput of safe assets, and that flow recast options into loans. By this we are not saying that the Bank would have described itself as a repo cash lender or option exchange. We are saying that the Bank adopted and did not alter policies that made it such.

Despite these parallels, it is worthwhile to consider some key differences between the receipt facility and modern repos. The Bank enjoyed considerable leeway in setting the terms for receipts because there were no equivalent private arrangements in precious metal assets.[15] In modern repo transactions, private and central bank cash lenders can and do adjust terms in response to market conditions. Haircuts are stated as a percentage of a collateral asset's market value, and these can increase with the riskiness of the collateral asset. Interest rates can also be adjusted to reflect a change in policy or an assessment of risk. Such adjustments can put pressure on market participants who fund themselves via repo, especially parties who finance long-term assets by rolling over short-term (often, overnight) repos (Gorton and Metrick 2012). Market risk on an underlying asset can lead to funding risk for parties financing their positions via repo.[16]

The Bank offered a rather different arrangement, whereby it assumed much of the market and funding risks. The term of a receipt was for up to six months rather than overnight. Redemption fees were held constant over long periods, although these fees would clearly meet the modern definition of a central bank policy interest rate.[17] Another difference was haircuts. The implicit haircut (market price less Bank price) on collateral (coins) could vary considerably, tending to be high when the value of the coins was high and low when the value of the collateral was low. The latter could result in people not redeeming receipts precisely when incentives to create receipts were substantial. In other words, unlike cash lenders in modern repo transactions, the Bank did not always try to protect its balance sheet via regular adjustments of valuations and haircuts, but instead it was willing to assume the risk of price drops by allowing coin collateral to "fall" to itself

---

[15] Private repo transactions did occur in stocks; see Petram (2011, 2014).

[16] The standard (Bank for International Settlements) definition of market risk is a party's risk of loss from declines in market prices; funding risk is the risk that a party will be unable to settle its obligations as they come due.

[17] There is no evidence that the Bank ever considered systematic variation of silver's interest rate as a policy tool. Regular variation of policy interest rates was not a common practice in central banking until the nineteenth century.

when receipts expired. This risk allocation could be of great benefit to the Bank's customers but potentially destabilizing to the Bank.

Why did the Bank feel comfortable taking on these risks? The best answer may be found in Johannes Phoonsen's original proposal to create a receipt facility. In effect, Phoonsen was arguing that by restricting itself to the most desirable kind of collateral (favored types of trade coins), the Bank would not be exposed to inordinate risk: "And in fact, real silver and gold [coin] is an imperishable form of security, unless the coin itself should also perish . . ." (Van Dillen 1921, 8). Either customers would not abandon such collateral or the Bank could eventually unload it at no loss. In anachronistic terms, the Bank would be exposed to the market risk of U.S. Treasury bills, a manageable risk. This chapter will show that in the subsequent implementation of his proposal, Phoonsen's assessment would prove largely correct for silver coins but less so for gold.

6.5 Receipts within the Monetary System

Conceptually, we have argued that receipt throughput relied on the outside price being greater than the Bank price (Figure 6.7), or, equivalently, throughput relied on the borrowing of Bank money through the receipt facility at a positive haircut. In a twist on modern repo, the receipt haircut might not discourage borrowers if the receipt was sold for a price that covered the haircut. As a result, the flow of coins into the Bank was not limited to people who also expected to repurchase the coins. Customers like Keyer and Pels could use the receipt facility to redeploy coins and Bank money.

In practice, we cannot directly verify that the silver coins that flowed through the Bank in Figure 6.3 had positive haircuts because we lack trade coin prices in bank florins. Receipts displaced an outside market for trade coins in Bank money; the Bank did not record receipt prices; and we have yet to find an account book of one of the specialized dealers in the receipt trade.[18] We can, however, turn to a related market, the local market for

---

[18] The rare observation of the Bank purchasing a receipt let us confirm the systemic pricing structure at one moment. In March 1791, the Bank purchased receipts for old Spanish dollars from Mexico at 6.6 percent. The bank price was 22 bank florins per mark, so the implied outside price was 22*1.066 = 23.45 florins per mark. Alternatively, silver bullion in March 1791 was 25.55 current guilders per fine mark (Posthumus 1946, 395), Spanish dollars were 0.9166 percent fine, and agio was 1.0013. The indirect market price was $\left(\frac{25.55 \text{ guilders}}{1 \text{ fine mark}}\right) * \left(\frac{0.9166 \text{ fine marks}}{1 \text{ mark}}\right) * \left(\frac{1 \text{ florin}}{1.0013 \text{ guilders}}\right) = 23.39$ florins per mark.

Table 6.1. *The implicit haircut*

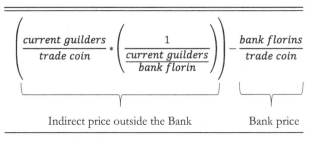

Indirect price outside the Bank	Bank price

Source: Authors' hypothesis.

silver and gold. For example, in November 1779, Spanish dollars from Mexico traded at 2.55 current guilders each (Mees 1838, 294). At that time, the agio was 1.0481 current guilders per bank florin. The combination of these two prices allowed for the calculation of an *indirect* outside price in bank florins of 22.22 per mark.[19] The Bank price was 22, and thus the implicit haircut was 22.22–22 = 0.22 florins or 1 percent of the Bank price.

Table 6.1 gives the general formula for the implicit haircut using Amsterdam's indirect markets. The process converts the guilder price of a trade coin into bank florins by means of the reciprocal of the premium in the agio market. It then subtracts the Bank price to get the implicit haircut. The result can be converted into a percent by dividing it by the Bank price.

The indirect outside price was a relevant substitute because of the system of monies described in Chapter 2. People used Bank money for bill of exchange transactions such as settlement and short-term (money market) lending. People used trade coins for transactions with distant markets. People used current money for domestic transactions such as taxes and consumption. People moved between these different monies through connective markets. The conceptual map in Figure 2.4 labeled three such markets as Bank, agio, and coin. Chapter 3 discussed the current guilder market for trade coins. Chapters 4 and 5 developed the agio market. The previous sections of this chapter showed how the receipt facility (a primary market) could combine with the resale of receipts (a secondary market) to form the Bank market.

In isolation, each market adjusted toward its own price ratio, but the three connecting markets did not operate in isolation. They formed a

---

[19] Spanish dollars (Spaansche piasters) of the 1728 standard were at 2.55 current guilders per coin, and 1,000 coins weighed 109.5 marks (Mees 1838, 294). $\left(\frac{2.55 \text{ guilders}}{1 \text{ dollar}}\right) * \left(\frac{1 \text{ dollar}}{0.1095 \text{ marks}}\right) * \left(\frac{1 \text{ florin}}{1.0481 \text{ guilders}}\right) = 22.22$ florins per mark.

Table 6.2. *No-arbitrage condition for bank florins, current guilders, and trade coins*

$$\frac{\text{bank florins}}{\text{trade coin}} * \frac{\text{current guilders}}{\text{bank florin}} = \frac{\text{current guilders}}{\text{trade coin}}$$

Source: Authors' hypothesis.

system because people could take the direct route through a single market or use a combination of the other two. The indirect route could be attractive if it delivered more bank florins than the direct market. For stability, the three market prices needed to align, so people did not switch markets in search of better deals (in modern terminology, they were no longer "engaging in arbitrage"). Ideally, this occurred when the product of two market prices equaled the third. This equation, technically known as a "no-arbitrage condition," can be stated as the equation in Table 6.2.

Amsterdam's monetary system aligned these prices through changes in flows between the types of money. If someone had trade coins and the indirect route paid better, then that person shifted an offer of coins from the Bank market to the local market. In economic parlance, the supply of coins for bank florins decreased, while the supply of coins for current guilders increased. Next, those extra guilders led to an increase in the demand for bank florins in the agio market. The stable alignment of these prices expressed in Table 6.2 came when people no longer altered such choices, that is, the flow of money was stable. In reality, things were never so simple, but it does show how Bank customers could view the indirect routes as setting a relevant alternative price for the Bank market.

This systemic perspective provided yet another view of the adjustment asymmetry created by receipts. When the Bank set a price for coins under receipt, it locked in the ratio of bank florins per trade coin in Table 6.2. If that ratio did not align with the other two market ratios, then pressure existed to reroute trade coins until the equality was satisfied, that is, the specie flow mechanism.[20] The ability to resell receipts altered the story by allowing the bank florin price to be comprised of the Bank price plus the receipt price. Because receipts were an option, their redemption value could not be negative, so the asymmetry emerged. A low Bank price plus positive receipt value, that is, a receipt being "in the money," could align

---

[20] If $\frac{\text{bank price in florins}}{\text{trade coin}} > \frac{\text{bank florins}}{\text{current guilder}} * \frac{\text{current guilders}}{\text{trade coin}}$ caused net inflows and thus the level of bank florins to increase, then eventually a combination of an agio $\left(\frac{\text{current guilders}}{\text{bank florin}}\right)$ decrease and local trade coin price $\left(\frac{\text{current guilders}}{\text{trade coin}}\right)$ increase would bring about equilibration.

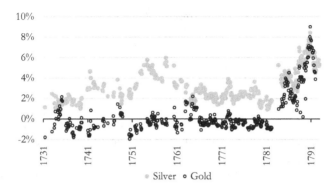

Figure 6.8. Implicit haircuts on bullion in Bank money, select months, 1731–1791
Sources: Posthumus (1946, 394–97) and authors' calculations.

the system. A high Bank price had no offsetting receipt value, so quantity adjustment was required: coins flowed into the Bank but not out.[21]

Returning to the issue of whether haircuts could help explain when customers found the receipt facility attractive (silver) or not (gold), we would want to calculate the implicit haircuts (Table 6.1) for each type of trade coin accepted by the Bank. The cashbooks revealed Bank prices. The financial press regularly reported agio prices. Dealers in trade coins, however, did not contribute price quotes to Amsterdam price currents (see Chapter 3). In the 1730s, however, the Dutch financial press started to report bullion prices in current guilders with increasing frequency. Because trade coins usually enjoyed a premium over bullion (see Chapter 3), these bullion prices can be treated as lower bounds that provided quantitative verification of our contention that outside prices were routinely above the Bank price for silver but not for gold.

In Figure 6.8, we took silver bullion observations, adjusted them to the fineness of Spanish dollars, converted them from current guilders to bank florins using the agio, subtracted the Bank price from that result, and then divided the difference by the Bank price to get a percent haircut.[22] The

---

[21] Before receipts, the agio price was anchored by a strong specie-flow mechanism with deposits creating a ceiling and withdrawals creating a floor (see Chapter 4). With receipts, low agios had a limited ability to decrease the quantity of bank florins. Instead, the pressure to exit Bank money could be expressed as large haircuts and throughput. Some of the lowest agios in Figure 2.5, such as 1759 and 1790, correspond with substantial silver throughputs in Figure 6.3. Statistically, low agios had weak reversion compared to high agios (Quinn and Roberds 2019, 767).

[22] For example, a haircut of 3 percent in January 1741 derived from 26 current guilders (cg) per fine mark fine (fm) of silver bullion; Spanish dollars at 0.9166 fine marks fine (fm) per

results are the gray dots. In all 464 extant monthly observations, the price of silver bullion in the current guilder market, as converted by the contemporaneous agio, was above the Bank price of 22 bank florins per mark. At least from 1730, silver had positive implicit haircuts, and the Bank price was as drawn in the supply and demand schematic in Figure 6.7.

Figure 6.8 also applies the same approach to gold.[23] The relevant gold coin was the Dutch dukaat that dominated gold receipts flows, when they occurred, for much of the eighteenth century. The Bank sought to maintain the traditional price of 5 florins per coin. The black circles were the resulting implicit haircut. The values were often negative, meaning that the lower-bound prices were often below the Bank price. A premium for being a trade coin might have lifted many of those haircuts into positive territory. Even so, gold would have often been near the edge. These near-zero haircuts contributed to gold's inflow surges, sporadic throughput, and abandonments. It also pressured the Bank toward lowering the price of gold coins when it did not for silver. When the Bank gave in to market pressure, the results also turned out to spell trouble.

6.6 Instability

A slight positive haircut was vulnerable to the outside price of gold falling *below* the Bank price. When that happened, the resale of receipts would no longer resolve flow imbalances. Instead, inflows would exceed outflows. To see a conceptualization of this situation, the schematic in Figure 6.9 recasts the market for Bank money with the Bank price above the outside price. Again, supply was customers like Keyser who had coins, wanted Bank money, and wanted to sell their receipts. Demand was customers like Pels who had Bank money, wanted coins, and were open to buying receipts

---

mark (m); an agio of 1.0519 current guilders (cg) per bank florin (bf); and a bank price for dollars of 22 bank florins (bf) per mark (m). The calculation was:

$$\frac{\left(26\,\tfrac{cg}{fm}\right)*\left(0.9166\,\tfrac{fm}{m}\right)*\left(\frac{1}{1.0519\,\tfrac{cg}{bf}}\right)-\left(22\tfrac{bf}{m}\right)}{22\tfrac{bf}{m}}=0.03\ .$$

[23] For example, a haircut of −1.1 percent in January 1741 derived from 374.53 current guilders (cg) per fine mark (fm) of gold bullion; Dutch dukaten at 0.986 fine marks (fm) per mark (m) (Polak 1998, 67); an agio of 1.0519 current guilders (cg) per bank florin (bf); and a Bank price for dukaten of 355 bank florins (bf) per mark (m). The calculation was:

$$\frac{\left(374.53\,\tfrac{cg}{fm}\right)*\left(0.986\,\tfrac{fm}{m}\right)*\left(\frac{1}{1.0519\,\tfrac{cg}{bf}}\right)-\left(355\tfrac{bf}{m}\right)}{355\tfrac{bf}{m}}=-0.011\ .$$

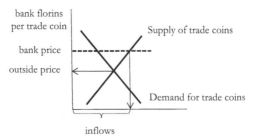

Figure 6.9. Primary Bank market without resale of receipts
Source: see text.

to get them. Throughput vanished because buyers could get a lower price outside the Bank, and sellers could get a higher price inside. The result was deposits that did not exit. For receipts, the price inversion created a negative haircut, and the resale market shut down. If sellers thought the situation transitory, then they might pay to prolong their receipts in hope of an eventual rise in the outside price. If more pessimistic, they could let the options expire. The situation was also unsustainable. Eventually, so many coins would enter the Bank that the price of those still outside would rise, and so much Bank money would be created that the agio would decline. Both effects would work to increase the outside price and dissipate abandonment incentives. In the meantime, a great deal of gold could fall into the Bank.

When the outside price of gold was below the Bank price, the Bank was left with two options: let gold levels build or lower the Bank price. The rub was that the Bank struggled to accept either outcome. Repeatedly, the Bank lowered the price of gold, which discouraged abandonment, but then the Bank later raised the price back toward its traditional value and reexposed itself. To see the conflicted nature of the Bank's approach to gold, this section presents detailed reconstruction of two episodes: 1719–1721 and 1726–1730.

At the start of fiscal year 1711, the Bank had no gold coins under receipt. The War of Spanish Succession had already dragged on for a decade, and economic activity was depressed. With peace in 1714, gold suddenly began to churn through the Bank. At first, the gold coins were French and Spanish. After the death of Louis XIV in 1715, however, the French Regency began to issue an intermittent series of gold coin ordinances (Velde 2003, 23–24). To generate seigniorage, each ordinance compelled people in France to remint gold into a new type of coin. Most of the recoinages also resulted in less gold per unit of account. The recoinages

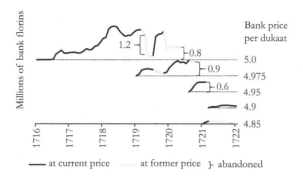

Figure 6.10. Gold dukaten under receipt, monthly, 1716–1722
Source: Authors' calculations.

pushed some of the old coins out of France and into the Bank. When the newer French coins had their turn to flee yet more debasements, the Bank did not accept them.[24] Some of these newer gold coins were diverted to Dutch mints. The mints enjoyed an upswing in production (see Chapter 3) as many coins were reminted in the Republic. The rebranded gold then entered the Bank as dukaten.

Figure 6.10 organizes the dukaten story from 1716 to 1722. The top line was the level of dukaten under receipt at a par value of 5 bank florins per coin. At the start of 1716, the Bank had no dukaten under receipt, and inflows began that summer. By the end of 1718, about 1.8 million were under receipt with a haircut of about 0.75 percent.[25] In February 1719, the Bank lowered the price to 4.975 florins per coin. In Figure 6.10, the new price is a new line with its own level of dukaten under receipt. The stock of coins in the Bank at the old price become gray to convey the legacy status of their receipts. The Bank would change price five more times over the next three years. The price went back up to 5 florins in August 1719, then back down to 4.975 in December, then down to 4.95 in September 1720, then down to 4.85 in February 1721, then up to 4.9 in April 1721. In total, Figure 6.9 has 7 black segments at five different Bank prices. It was a confusing time, as those jumps caused receipts for the same coins to coexist at different Bank prices. Figure 6.10 communicates this with coin amounts separated by their Bank price.

[24] The only time the Bank accepted these vintages through receivers under receipt was in 1726 with coins the Bank characterized as light, new French pistols (*ligte nieuwe Franse pistolen*).

[25] In November and December 1718, the Bank sold three sacks of abandoned dukaten at 5.0375 bank florins each for a haircut of 0.75 percent, being (5.0375-5)/5.

The cashbooks did not explain why the Bank prices were changed, and no record has been found of involvement by the City's governing council. The new prices appeared as another internal policy decision. Unfortunately, these years have lacked gold and agio price observations with which to calculate implicit haircuts, but we suspect that the Bank lowered its price because the outside price of gold had fallen below the old Bank price.[26] One indicator was the accumulation of inflows. Another was that after the Bank lowered prices, inflows slowed. The sequence suggested that the Bank lowered prices to discourage unwanted gold deposits. With this era coinciding with the rise and fall of John Law's system in France and the South Sea Bubble in Britain, the Bank may have feared becoming a dump box for gold. In contrast, the two price increases occurred when inflows were low and the Bank might safely move back toward a Bank price of 5.[27]

Another indicator was the behavior of customers with old receipts. As coins entered at the new price, receipts at the former price continued to exist. For example, inflows starting in February 1719 created receipts with the option to repurchase a sack at 4,975 bank florins plus fees. Older receipts had the option to repurchase the same sack at 5,000 plus fees. The haircut on the new receipts was a ½ percent larger and so less vulnerable to abandonment, especially if the Bank adjusted price to keep their haircut positive. In 1719, the new receipts were not abandoned. In contrast, two-thirds of the old receipts at 5 per coin were abandoned and 1.2 million fell into the Bank.[28] The rest were prolonged long enough to become current again when the Bank price, and presumably the outside price, rose again in August 1719. The difference in customer behavior suggested that the outside price had been between the two Bank prices.

The other receipt cohorts in Figure 6.10 tell a similar story. After the Bank price was restored to par at 5 in August 1719, the receipts at 4.975 thrived because they had a larger haircut. They had no abandonments, and their gray line segment turned to black when that price returned four

---

[26] The outside price being $\frac{\text{bank florins}}{\text{current guilder}} * \frac{\text{current guilders}}{\text{tradecoin}}$.

[27] A similar cycle did occur in silver in 1721 when 2.4 million florins of rijksdaalders were abandoned, and the Bank lowered the price from 2.4 bank florins per coin to 2.375. The traditional price was restored in November 1724.

[28] The cashbooks did not note a precise timing of this change in status, so we identified abandonments by a subsequent lack of receipt activity and eventual sale. Figure 6.9 applied all of the first round of abandonments to June 1719 for expositional clarity. The total abandonments for the later cohorts have been labeled when their receipt activities ceased.

months later. When the Bank reduced the price again in 1720, the same 4.975 receipts were suddenly abandoned, while the receipts at the new Bank price accumulated. The new 4.95 receipts were in turn abandoned in 1721 when the Bank lowered the price yet again. In total, customers abandoned coins worth 3.5 million bank florins – more than 2.4 tons of gold or about 25 percent of contemporary New World annual output. All the abandonments occurred in older receipts after the Bank had lowered the price. In contrast, when the Bank raised the current price to 4.9 florins each, the low-priced receipts at 4.85 were all redeemed or prolonged. The differences suggested that the Bank lowered price when the current price was headed toward abandonment, and it raised price when it would not set off abandonment. The Bank did not raise the price above 5 florins per dukaat.

Additional evidence that the Bank did not want all this gold was that the Bank soon began operations to sell the abandoned coins. Starting in 1722 and ending three years later, the Bank sold off all the abandoned gold dukaten. And that selloff had yet another, likely unintended, consequence: liquidation of the Bank's inventory displaced business at the gold receipt window. By selling large quantities, the Bank effectively created a new primary market for turning Bank money into gold coins that did not require a receipt. Much of the motivation for the receipt market was subverted. Customer-driven receipt flows nearly vanished until the Bank concluded its sales operations (see Figure 6.4).

The next era, 1726 through 1730, was another round of gold instability, and it highlighted what could happen when the Bank did not adjust the price of gold. Figure 6.11 reprises the framework of following gold dukaten

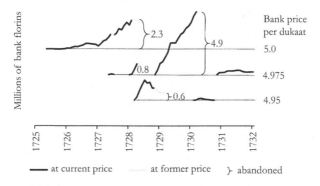

Figure 6.11. Gold dukaten under receipt, monthly, 1725–1732
Source: Authors' calculations.

by Bank price. With the completion of sales in 1725, the Bank attempted to reestablish a price at 5 florins and deposits resumed slowly. Soon enough, the previous pattern reemerged, again seemingly instigated by a large augmentation of coin values in France in 1726 (Velde 2009, 601). The example of Keyser and Pels in the introduction was at this turn of the tide. As abandonments such as our example mounted, the Bank dropped its price in May 1727. With the situation apparently calmed, the Bank price was quickly restored, but then the situation again deteriorated. The price was dropped in January 1728 and again in March. In the process, customers abandoned receipts covering 3.1 million in gold coins. The accumulation seemed to have peaked in mid-1728, and the Bank yet again relaxed and moved up the price by an increment in December.

Then the Bank changed policy. In 1729, when dukaten again began to accumulate, the Bank did *not* lower the price. It let 4.975 ride. Again, we do not know why, but the inflows were spectacular. These customers made almost no effort to redeem or prolong the receipts, and the mass abandonment of nearly 5 million bank florins followed. Receipts were so out of the money that customers even abandoned the older receipts at the more favorable 4.95. The Bank eventually dropped its price in February 1730, and inflows subsided. A weak throughput resumed after the Bank popped up the price nine months later. The Bank began to sell the abandoned gold in early 1732, and again receipt activity nearly vanished until the operation unwound years later (again see Figure 6.4).

Taken together, the two episodes (1719–1721 and 1726–1730) revealed the difficulties of targeting the Bank price too closely to the outside price. At a price of 5, the haircut was so slight that market swings easily led customers to dump gold at the Bank. The Bank had discomfort at becoming a "dealer of last resort" (Mehrling 2011) to the Amsterdam gold market, and repeatedly adjusted its price, presumably to better align with the outside market, but the Bank did not stick with any one of those prices. Either the Bank had coins it did not want, a price below 5 it did not want, or both. Also, the subsequent sale of abandoned coins suppressed the receipt process by opening a new primary market, making it even harder for gold to develop the receipt throughput enjoyed by silver. The Bank's role could shift uneasily from dealer of last resort to dealer of first resort, as big stocks of unwanted inventory were first accumulated, then liquidated.

Spurts of throughput in other eras, however, suggested that gold coins could have had more consistent flows through the Bank. What derailed the throughput were the cycles of abandonment, price adjustment, and eventual sale. The pattern of 1719 and 1729 was repeated in 1741, 1749, 1758, and 1771. Only after 1771 did the Bank stop trying to restore a Bank price of 5 florins, and, in 1776, the Bank even reduced the fee rate on gold coins to match silver at ¼ percent.[29] Perhaps gold would then have settled down into consistent throughput similar to silver's had not all of the Bank's operations soon been disrupted by the Fourth Anglo-Dutch War (see Chapter 7).

6.7 Conclusion

This chapter shows that for silver trade coins, the Bank's experience with the receipt system largely accorded with Johannes Phoonsen's optimistic prediction of how such a system would work. Through receipts, significant quantities of silver coins were attracted to the Bank, where they anchored the liquidity of Amsterdam's bill market. The majority of these coins then left the Bank within a year's time. The Bank harnessed but did not impede the global flow of safe silver assets.

The Bank's experience with gold coins, however, showed that its receipt facilities were not assured of robust throughput. A small haircut on gold rewarded Bank customers with value for their collateral but could give rise to destabilizing cycles of inflow and abandonment. Adjusting the Bank price to increase the gold haircut disrupted the goal of a stable, traditional Bank price. Selling off abandoned coins displaced the receipt market that was necessary for flow volume to build, and flow volume was necessary for the market deepening that made the entire framework reliable.

The more fundamental reasons for these inconsistent policies remain unclear. In an era when most of the world was on a silver standard (Irigoin 2018), the Bank would not have wanted gold as its principal backing asset. On the other hand, by 1720 the gold dukaat was well on its way to becoming the Republic's principal trade coin, and the Bank apparently felt the need to support its traditional price. Operating in the background were macro factors such as the ramp-up of gold production in Brazil, the South Sea Bubble, and John Law's system, developments that could not have been foreseen by Phoonsen in 1677.

The Bank's disparate experience with silver and gold showed that in order to flourish, a receipt facility required more than a set of rules. It required nuance. The Bank price had to be low enough to reward the resale of receipts, yet not so low as to discourage the many customers who

---

[29] The reduction in fee rate was ordered by the City at the request of bankers and merchants (Van Dillen 1925a, 426–427).

used receipts for both deposit and redemption. A low redemption fee helped but so did stability in both the fee and Bank price. One might harshly judge the Bank's gold receipt policies, but perhaps the more important lesson was the success that followed from not meddling with the terms for silver. This success allowed the Bank to let go of its stock of coins owned outright and lend more to the Dutch East India Company.

As a central bank, the Bank had erected a receipt policy that granted customers agency. For silver, that meant that throughput ebbed and flowed but remained substantial. For gold, throughput was burst and bust. These variations lead to the next set of policy decisions the Bank had to make: how to respond. This chapter has presented direct responses like price changes and sales of abandoned coins. Most responses, however, were less direct because the Bank did not adjust silver prices and silver was rarely abandoned. Instead, the Bank purchased and sold local silver coins that were not part of the receipt facility. These more nuanced responses, recognizable to modern observers as open market operations, counteracted receipt flow volatility and stabilized the overall level of Bank money. These open market operations are the focus of the next chapter.

A.6 Categorization of Metal within the Bank

Figure 6.1 separates Bank inventories into coins owned outright, coins under receipt (general) via receivers, and coins under receipt (specialized) via the assayer. The Bank, however, did not typically label coins as such, so each cashbook account was inspected for how the Bank acquired and relinquished the coins. To identify transactions as under a standard receipt, we looked for regularities identified in Chapter 5. Such deposits came through a receiver and arrived in sacks at stable Bank prices. Redemptions and prolongations occurred at standard fee rates. A partial exception was gold coins that we labeled as using receiver receipts. Gold dukaten did arrive through receivers and had a stable fee, but Bank prices did vary; see Figures 6.10 and 6.11. In contrast, assayer receipts entered through the assayer's account or directly into the master account. Also, fee rates and Bank prices often varied. While assayer receipts were not a major share of activity after 1713, their complexities made this era difficult to encode and reconcile. The remaining category of Figure 6.1 was owned outright, and it included all other silver and gold at the Bank.

Another significant complication was that a cashbook account often combined coins under receipt and coins owned outright with no explicit delimitation. For example, in January 1711, the Bank had 2.7 million florins of silver ducatons with no separation into under receipt or owned outright.

To discern the level (L) of ducatons under receipt, we identify the activities that could change that level. Coins under receipt left through redemption (r) or abandonment (a). New coins entered through deposit (d). The process of change can be described as the equation $L_t + d_{t+1} - r_{t+1} - a_{t+1} = L_{t+1}$, where the increment of time (t) is six months. A problem was that the Bank only recorded deposits (d) and redemptions (r). Even if there were no abandonments, the equation does not give the starting level of coins under receipt.

Luckily, receipts also involved prolongations (p). People only prolonged coins under receipt, and prolongations did not the change the level of coins under receipt. Prolongations provided two useful constraints on the level of coins.

One is $L_t \geq p_{t+1} + Max(0, r_{t+1} - d_{t+1} - p_{t+1})$. The basis of this constraint was that the coins under receipt at time t would be either prolonged or redeemed over the next six-months (t + 1). Receipts could also be abandoned, and, as the Bank did not explicitly record such, the constraint was a minimum instead of an equality. Another complication was that some redemptions might have been of newly deposited coins and other redemptions might have been of coins already prolonged. The limits to these potentialities were actual deposits, actual prolongations, and the fact that the net effect could not become negative, that is, deposits in excess of redemptions could not travel in time to become coins under receipt before their deposit.

A second constraint is $L_t \leq p_{t-1} + d_{t-1}$. It starts with the limitation that the level of coins under receipt resulted from prolongations and deposits over the previous six months. The level could be less if some prolongations or deposits were redeemed intra-period, so the constraint was a maximum.

Combining the two constraints created a window for the level of coins under receipt at a moment in time. The activity of the previous half-year created a maximum, and the activity of the subsequent half-year created a minimum. The earliest calculation was for the start of 1711. The minimum level of ducatons under receipt was 203,826 florins derived from activity in the subsequent six months. The maximum could not be calculated because no earlier cashbooks remain extant. We could, however, calculate a maximum for mid-1711 (1,359,426 florins) and subtract net deposits to estimate a maximum level for the start of the year of 754,194. The level of 600,000 florins assigned to ducatons under receipt in January 1711 falls within this range. Ducatons owned outright became the remainder of 2.1 million.

7

Two Banks and One Money, 1711–1791

On Thursday, March 13, 1721, Anthony Grill sold the Bank 938 kilograms of silver coins, a weight typical of a female walrus.[1] That scale was not unusual for the Bank, but the rest of the transaction was. Grill was the Bank's assayer, a salaried position that presumed a separate business as a specialist in precious metals (see Chapter 2). The Bank, through Grill, chose the time and scale of this transaction. Also, it did not go through a receiver, did not generate a receipt, did not use only whole sacks, did not use a stable Bank price, and did not involve trade coins. Instead, the Bank purchased 88,410 guldens in 147 sacks of 600 coins each plus 210 individual coins (ACA 5077/1339, 78). Gulden coins were local coins that circulated in the domestic economy at one guilder each (see Chapter 3), and receivers did not accept them for deposit. To repay Grill for the coins, the Bank created 84,000 florins in Bank money at a premium (agio) of 5¼ percent.[2] This was how the Bank conducted an open market purchase.

And, like a modern central bank, the Bank chained purchases together into operations. The next day, the Bank purchased more guldens from Grill at 5³⁄₁₆ and the day after that purchased more at 5⅛. Over the next two months, the Bank made 18 purchases that totaled 1.3 million coins (14 metric tons) at an average agio of 5.12 percent. The operation increased the amount of Bank money by about 5 percent. No aspect of the operation was public information, and the Bank did not record the goal of the operation. It could have been to make a profit, and the Bank did sell most of those coins at 4½ percent in a reverse operation that began in June 1724, but the

---

[1] For the transaction, see ACA 5077/1339, 78 and ACA 8077/1365, 26. Each coin weighed 10.61 grams (Polak 1998b, 76). Walrus weight ranges retrieved from https://seaworld.org on July 5, 2022.

[2] The calculation being $\left(\left(\frac{88{,}410 \text{ current guilders}}{84{,}000 \text{ Bank florins}} = 1.0525 \frac{\text{guilders}}{\text{florin}} \right) - 1 \right) * 100 = 5.25 \text{ percentagio.}$

rate of return would have been a mere 0.15 percent per year. Also, operations were too infrequent to have been a reliable source of income. Another motivation could have been to reduce high agios and inflate low agios, as when a modern central bank acts to keep market rates near target rates, but operations did not routinely interact with the agio in this way (Quinn and Roberds 2019). Instead, this chapter shows that the Bank used assayers to stabilize the total amount of Bank money. Why the Bank wanted a stable amount of money has remained a secret, but Chapter 6 did reveal why it was otherwise unstable. The success of the receipt system meant that customers routinely and substantially altered the overall amount of Bank money. The Bank used operations to alter it back in a process called sterilization by modern central banks.

This chapter is about seeing these two sides.[3] The receipt system described in Chapters 5 and 6 in effect added a new system for backing Bank money and modified, but did not eliminate, the old system. The new system was fully backed by trade coins and fully redeemable with receipts. It was a narrow bank, and customers determined the quantity and timing of transactions. Referring to the monetary map in Figure 2.4, this part of the bank interacted solely with trade coins, and the relationship was tight because the Bank actually did hold these coins until customers redeemed or abandoned their receipts.[4] For shorthand, we call this part of the Bank "the receipt bank," while acknowledging that money and receipts were distinct assets. Bank money paid for the release of coins, but the right to do so was bound to receipts, and redemption required both. This part of the Bank was attractive for customers who wanted to use Bank money while retaining control of trade coins, and the Bank managed this demand with benign neglect. Rates were kept low and stable, which encouraged customers to rely on those terms. That reliance supported the re-creation of millions of bank florins each year, and that volume varied considerably over time.

But not all Bank money was formed in tandem with receipts. When the Bank purchased coins outright or lent to the Dutch East India Company, it created balances without corresponding receipts. In the monetary map, this part of the Bank interacted with local coins (purchases) or just created Bank money (loans). This second system was not fully backed by safe

---

[3] We emphasize that this chapter's division of the Bank's balance sheet into constituent sub-banks, a receipt bank and a fiat bank, is a heuristic device and was never employed by the Bank in its own accounting.

[4] In modern parlance, the Bank did not re-hypothecate collateral.

assets such as trade coins; it had fractional reserves. Also, soon after the rise
of receipts, this money ceased to carry a right to redemption, and its coins
had no receipts. Our shorthand term for this part of the Bank is "fiat bank."
Fractional reserves without receipts worked because Bank money was
useful. Bank money could purchase or settle a bill of exchange, and it
could be easily converted into current Dutch money through the agio
market. This usefulness was essential for the receipt system also, as gaining
some Bank money for a while was an important reason customers parked
coins at the Bank. The balances created by purchases and loans were
identical to the balances created by the deposit of coin. This was a design
feature that made Bank money homogeneous. The differences between the
processes lay in what backed the money and who was in control.

This chapter will show how the two systems interacted and how the
Bank controlled, or not, the situation. A major quantitative finding is that
the Bank used operations to offset the variation in receipt flows created by
customers. For example, when customers deposited trade coins under
receipt, the Bank responded by selling local coins it owned outright.
Monetary control, however, could not always be maintained, as became
particularly evident during the Panic of 1763. To show all this, we disaggre-
gate the total stock of Bank money into the part controlled by customers,
backed by trade coins under receipts, and the part controlled by the Bank,
backed by loans and coins owned outright.

Customers also created linkages between the two systems. Trade coins
under receipt supported all Bank money through the availability of
redemption options. Customers concerned about the fractional-reserve
issues like loans gone bad could purchase a receipt to secure the explicit
backing of a safe asset. Conversely, the success of Bank money as a safe
asset made the placement of trade coins under receipt more attractive. This
system of mutual support was successful for decades but was not robust to
all circumstances, as was demonstrated by the fall of the bank florin that
began in 1781, when the loans and the seigniorage caught up with the
Bank. A run on the receipt system was a collapse of support that spread to
the rest of the Bank.

7.1 The Rest of the Story

Loans and purchases were the primary ways the Bank created its money
without receipts. Loans created fractional reserves and went to two primary
debtors: the Company and the City. To show how these actions affected
the balance sheet, Table 7.1 gives examples. In April 1715, the Company

Table 7.1. *Three changes to the Bank's balance sheet*

	A. A loan to the Dutch East India Company			
	Assets		Liabilities and Equity	
April 12, 1715	Credit at 3.5 percent	+200,000.0	Balances	+200,000.0
April 19, 1715	Debit	−200,000.0	Balances	−200,136.1
			Equity	+136.1
	B. A loan to the City of Amsterdam			
	Assets		Liabilities and Equity	
March 18, 1711	Credit	+95,522.40		
	Payment to the City Treasury of 100,000 gulden coins	−95,522.40		
January 28, 1724	Debit	−95,522.40	Equity	−95,522.40
	C. An open market operation			
	Assets		Liabilities and Equity	
March 13, 1721	88,410 gulden coins	+84,000.00	Balances	+84,000.00

Sources: ACA 5077/1275, 1; ACA 5077/1355, 16; ACA 5077/1339, 78; Van Dillen (1925b, 770).

borrowed 200,000 florins for one week. The loan created balances, was repaid in balances, and generated interest revenue in balances. In contrast, a 1711 loan to the City was paid in coin, did not earn interest, and was never repaid with coin. Instead, the City eventually wrote off its debt with a write-down of equity in 1724. In other words, the arrangement with the City was a loan in name only. The City had no obligation to repay the loan or forbear later profit taking, but it usually did enough to eventually make the Bank (nominally) whole. The last common process of money creation was the purchase of gold and silver, and Table 7.1 shows the transaction from the introduction.

7.2 Strength through Unity

What connected these activities to the receipt system was a joint monetary liability. Receipts, credits, and operations all created or destroyed the same Bank money. The exception was transactions with the City, which preferred to remove local coins, but in as much as the Bank acquired those coins through purchases with balances, even seigniorage was only one step removed from Bank money. Contrasting what customers were doing with

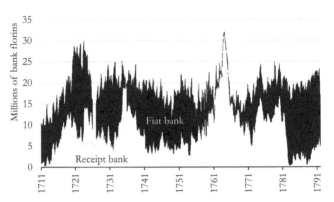

Figure 7.1. Total Bank money split into two banks, monthly, 1711–1792
Source: Authors' calculations.
Note: 1726 is missing.

receipts from what the Bank was doing with purchases and loans has required us to break that unified money into two parts: balances backed by trade coins under receipt and balances backed by everything else. More formally, we have separated total Bank money (M) into the balances (M_R) of the receipt bank and the balances (M_F) of the fiat bank. Receipt bank balances (M_R) have been defined as equal to trade coins encumbered by receipts, and fiat bank balances (M_F) have been defined as equal to the net of all the other elements of the balance sheet. By construction, $M = M_R + M_F$.

Figure 7.1 presents this decomposition: total Bank money parsed into the two banks from February 1711 through January 1792. Bank money equal to trade coins under receipt is the bottom and labeled receipt bank. Over it is the rest of the Bank money, labeled fiat bank. They stack (sum) to the total amount of Bank money. Most years have retained both ledgers and cashbooks, and the years without a cashbook have been successfully reconstructed with the exception of 1726 (for the details, see Quinn and Roberds 2019, Appendix A).

The figure confirms the story from Chapter 6: that receipt flows could and did vary considerably. The level of coins under receipt rose and fell in multi-year swings. The great crest was the Panic of 1763 when customers rushed trade coins into the Bank. The great collapse was the customer retreat from the Bank in 1781. Over eight decades, customers used the receipt facility at nearly every level in between. On top of the receipt bank was the fiat bank. It too had long-term undulations caused by large changes in loans and purchases. Despite the volatility in its components, the total amount of Bank money became rather constant. In time, variations in the two banks counteracted. As a result, the sum of the two banks, being the total level of Bank money, was much more stable than either component alone. Starting in 1727, the amount of Bank money averaged 19 million florins with a standard deviation of ±3 million. That was a major change from the earlier eras. The level of Bank money only hit 19 million for the first time in June 1718. The Bank well surpassed that level during and after the Mississippi and South Sea bubbles of 1720. Then it settled down.

Quinn and Roberds (2019) found evidence of this stability from 1736 forward. The extended dataset presented here places the start of the stable-money era in the mid-1720s, around the same time as the rise of receipts dominated by Spanish dollars (Figure 6.3). The move to a receipt bank built on foreign coins thus coincided with an apparent policy decision to offset those flows. We should again note that extant documents make no mention of a goal to keep the amount of Bank money around 19 million. As noted earlier, the Bank's traditional balance sheet was not public knowledge, so this dynamic within the Bank has only become evident with the reconstruction of transactions presented here.

To clarify what the two series measure, Table 7.2 illustrates the decomposition of Figure 7.1 in terms of the Bank's balance sheet. The left-hand side of Table 7.2 gives the consolidated balance sheet as recorded by the Bank for January 1711. The total on the sheet was set by the total amount of assets at 10.9 million bank florins.[5] On the right-hand side of Table 7.2, we reset the size to the total amount of liabilities by subtracting equity from both sides. That put assets less equity on one side and only monetary liabilities on the other, as account balances were the only type of liability the Bank incurred. The result was a "monetary balance sheet." Figure 7.1 used this balance sheet where we divided monetary liabilities by type of backing.[6]

This breakdown exists only as our own accounting device, because the Bank never designated specific balances as attached to any particular asset. Yet the focus on monetary liabilities has been an accurate depiction of how

---

[5] Following standard central bank accounting, in Table 7.2, "equity" refers to "balance-sheet equity, "the amount by which assets exceed liabilities" (Archer and Moser-Boehm 2013, 9). Equity calculations in this table are made with assets at book value, because (1) market values are not generally available, as discussed in Chapter 3, and (2) these were the values used by the Bank in its own accounting.

[6] As a heuristic device, our division of the Bank's balance sheet treats the first sub-bank as if its account balances were redeemable in coin; in fact, an account holder without a receipt would have had to purchase a receipt from someone else in order to redeem.

Table 7.2. *Two versions of the Bank's balance sheet of January 1711*

| Original balance sheet for one bank | | | | Monetary balance sheet for two sub-banks | | |
Assets		Monetary liabilities and equity		Assets less equity		Monetary liabilities
Metal	7.9	Balances	10.2	Metal under receipt	1.0	
Credit				Receipt bank sub-total	1.0	1.0
City	1.5					
Company	1.3			Metal owned outright	6.9	
Holland	0.2	Equity	0.7	Credit	3.0	
Total	10.9	Total	10.9	Less equity	−0.7	
				Fiat bank sub-total	9.2	9.2
				Total	10.2	10.2

Sources: Van Dillen (1925b, 765) and ACA 5077/1355.

the Bank actually processed information on the micro transactional basis. For example, when a customer redeemed a receipt for a sack of Spanish dollars, the monetary liability adjustment was −2,205.5 florins, being −2,200 for coins and − 5.5 for fees. The Bank did *not* record the offset as −2,200 in assets and a separate +5.5 in equity. Instead, it booked the offset as an "assets less equity" combination of −2,200 − (+5.5) = −2,205.5 (see Figure 5.8). Indeed, the Bank did not rearrange information into an asset-based balance sheet until the very end of the fiscal year in January.

From this adjusted perspective, the receipt bank's assets in 1711 were 1 million bank florins in trade coins under receipt. In legal parlance, the coins were "encumbered," meaning the Bank counted them on its balance sheet but did not control them. While the Bank did possess the coins, it was customers who controlled when this money was created or destroyed. The receipt bank had no equity, and any profits went to the fiat bank. The remaining 9.2 million florins in account liabilities were assigned to the fiat bank. These were backed by 6.9 million in unencumbered coins that the Bank owned outright and could freely dispose. The rest was backed by credit or equity, and those categories made the fiat bank fractional reserve. From 1711 through the 1770s, the stock of coins owned outright were twice the size of credits on average.

With the distinction between the two series made clear, Figure 7.2 offers another perspective on how the Bank created stability. It replots the same data from the stable era, 1727–1792, but puts each sub-bank on a different axis: the receipt-bank data on the vertical axis and the fiat-bank

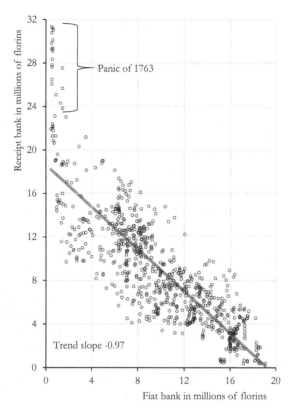

Figure 7.2. Two banks offsetting, by month, 1727–1792
Source: Authors' calculation.

data on the horizontal. Each had substantial variation, from nearly zero to 20 million or more. Yet, those extremes were persistently counteracted, with a tendency revealed in the plot by a negative overall slope. The trend line has a slope coefficient of −0.97 with a correlation of −.83. On average, each 100-florin increase (decrease) in the fiat bank was offset by a 97-florin decrease (increase) in the receipt bank. In modern jargon, changes in the receipt bank were sterilized by changes in the fiat bank. This process of stabilizing the level of Bank money around 19 million florins was highly regular over scale and time, but it did not have to be so. For example, a few observations from the Panic of 1763, being August 1763 through February 1765, showed how this trade-off could break down. Similarly, a plot of the same variables from before 1727 would violate this pattern. The stability shown here was not an accident. The Bank did not let money manage itself.

7.3 Operations

To stabilize the overall level of money, the Bank had to take deliberate action. The Bank had to choose when and how much to buy or sell coins. Through the policy of offering receipts as a standing facility, customers controlled the when and the how much of the receipt bank. The City controlled the Bank's equity, and the Company controlled the use of its line of credit. Nor did the Bank, unlike later central banks, vary its policy interest rates (either the redemption fees for receipts or interest charged for Company loans) as a way of controlling its balance sheet. This left quantitative interventions as the focus of Bank operations.

We contend that the Bank intentionally responded to the actions of its private customers, the Company, and the City. The Bank intervened with what it could readily control: coins it owned outright. Through the assayer, the Bank had been buying and selling coins and bullion for some time. Table 5.1 reports substantial coin sales in the 1660s. Chapter 6 mentions the Bank selling gold dukaten that had fallen into the Bank. What was new in the 1700s was that the Bank learned to regularly buy and sell current money in the form of silver gulden coins. As mentioned in Chapter 3, gulden coins were introduced in Holland in the 1680s, became a Republic-wide standard in the 1690s, and only started to gain substantial production volume early in the eighteenth century. While gulden coins became the standard for current money, the Bank did not accept them at the receipt window. As discussed in Chapter 2, the only primary connection between the Bank and gulden coins was when the Bank decided to buy or sell.

Trading in guldens offered a number of advantages for the Bank. The City wanted such coins from the Bank for its equity extractions, so some gulden purchases were always needed. Also, large-scale purchases and sales of local coins did not directly disrupt the foreign trade coin market that was the setting of the receipt facility. Chapter 6 has already shown how large sales of abandoned gold coins could displace the receipt facility. That fate was avoided for silver coins because they were rarely abandoned and the Bank infrequently purchased them.[7] The Bank could have purchased trade coins if it had wanted, but that option was not preferred.

Already in 1711, the assayer was buying and selling gulden coins. The apparent purpose was to have coins to surrender to the City and to make a

---

[7] In the late 1720s and early 1730s, the Bank occasionally purchased receipts and so caused Spanish dollars to fall into the Bank's ownership. Most of the coins were then melted into ingots for sale by the Bank to the local fine silver market.

Table 7.3. *Net monthly activity in local coins, 1716 through 1719*

	1716	1717	1718	1719
January	0	0	0	−65,646
February	0	17,767	0	0
March	64,000	0	0	0
April	96,000	0	0	0
May	214,000	−3,918	0	0
June	177,000	−85,672	0	0
July	166,000	−312,801	0	0
August	143,000	−408,434	0	0
September	0	−66,942	0	0
October	0	0	0	0
November	0	0	230,000	0
December	0	0	75,000	0

Source: Authors' calculations.

modest profit. For example, in February 1711, the Bank purchased 220,000 florins worth of gulden coins at agios of $4\frac{5}{8}$ and $4\frac{11}{16}$. About 40 percent of that was handed over to the City the next month. The rest was sold by the end of the year at slightly lower agios of $4\frac{3}{8}$ and $4\frac{2}{5}$. Recall that the agio was the ratio of current guilders per bank florin, so the Bank followed a buy (local coins) low and then sell high strategy for a gain of $\frac{1}{4}$ percent, that is, 25 basis points. In time, the Bank added larger operations in gulden coins. In 1716, the scale quadrupled when the Bank purchased 860,000 florins' worth at a modal agio of $5\frac{1}{8}$. A year later, the Bank sold the same for a marginal profit at a mode of $4\frac{3}{4}$. The profit margins were small, but the volumes had become large enough to be a stabilization tool.

Table 7.3 reports such activities in 1716 through 1719 as the net change in local coins owned by the Bank. Purchases were positive and created Bank money. Sales were negative and destroyed Bank money. The table gives the net change for each month, and all months with zero had no activity. Activity often came in spurts of buying or selling, and we will label these spurts "operations." We have defined an operation as the sum of mostly consecutive months totaling at least 400,000 bank florins in purchases or in sales.[8] This definition is another heuristic classification we

---

[8] The maximum gap between observations of the same sign was four months, and if the gap contained observations of the sign opposite to the operation, then the continuing observations had to more than compensate.

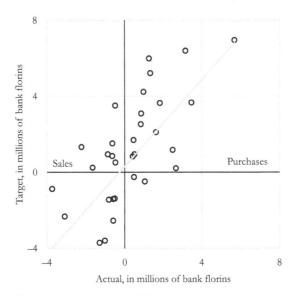

Figure 7.3. Gulden operations versus stabilization targets, 1711–1792
Source: Authors' calculations.

have adopted in order to gain insight into the Bank's activities. The Bank left no such descriptions.

Table 7.3 illustrates the activities we classify as operations in local coins. The Bank's activity from March through August 1716 became a purchase operation summing to 860,000 bank florins; May through September 1717 became a sales operation of –877,767. The other active months were either too small, too isolated, or of the wrong sign to be designated part of an operation. Over all the available data from 1711 through 1791, this filter identified 36 local coin operations: 18 purchases and 18 sales. A total of 30 million bank florins were purchased and 27 million sold. Figure 7.3 plots the total bank florin value of these operations on the horizontal axis. The largest purchase operation was for 5.7 million and the largest sale operation was for 3.8 million. Twenty of the operations were for ±1 million or more. On the vertical axis is a hypothesized target for each operation, which is derived as follows.

For operations to aid stabilization, their timing, direction, and scale needed to align with the overall level of Bank money. To gauge, in a rough sense, if operations contributed, we took the time frame of each operation and calculated the change that would have been necessary to move the overall level of Bank money to its long-term average of 19 million florins. The equation in Table 7.4 then gives a target size for each operation.

Table 7.4. *Hypothetical operation to stabilize Bank money at 19 million florins*

19 million − (Level at start) − (Change from other sources) = Target Change

Source: Authors' hypothesis.

The calculation used two known numbers for each operation: (1) the level of Bank money at the start and (2) the net change in Bank money during the operation from other factors. To find the target, we assume an end goal of 19 million. The result was the amount of deviation from 19 million at the end of each operation with the actual operation excluded. Figure 7.3 reports this predicted target operation size on the vertical axis. If an operation moved the level of Bank money to exactly 19 million, then it would be plotted along a 45-degree line running through the origin. The trend line in Figure 7.3 is not that line, but it is close. A simple linear fit to the data yields a slope of 1.14 instead of 1.00. The standard error of that fit is ±2.7 million, and the correlation between the two series was 0.65; so few operations were accurate to the ideal and some operations were counterproductive. Still, 83 percent of operations, by value, fall into one of the two aligned quadrants: actual purchases with positive targets, actual sales with negative targets. Sales of abandoned gold dukaten mentioned in Chapter 6 followed a similar pattern, albeit only in the negative quadrants. We would not go so far as to say that the equation in Table 7.4 constituted a policy rule for the Bank. On average, however, the timing and direction of the Bank's operations worked to stabilize its money stock.

The model of target interventions in Table 7.4 and Figure 7.3 has the virtue of simplicity but does not allow for more subtle effects resulting from the impact of an operation on other behaviors. For example, purchases have been found to have modest but dissipating short-term effects on receipt flows (Quinn and Roberds 2019, 761). As a result, the targets here were likely biased a bit too high on the purchase side and a bit too low on the sale side.[9] Another potential source of bias was an operation that might have been desired but could not occur. While the Bank could always purchase, it could only sell if it owned sufficient coins outright. More

---

[9] Additional econometric examinations are presented in Quinn and Roberds (2019) for the period 1736–1791. The relevant data and code are available from the *Journal of Economic History* through the website www.openicpsr.org.

elaborate econometric exercises have suggested that a lack of coins was sometimes a constraining factor (Quinn and Roberds 2019, 768).

No known internal statements describe what policy rules governed this open market activity.[10] Parsing the Bank's behavior to reveal its underlying policy has presented a deep challenge both to contemporary observers of the Bank and to subsequent scholars. Informed contemporaries knew that the Bank was up to something, and their theories focused on stabilization of the agio (Quinn and Roberds 2019, 737). After decades of study, Van Dillen agreed with these theories, stating that "[f]or many years [the Bank] bought in Bank money when the agio fell to 4¼ per cent and sold whenever it rose to 4⅞ per cent" (1934, 102).[11] Econometric analysis has found that operations did move the agio, but their timing did not correspond to that proposed policy (Quinn and Roberds 2019, 764, 767). If Bank policy was a form of bright-line agio threshold, then it failed to routinely translate into commensurate actions; and if quantity stabilization was policy, then it did. Lacking archival confirmation, we cannot state unambiguously that the latter was an official Bank policy.[12] As with many aspects of the Bank's operations, quantity stabilization may have originated as a technocratic fix rather than a conscious policy choice. But even with that caveat, the data shown here indicate that the fiat bank had a tool in open market operations that was used to stabilize Bank money around an apparent target of 19 million florins. This it achieved with noisy consistency over many decades. Perhaps unconsciously, this technocratic practice evolved into a monetary policy.

7.4 Monetary Control

To hit a target, one has to see it, and to control its monetary stock, the Bank had to know its size. This was no small challenge with the technology

---

[10] We are aware of only one surviving directive to the Bank's commissioners regarding open market operations. This is from 1782 and the directive instructs them, via the assayer, to maintain an agio of 4–5 percent, market conditions permitting (Mees 1838, 309; Van Dillen 1925a, 433–434). By this time, the agio had breached the target zone so that the directive was effectively a dead letter.

[11] This target range for the agio was first described by Van der Oudermeulen (1791, 59).

[12] Here we should caution that inferences from the Bank's data, as with most data in economics, are subject to identification issues. Plausible models of the Bank's activities with reasonable identifying assumptions might ascribe more of its open market activity to agio stabilization. We will, however, defer the investigation of such models to future research.

of the time. Chapter 5 discussed the importance of accounting to prevent fraud and showed how the Bank had access to a weekly summary of the volumes of different coins in its vaults. The anachronistic question has remained of how the Bank was able to keep accurate, real-time tallies of its money. The answer offered here is that it did not try to achieve both. The Bank favored accuracy over speed. With effort, the Bank could calculate its monetary total, and it did so at least twice a year in January and in July, when the Bank halted all operations to verify the balance of each customer and aggregate those balances into a total.[13] Otherwise, the Bank did not arrange its information processes to quickly deliver a monetary total. This reinforces the previous section that the Bank operations were intermittent, drawn out, and imprecise because operations were not fine tunings based on high-frequency data.[14]

To see what was going on at the source, Table 7.5 reports the typical master account (specie kamer) of folio 1278 of the main ledgers (*grootboeken*) that covered seven days in February 1765. Each entry had a date, a counterparty, its folio in the ledger, and the florin balance involved. Debits created balances, and this week only had two such entries: a fiat bank loan to the Company and a receipt bank repayment to the receiver Willem van Hoesen for deposits he took in through his account. Credits destroyed balances and did not go through receivers, and the folio listed each one. To save space, 47 of those credits have been consolidated into one line in the table. The rest are from the first day of the folio, Wednesday, February 6. Often, a credit was for one transaction, but sometimes more than one account paid for a redemption. For example, Anne Jacobsz & Volkart de Vries contributed 10,000 florins toward the repurchase of coins by Jan Elmenhorst Jansz. Notice that the master account did not specify what

---

[13] When the Bank constructed a balance sheet at the end of a fiscal year, the amount of Bank money expected through changes in the master account need not (and often did not) match the summation of actual account balances. Mistakes and fraud showed up as discrepancies between the two totals. In practice, the aggregation of account balances was not the official level of Bank money, and its discrepancies were kept off balance sheet (see ACA 5077/1324). Instead, the master account process shown in Figure 7.4 produced the official measure of Bank money used to create the final balance sheet.

[14] A modern take on the Bank's accounting is given by the famous CAP theorem of computer science (Townsend 2020, 44–45). The theorem states that a distributed data store (in this context, information on the master account) cannot simultaneously provide consistency (use of the most up-to-date information), availability (speedy access to information, even if not updated), and partition tolerance (ability to continue functioning in the presence of inconsistencies). In these terms, the Bank chose consistency and partition tolerance over availability.

Table 7.5. *One folio of the master account, February 6–12, 1765*

Date	Counter party	Counter folio	Florins
Debits (creation of Bank money)			
February 7	VOC (Company loan)	254	100,000.000
February 8	Willem van Hoesen (receiver transfer)	1308	44,920.000
			144,920.000
Credits (destruction of Bank money)			
February 6	Anne Jacobsz & Volkart de Vries voor [for] Jan Elmenhorst Jansz	1457	10,000.000
	Salomon & Willem Gerret Dedel	1449	126.500
	Jan Elmenhorst Jansz	1324	4,142.650
	Cornelis van der Oudermeulen & Comp.	1273	10,055.000
	Daniel Schroder	1288	51.575
	Daniel Schroder	1288	124.125
	Cornelis van der Oudermeulen voor [for] Cornelis van der Oudermeulen & Comp.	1058	12,000.000
	Henrik Hooft Danielz	215	5,091.350
	Joseph & Jacob David Proops	2391	3.000
February 7 to 12	47 transactions		283,332.775
			324,926.975

Source: ACA 5077/904, folio 1278.

collateral motivated this transaction.[15] That information was reported in the cashbook (*kasboek*). The master account was focused on monetary liabilities.

The discovery of how the Bank controlled its monetary accounts began with what the master account did not contain. It did not start with a carryover balance from its previous folio. The choice to ignore that information was unusual. Regular customer accounts carried over a net balance, so each folio contained the information needed to calculate that customer's overall balance. In contrast, the master account was designed to communicate flows: the total debits (144,920) and the total credits (324,926.975) of that folio and that folio only. The folio did not even calculate a net change. It wanted both gross accumulations. This made calculating the total

---

[15] The cashbook revealed that Elmenhorst repurchased 25 sacks of staten driegulden at 565 florins each: 14,125 in coins and 17.65 in fees (ADA 5077/1392, 92).

On February 6, 1765, Cornelis van der Oudermeulen & Company used two debits to pay 22,055 to redeem a receipt for 10 sacks of Mexican dollars.

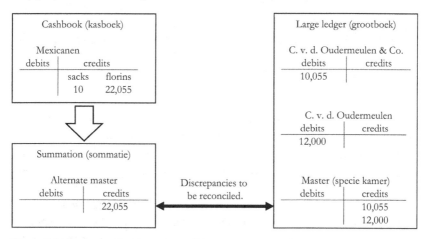

Figure 7.4. Example of system accounting
Sources: ACA 5077/904, folios 1278, 1275, 1058; ACA 5077/1392, folio 71; ACA 5077/1346, folio 2.

amount of Bank money a chore, as a clerk would have to go back to the last year-end balance sheet and then add the debits and subtract the credits of each subsequent folio of the master account. What this arrangement did produce were two sums that addressed a different question: whether the changes in the master account (monetary liabilities) matched changes in the cashbook (collateral assets). When the master account folio in Table 7.5 finished on February 12, the two totals (debits and credits) were compared to similar totals derived from what happened over in the vault. The purpose was to verify the accuracy of changes in Bank money.

Inaccuracy in accounts had threatened the credibility of the Bank in the previous century (see Chapter 5), and Figure 7.4 runs an example through a schematic of how the Bank used this information to gain control. On February 6, the firm of Cornelis van der Oudermeulen & Co. redeemed a receipt for 10 sacks of Mexican dollars. The asset side of this transaction was recorded in the cashbook (kasboek) as a 10-sack credit to the mexicanen account.[16] The cashbook also recorded that the florin value of the redemption *should* be 22,055 florins.[17] Note that the value combined coins (asset) and fees (equity) to align with monetary liabilities as per Table 7.2.

---

[16] A separate book recorded credits and other transactions that did not involve metal.
[17] Ten sacks weighing 100 marks each at a bank price of 2,200 florins per mark had a value as coins of 22,000. The fee rate as ¼ percent for an additional 55 florins.

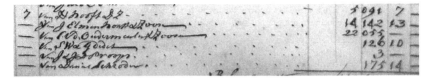

Figure 7.5. Summation credit entries for February 7, 1765
Source: ACA 5077/1346, folio 2.

That florin value was then copied to a new book called the summation (*sommatie*) that collected all the expected changes in Bank money. At the end of the folio, the master account was compared to the summation. In this case, Van der Oudermeulen's redemption was paid for with two transactions: 10,055 florins came from the firm's account and 12,000 came from his personal account. The description explicitly states that the personal payment was on behalf of the firm. That sum matched the expected value, so all was well. If they did not, then there was a discrepancy to be identified and reconciled.

To support our interpretation that the summation book summarized the cashbook and not the master account, Figure 7.5 reproduces the credit transactions from February 6, 1765, as they appeared in the summation book. The entries did not report the counter folios, and payments were consolidated into whole redemptions or prolongations of receipts. For example, the two Van der Oudermeulen payments became one redemption. Similarly, the payment by Anne Jacobsz & Volkart de Vries on behalf of Elmenhorst became part of Elmenhorst's redemption. Such payment details in the master account were not known and not relevant to the cashbook and hence the summation book. Even the sequence of entries was not the same.

What made this summation example atypical was the date, Thursday, February 7 (see the upper left of Figure 7.5). The clerk did not get around to recording the transactions of Wednesday, February 6, in the summation until the next day. Normally, a one-day discrepancy would not matter, but Table 7.5 has already told us that the master account jumped to a new folio at the start of that day. As a result, this summation folio included the credits shown, but those credits were *not* in the parallel master account that had been closed by the jump. The discrepancy occurred because the clerk did not know that the master account had begun a new folio because the information was not coming from the master account. And only then did something really unusual happen. The discrepancy was discovered, and the value of the mislaid transactions was subtracted (not shown here) from this summation folio and added to the next one so that both results aligned with the contemporaneous master account folios. The mistake was discovered and corrected because that was how the Bank made sure changes in assets matched changes in liabilities.

All of this goes to the point that about every week or two the Bank was going to considerable and sophisticated efforts to confirm the accuracy of known changes in the quantity of Bank money. One important benefit was that most mistakes were corrected quickly, if not instantaneously. Another benefit was that to conceal fraud, a bookkeeper had to compromise both sides of the process or the reconciliation process itself. As Chapter 5 showed, internal fraud could and did occur, but the reconstruction of these accounts, done to create the data presented in this book, has convinced us of the astonishing efficacy of this process. A cost, however, was that finding the current level of Bank money was cumbersome. The deep design principle was to control the process of accounting for the creation and destruction of Bank money by customers. After that, the Bank sometimes controlled those levels with stabilization operations.

7.5 Loss of Control

Let us once again indulge in anachronism and imagine that a modern expert (perhaps an official from the International Monetary Fund or even a monetary historian) could time-travel back to 1750 for a conversation with the Bank's commissioners. After being briefed on the Bank's approach to monetary policy, the modern expert would offer some frank advice. A policy of trying to simultaneously target the quantity of Bank money and its market price (the agio) could not be sustained over the long term. Moreover, because Amsterdam had the world's most open capital market, the Bank was subject to the famous trilemma of open economies: a monetary policy that simultaneously sought to peg a policy interest rate (receipt redemption fees) and an exchange rate (the agio) could provoke volatile capital flows and lead to a financial crisis, a currency crisis, or a combination of the two.[18] Continuing this fantasy, we can also imagine the commissioners' reply: these are interesting theories, but our policies have worked well since about 1727, so there will be no need to revise them. The expert would then be thanked and sent back to the twenty-first century.

---

[18] The agio was a domestic exchange rate, but its value would have had a large impact on cross-border rates; see the discussion of post-1780 events later in this chapter.

Soon after 1750, however, the scenarios envisioned by the expert began to manifest themselves. Demand for the Bank's receipt facility expanded sharply during the Seven Years War (1756–1763), with annual flows through the facility increasing to over 100 tons for silver (see Figure 6.3) and 5 tons for gold (see Figure 6.4). The agio also became volatile, dropping below 2 percent in 1759 before snapping back to normal levels in 1760, then falling below 2 percent – again in 1761 (see Figure 2.5). The usual mechanisms for controlling the agio and the stock of Bank money did not work under wartime conditions. People wanted to park trade coins at the receipt facility, for reasons explored in the next chapter, and low agios did not always motivate them to redeem their receipts. At the same time, by 1763, the fiat bank had already sold most all of the metal it owned outright, so sales operations ("drains" in modern central bank terminology) could not be employed to reduce the size of the fiat bank. The Bank was also unwilling to make the type of policy move that a modern expert might have recommended, that is, make receipts on trade coins more expensive so as to control capital flows.[19] Figures 7.1 and 7.2 show the end result of these developments; the Bank lost control of its money stock in 1763. Trade coin inflows beginning in August of that year caused the size of the receipt bank to well exceed its average of 8.6 million florins for the stable-money era.[20] As a result, the total level of Bank money also exceeded the long-term average of 19 million for the next 2 years.

In the summer of 1763, a panic hit the Amsterdam monetary system, and it convulsed. The stabilization policy developed in this chapter became counterproductive, and the Bank switched to crisis management. The crisis began in the bill of exchange sector, which had expanded rapidly during the Seven Years War to finance war-related activities (De Jong-Keesing 1939). The war ended in February 1763,[21] and the financial boom came to a tragicomic end in August 1763, with the collapse of a wildly speculative deal involving an Amsterdam merchant bank, Gebroeders de Neufville. That firm had become an aspiring member of the merchant bank elite amid the wartime expansion of bill credit. In April 1763, De Neufville, together with the Prussian war profiteer Johann Ernst

---

[19] As will be explained in the following discussion, ultimately the Bank did charge higher redemption fees, though only for less desirable types of collateral.

[20] The era being 1727 through 1791 excluding August 1763 through February 1765.

[21] The Treaty of Hubertusburg (February 15, 1763) ended hostilities between Austria, Prussia, and Saxony. This was the last peace treaty of the war. Earlier peace treaties were signed in St. Petersburg (May 5, 1762), Hamburg (May 22, 1762), and Paris (February 10, 1763).

Gotzkowsky, committed to purchase Russia's grain stockpile left in Prussia at the end of the war, much of this intended as cavalry horse feed. Like many European business deals at the time, it called for payment in reliable money – 1.2 million Dutch current guilders.[22]

Every aspect of this deal was dubious. The Russian merchant who negotiated the contract, Login Svešnikov, lacked full authorization to close the deal. The contract was nonetheless validated by the Russian crown. De Neufville and Gotzkowsky, for their part, did not have the wherewithal to make good on their purchase commitment, so they were counting on the Amsterdam bill market for funding. This was an optimistic expectation, given De Neufville's wobbly reputation in that market.[23] Finally, much of the contracted grain was spoiled by the time it could be gotten to market (Schepkowski 2009, 342). The deal came apart soon after the Bank reopened from its July accounting pause. One of De Neufville's favored counterparties in the Amsterdam bill market, Aron Joseph & Co. (a precious metals dealer in the taxonomy of Chapter 2), absconded on July 28, blowing an unrecoverable hole in De Neufville's funding (De Jong-Keesing 1939, 138). De Neufville was forced to stop all payments on July 30 (De Jong-Keesing 1939, 121).

The blowup of a dodgy deal for rotten horse feed now threw the finely balanced system of Figure 2.4 into chaos. Pressure on the system was experienced in every sector. The first explosion was in the bill market. De Neufville had defaulted on hundreds of bill-of-exchange "relations" in other cities, to the tune of 7.8 million guilders (De Jong-Keesing 1939, 101–110).[24] The relations were spread over Europe, but people knew that many were concentrated in Hamburg. People also realized that Gotzkowsky was headed to bankruptcy (with a relentless creditor in the person of the Russian Empress Catherine the Great) and, with him, many

---

[22] See, for example, Schepkowski (2009, 341). This deal has often been discussed in the literature on the Panic of 1763, including Sautijn Kluit (1865), Van Dillen (1922), Skalweit (1937), De Jong-Keesing (1939), Henderson (1962), Rachel and Wallich (1967), Schnabel and Shin (2004), and Quinn and Roberds (2015). The authors are nonetheless grateful to Taco Tichelaar for making them aware of many aspects of the grain deal and ensuing panic that are not emphasized in the literature.

[23] Reliance on short-term funding was nothing new to Gebroeders de Neufville. In early 1763, De Neufville rolled over 250,000 florins in funding each week through the Bank-money bill market (Quinn and Roberds 2015, 1160) and probably rolled over comparable amounts through current-money bills. De Neufville's bills were sold at a 1–2 percent risk premium over market rates (De Jong-Keesing 1939, 94).

[24] We do not know the distribution of these bills between Bank money and current money.

others in Berlin.[25] Bills drawn on these and many other places became unsaleable in Amsterdam. In response, Amsterdam's merchant banks sought to preserve their liquidity by protesting incoming bills from suspect locations (Quinn and Roberds 2015, 1152), thereby transmitting another punishing shock to those markets.[26] To compensate for lost bill funding, Amsterdam merchants had to bring Spanish dollars to the Bank to acquire sufficient balances with which to pay their bills coming due and to maintain precautionary liquidity. The resulting surge in coin inflows to the Bank is shown in Figures 7.1 and 7.2. These trade coins were "held captive" to the merchants' emergency liquidity needs and became unavailable for circulation outside the Bank. The bill-market shock was thus transmitted to the Bank-money and trade-coin portions of the map.

There were not enough trade coins to make every merchant liquid, however, even in Amsterdam, and the Bank was forced into a quasi-Bagehotian policy response.[27] Faced with an August 4 petition (five days into the panic) from all the major merchant banks, the City ordered the commissioners to lower the Bank's collateral standards, by taking in silver bars under receipt starting at 22.9 florins per fine mark.[28] The fee rate was ½ percent – a penalty of ¼ percent over the fee for silver coin. At the then-current agio of 2 percent, that Bank price for bullion translated to 23.4 current guilders and imposed a haircut of about 7 percent.[29] The bullion receipt facility proved popular despite these stiff terms, because at that time, Amsterdam was awash in low-grade silver following the demonetization of Prussia's wartime coinage (see Chapter 8). This emergency credit proved essential in helping the most vulnerable of the merchant banks settle their bills coming due, at a time when an additional

---

[25] As a creditor with a large army at her disposal, Catherine received a preferential settlement in the form of Gotzkowsky's art collection, 317 works in total (Schepkowski 2009, 346). Today, this forms the core collection of the Hermitage Museum.

[26] On the knock-on effects of the bill protests, see Schnabel and Shin (2004). The literature suggests that many of the protested bills were funding highly speculative activity, if not outright wisselruiterij.

[27] Referring to Bagehot's famous prescription for a central bank to lend freely during a crisis, on reasonable collateral and at a penalty rate (Bagehot 1979 [1873], 25–28, 96–99). Technically speaking, the Bank's crisis response came through its receipt window and was not seen as lending in the conventional sense.

[28] That price was 21 florins per mark for silver at least 91.66 percent (11/12) fine. Lower levels of fineness were to receive slightly worse prices per fine mark (Van Dillen 1925a, 412). As noted below, the agio went briefly negative at the outset of the panic before returning to 2 percent by late August.

[29] This calculation uses a value of 25.15 guilders per fine mark from November 1763 (Posthumus 1946, 394).

prominent failure would have been catastrophic (Quinn and Roberds 2015, 1167).[30]

Recovery from the panic was slow in part because the bill market shock also transmitted to the bottom half of the map. Like the Bank, Amsterdam's cashiers supplied liabilities (kwitanties) that were used to settle bills of exchange. Unlike the Bank, the cashiers relied on runnable quasi-banknotes (kwitanties) and demand deposits for funding. Amidst the general crisis of confidence, the cashiers unsurprisingly became subject to bank runs of the type well known from Anglo-American banking history (De Jong-Keesing 1939, 165). The ensuing surge in demand for local coins can be seen in the sudden, massive increase in production of gulden coins by Dutch mints (see Figure 3.6).

The panic thus shifted the loci of monetary demand from bills of exchange, the liabilities of cashiers, and trade coins, to Bank accounts and local coins. Connecting the two high-demand monies was the agio market, which now became dysfunctional. The agio dropped to –½ percent on August 6, the same day the Bank began accepting bullion on receipt (De Jong-Keesing 1939, 165). The desperation for local coins must have been severe, and we do not know whether that negative agio was for people buying cashier accounts or gulden coins. Normally, the two were interchangeable at par via deposit and withdrawal, but in banking panics, people favor coins, and a panic does not end until people again equate coins and accounts (Gorton and Tallman 2018). By late August, the agio rebounded back to 2 percent and began a slow climb to 3 percent in September. The size of the receipt bank continued to grow to a peak of 31.3 million in April 1764.

In summary, during the crisis period, the Bank tolerated growth of its money to whatever level receipt customers demanded. Even after the panic had passed, the Bank did not adjust receipt terms despite continued heavy use into 1765. The Bank became a passive lender of last resort: last resort because customers had few alternative ways to acquire Bank money, and passive because the Bank did not adjust the terms of its standing facilities. It let customers come as they always had. The exception was the command from the City to accept silver bullion under receipt. That policy was an expansion of facilities into lower-quality collateral during difficult times, and it bore similarities to the emergency credit policies of later central banks. The bullion policy also fit into the modern concept of a dealer of last

---

[30] Another emergency facility was created for a Bank customer with a unique connection to the Prussian crown. This facility is discussed in the next chapter.

resort, wherein a central bank lends on a wide range of collateral to non-banks in support of wholesale funding (Mehrling 2011). By such a definition, however, the Bank was always a dealer of last resort in trade coins, and its stalwart commitment to that policy during the panic reinforced confidence in the reliability of both receipts and Bank money.

7.6 Safe Asset

The Panic of 1763 was a traumatic experience for the Bank, but it was able to recover.[31] This section turns instead to the events of the early 1780s, which caused people to question the status of Bank money as a safe asset. This occurred when the two parts of the Bank ceased to work in a complementary fashion.

Safe assets have the property of trading with no questions asked, and that can be achieved when the cost to discover relevant information exceeds the benefits (Gorton 2017, 548). That was how early modern trade coins worked, and Chapter 3 presented coins as a technology that created informational opacity. Bank money was also a safe asset, and perhaps the safest asset in Europe for much of the eighteenth century. It moved with no questions asked and at high volumes. To help achieve this, the Bank, like other banks, created opacity through secrecy (Dang et al. 2017, 1005–1006). When circumstances caused customers to fear that the Bank's (secretive) fiat side was distressed and/or its receipt commitments were threatened, then questions were asked and redemptions could quickly turn into a run.

Differently from a deposit bank, the Bank's total withdrawal capacity was limited to receipts. There could be no all-encompassing run, and adverse reactions would have to shift from redemption to avoidance. Usage would decline and exchange rates weaken. This manner of decline was relevant because the success of Bank money relied on an international network of customers choosing to use bills of exchange payable in Amsterdam. Amsterdam merchants and merchant banks could also choose to draw on other places, such as London.

Fiat status also altered how dire a balance needed to become to threaten the safe-asset consensus. In the first decades of the Bank, insolvency threatened a par redemption mechanism because, literally, the Bank lacked sufficient assets to repay its monetary liabilities, and first-come-first-served

---

[31] Another financial panic with many similarities hit in 1772–1773 (see Wilson 1941; Koudijs and Voth 2016), but we defer investigation of that event to future research.

incentives would set off a redemption scramble. The Bank had such a run in 1672. With the 1683 transition to limited redemption, however, the question became when a deterioration in the Bank's balance sheet would prompt its customers to seek alternatives. One general answer, from the modern theory of central banking, is that such shifts are caused by impairments that undermine a central bank's ability to sustain its monetary policy (Fry 1993; Stella 1997). This situation has been called *policy insolvency*, noting that standard concepts of insolvency cannot be applied to central banks. Policy insolvency for the Bank occurred when it could not simultaneously maintain its traditional balance sheet of 19 million florins and a stable value of the Bank money in the agio and foreign exchange markets.

How spillovers from assets to monetary liabilities have affected central banks has become a large, complicated, and ongoing research program, and one persistent theme has been the behavior of a central bank's political authority.[32] For the Bank, that authority was the City, and it had two roles. One was exploitive. For example, the City regularly took coins from the Bank. Another was supportive, such as when the City pledged to back the Bank when founded in 1609. These roles were in tension, and Sims (2004) has suggested there are only two globally stable resolutions of this tension: (1) unreservedly exploit the central bank but back it fully (our shorthand: "sink" the central bank) or (2) limit support but resist exploitation ("float").[33]

The Bank, according to this classification, neither floated nor sank, but for many decades, it existed in a slightly submerged state. The City persistently exerted a strong downward pressure on the Bank's equity, but not enough to founder the institution, leaving the Bank sufficient space to pursue targets such as quantity stabilization. In modern terminology, the Bank was often balance-sheet insolvent but not policy insolvent. This situation can be seen, for example, in Table 7.2, where the Bank's nominal equity (0.7 million florins) was exceeded by the value of its loans to the City (1.5 million), loans that would never be repaid. The true equity of the Bank was thus negative (−0.8 million), but this was likely not a source of concern at the time, because the earning power of the Bank was sufficient to amortize this position within a few years.

---

[32] For a sampling of this literature, see Fry (1993), Stella (1997), Sims (2004), Stella (2005), Klüh and Stella (2008), Archer and Moser-Boehm (2013), Del Negro and Sims (2015), Bassetto and Sargent (2020), and Buiter (2021).

[33] Sims' argument is couched in terms of a modern central bank whose assets consist of government debt, but we believe its logic would carry over to institutions such as the Bank.

An even more technical statement of the situation (cf. Archer and Moser-Boehm 2013, 9) would be that the Bank had positive *comprehensive net worth*, which is equity adjusted for the present value of probable future income. Operating in the background was the City's willingness and ability to inject capital (literally, put coins back) into the Bank should a crisis situation develop. The general effectiveness of this combination was enhanced by strict secrecy. Outside observers did not know of the takings, so they assumed the vaults held more coin than they did, and the need for backing seemed remote.

The receipt system added to stability by helping divert customers who might ask questions. In Amsterdam, a concerned customer, say, with inside information or just a general fear, could purchase a receipt. The cost was a few percent, the market was reliable, and the gain in commitment was specific. Receipts were a more relevant and less costly solution than efforts to penetrate Bank secrecy. This pressure valve would allay more general fears that others might discover and act on more general information, such as the balance sheet. For the Bank, receipts let individuals pierce the shroud of secrecy without revealing anything about the overall shape. The receipts were, from a modern perspective, tradeable put options on the bank florin, and a confident Bank could afford to write many such options. To outsiders, the presence of many unexercised put options in the Amsterdam market could have served as a reassuring signal that nothing was amiss with the Bank (Calomiris and Kahn 1991). At the same time, the price of receipts could communicate balance-sheet risk. In the extreme, a receipt run (mass redemption) could signal distress in a manner similar to a traditional bank run.

The long run of Bank money as a safe asset came to an end with the Fourth Anglo-Dutch War (1780–1784). The British government declared war on the Dutch Republic in December 1780. The British were frustrated that the Dutch, an erstwhile ally, asserted neutrality, yet supplied military materials to France and the United States, both countries with which Britain was at war. The British navy blockaded the Republic, captured merchant shipping, and seized Dutch colonies (De Vries and Van der Woude 1997, 455). An armistice came in January 1783 and a formal peace in May 1784, but by then the Dutch East India Company (VOC) had lost much of its economic power in Asia. The VOC's business model was shattered, its balance sheet was insolvent, and the Republic had no clear legal process to dissolve a government-sponsored enterprise. As early as February 1781, the province of Holland gave the Amsterdam Chamber of the VOC (the Company) permission to suspend debt repayments (Steur 1984, 116).

The Company's woes became the Bank's woes. At the start of the war, the Company owed the Bank 1.9 million florins, and it borrowed 2.9 million more in January 1782, just before the books closed for the Bank's fiscal year-end accounting (Van Dillen 1925b, 789; Quinn and Roberds 2016, 85). The total of 4.8 million was in the top 6 percent of the Company's monthly debt levels going back to 1666. The largest debt level had been 7.9 million in October 1741 (cf. Figure 2.3). The issue was not the scale of lending, but rather the scale of non-performance. One quarter of the Bank's assets now looked to receive nothing from the Company for years, and the debts would eventually become a nearly complete loss. At the same time, again in February 1781, the City lent 1 million gulden coins from the Bank to the Province of Holland on a 40-year annuity. The plan was for the subsequent annuity repayments to slowly restore the coins to the Bank.[34] The City used the Bank to support the Company and the Province of Holland in difficult times.

The times got worse as the disastrous war progressed, and the City expanded its exploitation of the Bank. In early 1782, the City took another 1.2 million in gulden coins for another provincial annuity.[35] Also, the Bank inexplicably lent 300,000 more to the Company. In addition, the Bank reopened and funded an account for the City loan chamber (*Stadsbeleeningkamer*) in February. The loan chamber had been a small experiment during a financial crisis in 1773, and it was revived with scale at this time (Breen 1900; De Jong 1934). The City used the loan chamber to make loans to local merchants.[36] Initially, the chamber had been guaranteed by a private syndicate, but by the end of 1782, responsibility had been transferred to the City, and the chamber's debt with the Bank totaled nearly 1 million florins (Van Dillen 1925b, 790). The chamber did pay interest and repay some principal, but the loan chamber continuously drew

---

[34] Also, despite the total level of Bank money being at 21 million at mid-year, the Bank began its largest gulden purchase operation of 5.7 million in July, one that would continue through September 1782 (Quinn and Roberds 2016, 82–83).

[35] Again, the subsequent annuity payments were intended to slowly restore the coins back to the Bank.

[36] The Loan Chamber was not a facility to discount bills of exchange but a secured lending facility. Eligible collateral at the facility categorically excluded bills but allowed non-perishable real goods and securities of various types, even Company debt at a 25 percent haircut (De Jong 1934, 322). More controversially, a 1784 application by three Amsterdam merchants (Willink, Fijnje, and Van Staphorst) requested a loan against United States bonds. The applicants were informed that they could expect a 40–50 percent haircut on such speculative collateral, after which they withdrew their request (Breen 1900, 147–48).

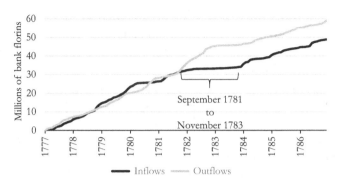

Figure 7.6. Cumulative receipt inflows and outflows, monthly, 1777–1786
Source: Authors' calculations.

new credits from the Bank, so the actual performance of the backing merchant loans remains unknown.

In mid-1782, a desperate Company pitched a debt restructuring scheme (De Korte 1984, 81). The Company gave short-term creditors like the Bank the opportunity to convert into a long-term form that also brought potential backing by the province of Holland. To participate, the creditors had to advance at least another 50 percent of their existing position. The City approved, and the Bank lent 2.85 million more (Van Dillen 1925a, 439–440). As a result, overall credit had quadrupled in two years of war, and 70 percent was now non-performing.[37]

Did all of this affect demand for Bank money? Customer behavior suggests that it precipitated a receipt run.[38] Figure 7.6 presents the cumulative receipt inflows and outflows by month starting in February 1777, when the receipt bank was 11.8 million florins. The flows run rather evenly through August 1781 with 32 million in and 32 million out. Then, in September 1781, inflows stalled for over two years. Outflows kept going until the stock of coins under receipt fell to 0.4 million. The receipt bank almost disappeared (see Figure 7.1). Receipt throughputs did not begin to revive until November 1783.

Trust in receipts broke, and safe-asset theory would suggest that customers feared questions such as whether the Bank was exposed to the Company, whether the City was taking coins from the Bank, whether the

---

[37] The debt level was 2.7 million on January 1, 1781, and 11.1 million on January 1, 1783.
[38] It was conceivable that the Amsterdam market suddenly ran out of silver, but contemporary Dutch mint production did not collapse, and the price of silver bullion did not skyrocket (Posthumus 1946, 395).

Figure 7.7. London-on-Amsterdam exchange rate of two-month bills, monthly, 1711–1793
Source: Castaing's *Course of the Exchange,* transcription provided by Larry Neal.
Note: Original series is London prices in Flemish shillings (schellingen; see Chapter 2) and has been converted at 0.3 florins per shilling.

new loan chamber had adequate collateral, and whether the City was going to seize trade coins under receipt. While the last concern did not material- ize, a receipt run only required that it become a relevant possibility. Public signs of difficulties, such as the Company's default and the activation of the loan chamber, could have been sufficient. Leakage of inside information into Amsterdam's elite financial community was another and reinforcing possibility. "When the war was over (1784) neither the Company nor the Loan Chamber, nor the [City] Treasury were in a position to repay the advances received. Unfavorable rumors regarding the Bank commenced to circulate" (Van Dillen 1934, 114).

The run depleted the ability of receipts to allay, and may have reinforced, balance-sheet fears. The breakdown of the safe-asset consensus transitioned from redemptions to a decline in the price of florins that could not be redeemed. The clearest measure of this was the slow weakening of the bank florin relative to the British pound. Figure 7.7 reports the ratio of Bank money per pound sterling for two-month bills of exchange drawn in London on Amsterdam from 1711 through 1793. The bank florin was particularly strong when the war began, but it weakened over the next dozen years. By 1793, Bank money had lost over 10 percent relative to its previous long-term relationship with the pound.[39] The collapse broke a

---

[39] From 1711 through 1780, the average monthly exchange rate was 10.7 bank florins per pound.

trading range that had held for at least eight decades and reflected a migration of the international community out of Bank money. Bank money also weakened relative to current money as can be seen in the agio series in Figure 2.5.

City leaders in the 1780s could have reasonably seen the situation as a one-time deviation that would snap back. Indeed, Flandreau and Jobst (2009, 660) found a lingering resonance of Amsterdam's pre-eminence in the European bill market persisted as late as 1900. Instead, the florin's decline continued, and by late 1790, the agio turned negative, a situation that previously only occurred during the 1672 run on the Bank and during the 1763 run on cashiers, and those episodes lasted only a few days (cf. Figure 2.5). The receipt collapse was fast, but the exchange rate collapse was more persistent.

In 1791, a lawyer representing disgruntled Amsterdam merchants petitioned the City for action, arguing that existing policies would not change international attitudes toward the Bank: "Even if the distrust which exists abroad is baseless, it will be – as long as Bank money stays at the low rate to which it has fallen or falls further – impossible to convince any foreigner that 100 bank florins represents 105 guilders current money" (Van Dillen 1925a, 450). The petition wanted the Bank to sell coins until the agio was restored to 5 percent. Another petition wanted the resuscitation of convertibility into local coins, and yet another wanted the City to open the Bank's books (Van Dillen 1925a, 455, 457).[40]

Under this pressure, the Bank experimented with redemption rights into local coins.[41] At the start of January 1791, the Bank owned 2.2 million in local coins, and that month the Bank offered cashiers those coins at an agio of −1 percent, just below the market of −0.6. Cashiers withdrew 0.3 million. In February, the Bank raised the redemption agio to zero, and the experiment was quickly stopped after cashiers withdrew 1.6 million in two weeks and reduced the Bank's holdings of local coins to 0.3 million. The Bank gave up on the restoration of the agio through convertibility.

Attention turned to recapitalization, and the City council appointed a commission that recommended a bond issue to fund an infusion of

[40] Another indication that the balance sheet was still private was that the lawyer, Nicolaas Bondt, guesstimated the level of Bank money at 40 million when the most recent tally of July 1790 was 22.2 million (Van Dillen 1925a, 449; ACA 5077/1349, 136).

[41] Before this, in November 1790, the Bank had offered to redeem Bank money in silver bars at 26 florins 5 stivers (banco) per mark, a de facto depreciation of about 10 percent (Van Dillen 1925a, 447). There were few takers.

6 million (Van Dillen 1925a, 458–459).[42] Quinn and Roberds (2016, 95) estimated the Bank's comprehensive net worth by that time was about –6.5 million florins, so the proposal was of an appropriate scale.[43] The City did issue bonds that allowed the Bank to destroy 6 million bank florins of balances, which occurred in stages from April 1791 to January 1792 (Quinn and Roberds 2016, 95).[44] However, the City simultaneously took back 1.7 million in local coins from the Bank.[45] The Bank additionally wrote off 1 million of the loan chamber's 1.9 million debt and handed back to the City 1 million in provincial annuities (see Figure 5.13). These extractions undid 60 percent of the recapitalization and the Bank remained policy insolvent.

More critically, the City's maneuverings did not restore foreign confidence. The exchange rate on Amsterdam continued to decline. The last extant cashbook is from 1791 and marks the end of our balance-sheet reconstruction. Subsequent events do not require delicate filtering of the data, however. The year 1793 had brought war with France, the next year an invading army, and the next year the end of the Dutch Republic. Based on annual balance-sheet information, Bank money grew in 1792, shrank back by about the same amount in 1793, and then contracted substantially in 1794 (Van Dillen 1925b, 795–797). The new municipal government in 1795 quickly revealed the Bank's balance sheet. The receipt bank was again tiny at 0.7 million. The fiat bank was 11 million, of which 16 percent was backed by metal and 57 percent was backed by debt of the bankrupt Company (Van Dillen 1925b, 480, 797). The London bill market ceased exchange rates quotations on Amsterdam in January 1795. Although the Bank was not shuttered until 1818, "More and more, the merchants grew accustomed to paying their bills outside the Bank, in current money" (Van Dillen 1934, 115).

---

[42] The bonds that were subsequently issued paid 3.5 percent and the issue was undersubscribed at 5.174 million.

[43] This estimate of net worth is based on conjectural market values for Company debt. By contrast, the Bank's pre-1780 comprehensive net worth, with Company debt carried at book value, had averaged slightly more than 1 million bank florins.

[44] The City used the proceeds of the bond sale to purchase balances through the agio market. Those balances were destroyed by debiting the City's account and crediting the master account. As assets remained unchanged, the loss of balances resulted in an offsetting increase in equity to create a capital injection.

[45] In March 1791, the Bank had reloaded its stock of gulden coins by having 2.8 million in silver bullion minted into local coins. When the City took these coins, assets (coins) and equity were reduced on the balance sheet.

7.7 Conclusion

The practical business of central banking was famously summarized by John Maynard Keynes in his *Treatise on Money*: "The first necessity of a Central Bank, charged with responsibility for the management of the monetary system as a whole, is to make sure that it has an unchallengeable control over the total volume of bank-money . . ." (Keynes 1930, 225). Through the sterilization of receipt-window swings and the putting aside of such stabilization during the Panic of 1763, the Bank evidently sought to confront this necessity and to manage the monetary system as a whole. The consistency of these actions suggests that they were undertaken with a vision regarding the role of an institution that we would now call a central bank.

The broader policy goal was to maintain the status of Bank money as a safe asset, one that supported an extensive system of bill-based trade credit and merchant banking. This goal was in part achieved through the issue of discrete packets of information in the form of receipts. A receipt provided a crude but relevant signal of the Bank's condition, by awarding its holder the right to instantaneously convert their Bank money into trade coins. Receipts qua put options were powerful but double-edged instruments. When confidence was high, receipts made it easier for people to accept the mystery of the larger picture and to accept Bank balances sans receipts as an irredeemable asset with an opaque backing. When confidence was low, receipts became an instrument of flight that signaled distress, and demand for Bank money faltered.

The Bank's secrecy meant that outsiders could not see beyond its smooth exterior to observe the volatility of the receipt bank or the fiat bank's open market operations. Beneath the Bank's opaque and generally peaceful façade, however, lay the monetary turbulence of eighteenth-century Europe. Amsterdam's location near the center of Europe's monetary system meant that any instability would inevitably be felt there, the Bank's efforts at money management notwithstanding. The next chapter provides an example of how geopolitical struggles could spawn destabilizing cross-border monetary shocks, with stressful consequences for the Bank and for the platforms sketched in the monetary map of Figure 2.4.

8

Prussia's Debasement during the Seven Years War: the Role of the Bank

Eighteenth-century Europe did not lack in monetary turbulence, and every breeze would have been felt in Amsterdam. Tracking this turbulence through millions of Bank ledger entries can pose data challenges, however. The exceptional events were those disruptive enough to visibly impact the Bank's master account, two examples being the rise and fall of John Law's system (Chapter 6) and the Panic of 1763 (Chapter 7). This chapter considers another exceptional episode: Prussia's debasement of its coinage during the Seven Years War.[1] Like the John Law and 1763 episodes, Prussia's debasement generated large flows through the Bank's master account, and an extensive historiography facilitates interpretation of these flows.[2] The mechanics of the debasement and its subsequent reversal also illustrate the Bank's role in the monetary systems of Amsterdam and early modern Europe more generally.

This story has a quiet beginning, with an ostensibly touristic visit to the Dutch Republic in June 1755. This tour would, however, have lasting implications for the Bank and for the course of European history, for the tourist in question was Frederick II, King of Prussia (later known as Frederick the Great), a ruler who would soon plunge his country into a prolonged war.[3]

---

[1] The Seven Years War began in August 1756 and was a three-continent conflict involving many countries; on the course of the war, see, for example, Szabo (2008) and Baugh (2014).

[2] A partial list of the literature on the Prussian debasement includes Büsch (1797), Koser (1900), Schrötter (1908, 1910, 1913), Bahrfeldt (1913), Stern (1950, 1971), Redlich (1951), Gaettens (1955), Schnee (1955), Rachel and Wallich (1967), Hoensch (1973), and Kluge (2012, 2013). As discussed later, the unwinding of the Prussian debasement was a contributor to the extraordinary flows through the Bank experienced during 1763.

[3] On Frederick's visit to the Republic, see Rödenbeck (1840, 275). We are again grateful to Taco Tichelaar for pointing us to this reference.

The full itinerary of Frederick's trip to the Republic will never be known – this was a secretive journey where the king traveled incognito, traveling by *trekschuit* (horse-drawn boats that served as public transit) and accompanied only by a single servant. But his schedule likely combined business with pleasure, for much of Frederick's time in the Republic was spent visiting Isaac de Pinto, a retired banker, famed Enlightenment thinker, and acknowledged expert on matters of economic policy.[4] Both Frederick and De Pinto were connoisseurs of fine art and this shared interest would have provided a pretense for their meeting. But Frederick's conversations with De Pinto likely touched on more practical matters.

Prussia's relations with three larger neighbors – Austria, France, and Russia – were deteriorating and would soon tip over into war. Prussia's options for financing a war were always limited and the country had recently experienced a downward shock. Like many states at that time, Prussia had no central bank, no bond market, and essentially no credit. Its military budget was a largely pay-as-you-go affair, augmented during wartime with subsidies from allies and "contributions" (tribute) from conquered territories (Koser 1900). If Prussia's financial infrastructure had been more advanced, or its military prospects had been brighter, then Frederick might have used his time in the Republic to meet with a merchant-bank lender. That he instead chose to visit the more theoretically inclined De Pinto was a reflection of his desperate circumstances.

Frederick had been counting on revenues from seigniorage to bolster his war budget. To that end, he hired an outside expert on coinage, Johann Philipp Graumann (sometimes written as Grauman), and had given Graumann almost complete control of Prussia's coin production (Schrötter 1908). Graumann failed to deliver his promised amounts of seigniorage, however, causing Frederick to dismiss him and to outsource coin production to two "mint entrepreneurs," Moses Fränkel and Nathan Veitel Heine Ephraim, prominent Jewish merchants in Berlin.[5] Both entrepreneurs had previously worked as silver suppliers to Graumann, and they would have been well known to the king. Frederick must have nonetheless felt discomfort with an arrangement that relied on Jewish entrepreneurs,

---

[4] Rödenbeck's account suggests that Frederick met with De Pinto at the latter's richly decorated canal house in Amsterdam, but in reality, the two may have met at De Pinto's country estate.

[5] Fränkel and Ephraim's coinage contract with the Prussian crown is reproduced in Schrötter (1908, 520–521). Although Fränkel, Ephraim, and other mint entrepreneurs essentially acted as Frederick's bankers, under the cultural conventions of the time they could not be called "bankers."

who, by tradition, were excluded from Prussian citizenship.[6] Outsourcing of coinage was also forbidden under the laws of the Holy Roman Empire (or "Empire"), of which most of Prussia was still a part.[7] We can therefore surmise that the terms of the entrepreneurs' (top secret) contract were the subject of discussions between the king and the financial expert De Pinto.

What happened after Frederick's return to Prussia is not a matter of conjecture but of historical fact: Fränkel and Ephraim were fired and replaced with a consortium of three other mint entrepreneurs, Herz Moses Gumperts, Moses Isaac, and Daniel Itzig (Schrötter 1910, 239–46).[8] These new entrepreneurs were, like their predecessors, Jewish merchants who had earlier worked as suppliers to Prussia's mints. Frederick's decision to outsource mint operations to this group proved to be an auspicious one, for there were few people who better understood the idiosyncrasies of eighteenth-century money, or who were more capable of exploiting these idiosyncrasies. Over the course of the Seven Years War, this consortium and its successors would create and circulate immense amounts of debased coin. By a conservative estimate, the entrepreneurs processed 800 tons of silver, providing a steady stream of seigniorage revenue to fund Prussia's war efforts.[9] Prussia finished the war with a thoroughly debased money stock, but in contrast to other warring powers, no debt.[10]

---

[6] It is noteworthy that De Pinto himself was a prominent member of the Amsterdam Jewish community. His family had Portuguese rather than German origins, however, and to our knowledge, De Pinto had no business or family connections to the Prussian mint entrepreneurs. However, De Pinto would have been well acquainted with parties in Amsterdam who would later support the entrepreneurs' operations.

[7] The Holy Roman Empire was a loose confederation of mostly ethnic German states in central Europe. The Empire tried to enforce a unified coinage policy, which included a ban on outsourcing. Prussia's easternmost territories lay outside the Empire, which may have left some legal wiggle room for coins minted there.

[8] Isaac is sometimes spelled Isaak and Gumperts is sometimes spelled Gumpertz, Gumprecht, or Gompertz.

[9] Koser (1900, 43) gives a wartime revenue breakdown for Prussia of 42 percent tribute from conquered territories, 16 percent from British subsidies, and 17 percent from inflation (seigniorage), with the remainder coming from domestic rents and taxes. For comparison, the United States financed 19 percent of its World War II expenditures through inflation (Hall and Sargent 2021).

[10] Britain's debt at war's end was 133 million pounds or 119 percent of its GDP (Hills, Thomas, and Dimsdale 2010); France's debt was 220 million livres (98 million British pounds) or 40–50 percent of its GDP (François Velde, personal communication); Austria's debt was 285 million Austrian gulden (32 million British pounds; see Dickson 1987, 39) or 89 percent of its GDP or about 320 million Austrian gulden (Clemens Jobst, personal communication).

The Bank pervades this story because the starting points for the entrepreneurs' operations were the precious metal markets in Hamburg, London, and especially Amsterdam. To create large quantities of debased silver coins, one first had to acquire large amounts of silver, and the liquid pool of trade coins held at the Bank was a natural place for the entrepreneurs to source their silver supply. Many of the entrepreneurs' operations can thus be matched to transactions recorded in the master account of the Bank. These transactions are suggestive of the scale of the Prussian debasement and illustrative of the Bank's capabilities. Before describing the entrepreneurs' operations, we first describe Prussia's prewar monetary regime and its connection to Amsterdam.

8.1 Beating the Dutch at Their Own Game

Five years before Frederick II's trip to the Dutch Republic, the stage was already being set for his wartime debasement, with a coinage reform initiated by Johann Philipp Graumann, Prussia's newly installed mint master. Though Graumann's reform did not succeed in its goal of delivering promised revenues to the Prussian treasury, it created a streamlined cross-border production framework that would later allow Frederick's mint entrepreneurs to earn exceptional amounts of seigniorage.

Graumann was an expert on coinage who had previously worked as mint master in Brunswick. He attracted Frederick's attention by publishing a polemical essay on the state of European coinage (Graumann 1749) and was installed as Prussian mint master in 1750 (Gaettens 1955, 149). The arch-mercantilist Graumann viewed Dutch trade coins, which circulated in Germany at premia over their bullion values, as little more than instruments of fraud.[11] Graumann particularly hated the Republic's most important trade coin, the gold dukaat, in part because of its convenience premium and in part because it often circulated in a clipped state due to its lack of milling (see Chapter 3). Compounding the defects of the dukaat, in Graumann's view, was the Dutch mints' habit of producing substandard or "light" dukaten for circulation abroad (Graumann 1762, 128–29).

Prussia's native coinage was at this time governed by the common standard of the Empire, known as the Leipzig standard, which set a mint equivalent of 12 currency units (*Thaler*) per fine mark for large silver coins.[12] By the 1740s,

---

[11] See Greitens (2020) for a critical review of Graumann's writings on money.
[12] On the Leipzig standard, see, for example, Hoensch (1973, 115). The Thaler was both a coin and a unit of account. The German plural of Thaler is Thaler, and the modern

however, market prices of silver were running at 13 Thaler per mark or more, so Prussian coins produced at the Leipzig standard tended to become easy prey for persons (including Dutch traders) who could offer desirable foreign coins in exchange. In 1747, Austria began minting coins at a more realistic 13-Thaler standard, adding pressure on Prussia to reform its coinage (Hoensch 1973, 118). Lacking natural sources of precious metal, Prussia obtained the raw material for its mints by requiring Jewish residents of Prussia to annually deliver fixed quantities of silver, which they obtained through trade in eastern Europe (Stern 1971, 56). Because Prussia paid below-market prices for these deliveries, the silver quotas amounted to a form of tax. Mint production under this system was light, using only 0.69 tons of silver in its most active year of 1748 (Schrötter 1908, 108–9). Graumann saw the quota system as outmoded and was envious of the Republic's ability to circulate its trade coins abroad. What he proposed to Frederick was no less than a Prussian takeover of the Republic's role as provider of trade coins to Germany and the Baltic.

Graumann's plan had three major components. The first of these was to set a new coinage standard for Prussia (Koser 1900, 12). Graumann's Thaler coin bore the ambitious name of *Reichsthaler* ("Imperial dollar," implying validity over the whole of the Empire) and was meant to displace foreign silver trade coins such as the Dutch rijksdaalder and other German coins. The Reichsthaler's mint equivalent was set higher than the Leipzig standard and higher than market silver prices, at 14 Thaler per fine mark. A new Prussian gold coin, similarly meant to compete with foreign coins such as the Dutch gold dukaat, was also given an ambitious name: the *Friedrichsdor*, a flattering reference to another popular trade coin, the French Louis d'or.

The second component of Graumann's plan was to mint lots of coin, his reasoning being that supply would create its own demand: if many Prussian coins were available, then people throughout the Baltic or even throughout Europe would use them. In his 1752 *Testament Politique*, Frederick describes Graumann's goal of producing 20 million Thaler per year of coins at a 5 percent profit margin, generating 1 million Thaler in seigniorage (Volz 1913, 124–25).[13] If these were (for example) all full-weight silver coins, then vast amounts of silver – 334 tons – would have

---

spelling of Thaler is Taler. The Prussian mark weight was equal to 233.8555 grams, slightly less than the Dutch mark (Chapter 3, note 13).

[13] The Testament was a statement of governing principles intended for Frederick's own use and for the use of his successors. The section on coinage summarizes Graumann's plan as presented to Frederick.

been required.[14] In preparation for large production volumes, Graumann expanded the number of Prussian mints from two to six.

The third component of Graumann's plan was to scale up the supply of raw material to the mints. The traditional quota system was scrapped and replaced by a new system, under which supply was contracted to merchants with sufficient standing to purchase large amounts of metal abroad, on their own credit (Stern 1971, 232). The most prestigious contract, to supply silver to the Berlin mint, went to a consortium of the Christian banker Seegebarth and the Jewish firm of Gumperts. Other silver delivery contracts went to Jewish firms, all of which were well known at the Prussian court and many of which would later function as mint entrepreneurs.[15]

The catch in Graumann's plan was that the debts incurred by suppliers in places such as Amsterdam (for example, bills of exchange drawn on Berlin) would eventually have to be repaid in Prussian coin. If repayment were to occur in Prussia's flagship coin, the Reichsthaler, then the gamble was that silver could be acquired at a price that translated to less than 14 Reichsthaler per fine mark, the Reichsthaler's mint equivalent.[16] A complementary strategy would have been to pay off some bills in Prussian small coins (*Scheidemünzen*) with even higher mint equivalents, again presuming that these would be valued above their fine content. These strategies may have appeared reasonable, given the premia attached to Dutch trade coins in Baltic markets (as high as 8 percent according to Graumann, cf. Chapter 3).

At first, it appeared that the gamble might pay off, in part because Graumann had chosen an opportune moment to begin an assault on his despised rivals, the Dutch mints. The States General had outlawed the payment of mint commissions in 1749. Graumann's suppliers apparently entered the Amsterdam market not long after, and the effects of their activity quickly became evident. By November 1750, the Republic's General Mint Masters were pleading to the States General to rescind the ban on commissions, citing "a large reduction in the local business of gold and silver coinage," because "every day much gold and silver is transported

---

[14] More realistically, Graumann would have anticipated minting a mixture of gold and silver coins.

[15] A fourth proposed component of Graumann's plan was to found a Prussian version of the Bank of Amsterdam, as a way of attracting precious metal to Berlin. This proposal was successfully resisted by Berlin banks however, which feared competition from a public bank (Schrötter 1908, 138; Rachel and Wallich 1967, 522–526).

[16] In this instance, Reichsthaler refers to both a coin and a unit of account.

to the Prussian mints, where significant quantities of gold and silver Fredericks are minted" (Van Dillen 1925a, 387). Continued political pressure on the States General caused it to suspend the ban on commissions in February 1751.

Perhaps due to renewed Dutch competition, it was then Graumann who began to experience market pressures. A May 1751 letter from Frederick forbade Graumann to pay more than 13.1267 Reichsthaler per mark for silver, but that limit was breached a short time later (Schrötter 1908, 123–28). Sometime around October 1751, the Gumperts–Seegebarth consortium arranged for the purchase of 3.5 million Reichsthaler worth of silver (about 58 tons) in Amsterdam, at a price that translated to a barely profitable figure of 13.875 Reichsthaler per mark (Schrötter 1908, 253).[17] This outcome led to the cancellation of the Gumperts–Seegebarth supply contract, but the other suppliers could not do much better. By early 1752, the average price paid by Prussian mints was 13.53 Reichsthaler per mark, and by 1753 this average had risen to 13.84 Reichsthaler, leaving Graumann a disappointing gross margin of only 0.26 Thaler per coin (1.17 percent) on the minting of large silver coins (von Schrötter 1908, 482).

Coinage of gold under Graumann's scheme proved even more problematic than silver. The mint equivalent for the Friedrichsdor was set at 193.145 Reichsthaler per mark fine gold (Koser 1900, 12) with an implied legal gold–silver ratio of 13.796, substantially below the contemporary market ratio of about 14.5. The expectation seems to have been that the Friedrichsdor would immediately command a 5 percent premium. Mint gold deliveries were contracted primarily to two prominent Berlin banks: Splitgerber & Daum and Friedrich Wilhelm Schütze. These firms were flattered to have such a prestigious contract but found it difficult to acquire gold at a profitable price, because the anticipated liquidity premium did not materialize (Rachel and Wallich 1967, 242–43). In the end, few gold coins were produced. Lack of production reinforced a market preference for the familiar Dutch gold dukaat, which commanded a 4 percent premium over the struggling Friedrichsdor (von Schrötter 1908, 128).

By 1754, Graumann's attempted reform was at an impasse. The envisioned premia on his silver coins had not materialized and silver prices had crept up to the point where coin production was no longer profitable. Gold coinage was virtually nonexistent. Frederick was not sure who to blame

---

[17] Such a large purchase would have made a splash in the Amsterdam silver market. So far, however, we have been unable to conclusively identify the consortium's counterparties in Amsterdam.

and suspected malfeasance on the part of the suppliers. In May 1754, he approached a Berlin banker, David Splitgerber, with a proposal that contracts for the metal deliveries be taken over by a consortium of Christian merchants. These firms were well aware of the attendant risks however and politely declined Frederick's offer (Schrötter 1908, 139).

The year 1755 saw several events that would transform Graumann's sputtering monetary system into a "virtual printing press" of seigniorage revenue. The first of these, unsurprisingly, was the firing of Graumann as mint master. Graumann was kept on at full salary as an informal advisor to the king, however, perhaps out of personal affection or perhaps from fear that Graumann might be hired by a rival prince (Gaettens 1955, 150). Operation of Prussia's four outlying mints – Königsberg and Breslau in the east, Aurich and Cleve in the west – were then (secretly) outsourced to Fränkel and Ephraim, in conflict with Imperial law.[18] Contracted rates of seigniorage were 4 percent for the eastern mints and 3.5 percent for the western mints (Rachel and Wallich 1967, 293). Frederick's uneasiness with the terms of this contract may have helped motivate his June trip to the Dutch Republic.

Soon after Frederick's return home, Prussian coinage policy embarked on a more aggressive phase. Supervision of all minting activity was turned over to a trusted subordinate, Major General Wolf Frederick von Retzow, someone who harbored a deep dislike of Ephraim. By early October, Retzow had canceled the contract with Ephraim and Fränkel and had signed a contract with Gumperts, Isaac, and Itzig (Schrötter 1910, 239–46). The new contract was both ambitious (100 tons of silver was to be minted each year) and more favorable to the Prussian crown (an amount equal to 5.2 percent of the minted silver was to be paid over on a strict quarterly schedule). This contract marked a sharp turning point in Prussia's success as a coin producer and a major conceptual shift in its coinage strategy, developments that are described in the next section.

8.2 A Change of Tactics

Frederick's mint entrepreneurs were able to succeed where Graumann failed, by making two adjustments to his overall plan. One adjustment was to emphasize coin production at locations distant from the Prussian heartland, with the idea that these coins would be less likely to impact exchange rates on Berlin. A clause in the entrepreneurs' October 1755 mint

---

[18] For convenience and for consistency with the sources, this chapter employs historical names for places such as Königsberg (modern Kaliningrad), Breslau (Wrocław), and Cleve (Kleve). We again note that the mint in Königsberg lay outside the Empire.

contract, for example, authorized the Gumperts–Isaac–Itzig consortium to produce indefinite amounts of small coins at a mint in a detached western province (Cleve, near the Dutch border), at a gross profit margin of 18 percent (Schrötter 1910, 15). As a sweetener, the profit from this subsidiary coinage could in principle be retained by the entrepreneurs, with no portion pledged to the crown. The entrepreneurs were still on the hook for quarterly payments of contracted seigniorage, however.

The second adjustment occurred because the entrepreneurs realized that they, like Graumann, would ultimately face the problem of how to purchase large amounts of silver in markets such as Amsterdam without being front run by rival parties in those markets. Their solution was to circulate Prussian-minted coins in yet more distant places, primarily in eastern Europe, in exchange for full-weight coins already present in those locations. Full-weight coins obtained in this fashion could then be used to pay the bills coming due for the initial silver purchases. In other words, credit purchases of full-weight coins (notably, in Amsterdam) would be repaid by transfers of other full-weight coin obtained in eastern Europe, including, of course, the ever-popular Dutch trade coins like the dukaat. The lead mint entrepreneur, Herz Moses Gumperts, endorsed this strategy in a candid memorandum to Prussian mint officials, dated October 20, 1755 (Schrötter 1910, 248):

Because much gold and silver are still present in Poland, we are therefore able to exchange this for Prussian-Polish monies, so it is not necessary to enrich the English, Dutch, and Hamburgers by pushing up gold and silver prices and the exchange rate.

To implement their strategy, Gumperts' consortium needed to produce coins that would be readily accepted in places such as Poland, something the original coinage contract did not allow for. The entrepreneurs proposed a simple modification to handle this problem, as Frederick explained to Retzow in a letter dated November 6, 1755 (Bahrfeldt 1913, 102–3). This was for Prussia to circulate its own versions of Polish *Tympfe* coins, so close in appearance to the originals that the two "cannot be distinguished from one another." The state-sponsored counterfeiting was to be limited, however, to Prussia's two easternmost mints in Königsberg and Breslau.

Poland was an especially profitable market for the entrepreneurs.[19] At this time, Poland lacked its own national mints, so people there were

---

[19] Hungary, Russia, other German states, and of course Prussia itself are also mentioned as target markets for Prussian debased coin (Schrötter 1908, 111). However, the literature is in agreement that the single largest and most reliable market for Prussia's debased coins was Poland. Poland remained neutral during the Seven Years War.

accustomed to using coins produced elsewhere, under either foreign or pseudo-Polish imprint.[20] Poland shared a king with Saxony under a personal union, so much of Poland's "native" coinage was minted in Saxony.[21] Under Graumann's management, Prussian mints in Königsberg and later Stettin had produced some copies of the Saxon coins, controversially because their fineness was less than either legitimate Saxon or normal Prussian coins (Hoensch 1973, 121–23). These kinds of operations would be expanded under the entrepreneurs.

How were the entrepreneurs' coins distributed and what did they receive in return? No records remain for this shadowy phase of the entrepreneurs' operations, but its general outline is well described in the literature. The actual trading was done by a network of small-time traveling merchants, known euphemistically as "purchasers" (*Aufkäufer*), whose job it was to exchange Prussian-produced coins for coins with higher fine content (Gaettens 1955, 164). Members of the Polish nobility were frequently targeted in such exchanges. Thanks to Poland's large exports of agricultural products to western Europe, many foreign coins found their way into Poland.[22] Polish nobles were known to have accumulated coin hoards through such trade (Schrötter 1908, 102) while simultaneously racking up debts with merchants in commercial cities.[23] The offer of more nominal purchasing power through an exchange for debased coins may have thus been tempting for nobles who were coin-rich but heavily indebted. In general, people were willing to take the entrepreneurs' coins, either through ignorance of their true fine content or trust in their higher local value, or perhaps a combination of both. Bribery of Polish officials also facilitated the coins' acceptance (Schrötter 1910, 60).

The entrepreneurs occasionally resorted to more daring tactics. After war began with Austria, purchasers were sent to follow the Austrian army, exchanging full-weight Austrian coins in return for debased Prussian coins (Schrötter 1910, 75).[24] And on several occasions, when Austria lacked

---

[20] On contemporary coins in Poland, see Hoensch (1973, 114). Some coins were produced by municipal mints operating in commercial cities: Danzig (Gdansk), Thorn (Torun), and Elbing (Elblag); see Wójtowicz (2006, 9).

[21] This king was known in Poland as August III (1696–1763), and confusingly, in Saxony as Frederick August II.

[22] Attman (1983, 76), for example, estimates England's bilateral yearly trade deficit with Poland and Prussia combined to be 500,000 Dutch rijksdaalders (equivalent in value to 13 tons of silver) over 1751–1755.

[23] See Hoensch (1973, 138). Such debt often arose from advances against grain harvests (Braudel 1984, 256).

[24] In contrast to Prussia, Austria did not finance its war through seigniorage, but instead relied on extraordinary taxes and loans (Dickson 1987, 124–129; 388). Some of Austria's

sufficient coin to pay its troops, it resorted to paying them in debased coins produced by the entrepreneurs and obtained through their exchange for full-weight Austrian coins (Rachel and Wallich 1967, 30). These secretive exchanges were arranged by an intermediary in Dresden who is thought to have been a Saxon nobleman, Count Bolza (or Boltzan).

To summarize the differences between Graumann's coinage strategy and that of the entrepreneurs: Graumann borrowed precious metal abroad and repaid these loans in Prussian coins. He expected that premia would emerge for Prussian coins that would make this strategy profitable, but in practice that did not occur. The entrepreneurs, like Graumann, borrowed abroad to create Prussian or pseudo-Saxon/Polish coins, but they did not repay their loans directly with these coins. Instead, debased Saxon-Polish imprint coins were diffused over wide areas in small batches by a network of purchasers. Value was created when these small batches of lower-fine-content, but locally valuable coins could be exchanged for full-weight coins already held by the local populace. The full-weight coins obtained in this fashion could then be used to (1) pay bills drawn on the entrepreneurs, (2) pay seigniorage due to the Prussian crown, (3) buy bills on foreign markets in order to purchase more silver, or (4) be retained by the entrepreneurs as profit.

It is worth noting that the novelty of the entrepreneurs' plan lay in its scale rather than its technique. Predatory circulation of debased coin had a long tradition in the politically fragmented Holy Roman Empire (Volckart 2018) and trading for silver in eastern Europe would have been a familiar business for the entrepreneurs, in part to fulfill Prussia's silver delivery quotas. But, because Frederick's needs were now orders of magnitude greater, this business would expand accordingly.

8.3 War Finance

The first half of 1756 witnessed a sequence of dramatic events known as the "Reversal of Alliances" or the "Diplomatic Revolution." The upshot of these events was that Austria and France, traditional enemies, now formed an alliance against Britain and Prussia. This realignment bolstered the neutrality of the Dutch Republic for the duration of the Seven Years War, since a French invasion of the Republic would need to cross the Southern Netherlands (modern Belgium), then under control of France's

---

loans were financed through Amsterdam and others by its public bank, the Vienna Municipal Bank, which issued a small amount of paper currency at the end of the war (Jobst and Kernbauer 2016, 23).

new ally Austria (Baugh 2014, 179). This outcome was favorable for Frederick and his entrepreneurs, in the sense that Amsterdam remained free to serve as a springboard for the entrepreneurs' operations.[25]

For Frederick, a less favorable consequence of this realignment was that Russia chose to join with Austria and France against Prussia. Rather than wait to be crushed by the armies of three larger enemies, Frederick decided to begin the Seven Years War in August 1756 with a preemptive invasion of neighboring Saxony (Blanning 2016, 224–26). By October of that year, Saxony was in Prussian hands, and the formerly discredited entrepreneur Ephraim had moved in to take over the Saxon mints in Leipzig and Dresden (Koser 1900, 13). This takeover was a particularly attractive proposition, in part because Saxony had its own silver mines, which supplied the mint in Dresden.[26] Also attractive was the fact that these mints had the original dies for the Saxon coins supplied to Poland.

Ephraim's takeover transformed the Saxon mints from somewhat conservatively managed providers of Saxon-Polish coin into aggressive rivals to Gumperts' consortium. From this point through the end of the war, Prussian coin production became a big business, one that was outsourced through a sequence of coinage contracts with multiple entrepreneurs. Coinage standards at all mints were relaxed (i.e., mint equivalents were increased) throughout the war, each relaxation accompanied by official grumbling but followed by an acquiescence to the need for more revenue. Table 8.1 gives an overview of the different contracts and amounts of silver coin production under each contract; gold coinage is discussed in a subsequent section. Many of the figures in the table are based on historians' reconstructions, since Frederick later destroyed most of the contracts.[27] The production figures in particular (column 6 in the table) are estimates derived from seigniorage amounts and mint equivalents. The estimated figures are nonetheless indicative of the production quantities needed to satisfy Frederick's demand for revenue.

The table also shows how the contracts changed over the course of the war. Separate contracts were maintained for Prussia and Saxony up through 1758, when the Gumperts' consortium managed to wrest control

---

[25] The continued neutrality of the City of Hamburg was also beneficial for the entrepreneurs, since much of the metal obtained in Amsterdam was channeled to Prussian mints via Hamburg (Schneider 1983, 65).

[26] See Redlich (1951, 171). Saxony's mint in Leipzig, however, was dependent on silver supplied by the entrepreneurs.

[27] Mint equivalents are taken from Koser (1900) and Schrötter (1910), passim. Aspects of the coinage contracts are extensively discussed in the subsequent literature.

Table 8.1. *Overview of Prussia's silver coin production, 1756–1762*

Year	Contracted mint locations	Entrepreneurs	Maximum mint equivalent Prussia	Maximum mint equivalent Saxony/ Poland	Estimated annual production (tons of silver)	Tons of Bank silver redemptions
1756	Prussia	Gumperts, Isaac, Itzig	14	15–16	100+	72
1757	Prussia	Gumperts, Isaac, Itzig	14		100+	78
1757	Saxony	Ephraim		18	?	
1758	Prussia	Gumperts, Isaac, Itzig	14–18		100+	166
1758	Saxony	Ephraim, later Gumperts, Isaac, Itzig		19.64	100+	
1759	Prussia & Saxony	Ephraim, Isaac, Itzig	19.75	30	220–335?	85
1760	Prussia & Saxony	Ephraim, Itzig	19.75	30+	350?	152
1761	Prussia & Saxony	Ephraim, Itzig	19.75	40+	200+	94
1762	Prussia & Saxony	Ephraim, Itzig	19.75	40+	200+	58

Sources: Koser (1900, passim), Schrötter (1910, passim), and authors' calculations.

of the Saxon mint contract from Ephraim (Rachel and Wallich 1967, 299). Gumperts died shortly thereafter, leading to a merger of the two groups and a unified contract for Prussia and Saxony, though with separate standards for each imprint. Moses Isaac dropped out of the consortium in 1760. For the first two years of the war, Prussian-imprint coins were kept at Graumann's original 1750 standard (a mint equivalent of 14 Reichsthaler per fine mark), but were then debased by about 41 percent, to 19.75 Reichsthaler/mark. Saxon imprint coins started the war at a lower fineness than their Prussian counterparts and were more heavily debased throughout. We believe that the latter constituted the majority of coins actually produced by the entrepreneurs, for reasons given below.

The rather impressive magnitudes in Table 8.1 (high fractions of contemporary world silver production) likely understate the wartime monetary expansion experienced in Prussia and neighboring areas. This is because debasement was not limited to Prussia. Schrötter (1910, 77) lists 22 jurisdictions, most of them tiny principalities, that produced copies of debased Prussian/Saxon coins during the Seven Years War, often with even less fine content than the originals. These were probably distributed in the same way as for the Prussian/Saxon coins. The mint operations for one of the most prolific counterfeiters, the principality of Anhalt-Bernburg, were initially handled by none other than Prussia's entrepreneurs Isaac and Itzig, in partnership with one of their relatives (Rachel and Wallich 1967, 303). From 1759, Prussia responded by authorizing its entrepreneurs to produce "other" coins, meaning the facsimiles of the native coins of the copycat principalities (Gaettens 1955, 156). This back-and-forth of competitive counterfeiting would continue through the end of the war.[28]

The profitability of all these operations depended on keeping down the cost of silver supply. Table 8.2 offers some evidence that the Prussian entrepreneurs were quite successful in this dimension. The table reports reconstructed silver price series for Berlin over 1756–1764, where the reconstructed series consist of market silver prices in Amsterdam and Hamburg, converted to Prussian Reichsthaler at market exchange rates (i.e., at prices for bills drawn in Berlin on Amsterdam and Hamburg).

---

[28] The Prussian entrepreneurs' most serious competition came from a mint managed by Heinrich Karl Schimmelmann, a renowned war profiteer. Schimmelmann produced a variety of counterfeit coins from the safety of a Baltic village located in a Danish protectorate. These were regularly delivered to Hamburg for sale and further circulation (Kluge 2013, 140).

Table 8.2. *Reconstructed prices of silver purchased from Berlin, Reichsthaler per fine mark*

Date	Mint equivalent, Prussia	Mint equivalent, Saxony/Poland	Price of silver sourced from Amsterdam	Price of silver sourced from Hamburg
May 1756	14	15–16	14.7	14.1
July 1757	14	18	14.7	14
August 1758	14–18	19.64	15.3	14.5
July 1759	19.75	30		17.6
October 1760	19.75	30+	22.2	21.7
November 1761	19.75	40+	21.7	20.8
November 1762	19.75	40+	23.0	21.5
October 1763	19.75		22.4	21.3
January 1764	14*		14.4	13.9

Sources: Exchange rates are from Schrötter (1910, 522); Amsterdam silver prices are from Posthumus (1946,182); Hamburg silver prices are from Hamburg Preis Couranten.
Notes: The reconstructed prices are the projected cost of silver bought in Amsterdam and Hamburg using bills of exchange drawn in Berlin. Prussian administration of Saxon mints ended in early 1763. *Mint equivalent as of March 1764.

Two facts are evident from the table. First, as Graumann had earlier discovered, there was little money to be made by producing Prussian-imprint large silver coins. Reconstructed silver prices are always at or above the Prussian mint equivalents except during 1758–1759, when silver prices took almost a year to catch the upward drift of Prussian coins to 19.75 Reichsthaler per fine mark. Second, as Gumperts had pointed out in his memo, minting of Saxon-Polish coins was very profitable. The reconstructed silver prices rise as high as 23 Reichsthaler per fine mark by 1762, but by this time, the entrepreneurs were producing Saxon-Polish coins at 40 Reichsthaler per fine mark or even higher mint equivalents.

As with Table 8.1, the reconstructed data in the figure must be interpreted with caution. The actual prices paid by the entrepreneurs would have incorporated some adjustment for risk. By late 1760, for example, Prussia's military reversals and other unfavorable developments caused the entrepreneurs to buy silver at prices as high as 28 Reichsthaler per fine mark, which is double Prussia's prewar mint equivalent (Schrötter 1910, 51).[29]

[29] This elevated price may reflect the impact of an Imperial embargo on silver shipments to Prussia, enacted in August 1759 (Hoensch 1973, 128). Or it may simply reflect risk assessments by the entrepreneurs' counterparties abroad.

8.4 Entrepreneurs' Activity in Amsterdam

The entrepreneurs' first logistical challenge would have been to acquire sufficient precious metal as raw material. The pool of trade coins held at the Bank would have been a tempting source of supply for several reasons. First and somewhat ironically, the reliable fineness of these trade coins enhanced their appeal as raw material for debased coins. To reach a target level of debasement, it helps to know the fineness of the input metal, and as was discussed in Chapter 3, gaining such knowledge was a slow and expensive process. Other attractions of Amsterdam were its dense credit markets and its lack of export controls on precious metal.

We focus first on flows of silver coins. The rightmost column of Table 8.1 records withdrawals of silver coins held under receipt at the Bank during the period when Prussian entrepreneurs were active. A comparison of Bank redemptions to the entrepreneurs' production (column 6 in the table) indicates that the Bank withdrawals could have easily supplied a large portion, though not all, of the silver needed for the entrepreneurs' operations. We should also note that the production figures in the table represent flows rather than stocks. A secondary source of silver for the entrepreneurs' production would have been coins acquired by the purchasers. Silver obtained in this way could be continuously "recycled" by melting down silver coins that were in many cases already somewhat debased (very prevalent in the later stages of the war) and reminting these into even more debased coins.

One channel through which the entrepreneurs could tap into the Bank's silver pool was through their family connections in Amsterdam. A search of the Bank's master account confirms that the entrepreneurs did make use of this channel. We consider two prominent and relatively easily traceable examples.[30] The first clear example of a family member doing large withdrawals shows up in 1756, with Nathan Veitel Heine Ephraim's nephew in Amsterdam, Joseph Marcus Ephraim. Figure 8.1 shows the cumulative amount of silver that Joseph Marcus Ephraim removed from the Bank over the relevant time frame. Our sample begins in 1754, but Joseph only started to remove silver after his uncle Nathan gained the Saxon mint contract at the end of 1756. Joseph then removed 6 tons of

---

[30] The authors are grateful to Harmen Snel of the Amsterdam City Archive for help in sorting through the entrepreneurs' family relations. There were doubtless more relatives and near-relatives involved with the entrepreneurs' operations than the two examples presented here.

Figure 8.1. Joseph Marcus Ephraim's use of silver receipts, monthly, 1754–1762
Sources: Authors' calculations.

silver from the Bank over the next 18 months. He did this by redeeming receipts for Spanish and French trade coins, for which he needed both receipts and Bank money. We do not know how Joseph Marcus Ephraim acquired the receipts, because the Bank's ledgers did not track transfers of receipts, which traded over the counter. The ledgers did track who paid the Bank to prolong or redeem a receipt, and that is the information presented in Figure 8.1.

The Bank's ledgers indicate that Joseph was building a long position in silver well before his redemptions began. We know this because starting in May 1756, Joseph paid the Bank ¼ percent to prolong receipts for an additional six months. This silver had entered the Bank at least six months prior to the prolongation date. Figure 8.1 plots the amount of silver kept under option by those prolongations. Joseph's receipts grew to control 2.1 tons of silver by November 1756, and this process illustrates how entrepreneurs could lock in silver prices – and avoid full revelation of their trading positions – well before the far more expensive process of removing the silver. These positions could be highly geared, since receipts sold at a few percent of the silver controlled (Dehing 2012, 125).

Exercising the options in the receipts required liquidity, and Joseph Marcus Ephraim took full advantage of Amsterdam's credit markets when it came time to cash out his position.[31] Joseph was a scion of a wealthy family but did not have funds on hand to mobilize the quantities of silver

---

[31] As noted in Chapter 5, long positions in receipts were in options on collateral (trade coins) rather than in the collateral itself. As is shown in the next examples, this distinction did not impede the entrepreneurs' ability to mobilize collateral.

Table 8.3. *Bank balance-sheet effects of a silver removal, January 28, 1757, in bank florins*

Assets	Liabilities
−22,000 in silver coins to Joseph Marcus Ephraim	−12,000 in balances from Bitter & van Hoven −3,000 in balances from Eliaser Samuel Levy −7,055 in balances from Jacob van Thiel
	+55 to the Bank's equity, being ¼ percent of the silver removed.

Source: ACA 5077/406, folio 1275.

Figure 8.2. Payment with a third party, January 28, 1757
Source: ACA 5077/406, folio 1275.

required by his uncle. He did have access to sufficient credit. In 1757, Joseph spent 357,291 bank florins acquiring silver (Figure 8.1), yet he began that year with a balance of only 41 bank florins (ACA 5077/1180, folio 18). We do not know on what terms Joseph was able to obtain financing, but from the Bank's master account, we do know that at least nine different creditors were involved. For example, on January 28, 1757, Joseph Marcus Ephraim withdrew a fifth of a ton of silver from the Bank. The removal was paid for by a combination of three others: Bitter & van Hoven, Eliaser Samuel Levy, and Jacob van Thiel.[32] Table 8.3 pulls the transaction together to show, from the Bank's perspective, how Joseph withdrew the silver while having others pay for it.[33]

Even more suggestive of third-party funding is that the participants had the Bank record Joseph's involvement. Figure 8.2 reproduces the actual entry in the Bank's ledger wherein the Bank was credited for 7,055 bank florins from Jacob van Thiel. Thiel's payment is explicitly recorded as for

---

[32] In the merchant classification of Chapter 2, Ephraim and Levy were precious metal dealers; Van Thiel (certainly) and Bitter & Van Hoven (most likely) were cashiers.

[33] The other known creditors in 1757 are Alexander & Eleasar van Emden & Soon; de Harder & Clasing; Egbert & Anthony van der Bergh; Levy & Simon Marcus; Nicolaas Bleeker; and Salomon & David Levy.

("*voor*" or just "*v*") Joseph Marcus Ephraim. The routine elements recording the payment are the date, Thiel's name, the bank florins, and the counter folio: in Figure 8.2, that folio is 2203 where Van Thiel's account is debited. While Ephraim removed the silver, his name is not relevant to the double-entry payments system run by the Bank. Rather, the notation gave Thiel a legal record that the payment was provided so Joseph could remove the silver. It acted as proof that consideration was paid by Thiel to the benefit of Joseph and implies that Thiel and Joseph had a contract conditional on the removal of the silver.

We explore this detail because 40 percent of Joseph Marcus Ephraim's 1757 silver withdrawal was paid for by others. The notation makes clear that by the time of the actual withdrawals, Joseph was not concealing why he needed funding, because these payors had the Bank explicitly record that the payments were for the removal of silver (the price of the silver would have been locked in with the purchase of receipts). We will use the term "extra payors" to designate parties such as Thiel who provided funding to parties such as Joseph Marcus Ephraim for the purpose of withdrawing silver from the Bank.

This process was one way that Amsterdam provided credit that Ephraim and others could take advantage of. We say others because use of extra payors increased from 8 percent of silver removal transactions at the Bank from 1754–1756 to 15 percent in 1757 and 1758. Figure 8.3 gives the number of transactions that removed silver from the Bank with one, two, or three extra payors. The year 1758 even brought four examples of transactions with four payors and one with five payors (not shown). The use of multiple extra payors is one way through which people could spread

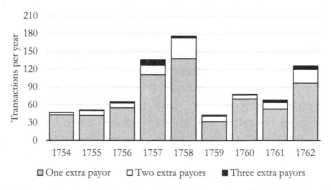

Figure 8.3. Transactions removing silver using extra payors, 1754–1762
Sources: Authors' calculations.

Table 8.4. *Top users of "voor" notation, 1754 through 1762*

Rank	Name of creditor	Profession	Instances
1	Weduwe van der Hoogt en Zonen	Cashier	127
2	David van Heyst	Cashier	67
3	Nicolaas Bleeker	Cashier	63
4	Estienne Ferrand	Cashier	58
5	Jacob van Thiel	Cashier	56
6	Gerrit Muller	Cashier	50
7	Johannes Verhoeff	Cashier	46
8	Borchers & Mysenheim	Cashier	44
9	Weduwe Abraham Beck en Zoon	Cashier	36
10	Frederick Jacob & Hendrik Cramer	Cashier	34
Out of 210			Out of 1,314

Sources: Profession based on listing in Van Dillen (1925a, 1414–25), and De Jong-Keesing (1939, 82). Instances derived from authors' calculations.

the funding load of large receipt redemptions, and the rise in multiple-payor transactions is suggestive of the increasing size of the underlying deals.

While a wide variety of people paid for others to remove silver, this practice was most common among cashiers. Table 8.4 lists the ten accounts that most frequently paid for others to remove silver from 1754 to 1762. All ten are known cashiers, and together they account for 43 percent of all such instances in the sample. This tier of financial intermediary helped fund Joseph Marcus Ephraim's acquisitions. Of the nine extra payors used by Ephraim in 1757, six are identifiable as cashiers from a listing given in De Jong-Keesing (1939, 82), and these include the active players Nicolaas Bleeker and Jacob van Thiel (Table 8.4).

The next example of a familial supplier to the Prussian entrepreneurs is provided by the silver smelter Moses Philip, whose trading strategy is similar to Joseph Marcus Ephraim's in some respects. We believe that Philip was likely part of Ephraim's enterprise at this stage, because Philip's granddaughter, Goedje, later married Nathan Ephraim's son Benjamin Veitel Ephraim (in 1761; see Michaelis 1976, 218). Philip came into these operations later than Joseph Marcus Ephraim however and did not try to first build up a large position in receipts.

Figure 8.4 shows that Philip began to rapidly acquire silver in September 1757 and eventually pulled out 15 tons over the subsequent year. Of that, one-third was paid for by 28 different people: 11 are known

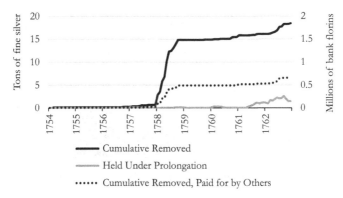

Figure 8.4. Moses Philips' use of silver receipts, monthly, 1754–1762
Sources: Authors' calculations.

cashiers, and three extra payors (Nicolaas Bleeker, Eliaser Samuel Levy, and Jacob van Thiel) are shared in common with Joseph Marcus Ephraim. Another suggestive dimension is that 11 of the 28 names are members of the German Jewish merchant community, most being known precious metal dealers: Benjamin & Samuel Symons, Benjamin Isaac de Jong, Eliaser Samuel Levy, Isaac Philip Bock, Jacob en Levi Philips, Joachem Moses, Joseph Isaac de Jong, Levy Bing & Zonen, Michael Levy, Philip Salomons, and Salomon Jacobs & Zonen Nathan en Simon. Philip seems to reach into that network to raise the 1.5 million bank florins he spent on silver. Moses Philip needed the funding, for he started 1758 with an account balance of only 2,777 bank florins (ACA 5077/1183, folio 25).

Figures 8.1 and 8.4 show that Joseph Marcus Ephraim and Moses Philip together pulled about 21 tons of silver coins from the Bank during 1757–1758. This was a significant quantity, especially if we consider that a Prussian foot soldier at this time was paid about 25 grams of silver a month (Kluge 2012). The lumpy pattern of transactions and the involvement of third parties indicate that these transactions were something extraordinary for both Ephraim and Philip, unusual deals that justified the degree of leverage involved. It is also clear from Table 8.1 that these family-oriented deals would have been insufficient to supply the Prussian entrepreneurs, who needed something in the order of 200 tons of silver for their 1758 contracts alone. So, who provided the entrepreneurs with the rest of their silver?

Figure 8.5 offers a somewhat surprising answer to this question. The figure reports withdrawals by Bank customers who removed at least 10 tons of silver in a year over the time when the entrepreneurs were active. Before

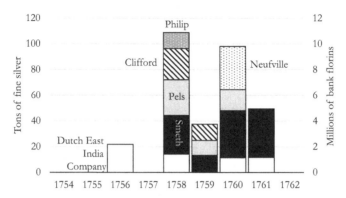

Figure 8.5. Acquirers of at least 1 million florins in silver in a year, 1754–1762
Sources: Authors' calculations.

1758, only the silver-hungry Amsterdam Chamber of the Dutch East India Company engaged in such large redemptions, and 10 tons was the Company's average annual removal from 1754 through 1762. In 1758, four accounts suddenly joined the 10-ton club: Moses Philip, who removes an already impressive 12 tons, but also three merchant banks – George Clifford & Zonen (24 tons), Andries Pels & Zonen (28 tons), and Raymond & Theodoor de Smeth (30 tons).[34] Of these, Philip is evidently the smallest participant. Collectively, the four removed 94.6 tons of silver in 1758.

Like Ephraim and Philip, the big merchant banks used leverage to access so much silver so quickly. But unlike the smaller players, the banks did not need special arrangements with extra payors to finance their activity. In 1758, Pels and Clifford used no extra payors, while the De Smeth firm used extra payors in only two transactions, to cover just 1 percent of its silver removals. Instead, these merchant banks could secure millions of bank florins by selling bills of exchange drawn on their foreign counter-parties, and they did need to secure funding. Collectively, the three merchant banks started 1758 with just under 1 million in bank florins, yet they removed just under 8 million bank florins in silver that year.[35] It appears that the scale of silver demand went beyond the capabilities of merchants like Joseph Marcus Ephraim and Moses Philip. The merchant banks accommodated this demand.

---

[34] In July 1759, the firm of George Clifford & Zonen George, Jan, en Henry re-formed as George Clifford & Zonen.

[35] In January 1758, Pels had 506,224 bank florins, Clifford 269,658, and De Smeth 176,950 (ACA 5077/1183, folios 25, 26).

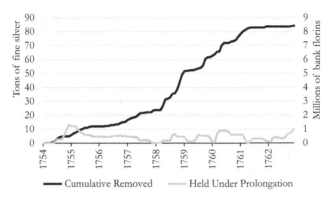

Figure 8.6. Andries Pels' use of silver receipts, monthly, 1754–1762
Source: Authors' calculations.

Apart from size, another distinguishing feature of the banks is that they were continuously active in the silver market. Figure 8.6 shows the cumulative silver removals by Andries Pels & Zonen, the largest merchant bank of the day, from 1754 through 1762. Pels acquired silver each year before 1758, while Ephraim and Philip did not. What wartime changed for Pels was the scale: the firm's rate of silver removal quadrupled in 1758. Instead of starting from new, the largest financial firms of the era simply stepped up their existing business to generate the funding necessary to remove such a concentration of high-quality silver. This pattern illustrates the dominant role of the merchant banks in the Amsterdam market, as parties with the credit capacity to exploit such large-scale trading opportunities.

This pattern also indicates that the big banks were not the only parties to profit from the wartime boom in silver trading. Other players in the game were the people who brought trade coins into the Bank and sold off receipts, the people who financed receipt redemptions through purchases of the banks' bills of exchange, and the Bank itself when it collected fees on receipts. During the Seven Years War, all these activities occurred at a heady pace not witnessed before. An Amsterdam merchant, Thomas de Vogel, expressed the mood of the moment in a letter to his Hamburg correspondent: "business is presently miraculous."[36]

To be clear, the Bank does not record the business relationship between merchants in Amsterdam and the entrepreneurs in Prussia and Saxony, but the circumstantial evidence is powerful. When Frederick's mint

---

[36] Quoted in De Jong-Keesing (1939, 68). The quote is not dated but is from correspondence during 1760 or 1761.

entrepreneurs needed close to 200 tons of silver in 1758, an extra 110 tons of silver suddenly left the Bank, and most of that was through three merchant banks, the only parties (beyond the needy VOC) with the financial muscle needed to mobilize silver at this scale. Some portion of this silver withdrawal may have gone to other wartime uses.[37] Even so, Figure 8.5 provides evidence that much of the silver needed for the 1758 debasements was provided by these dominant players in the Amsterdam market. It also raises some questions, however.

Section 8.7 will show that when the unwinding of the debasement got caught in the Crisis of 1763, Clifford, Pels, and De Smeth were all members of a small group of banks with claims on the Ephraims' unprocessed war coins. Hence, one question is whether the relationships of 1763 were already formed in 1758. Another relevant question is why such large, highly respected, and well-informed merchant banks would have suddenly and simultaneously chosen to extend large amounts of credit to the mint entrepreneurs. Here we can only point out that such credit would have been short term. Plus, the entrepreneurs were known to pay their bills.

The sequence of silver withdrawals decelerates somewhat in 1759 (see Figure 8.5), but then resumes. A total of 150 tons of silver flowed into and quickly out of the Bank's vaults during 1760 (cf. Figure 6.3). Figure 8.5 breaks down the 1760 outflows and shows that the cast of large withdrawers changed somewhat. The merchant banks Pels and De Smeth resumed large withdrawals, but Clifford dropped out of the large-withdrawal group, to be replaced by Gebroeders de Neufville, the merchant bank whose 1763 failure was discussed in Chapter 7.[38] De Neufville's silver withdrawals started later than the other merchant banks, but over 1759–1760, they redeemed receipts for 50 tons worth of silver (Figure 8.7). The De Neufville firm apparently did not enjoy the same access to the bill market as the other merchant banks but relied on extra payors for funding half of its withdrawals. Again, we cannot ascertain whether these withdrawals went directly to the entrepreneurs, but entrepreneurs' need was great and the

---

[37] Notably, British subsidies to Prussia began in 1758 and for that year were partly paid in silver (2.7 million Reichsthaler or about 44 tons at prewar parity). Some if not all of this subsidy was likely channeled through Amsterdam, contributing to the large silver withdrawals for that year. The British subsidies are discussed below.

[38] We do not know why Clifford dropped out of the large withdrawal group, but note that beginning in 1760, Clifford floated a number of loans for Austria. The 1760 Austrian loan was for 400,000 Austrian gulden, followed by a 242,000 gulden loan in 1762 (Dickson 1987, 406–407). These loans were secured by Austrian copper and mercury production (Dickson 1987, 410).

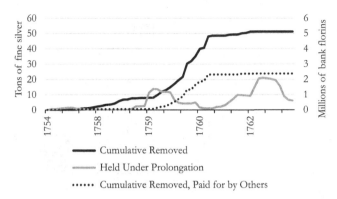

Figure 8.7. Gebroeders de Neufville's use of silver receipts, monthly, 1754–1762
Source: Authors' calculations.

circumstantial evidence is strong. Figure 8.7 also shows that De Neufville again built a long position in receipts over 1761–1762, perhaps in anticipation of another silver supply deal, but was unwilling or unable to cash out this position.

8.5 Amsterdam and Prussia's Gold Coinage

Amsterdam also played a role in providing raw material for Prussia's wartime gold coinage, though by a different process than for silver. The funding for Prussia's gold coinage was provided by British subsidies to Prussia, which were paid over four years of the war. In 1758, Britain agreed to an annual subsidy of £670,000 and paid these amounts from July 1758 through 1761 (Schrötter 1910, 55–58; Koser 1900, 24). In 1758, a portion of these subsidies were paid as silver, but all later subsidies were paid in gold. As had occurred earlier under Graumann, deliveries of gold were handled not through the entrepreneurs but through Berlin banks. Deliveries occurred via Hamburg using bills drawn on Amsterdam, and coins minted from these deliveries were produced at the central Berlin mint and sent directly to the Prussian treasury. The main coins produced were Prussian copies of Saxon-Polish gold coins known as *Augustdor* (after the Saxon-Polish king August III). As the debasement of silver coins progressed, the Augustdor were debased proportionately so as to discourage arbitrage between silver and gold coins (Koser 1900, 24; Schrötter 1910, 55, 80; Rachel and Wallich 1967, 220; Kluge 2013, 137).

Did the Bank help supply this gold also? Timing and scale again suggest yes. Figure 8.8 follows the example of the silver in Figure 8.7 and only

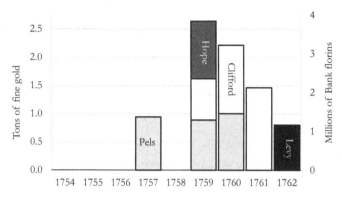

Figure 8.8. Acquirers of at least 1 million florins in gold in a year, 1754–1762
Sources: Authors' calculations.

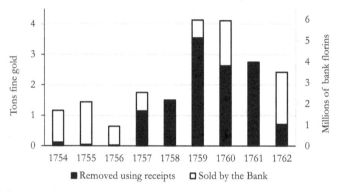

Figure 8.9. Gold outflows by channel, 1754–1762
Sources: Authors' calculations.

shows accounts that removed at least 1 million bank florins in gold in a year from the Bank. Again, large gold outflows suddenly emerged but now a year later, in 1759. These removals are a combination of repurchases using receipts and of direct purchases of gold coins that the Bank owned outright and chose to sell (see Chapters 6 and 7). Once again, the great merchant banks led the surge, with Hope & Co. joining Pels and Clifford. An unexplained curiosity is that in 1762, the firm Salomon & David Levy, precious metal dealers, jumped into large-scale gold purchases, and they did so with heavy use of cashiers.

Figure 8.9 shows that total gold flowing out of the Bank in 1759 and 1760 amounted to about 4 tons, enough to supply the bulk of annual British subsidy (670,000 pounds or about 4.9 tons). Most gold left the Bank via receipt redemptions but a significant portion was sold off in discretionary open market operations. The outflow begins to wind down in 1761, the final year of the subsidy.

While most of the British gold undoubtedly went to pay Prussia's military expenses, a portion of it may have gone to seed the entrepreneurs' silver purchases. In October 1760, Ephraim and Itzig sustained losses of 240,000 Reichsthaler on their bill positions following a short-lived Russian occupation of Berlin (Rachel and Wallich 1967, 306–7). Stung by this loss, Ephraim proposed that funding for the future production of silver coins should now come from stocks of gold coin held by the Prussian treasury:[39]

The Privy Councilor Köppen finds it urgent of late to have an important quantity of silver coined by June [1761]. Difficult as it may be [to accommodate this request], we [the entrepreneurs] wish to sacrifice ourselves once more and have only requested a parcel of Augustdor, for which we would pay a premium, in order to facilitate the purchase of the necessary Dutch bills.

This proposal was rejected, but others may have followed. The literature unfortunately does not record whether the entrepreneurs were later successful in gaining direct (i.e., gold-coin) funding from the Prussian treasury.

8.6 The Great Unwind

Prussia's war ended on February 15, 1763, with the signing of the Treaty of Hubertusburg. The advent of peace would not end Prussia's relationship with the mint entrepreneurs however, nor would it end the entrepreneurs' reliance on Amsterdam. Prussia emerged from the war with its sovereignty and territory intact, but with serious economic problems, including the loss of a tenth of its population, along with much of its forests and livestock.[40] The wartime debasement had provided fiscal relief, but the resulting inflation created political headaches for Frederick. By early 1763, wheat and rye prices in Berlin were running at four times their prewar level (Skalweit 1931, 647–48). Although no precise figures are available, contemporary descriptions suggest that by the end of the war, most of Prussia's circulating coin consisted of the heavily debased Saxon-Polish coins, higher-fineness coins having long since been bought up by the

---

[39] Letter from Ephraim to Frederick's Privy Councilor Köppen, reproduced in Schrötter (1910, 311–312).

[40] On Prussia's postwar economic conditions, see De Jong-Keesing (1939, 50), Henderson (1962, 89), and Schieder (1983, 222).

purchasers. Adding to the monetary misery were the even more debased coins produced by other jurisdictions.

A financial statement compiled by Frederick's advisors at the end of March 1763 is informative about the state of money in Prussia at the end of the war (Koser 1900, 37). The statement records a 14.2 million Reichsthaler balance of items that the Prussian treasury viewed as cash equivalents. Only 2 million of this balance was true hard cash in the form of Dutch gold dukaten or moderately debased Prussian (i.e., Saxon-Polish) gold coin. The total also included 3.7 million Reichsthaler in payments due from various parties, including 2.2 million in seigniorage due from the entrepreneurs and 817,000 due from the Prussian war profiteer Johann Ernst Gotzkowsky, soon to go bankrupt from the sketchy Russian grain deal. The remainder (8.5 million Reichsthaler) consisted of heavily debased silver and gold war coins. Simply put, there seems to have been almost no full-weight coin left in Prussia at the end of the war, even in the royal treasury.

The prevalence of debased coins created a public relations problem for Frederick. His mint contracts were of course top secret, but among the populace, the reputations of the king and his mint entrepreneurs were uncomfortably close. A popular jingle described war coins as having "Frederick on the outside, Ephraim on the inside" and a few brave jokesters circulated obviously fake coins imprinted with Frederick calling Ephraim "my beloved son, with whom I am well pleased" (Vehse 1851, 273). A coinage reform that had begun with Graumann's attempt to displace foreign trade coins had ended up flooding Prussia with grossly substandard coins of foreign (Saxon-Polish) imprint.

A more serious issue was the impact of inflation on the Prussian nobility, a class who lived off fixed rents and who had suffered heavy casualties during the war (Skalweit 1937, 19; Blanning 2016, 437–38). A real estate bubble was encouraged by a combination of inflation with a Prussian law that only allowed rents to increase when property changed hands (Beutin 1933, 238; Skalweit 1937, 20). Most Prussian nobles were unable to capitalize on this trend however, unlike the prosperous war profiteers, leading to intense resentment of the latter by the former.[41] Wealthy creditors were also disadvantaged by debtors discharging their

---

[41] The nobles' inability to extract full value from their land holdings was a contributing factor in the postwar formation of credit cooperatives known as *Landschaften* (Wandschneider 2015). The Landschaften issued joint liability bonds that were viewed as highly secure, allowing the nobility to borrow against their real estate wealth.

obligations in debased coin, despite an ordinance limiting this practice (Schrötter 1910, 162–63). The wartime inflation had disrupted the class structure of the Prussian society.

The only way to undo this humiliating and politically hazardous state of affairs was to reinstate Prussia's prewar coinage standard (i.e., the 14-Reichsthaler Graumann standard). To this end, in May 1763, Frederick set a transitional standard of 19¾ Reichsthaler per fine mark for large silver coins, in effect demonetizing the Saxon-imprint war coins (Gaettens 1955, 159–60). The edict did not commit to an immediate return to prewar parity but anticipated that event by making taxes payable only in full prewar-weight (14-Reichsthaler) coin, or in moderately debased 19¾-Reichsthaler coin at a 41 percent discount.

In another strange twist, implementation of this transition again required the services of Ephraim and Itzig, the two entrepreneurs most identified with the wartime debasement. The entrepreneurs' services were needed because recoinage entailed serious logistical challenges. Large quantities of debased coin had to be processed ("affined") in order to remove its silver content, which could then be combined with copper in the right proportions to mint full-weight coin. The traditional affining process, known as cupellation, had been known since ancient times, but in this era few people understood how to manage it on an industrial scale.[42]

The low fineness of the war coins hindered this process. One Dutch mint master described the typical silver content of Prussian war coins at 5/12 or 42 percent, making them hardly worth the expense of getting them up to the 11/12 content required by the Republic's mint ordinances.[43] Other assessments of the war coins are less charitable. A German coinage expert described the silver content of crude silver bars flooding the postwar Hamburg market as 5/16 to 6/16 fine (31–38 percent; Justi 1765, 9).

---

[42] The standard cupellation recipe, described in Justi (1765, 11), called for 13 times as much lead as debased coin to be heated in a furnace charge. One-fourth to one-third of the lead and two-thirds of the copper in the coins were "chased" during the process, that is, discharged as vapor into the surrounding atmosphere or absorbed into the furnace lining. The end products were silver and an oxidized lead–copper byproduct (litharge). Justi advocated the use of a second technique, called liquation, which reduced the amount of lead input to three times the weight of the debased coin. This technique was employed by the Ephraims for at least some of their operations in the Netherlands.

[43] This was Johan Ernst Novisadi, master of the Utrecht mint (De Jong-Keesing 1939, 51). An 11/12 fine content was required for the most popular Dutch domestic coin, the gulden (Polak 1998b, 76).

These bars would have been obtained by melting down war coins. Similarly, a 1767 report by a French visitor to a smelter near Amsterdam records a typical fine content of roughly one-third for war money (Zappey 1982, 198). Mint officials in Prussia lacked the facilities and metallurgical expertise to process such heavily alloyed material, meaning that once again this task had to be outsourced to the entrepreneurs.

The entrepreneurs did not set up their affining operation anywhere in Prussia, but in Muiden, a village near Amsterdam. The path from Berlin to Muiden is circuitous. In anticipation of Prussia's postwar needs, Nathan Veitel Heine Ephraim had dispatched his youngest and most ambitious son, Benjamin Veitel Ephraim, to Amsterdam in 1761, where he married the granddaughter of the silver smelter Moses Philip. Philip had contact with several affining operations that operated in towns near Amsterdam, including Muiden. These were eventually taken over by Benjamin Veitel Ephraim, who after the war relocated to Muiden in order to personally supervise affining operations there (Zappey 1982, 202).

Muiden, though physically remote from Prussia's mints, did have advantages as a base of operations. Since the entrepreneurs were non-citizens, their legal status in postwar Prussia was never fully secure and the neutral, relatively tolerant Dutch Republic would have been a safer domicile. Other factors in Muiden's favor would have been its proximity to Amsterdam's financial markets, the Republic's lack of controls on the import and export of silver, and the willingness of Dutch authorities to tolerate private smelting facilities that competed with the Republic's mints.[44] More tangible advantages would have been the clustered availability of necessary inputs: lead as a catalyst, peat as fuel, and skilled labor to manage the affining smelters. One of Ephraim's managers, Johann Heinrich Müntz, left behind a detailed technical manual with drawings of the affining facilities. These drawings leave little doubt as to the scale and sophistication of the Ephraims' affining facilities. Figure 8.10 shows one of these drawings.

Of course, Benjamin Veitel Ephraim was not the only person in the Republic to see the opportunity in affining war coins. Another affining operation was set up in 1762 near Haarlem by none other than De Neufville (Müntz 1769–1770, 4) and this was likely not the only rival

---

[44] Dutch officials inspected the Muiden facilities but did not object to their operation. By contrast, a 1759 Imperial edict prohibited all private smelting of precious metals, subjecting affining operations within the Holy Roman Empire to legal risk (Schneider 1985, 21).

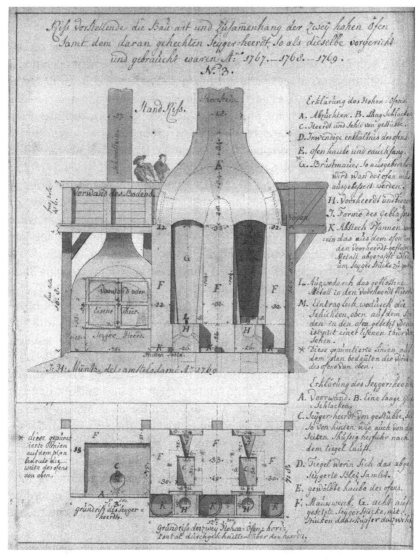

Figure 8.10. One of the Ephraims' furnaces in Muiden, circa 1767.
Source: Müntz (1769–1770, 68). Image courtesy of Baker Library, Harvard Business School.
Note: Müntz's manual would have been eagerly read in parts of Europe overrun with debased
Prussian war coins. Shown is an advanced postwar (1767–1768) design.

to the entrepreneurs. De Neufville's affinery suffered from technical
defects, but Figure 3.5 suggests that a more capable set of rivals were the
Dutch mint masters, who in 1763 and 1764 processed record amounts of
silver into gulden coins.

8.7 The Challenges of Reinforcement

Engineering a reinforcement, or reverse debasement, involved a supply chain with many similarities to the entrepreneurs' debasement operations, only with the flows of metal and credit reversed. Debased coins available in Prussia and other places in central Europe were purchased on credit, transported to Muiden for processing, and then sent back to Prussia for minting into prewar-standard coins. This process was an even riskier proposition than the original debasement cycle, however, because the underlying collateral of war coins was effectively junk collateral until it could be affined. In contrast to the trade coins employed in the original debasement cycle, war coins no longer functioned as a medium of exchange in many places. Demonetized war coins were sometimes further commoditized by melting them into bars, whose low fine content was difficult to mobilize until the silver had been extracted (Büsch 1797, 123). The entrepreneurs' leveraged long positions in war coins thus exposed them to substantial liquidity risk.

The documentary evidence for the entrepreneurs' reinforcement operation is sparse. The first and most important postwar contract with the Prussian crown was for the delivery and reminting of 3 million Reichsthaler (50 tons of silver) in 1763 (Rachel and Wallich 1967, 321). This contract, of which no copy exists, had to be canceled due to subsequent events. Other aspects of the reinforcement are also unclear, particularly how the entrepreneurs were able to obtain the necessary silver, or to what extent their purchases were subsidized by the Prussian treasury. Schrötter (1910, 185) puts the entrepreneurs' transport and affining costs at 1/3 to one Reichsthaler per fine mark, suggesting a breakeven silver price for the entrepreneurs of around 13 Reichsthaler for the minting of full-weight coins.[45] However, Amsterdam and Hamburg market prices for fine silver in mid-1763 translate to Berlin prices well in excess of the transitional standard of 19¾ Reichsthaler per fine mark (cf. Table 8.2).

This divergence suggests that the entrepreneurs may have again relied on a network of purchasers to assemble the necessary stocks of war coin at favorable prices. This hypothesis gains some support from a chance encounter recorded by a contemporary German academic, Johann

---

[45] The affining cost cited by Utrecht mint master Novisadi is at the lower end of this range, ¾ guilders per fine mark (De Jong-Keesing 1939, 51). Novisadi's transport costs would have been much lower than the entrepreneurs'.

Beckmann.[46] While traveling through northern Germany in October 1762, Beckman stumbled upon a wagon train of Prussian war coin headed to the Dutch Republic for processing.[47] He noted that these coins sometimes traded locally as if they were one-third silver, although he guessed their true fine content to be closer to 44 percent. The reminting of such coins thus offered up profit opportunities for people willing to bear the associated risks.

The best evidence on the entrepreneurs' reinforcement operations comes from their involvement in the Panic of 1763, an event described in Chapter 7. For Ephraim and Itzig, the freeze-up of the Amsterdam bill market in August 1763 meant that a critical source of funding was suddenly cut off. In particular, the return of bills (and an inability to draw new bills) on Amsterdam to fund purchases of war money meant that they now owed their creditors payments in cash, meaning better-quality coin. The entrepreneurs summarized their predicament in a letter to Frederick dated August 8, 1763, that politely begged for a bailout (Rachel and Wallich 1967, 454):

> Your Royal Majesty is without doubt aware of the enormous bankruptcies that are now occurring in Amsterdam. The sums at stake are many millions and the largest houses in Holland and Hamburg have lost sometimes half, sometimes their entire fortunes, so that no more bills may be drawn on those places. ... Though the ongoing evil does not affect us directly, our credit has been so thoroughly disrupted that we must immediately settle our bills in cash, which seems impossible without Your Majesty's assistance. We therefore request of Your Majesty: to advance to us through Privy Councilor Köppen three million [Reichsthaler] in the newest Augustdor for three months against sufficient collateral, such as what we may furnish with silver at the mints. By means of this [loan], we, as well as other mint contractors, shall be relieved of much distress.

The letter's reference to "silver at the mints" was a euphemism for war coin or silver bars in various stages of processing, meaning that what was being proposed was effectively a loan of more liquid (although debased) gold coin against silver war money. In response, Frederick proposed an interest-free loan of 2,460,000 Reichsthaler to the entrepreneurs, on the condition that they in turn lend 400,000 out of this loan to the distressed war profiteer Gotzkowsky. Ephraim and Itzig feared entanglement with Gotzkowsky and suggested a loan of 2 million with no strings attached.

---

[46] Kernkamp (1912, 320), cited in De Jong-Keesing (1939, 51).

[47] Peace negotiations were already underway in the autumn of 1762, and it is likely the war coins Beckmann encountered were being exported in anticipation of their demonetization.

Frederick assented to this proposal, and on August 12, wagons of gold coins were dispatched to Hamburg under heavy guard (Van Dillen 1922, 247; Rachel and Wallich 1967, 454–56). Frederick did not let his money speak for itself, but sent word through Prussia's representative in Hamburg, Privy Councilor Hecht, that the entrepreneurs were indeed too big to fail and should be treated as such (Michaelis 1976, 214).[48]

Even these generous gestures of support were not sufficient. In particular, they could not liquefy the entrepreneurs' stocks of war coins that were now awaiting processing in the Dutch Republic. This required a second intervention from an unlikely source, the Bank, which expanded its receipt facility in a customized fashion to accommodate Benjamin Veitel Ephraim. The Bank's exact motivations for this bailout action are not recorded, but again can be guessed. On August 30 (a month into the panic), the governments of both the City of Amsterdam and the Province of Holland had received urgent letters from Frederick, requesting an accelerated (and for Prussian creditors, preferential) resolution of Gebroeders de Neufville's imminent bankruptcy, as well as expressing a special concern for De Neufville's affining operations (De Jong-Keesing 1939, 122; Zappey 1982, 198). These politically sensitive requests were not granted, but Frederick had made his sentiments clear. Complicating the situation was the fact that the illiquid Benjamin Veitel Ephraim owed big amounts to some big names: the Amsterdam banks Pels, Clifford, De Smeth, and Harmen van de Poll. Recall that three of these parties (Pels, Clifford, and De Smeth) appear to have been great suppliers of silver back in 1758 (cf. Figure 8.5).

The Bank's solution to the younger Ephraim's predicament, implemented over the first two weeks of September 1763, was to lend Benjamin 365,000 bank florins against an unusual form of collateral that is recorded only as "barrels" (*Vaaten*), meaning almost certainly barrels of Prussian war coins. In Chapter 7, we noted that the Bank granted its other customers credit against silver bullion during this panic episode, but the younger Ephraim was the only customer of this expanded facility. The highly accommodative nature of this arrangement is underlined by the fact that the war coins were very impure, difficult-to-assay assets of variable quality, a far cry from the trade coins the Bank ordinarily dealt in. There

---

[48] Despite Frederick's efforts, the entrepreneurs later (September 14) received letters from the Hamburg magistrate informing them that any of their claims on Hamburg counterparties would not be given preference over claims by other merchants (Rachel and Wallich 1967, 459).

Table 8.5. *Payouts from B. V. Ephraim via the Bank's Vaaten facility, September 1763*

Payee	Type	Probable earlier connection to mint entrepreneurs	Amount (bank florins)
De Smeth	Merchant bank	Silver supplier	80,000
Pels	Merchant bank	Silver supplier	73,000
Moses Philip	Silver smelter	Silver supplier and relative by marriage	70,000
Van de Poll	Merchant bank	–	58,000
Clifford	Merchant bank	Silver supplier	48,000

Sources: ACA 5077/443, folio 14 and 5077/1390, folios 30-1.

were limits to the Bank's generosity however. The funds created through the facility were treated in the Bank's ledgers not as a credit to Benjamin's Bank account, but instead as immediate credits to his counterparties: De Smeth, Pels, Van de Poll, and Clifford (see Table 8.5). The ledgers also record a 70,000-florin credit to the account of Benjamin's grandfather-in-law, Moses Philip.

These exposures seem small when compared to the millions apparently fronted by the merchant banks during the war (see Figure 8.5). It is possible, however, that timely payments from Benjamin Ephraim were critical for De Smeth, who was under pressure due to a 319,000-florin exposure to the bankrupt De Neufville (De Jong-Keesing 1939, 110). Failure of De Smeth, another large merchant bank of a size comparable to De Neufville, would have sparked knock-on bankruptcies in Amsterdam and Hamburg and worsened the extent of the panic.

Thanks in part to the emergency credit arrangements, the entrepreneurs were able to recover from the panic within a few months' time. Benjamin Veitel Ephraim's extraordinary credit at the Bank of Amsterdam was repaid by January 12, 1764. Repayment of the entrepreneurs' larger loan from Frederick took slightly longer and did not occur until February 18, 1764 (Rachel and Wallich 1967, 454). However, the total production of silver coin at Prussian mints over March–December 1763 was a robust 178 tons (Schrötter 1910, 521), indicating that the entrepreneurs were able to restore mint output once the shock of the panic had passed. By January 1764, the effective silver price for Berlin went below 14 Reichsthaler for the first time since 1755 (Table 8.2), indicating that the markets sensed a return to the prewar (Graumann) standard.

The Graumann standard was officially restored on March 29, 1764, at which time the operation of Prussia's mints was returned to government officials (Gaettens 1955, 161). Simultaneously, the mints were authorized to offer repurchase of war coins at various discounts ranging from 41 to 73 percent (Schrötter 1910, 183). March 1764 also saw the reinstatement of compulsory silver deliveries by Jewish residents. As had occurred before 1750, Prussia paid a fixed submarket price for these deliveries, of 12 Reichsthaler per fine mark. The delivery quota was initially set at 1.9 tons of silver in total and was later raised to a nominal level of 7 tons. In practice, exemptions from the quota were granted for persons operating industrial enterprises within Prussia (Schrötter 1913, 128–30).

Despite these efforts to place some distance between Frederick and the by now thoroughly unpopular figures of Ephraim and Itzig (associated in many minds not only with wartime debasement but also the postwar panic), some aspects of Prussia's coinage continued to be managed by its erstwhile mint entrepreneurs. The official channels of silver quotas and voluntary reminting of war coins proved insufficient to supply the mints, and the same network of purchasers who had disseminated the debased war coins was now tasked with removing these from circulation. Schnee (1955, 142) describes 44 purchasers as active in one province alone (Pomerania) in 1766, and directed efforts to remove wartime coinage from circulation continued until about 1770 (Schrötter 1910, 235).

The need for entrepreneurs' affining services also persisted. A July 1764 contract with the Prussian crown awarded the Ephraims the exclusive right to process war coins at their affinery in Amsterdam (i.e., Muiden), promising a fixed price of 13 Reichsthaler per fine mark for affined silver (Schrötter 1910, 423–26). The contract remained in effect for three months until a domestic affinery could be set up behind an Ephraim property in Berlin. The younger Ephraim's affining operations in Muiden continued in operation until 1769, when he became implicated in an insurance fraud and was forced to flee back to Prussia (Müntz 1769–1770, 48).

The last echoes of Prussia's wartime inflation were felt in the country where most of the war money had been dispensed, Poland. There, the destabilizing flood of debased coins from Prussia led to a recognition that Poland needed its own national coinage. However, lengthy debates, court intrigues, and a royal succession delayed any monetary reform. Finally, in December 1765, the new Polish king Stanisław II August was able to enact a standard based on the 1753 Austrian-Bavarian Convention standard (10 *Conventionsthaler* = 80 *złotych* per mark of fine silver), rather than the locally unpopular Graumann standard. Implementation of new coinage proved as problematic in Poland as it had in Prussia, meaning that war coins continued to circulate for some years afterward, their poor reputation and official demonetization notwithstanding (Hoensch 1973, 149–75).

8.8 Conclusion

Prussia's wartime debasement was a private-sector extension of the system developed by its prewar mint director Graumann and enthusiastically embraced by Frederick himself. Although the literature sometime presents the debasement as an exercise in fraud, a closer examination reveals that "the thin line between debasement and counterfeiting" (Volckart 2018) was never clear-cut. Graumann's original plan was for Prussia to capture premia such as already existed for Dutch trade coins like the silver rijksdaalder and the gold dukaat. The irony was that Graumann's plan relied on a ready supply of precious metal from Amsterdam. Successful implementation of the plan also required predatory circulation of Prussian-produced coin in neighboring countries. Graumann's failure to grasp this practicality led to his dismissal and replacement by the mint entrepreneurs.

Contractual limits on the entrepreneurs were eased with the outbreak of war and got easier as hostilities dragged on. The absence of restraint facilitated money creation: a reasonable guess of the quantity of silver the entrepreneurs processed is around 800 tons for the years 1758–1761. This figure is an estimate of gross flows that were partly accommodated through the recycling of coin already in circulation. However, evidence presented above suggests that much of the entrepreneurs' silver was obtained from coin withdrawals at the Bank, which totaled 555 tons for this same period (again, flows). The same evidence indicates that access to credit, especially credit in the Amsterdam bill market, was crucial in allowing the entrepreneurs to obtain such extraordinary quantities of precious metal.

At the end of the war, much of Prussia's debased silver returned to the Dutch Republic for affining before it could be reminted as full-weight coin. Amsterdam's bill market played a big part in financing this operation. When credit from Amsterdam collapsed in August 1763, the entrepreneurs needed emergency loans of 2 million Reichsthaler (about 2.2 million bank florins) from Frederick and 365,000 bank florins from the Bank to replace their lost liquidity.

The wartime debasement carried reputational costs for Frederick, but his famous defense was unapologetic: "When two rulers are at war, the best peace treaty will go to the one with the last Thaler in his pocket" (Buchner

1862, 343). A question has been where Frederick got his hands on so many Thaler(s), particularly since Prussia had essentially no credit, limited access to natural sources of silver, and no central bank. One answer is that much of Prussia's war money originated in Amsterdam. Although Prussia lacked a central bank, its mint entrepreneurs could tap the pool of silver held at Amsterdam's central bank. Prussia could not monetize its own debt, but it could monetize bills drawn on the entrepreneurs. These arrangements were clumsy by modern standards but sufficient to keep Frederick's pockets well supplied for most of the war.

9

The Bank's Place in Central Bank History

To conclude, we place the Bank of Amsterdam into a selective history of central banks in order to evaluate its modernity. This history is selective, in part because the journey to the present state of central banking has not been a smooth procession from Amsterdam through London to New York.[1] The Bank and its old ways died at the end of the eighteenth century, to be displaced by the new type of central bank invented by the Bank of England and manifested in the Netherlands in 1814 by the founding of De Nederlandsche Bank.[2] This model of central banking would eventually spread to all countries, including the United States in 1913, and be heavily modified in response to later events. Our take on this history is that the key feature of the post-1683 Bank has persisted: managed central bank liquidity, as embodied in the fiat portion of the Bank, paired with on-demand liquidity in exchange for safe assets, as manifested by the receipt portion of the Bank. This chapter will describe two cycles of extinction and subsequent reinvention of this idea.

This combination first evolved and has since reevolved from the implementation side of central banking. There is in every central bank a division between "white-collar" (policy) and "blue-collar" (implementation)

---

[1] A full survey of central bank history since the demise of the Amsterdamsche Wisselbank would require multiple volumes. This chapter instead only focuses on two well-documented Anglo-Saxon institutions (the Bank of England and the US Federal Reserve), which are commonly seen as inheriting the Wisselbank's dominant role in international finance.

[2] De Nederlandsche Bank was founded in 1814 and was meant to supersede the Amsterdamsche Wisselbank (De Jong 1930,1934; Uittenbogaard 2014). To the consternation of Amsterdam merchants, the design of this new institution did not incorporate a receipt facility. "As late as 1823 Van der Hoop stuck to his guns, grumbling that the abolition of the Wisselbank had killed the bullion trade, and he was not alone" (Jonker 1996, 165).

functions (Bindseil 2014, 11). The white-collar function is the formulation of principles by which monetary policy is conducted. Scholarly discussions of central banks are often focused on their white-collar aspects. To cite one prominent example, James (2020) describes a trend in central banking from the 1990s, in which policy has become increasingly oriented around rule-based approaches such as inflation targeting. The job of applying white-collar principles is, however, usually left to a less visible division of the central bank, the blue-collar function, whose task it is to actualize policy. A gentler name for the blue-collar function is "policy implementation," a term that implies rigid subordination of the implementation function to principles. In practice, however, shifting market realities can place hard limits on policy choices, leading to thoroughgoing changes in the latter.

Shifts in implementation can also bind policy through the force of another dialectic, rooted in the tensions surrounding central bank credibility.[3] To insulate monetary policy from political pressures, central banks are often set apart from direct political control. To credibly limit the range of that independence, central banks also exist as organizations whose charters impose tight restrictions on what they may own and do. Restrictions may enhance a central bank's legitimacy by delineating the appropriate use of its power (Tucker 2018), but there are always temptations to deviate during unforeseen market circumstances: "this time is different," in the words of Reinhart and Rogoff (2011). The political economy of time and place can pressure a central bank to experiment through different implementations, possibly compromising a reputation built on predictability. Attempts to manage this rules-versus-discretion trade-off have been a driving force in the evolution of central banks.

Earlier chapters have discussed how these forces shaped the Bank. The Bank's original 1609 charter envisioned a tightly constrained, mostly blue-collar institution, one that would take in trade coins, reliably pay them out, and keep a clean set of transfer books. The simplicity of these tasks meant that political independence was not seen as necessary. The Bank's collar then got whiter (and its discretion greater) as time progressed, but the impetus for whitening came not so much from legislative mandates as from practical adaptations. Commonality of interests within Amsterdam's ruling class meant that the Bank did not suffer for legitimacy. The end

---

[3] This is a topic with a large literature that we will not attempt to survey here. For a concise review of various historical approaches to ensuring central bank credibility, see Bordo and Siklos (2016).

result was a central bank with a split personality: a blue-collar receipt bank with virtually no room for discretion, attached to an esoteric fiat bank subject to few bounds other than market discipline ("honor," in contemporary terminology). We will argue that this pinstriped (half-blue-, half-white-collar) design was highly advanced, if not completely unique, for its time and was revived by the Bank of England 161 years later, albeit in modified form.

As noted in the introduction, recent years have seen a greater revival of the old blue-collar toolkit. Modern central banks have adopted fiat money, and the dominant form of that money has shifted from notes to accounts. How those fiat accounts are created and destroyed is mostly through various types of open market operations but can also occur through repurchase operations, including repo facilities. In these ways, the Bank of Amsterdam was ahead of its time: arguably, it was the first modern central bank. What modern central banks have not yet done is to promote all-comers' standing repurchase facilities as their primary mode of market interaction. We would argue that the Bank's experience offers lessons in the promise and peril of using these tools in that way.

9.1 From Then to Now

The evolutionary path from the earliest public banks, through institutions such as the Bank of Amsterdam, to modern central banks, has involved multiple waves of speciation and extinction. Ideas such as fiat money and repo facilities have been experimented with, abandoned, and occasionally rediscovered. The pattern of progression has been one of punctuated evolution: concepts borrowed from other central banks are combined with practical adaptations to yield small changes in policy frameworks, which occasionally break through to yield wholly different kinds of institutions. The next sections review some of these evolutionary episodes.

The Bank's history illustrates the basic pattern. Its original design was not a new concept but an adaptation of a Venetian public bank, the Banco della Piazza di Rialto. Nor was the Rialto Bank an entirely original institution, but one whose design borrowed from earlier public banking institutions such as Barcelona's Taula di Canvi (founded 1401) and Genoa's Casa di San Giorgio (founded 1407), as well as Venice's rich tradition of private banking (Ugolini 2017, 35–45). The success of the Bank of Amsterdam helped spread the idea of public banks to various jurisdictions in northern Europe, including several Dutch cities (Delft 1621, Middelburg 1616, Rotterdam 1635), Hamburg (1619), Nuremberg (1621), Stockholm

(1657), Leipzig (1698), and Vienna (1706). By one count, 25 public banking institutions were active in Europe by the close of the seventeenth century.[4]

Each of the early public banks has a unique life story, but the common motivation for their founding was local dissatisfaction with existing arrangements for banking, payments, or public credit. A public bank was envisioned as a more trustworthy intermediary between creditors and debtors, payors and payees, state and citizens, ideally so trustworthy that its liabilities (meaning usually ledger balances) would be seen as safe assets within a given community. Trustworthiness was promoted by various forms of legal privilege: monopoly charters, freedom of accounts from attachment, dedicated revenue streams, etc. When successful, claims on the public bank would then emerge as a highly liquid, mostly safe asset, one that expanded the scope for trading in all sorts of financial claims.

The market reality was that privilege did not always equate with safety: the only universally accepted safe assets of the era were high-quality trade coins, whereas the backing assets of the early public banks typically consisted of a variety of coins and various kinds of debt. The hope was that if good coins were concentrated within a credible municipal bank rather than dispersed outside it, then a higher volume of safe-asset transactions could be sustained with a lesser stock of coin, via giro payments. Hope rarely triumphed over experience. If account balances at the public bank were made redeemable in high-quality coin in order to uphold their safe-asset status, then the bank's coin stock could be depleted in a run as circumstances shifted. Or if redeemability was diluted in order to prevent runs, then the bank could not pretend that its liabilities were safe assets.

The great number of early public banks gave rise to many approaches to this problem. Two endpoint cases merit special mention. One is Venice's second attempt at a public bank (Banco del Giro, 1619–1800), which did not offer on-demand redeemability of its accounts until 1666, and operated on a managed fiat standard during its first decades (see, e.g., Roberds and Velde 2016a, 336–39; Ugolini 2017, 226–27). A second endpoint was offered by the Bank of Hamburg (Hamburger Bank, 1619–1875). After 150 years of experimentation, the Bank of Hamburg decided (in 1770) to sidestep the convertibility issue, and instead simply offer to buy its

---

[4] See Clapham (1945a, 3). A classic reference on pre-Napoleonic public banks is Van Dillen (1934). More recent surveys can be found in Roberds and Velde (2016 a, b, c), Ugolini (2017) and Bindseil (2020). Summary tables of these institutions are given in Roberds and Velde (2016c, 42–43) and Bindseil (2020, 76).

customers' silver at one price and sell it back to them at a slightly higher price.[5] Partly due to this policy (and due to conservative lending policies) Hamburg was one of the few early public banks to survive the disruptions of the Napoleonic era.

These special cases aside, the more common outcome was an unsatisfactory fudge. A public bank would promise some degree of redeemability, but people knew such promises could not always be kept. Depositors would run at a hint of trouble. The consequence was, in more favorable circumstances, temporary suspensions of redemptions (as occurred in Hamburg during 1672), or in less favorable ones, closure and liquidation of the bank (as occurred with Genoa's Banco di San Giorgio, shuttered in 1444).

The Bank of Amsterdam's release from this quandary was to combine elements of the endpoint cases into a single institution. Functionally this was accomplished by the unbundling of Bank deposits into transferable account balances and negotiable rights to withdrawal (receipts). A clean unbundling had to work around some blue-collar bookkeeping problems, which led to Bank account balances becoming a fiat money (Chapter 5). Post unbundling, risk-averse Bank customers came to see the Bank as 100 percent backed by trade coins. The seemingly fully backed Bank did have a less visible, fractionally backed counterpart, which smoothed fluctuations in the more visible receipt bank through open market operations (Chapter 7). The Bank's true structure was sufficiently obscured that even well-informed outsiders such as James Steuart could only guess its form. This opaque design nonetheless supported the Bank's credibility over nearly a century, from 1683 until the early 1780s.

9.2 Creative Destruction

The next big evolutionary leap occurred in an inhospitable habitat: England. For most of the seventeenth century, England was an unlikely

---

[5] See Roberds and Velde (2016a, 351). The Bank of Hamburg, founded in 1619, had many parallels with the Bank of Amsterdam, including a two-bank structure (separate deposit and lending arms) and a distinct, legally recognized unit of account for bank money (the *mark banco*). In an 1816 essay (26), David Ricardo urged that the Bank of England orient itself around a policy for gold analogous to Hamburg's for silver. It is unknown to what extent Ricardo's proposal was influenced by the earlier experience of Hamburg and other public banks. Detailed investigation of the Bank of Hamburg has unfortunately been hindered by the almost complete destruction of its records during the nineteenth century.

location for any institution resembling a public bank, much less for a central banking revolution that would sweep away the old style. Events such as the 1672 "Stop of the Exchequer," a de jure moratorium on royal debt payments, did not inspire confidence in the monarchy (Li 2019). Confidence in money was also low, because coin circulating in England during this period tended to be severely clipped and worn (Quinn 1996, 481). To the astute English diarist Samuel Pepys (1902 [1666], 447), the possibility of an Amsterdam-style chartered bank operating in London seemed remote:

The unsafe condition of a Bank under a Monarch, and the little safety to a Monarch to have any; or Corporation alone (as London in answer to Amsterdam,) to have so great a wealth or credit, it is that makes it hard to have a Bank here.

It is also unlikely that the Stadholder Willem (soon to be William) III was contemplating public banks when his invasion force crossed the English Channel in 1688 (funded in part with bills payable through the Bank of Amsterdam). The more pressing matter was the forcible unseating of James II, William's father-in-law and uncle, from the English throne. But after a quick military triumph and a constitutional convention, the new King William III was in a position to attempt additional conquests, if only the necessary funds could be found. Sourcing these funds required some financial engineering.

Government defaults and coin debasement were common fiscal strategies in early modern Europe, but neither had the parliamentary support that William would need under England's evolving constitution. A more fundamental problem faced by William was English resistance to Continental levels of taxation (Fritschy 2017, 251–310). Parliament also insisted on short-term funding, so long-term borrowing was "expensive, small in its relative amount, and tentative and experimental in form" (Dickson 1967, 47). The earliest attempts at more stable funding were tontines and lotteries, instruments that suffered from illiquidity. A different approach was some type of fund that allowed investors to easily liquidate their stake. William Patterson proposed a "transferable fund of interest" supported by interest-paying short-term bills that would need to be routinely rolled over, and Michael Godfrey proposed a corporation with transferable shares and short-term bills (Kleer 2017, 30–33). Both of these "projectors" would become directors of the new Bank of England.

England's projected bank drew on the example of Genoa's Casa di San Giorgio, a nominally independent institution that was privately owned but dedicated to public finance (Clapham 1945a, 15–16). Under the proposed design, William would obtain his first round of war funding immediately and without coercion, voluntarily paid over as capital by the bank's shareholders. Investors would gain shares more liquid than contemporary forms of government debt. The new bank would hold interest-bearing state debt backed by customs duties and issue lower-cost debt in the form of circulating notes, as well as receive an annual management fee.[6] London merchants could use the bank's notes (under optimistic projections) as an alternative to scarce good coin. Shareholders could (again, optimistically) earn a nice return on their leveraged capital via the spread on the state's versus the bank's debt. Confidence in the scheme was to be reinforced by new taxes, levied by Parliament, and by redeemability of the bank's liabilities into coin.

This proposal (the winner out of 70 schemes considered) was realized in 1694 when Parliament chartered the Bank of England and the bank's initial stock issue sold out within 12 days (Clapham 1945a, 19–20). The chartered bank did finance much state debt, albeit only debt that had been authorized by Parliament. Lingering public distrust meant that the bank's existence was only assured for a limited term (11 years in the initial charter), but forecasts of the bank's profitability were proved correct and the Bank of England has been in operation ever since. Its success made it into a prototype for subsequent central banks. England's bank was in its conception a very different type of institution from Amsterdam's and Table 9.1 highlights some major differences between the two institutions.

Despite its somewhat speculative beginning, England's public bank soon showed itself as advanced over Amsterdam's in at least four respects. The first advancement was political, the upscaling of the public-bank concept to a national level.[7] This was no small accomplishment, because skepticism of a public bank in a monarchy, as recorded in the passage by Pepys, was deep and widespread. Two earlier attempts to found public banks in England had failed (Clapham 1945a, 13). Michael Godfrey, the first Deputy Governor of the Bank of England, attempted to allay public uneasiness in a colorfully worded essay:

Another comes cock-a-hoop, and tells ye, that he or his grandsire, uncle, or some of the race, have been in some country or other, and in all their peregrinations they

---

[6] In addition to notes, the Bank of England also offered transactions accounts (known as "drawing accounts," to distinguish them from accounts at the bank's discount window). These accounts were less critical than in Amsterdam because they lacked a privileged status as a settlement medium for bills of exchange.

[7] Such an upscaling had already occurred in Sweden with the 1668 chartering of the Bank of the Parliament (Riksens Ständers Bank); see Heckscher (1934).

Table 9.1. *Salient features of the post-1683 Bank of Amsterdam and the early Bank of England*

	Bank of Amsterdam	Bank of England
Chartering entity (date)	City of Amsterdam (1609)	Kingdom of England (1694)
Ownership	Public (municipal)	Private under public charter
Term of charter	Perpetual	Initially to 11 years; subsequently renewed
Initial capitalization	None	Private shareholders
Profits	Paid to City Treasury at the end of each year	Paid as dividends to shareholders, with some portion (the "Rest") retained as a capital buffer
Monopoly privileges	Settlement of all bills of exchange payable in Amsterdam (later relaxed)	Only large issuer of banknotes in London (from 1708)
Principal types of assets	Bullion, coin, VOC debt	Bullion, coin, English national debt, bills of exchange
Principal types of liabilities	Ledger accounts	Accounts and banknotes
Redeemability of liabilities	From 1683, only with receipt	Unconditional
Unique unit of account?	Yes (bank florin)	No
Total liabilities (million bank florins)		
– in 1750	17.96 (accounts)	45.4 (notes); 20.1 (accounts)
– in 1788	18.41 (accounts)	114.8 (notes); 27.3 (accounts)

Sources: Clapham (1945a, 295–96), Van Dillen (1934, 120–21), Broz and Grossman (2004, 51), exchange rates from Castaing's *Course of the Exchange.*

never met with banks nor storks anywhere but in republics. And if we let them set footing in England, we shall certainly be in danger of a commonwealth (Godfrey 1694, 8).

Godfrey went on to argue that a chartered bank was necessary if England, as a kingdom, wanted to enjoy the same commercial success as seen in republics. If London wanted to be as rich as Amsterdam, the English would have to learn from the Dutch:

Whatever the groundless jealousies of men may be, none can reasonably apprehend any other consequences of this [bank's] design to government and nation, but that it will make money plentiful, trade easy and secure, raise the price of lands, draw the species of gold and silver into the hands of the common people, as we see it in Holland, Genoa, and other places . . . (ibid., 15).

Less emphasized in Godfrey's writings was a second advanced feature of the Bank of England, which was its substantial private equity capital, a necessity given the kingdom's fiscal urgency and the Bank's leveraged design. Accumulated profits could be to some extent retained, bolstering the resiliency of the bank, and shareholders could be called upon to inject additional capital. This structure contrasts with the Bank of Amsterdam, which as a municipal agency had no initial capital and was required to pay out its accumulated earnings, leaving little or no cushion for stress situations (see Figure 5.13).

Also unlike Amsterdam, the Bank of England was never granted a privileged status in the settlement of bills of exchange.[8] London merchants did lobby for a homegrown version of Amsterdam's coin receipt facility, but they did not get one (Magens 1753, 35). These shortcomings were more than made up for by a third advance over the Bank of Amsterdam, which was the issue of bearer notes.[9] The earliest Bank of England notes, high-denomination and often interest-bearing, were not what we would recognize today as circulating currency.[10] Initially, notes were a tiny part of the bank's balance sheet, but the recoinage crisis of 1695 spurred demand that never subsided (Kleer 2017, 36–47). Once the bearer notes gained a sufficient network of circulation, they represented an advance over account-based bank money. People did not need to have a bank account to pay and receive bank funds, broadening the market for such money and bolstering the Bank of England's market footprint. Bookkeeping costs were likewise reduced. Occasional cases of fraud were kept to a minimum by restricting note issues to large and uniform amounts. Rival banknote issuers in metropolitan London were effectively suppressed when the Bank renewed its charter in 1708, gaining a clause that prohibited other

---

[8] Centralization of settlement within London did occur in the nineteenth century, as discussed later.

[9] The issue of bearer notes by public banks had been successfully pioneered in Naples during the late sixteenth century (Costabile and Nappi 2018; Velde 2018), so this was another borrowed idea. While the idea of public banknotes was not new, a successful large-scale implementation was a triumph. As described earlier (Chapter 5), the Bank of Amsterdam's attempts at bearer note issue had resulted in egregious fraud and public humiliation for its Bank.

[10] See Richards (1934, 219–230). As the notes gained in popularity, interest was eliminated and denominations were reduced.

note issue by other banks having more than six partners (Richards 1934, 212).

The popularity of its banknotes allowed the Bank of England a high degree of presence in the London money market. This popularity was reinforced by a fourth advanced feature, which was the ability to directly funnel liquidity to the London bill market by discounting bills of exchange.[11] At first, the privilege of discounting was restricted to customers who banked solely with the Bank of England, but later was extended to any market participant judged to have sufficient standing (Richards 1934, 255). Like Amsterdam's receipt redemption fees, the early Bank of England's discount rates were rarely varied, remaining between 4 and 5 percent over the eighteenth century (Clapham 1945a, 299).

These various adaptations – national chartering, leverage combined with strong yet liquid capitalization, note issue, and credit to private parties – came together to yield a successful new species of public bank, one that was firmly connected to state finance. Success brought additional burdens, as the Bank of England was compelled to take on more and more state debt in each re-chartering, but the Bank managed to reduce its share of the debt with a pivot toward debt administration (Broz and Grossman 2004, 51). By the dawn of the French Revolution, England's bank had survived and grown to almost eight times the size of Amsterdam's, largely on the strength of its note issue (cf. Table 9.2).

9.3 The Two-Bank Solution

The triumphant success of the Bank of England was reflected not only in its size, but its ability to weather the Napoleonic-era troubles that either crippled or extinguished many of its public-bank counterparts, the Bank of Amsterdam included. The Bank of England suspended convertibility in 1797 but was able to resume in 1821 (O'Brien and Palma 2020). England's successful model of a nationally chartered, note-issuing public bank became the new norm for public banks. Note-issuing institutions resembling the Bank of England (more or less) could be found in most developed countries by the close of the nineteenth century, by which time they were

---

[11] In Amsterdam, this discounting role would have been played by its private merchant banks (cf. Chapter 2). Shifting a portion of the discounting business to a public bank may have been less efficient during normal times (Calomiris and Haber 2014, 93–99) but expanded the Bank of England's ability to support the bill market during crisis episodes. In the nineteenth century, the discount rate would become an important instrument of monetary control.

increasingly called "central banks."[12] The dissolution of the Bank of Hamburg and its merger into the Prussian State Bank in 1873 (soon to become the Reichsbank) ended the last major example of a ledger-money, municipally chartered public bank (Roberds and Velde 2016a, 352–53).

This success story did not mean that the Bank of England was wholly excused from the safe-asset issue that had dogged its predecessors. The bank's purpose was to extend credit, through its lending to the state and its discounting of private bills. Was it lending too much or too little? Bank liabilities (notes and accounts) were redeemable in coin but would the Bank's metallic reserve be sufficient to meet redemption demands? Over time, these questions grew more pressing because the bank, like other early public banks, shielded most details of its balance sheet from public view. This opacity came under increasing political pressure after 1832, however (Horsefield 1953, 125). The resolution of these concerns, as embodied in the famous debates of the "Banking School" and the "Currency School" and the subsequent passage of the 1844 Bank Charter Act (known as Peel's Act) would entail a two-bank solution with similarities to the solution embraced by Amsterdam in 1683.

This is not the place to recount the history of this debate and the act, but we will point out that the two-bank solution had its origins in an 1824 essay by an author with family roots in Amsterdam – David Ricardo (Ricardo 1824; Horsefield 1953, 116), who would have been well acquainted with the operation of the receipt window. Soon thereafter (by 1830), the Bank of England tried out its own, rather informal version of Ricardo's recommended "currency principle" (i.e., 100 percent metallic backing of all circulating banknotes, issued by a single-purpose National Bank). This modified currency principle, known as the Palmer rule, called for 100 percent *marginal* backing of the Bank of England notes, combined with a policy that the bank's total securities holdings would not exceed some fixed level (Horsefield 1953, 113–14).[13] A financial crisis that began in 1837 revealed that this informal approach would not be sufficient. Under pressure from crisis liquidity demands, the Bank of England was eventually forced (in 1839) to discount bills with the Banks of France and Hamburg in order to maintain the value of the pound and to reinforce its own liquidity

[12] The well-known examples include the Banque de France (1800), Austria's National Bank (1816), Germany's Reichsbank (1875), the Bank of Japan (1882), and many others. An outlier was the United States, which did not permanently establish a central bank until the 1913 creation of the Federal Reserve System.

[13] At this point the Bank of England was still privately owned, so implementing Ricardo's ideal of 100 percent backing would have curtailed profits to its shareholders.

(Clapham 1945b, 169). This embarrassing turn of events led to the passage of Peel's Act in 1844.

The act split the Bank of England into two sub-banks, known as "departments." This was a de jure rather than the de facto division as occurred in late seventeenth-century Amsterdam.[14] The underlying idea was similar, however. The Bank of England would be stabilized by creating a narrow sub-bank within the bank, one whose liabilities would be firmly tied to reliable metallic assets and freely available to market participants. In the case of the Bank of England, the narrow bank was known as the "Issue Department," which was legally constrained (rather than informally, as before) to hold at most £14 million in securities, otherwise only coin (mostly in gold) and bullion. Issue of banknotes was restricted to this department (Clapham 1945b, 183). The Bank of England was also obliged to purchase any offered gold bullion with its banknotes, at a price above a specified minimum. As before, notes were redeemable in British gold coins ("sovereigns") at a slightly higher price, which could not be varied. Central bank money could be created on demand by selling bullion to the bank, and extinguished by redeeming notes.

Customer bank accounts were to be kept at a second sub-bank, the "Banking Department." The Banking Department was allowed to discount bills and hold variable amounts of securities. Its reserve was to be mainly held in the form of notes issued by the Issue Department ("own notes"). Table 9.2 illustrates the two-bank structure for the Bank of England's balance sheet. After the passage of Peel's Act, balance sheets such as the one in the table were published each week in a document known as the Return.

Here we should point out some parallels and distinctions between the post-1844 Banking Department and the post-1683 fiat sub-bank of the Bank of Amsterdam (Chapter 7). A key similarity was that each sub-bank was firmly bound to a more mechanistic sibling, that is, the fiat bank to the receipt bank in Amsterdam, the Banking Department to the Issue Department at the Bank of England (cf. Table 7.2). A key difference was that Amsterdam's fiat sub-bank was less constrained by this connection than was the Banking Department. This was because the customer accounts held with the Banking Department, while thought to be less money-like than circulating notes, still carried the right to redemption in

---

[14] Like the Amsterdam sub-banks explored in Chapter 7, the two divisions of the Bank of England were basically accounting constructs and not separate operational entities. This was different from Ricardo's original 1824 proposal, which required that note issue be devolved to a wholly separate institution, the proposed National Bank.

Table 9.2. *Two versions of the Bank of England's balance sheet of February 22, 1851*

As a consolidated bank				As two banks			
Assets		Liabilities and equity		Assets		Liabilities and equity	
Gold	15	Notes	28	Gold	14	Notes	28
Credit	40	Balances	17	Credit	14		
Own notes	9	Bills	1	*Issue Department*	28		28
		Equity	18	Gold	1	Balances	17
Total	64	Total	64	Credit	26	Bills	1
				Own notes	9	Equity	18
				Banking Department	36		36

Memo: In this table, the Proportion, being Banking department gold (1) plus notes (9) divided by balances (17) plus bills (1), is 55.5 percent.

Source: Bank of England Balance Sheets; figures are pounds sterling, rounded to the nearest million.

gold at a fixed price; that is, these were not fiat money.[15] This feature, in combination with the weekly publication of the Return, meant that the Banking Department would be subject to intense market discipline and would need to manage its balance sheet accordingly. Proponents of Peel's Act thought that this arrangement would enhance the stature of the Issue Department, thought to always be liquid due to its tight backing constraints, and downgrade the Banking Department to a secondary entity operating essentially as a commercial bank, one of many in London.[16]

The great story of nineteenth-century central banking is that this attempt to straitjacket the Bank of England into a mostly narrow bank was largely negated by subsequent developments, a triumph of blue-collar market forces over the white-collar intents of Peel's Act. The British

[15] It should be acknowledged that liabilities of the Issue Department (notes) and Banking Department (accounts) were not indistinguishable, as was the case with the liabilities of the constituent sub-banks of the Bank of Amsterdam. In practice, however, notes and accounts became closer substitutes than was imagined in 1844.

[16] See Clapham (1945b, 187–188). Peel's Act also limited currency issue by other English banks, eventually causing the Bank of England to become the near-monopoly issuer of circulating banknotes (ibid., 183–184). The intent was to concentrate much of the gold reserve of the nation within the Issue Department.

monetary landscape shifted, the Banking Department thrived, and the Bank of England developed techniques for active monetary control. The next section briefly describes some of these techniques and compares them to the ones employed by the high-tide Bank of Amsterdam.

9.4 Monetary Maps: 1750 and 1900

A comparison must first acknowledge that the mid-eighteenth-century Bank of Amsterdam and the late-nineteenth century Bank of England operated in very different worlds. Global economic output roughly tripled over the course of the nineteenth century (Bolt and Van Zanden 2020), and the global trade ratio rose from 7 percent of world GDP to 22 percent (Estavadeordal, Frantz, and Taylor 2003). Increased availability of consumer goods pushed their prices down in most countries (O'Rourke and Williamson 2002). The almost nonstop European wars of the early modern period gave way to a century of "armed peace" (Hoffman 2015).[17] A major contributing factor to this atmosphere of peace and prosperity was monetary stability. Gold displaced silver as the monetary standard, as large lodes were discovered in California, Australia, Alaska, and South Africa. By 1880, most developed countries had adopted some version of a gold standard, resulting in a system of stable exchange rates known as the Classical Gold Standard (CGS; see, e.g., Eichengreen and Flandreau 1997).

Despite this increase in the breadth, scale, and stability of economic activity, the monetary architecture of the CGS retained similarities with earlier eras. Payments and credit were oriented around the widespread availability of gold, but most trade did not consist of gold coins being swapped for goods. The great majority of money, 90 percent of it by 1913, existed not as gold but as paper claims thereto (Triffin 1997). Central banks, of which the leading example was the Bank of England, played critical roles in maintaining confidence in this fractional-reserve monetary system (Jobst and Ugolini 2016). The overriding role was, of course, preserving confidence in the convertibility of currencies to gold, but this had to be balanced against central banks' responsibility to provide credit to their financial sectors, particularly in crisis periods.

The key monetary instrument supporting international trade remained the bill of exchange, especially bills of exchange drawn on major financial

---

[17] Major conflicts did occur during this period in China, Latin America, and the United States. These were, however, more remote from the center of the world financial networks and arguably less disruptive to global monetary equilibrium.

centers, and above all bills on London (Accominotti, Ugolini, and Lucena-Piquero 2021). Bills drawn on (and accepted by) reputable London counterparties were seen as claims whose safe-asset status was guaranteed by their convertibility into claims on London banks, and ultimately, into claims on the Bank of England, which were redeemable in sovereigns. The core architecture of the CGS-era was thus not fundamentally different from the era of the Wisselbank.

At the pinnacle of the global safe-asset pyramid sat the Governor of the Bank of England, someone whose job required more than a modicum of sang froid. Each morning, the Governor would peruse a summary of the previous day's monetary data, focusing on a single critical number: the Proportion, or reserve ratio of the Banking Department (Sayers 1976, 30; cf. Table 9.2). The Governor would have had cause for nervousness during these perusals, because (1) the Proportion was typically lower than the Amsterdam fiat bank's reserve ratio,[18] (2) this number was revealed at the end of each week in the Return, and (3) virtually all of the Banking Department's liabilities were redeemable in gold on demand. Maintaining the Proportion at a level that assured confidence in the pound sterling, and hence, confidence in the worldwide gold standard, was therefore a major concern of Bank of England policy.

The officially designated tool for this job was the interest rate at the bank's discount window, known as the Bank rate, which was varied in order to manage the demand for discount credit. The official policy was to "play by the rules of the gold-standard game," by raising the Bank rate whenever gold became scarce on the London market (Keynes 2010 [1931], 220). A policy focus on interest rates was something new and something that would not have been considered in earlier eras. Changes in the Bank rate were rare before 1844 but frequent thereafter (Clapham 1945b, 429–32; Anson et al. 2017, 37). The Bank rate averaged about 4 percent but could rise sharply during crisis periods, even touching double digits (10 percent) for a brief period in 1857. The resulting policy framework was neatly summarized in a statement to the U.S. National Monetary Commission:

The Bank rate is raised with the object of either preventing gold from leaving the country, or of attracting gold to the country, and lowered when it is completely out of touch with the market rates and circumstances do not render it necessary to induce the import of gold.[19]

---

[18] The distribution of the Proportion over the CGS era is shown in Figure 9.1.
[19] National Monetary Commission (1912, 26), quoted in Sayers (1976, 29).

Table 9.3. *Comparison of monetary environments, Amsterdam 1750 and London 1900*

	Amsterdam circa 1750	London circa 1900
Central bank	Bank of Amsterdam	Bank of England
Deposit banks	Cashiers	Clearing banks
Units of account	Dual: bank florin and current florin	Unified: pound sterling
Redeemability of central bank accounts	Limited to receipts	Unconditional
Main settlement platforms	Dual: Bank giro transfers and cashiers' clearing	Unified: London Bankers Clearing House
Dealers in bills of exchange	Merchant banks	Primary: Merchant banks (acceptors) and discount houses Secondary: clearing banks, Bank of England
Dealers in precious metal	Private dealers	Bank of England
Principal metallic assets	Silver trade coins	Full-weight British gold coins (sovereigns), gold bullion
Secondary metallic assets	Local (gulden) coins, gold coins	Foreign gold coins

Sources: Ugolini (2013), Accominotti, Ugolini, and Lucena-Piquero (2021).

Subsequent research has revealed, however, that the discretionary policies pursued by the CGS-era Bank of England were more complex and secretive than this summary suggests. Policy devices known to earlier central banks continued to be employed. The full range of policies was first described by Sayers (1936, 1976), who, lacking access to the relevant archives, reconstructed these from financial press reports. With increased data availability, Sayers' descriptions have been expanded and revised in more recent research, including Ugolini (2013, 2016) and Accominotti, Ugolini, and Lucena-Piquero (2021). The CGS-Bank of England's policies were undertaken in a market environment with some resemblance to the Amsterdam environment described in Chapter 2 and mapped in Figure 2.4. For comparison, Table 9.3 summarizes the two environments.

The CGS-era Bank of England did play some roles that went well beyond the remit of the Bank of Amsterdam. Large inventories of sovereigns were needed for potential banknote and account redemptions, eventually causing the Bank of England to become the monopolist gold dealer for the London market (Ugolini 2013, 66–67). The Bank of England also maintained a presence in the bill market, an activity that was restricted to private parties (merchant banks) in 1750 Amsterdam. Many bills on London were also traditionally drawn on merchant banks (also called acceptors), but once accepted, could be sold on to specialized bill brokers (discount houses), deposit banks (clearing banks), and the Bank of England itself (Accominotti, Ugolini, and Lucena-Piquero 2021). Heavy involvement in this business (over 23,000 bills were handled by the bank's Discount Office in 1906) was necessary in order to keep the Bank rate "effective," that is, allow the Bank of England to exert direct influence on the London money market.

Despite this scale of activity, there were forces at work that tended to diminish the Bank of England's market footprint. A development that the framers of Peel's Act did not foresee was the expansion of checkable commercial bank deposits as an alternative to circulating notes. London's banks, legally prohibited or discouraged from note issue by the act, developed checks as an alternative payment instrument (Michie 2016, 82). Deposit banking, relegated to second-class firms (cashiers) in eighteenth-century Amsterdam, became the business model of the largest institutions in the London money market, the joint-stock (limited-liability) clearing banks. In 1864, the Bank of England integrated into this system by joining the London Bankers' Clearing House, a commercial banks' system for clearing and settling check payments (Matthews 1921, 26). Because the Clearing House settled on a net basis, however, the clearing banks did not need to maintain large balances with the Bank of England for settlement purposes. As the clearing banks expanded, the Bank of England came to occupy an ever-smaller niche in the British banking system, frustrating its efforts at monetary control (Ugolini 2016, 28).

The Bank of England responded to this situation by employing techniques that allowed it to punch above its diminished market weight. An important technique, a throwback to the methods of the Bank of Amsterdam, was to trade in secondary types of precious metal assets. Peel's Act did not regulate the Bank of England's dealings in foreign gold coins, perhaps because few countries other than Britain were on the gold standard as of 1844 (Ugolini 2013, 69). As the gold standard spread internationally, however, the Bank of England came to deal in more and more of these coins, which traded at variable prices in the London market.[20] Open market purchases (sales) of these coins could be employed

---

[20] Various types of gold coins carried liquidity premia in certain markets. Relative to the early modern era, however, steam navigation, telegraphic communication, and free

to reinforce discount-rate increases (cuts). Peel's Act did not specify bid and ask prices for foreign coins, leaving the Bank of England substantial freedom to adjust these to market conditions.[21] Such open market operations, known as "gold devices," resemble the Bank of Amsterdam's earlier dealings in gulden coins. Peel's Act also allowed the Bank of England the right, which it occasionally exercised, to raise its bid price for gold bullion. Such price rises could be employed to amplify the gold-attracting effects of an increase in the Bank rate.

Because the Bank held large stocks of marketable government and private securities, it could have bought and sold these as an alternative way to implement policy. In practice, however, it preferred to use gold devices and another, more secretive type of transaction, one that could obscure the weekly balance-sheet disclosures required by Peel's Act. These transactions, essentially reverse repos, consisted of the bank selling securities to private parties while committing to repurchase the same securities at a later date.[22] Corporate bonds and stocks were used for such operations, because holdings of these assets were included in a broad, hard-to-decipher category in the weekly Return (Ugolini 2016, 17–18). These transactions were not publicized but were frequently rumored in press reports, and were taken as a signal of impending increases in the Bank rate (Sayers 1936, 43–44). Through this technique the Bank avoided revealing the magnitude of its liquidity-draining operations, as would have been more obvious if it had dumped large quantities of government securities or gold assets.

Applied in concert, these devices allowed the CGS-era Bank of England a high degree of discretionary monetary control. When they sometimes proved insufficient, however, was during times of monetary stringency when the Bank's need to preserve its own liquidity could conflict with a need to function as lender of last resort. In such situations, two backup mechanisms were available. The first of these was the "Chancellor's letter,"

capital movement kept these premia within comparatively tight bands, known as "gold points" (Officer 1996). The price floor for all gold assets in London was the Bank of England's bid price for gold bullion.

[21] See Ugolini (2013, 76–83). The bid-ask spread allowed by Peel's Act for officially recognized gold assets ranged as high as 0.8 percent, giving the Bank of England freedom to deal in foreign gold at prices within this spread.

[22] A reverse repo is the opposite side of a repo transaction. In these transactions, the Bank of England essentially "borrowed" funds from its counterparties, paying interest for such borrowings. The Bank of England as a general matter did not pay interest on customer accounts, but reverse repos allowed it to pay interest without admitting as much. Several variations on this basic technique were employed by the CGS Bank of England; see Sayers (1936, 24–44).

referring to the Chancellor of the Exchequer. A Chancellor's letter was a declaration by the government, issued during times of stringency, that allowed for temporary removal of the paper wall around the reserves of the Issue Department. The letters carried an implied fiscal backing for the Bank of England (still a private entity) and allowed the Banking Department to access the Issue Department's reserves. Once a letter had been issued, the Bank of England could expand crisis lending with more confidence (Anson et al. 2017, 50). In some cases, the mere news that such a letter had been sent was enough to stop the threat of bank runs and allay a crisis. Somewhat ironically, there was often more enthusiasm from the government than from the still-private bank regarding the issue of such letters (Calomiris and Haber 2014, 188).

A second mechanism was for the Bank of England to enter into agreements with other central banks to obtain sufficient gold to quench panic demands in London. The most frequent counterparty in such agreements was the reserve-rich Banque de France (Flandreau 1997). These agreements were never automatic and were usually the outcome of secret, often uneasy negotiations. They were also a throwback to the measures employed over 1837–1839, which contributed to the passage of Peel's Act. However awkwardly, foreign liquidity provided through this mechanism allowed the Bank of England to weather potentially existential shocks such as the Barings Crisis (1890) and the Crisis of 1907.

The net impact of these techniques is shown in Figure 9.1, which plots the distribution of the Proportion of the Banking Department over the CGS period (1880 through 1913), taken from the weekly Returns. For comparison, the figure shows the distribution of reserve ratios for the fiat sub-bank of the Bank of Amsterdam, using monthly data from February 1711 (the beginning of reliable data) through January 1780 (the beginning of the Bank's difficulties with the Dutch East India Company or VOC). Both series stop on the eve of a major war that disrupted the prevailing monetary environment.

The figure shows that by applying a broader range of policy tools, the Banking Department was typically able to operate with a smaller reserve ratio than the fiat portion of the Bank of Amsterdam.[23] The median Proportion over the CGS period was 46 percent as compared to a 70 percent median reserve ratio for Amsterdam's fiat sub-bank. A lower reserve ratio created space for credit operations. Regular publication of the Return

---

[23] Moreover, the Banking Department's reserves were not exclusively metallic assets, but also consisted of claims on the Issue Department (own notes).

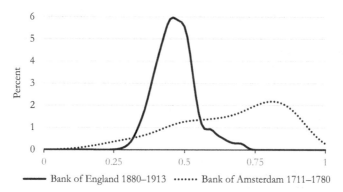

Figure 9.1. Distributions of reserve ratios for the Banking Department of the Bank of England (The Proportion) and the fiat sub-bank of the Bank of Amsterdam
Sources: Bank of England Historical Balance Sheets and authors' calculations; histograms with Gaussian smoothing.

apparently meant, however, that the Bank of England felt the need to maintain the Proportion within tight bounds: the interquartile range of the Proportion covers only a 10 percent interval (41–51 percent) as compared to a 30 percent interval (52–82 percent) for the fiat sub-bank's reserve ratio. While Amsterdam secretly stabilized the overall quantity of money, London publically stabilized the proportion of money.

To summarize this section, the CGS-era Bank of England relied on some new techniques to implement policy: well-publicized changes in the Bank rate, clandestine reverse repos, Chancellors' letters, and side deals with other central banks. At the core of this policy framework, however, was a two-bank structure resembling the one that had emerged in Amsterdam almost two centuries earlier (though perhaps more honored in the breach via Chancellors' letters). In addition, the Bank of England complemented its other policy moves with gold-device operations, a technique out of the Bank of Amsterdam's playbook. The Bank of England was not the only CGS-era central bank to utilize such operations. The Bank of France had a strong distaste for interest rate changes and much preferred quantitative interventions as a way to manage money-market pressures (Bazot, Bordo, and Monnet 2016). A recent survey of CGS-era central banks (Bazot, Monnet, and Morys 2022) provides evidence that similar interventions were employed by other central banks, in part to smooth interest-rate movements emanating from the Bank of England.[24]

---

[24] Other aspects of nineteenth-century central bank policy frameworks are surveyed in Jobst and Ugolini (2016).

9.5 The Once and Future Bank

While the CGS-era Bank of England did employ some techniques of the old Dutch masters, key features of the Bank of Amsterdam remained in the historical background until another extinction event – World War I – undermined the late-nineteenth-century paradigm. The Classical Gold Standard vanished during the summer of 1914, never to return. The 1920s substitute, known as the Gold Exchange Standard, proved unstable and did not enjoy the functionality of its prewar predecessor (Bordo and James 2014). The CGS-era monetary infrastructure was also undermined by World War I. The London bill market, formerly the focal point of the international monetary system, contracted massively. At the center of this market, the 1920s-era Bank of England struggled to find bills to discount.[25] "Monetary policy" in London and elsewhere increasingly came to mean central bank transactions in government debt, an asset that was in greater abundance after 1914.

Subsequent developments have brought new relevance to the old Bank of Amsterdam. The dissolutions of the Gold Exchange Standard over 1931–1933 (see, e.g., Eichengreen 1992) and the postwar Bretton Woods system in the 1970s (see, e.g., Bordo 1993) brought a return to fiat money. Many privately owned central banks were taken over by governments following World War II, although typically with some degree of statutory independence. The increased preference for electronic payments instruments over banknotes has reestablished the primacy of accounts. The growth in sovereign debt and its quasi-monetary functionality has thoroughly revived repo. Along these dimensions, we would argue that the Bank of Amsterdam came closer to being a modern central bank than many of its better-known successors.

The reappearance of repo merits additional discussion. Earlier chapters have described how merchants in eighteenth-century Amsterdam were able to mobilize safe assets through a repo-like mechanism offered through the Bank. From this experience, it does not seem surprising that modern finance has rediscovered repo as a way of liquefying collateral. Modern repos need not occur through central bank facilities, but instead may occur

---

[25] Sayers (1976, 278–279). The original vision for the Federal Reserve, as articulated by Paul Warburg, was for the Fed to help create a U.S. bill market comparable in stature to the prewar London market (Meltzer 2003, 70). Warburg was the scion of a prominent Hamburg banking family and was well acquainted with European financial institutions. Warburg's vision for the Federal Reserve was undermined by the events of World War I.

as market transactions between private parties. Many modern central-bank implementation frameworks make wide use of repos, however, a noteworthy example being the original policy framework of the European Central Bank, which relied almost exclusively on repos (European Central Bank 2001). On the other hand, modern central banks, unlike the Bank of Amsterdam, have hesitated to offer accounts and standing repo facilities to any and all significant players in their associated money markets. Repo markets have emerged as an alternative channel for converting safe assets to market liquidity.

Use of repurchase agreements increased during the 1970s, in part because repos offered a convenient, lightly regulated way for money market participants to take advantage of then-prevalent higher bond interest rates. Repos' legal standing in the United States was strengthened by 1984 legislation that established an exemption from bankruptcy stay (known as a "safe harbor"), for repos in Treasuries and related assets, which was later extended to repos in broader categories of assets.[26] Such laws have increased the moneyness of repo transactions by enabling the "collateral doubling" feature of repos, noted by Graumann (1762), in which a cash lender and cash borrower may both think of repo collateral as being effectively subject to their control.

Receipt transactions in eighteenth-century Amsterdam created central bank balances that could easily circulate through the local money (bill) market. Modern repo market transactions (between private parties) do not create central bank liquidity but can still take on a money-like character. In some situations, a cash lender in a repo transaction may have leeway to repledge collateral in order to obtain cash from other parties, an action that may be repeated several times over.[27] Singh (2011) refers to this collateral recycling as "velocity," an allusion to repo's monetary functionality.[28] This collateral multiplication feature of repo finance has been a major

---

[26] See, for example, Garbade (2006), Gorton and Metrick (2010), and Sissoko (2010). This safe-harbor exemption allows repo cash lenders the right to immediate liquidation of collateral in the event of a default. As noted earlier, the option-like structure of receipts effectively granted the Bank of Amsterdam immediate control of collateral upon expiration of a receipt.

[27] See Singh (2011). The "cash" in such transactions may or may not consist of central bank money. Repledging of collateral may be termed "rehypothecation" or "reuse" depending on precise circumstances of the transaction. Singh notes that United States law sometimes places limits on the repledging of collateral, depending on whether the original transaction is formally considered a repo or a securities lending transaction. Other jurisdictions do not place such limits on repledging.

[28] See Pozsar (2014) for examples of collateral recycling.

contributor to the growth of "shadow banking" (Gorton and Metrick 2010; Pozsar et al., 2010; Pozsar 2014), a generic term for quasi-monetary financial arrangements outside the scope of traditional, highly regulated deposit banking.

Although private repo dominates, repos also play important roles in modern central banking. The Federal Reserve, in particular, has long made use of repos. Fed repos began as early as 1917, when the Fed utilized repos in U.S. Treasury bonds to facilitate war finance (Garbade 2012, 193). After a long pause in the 1930s and 1940s, the Fed reinstated repos during the 1950s, as a way to smooth short-run fluctuations in prices of Treasuries (Garbade 2021, 152–66). Fed usage of repos was expanded in the 1960s to include repos in longer-term Treasuries, repos in agency securities (those of government-sponsored enterprises), and reverse repos (Garbade 2021, 351–70). In this era, the main purpose of repo operations was to allow the Fed's balance sheet to quickly expand or contract in response to temporary factors, without signaling a change in Fed policy.

This use of repos for "temporary operations" became less common after the 2008 Global Financial Crisis, when the Federal Reserve's balance sheet expanded and it started paying interest on reserve balances. Commercial banks' reserve balances expanded, lessening the need for such high-frequency interventions. On the other hand, the Fed's use of reverse repos has expanded dramatically since 2013, as a way of managing a larger balance sheet in the wake of the Global Financial Crisis and the March 2020 pandemic-induced liquidity scramble (discussed below).

The immense size of modern repo markets shows that repo has developed well beyond what was possible in eighteenth-century Amsterdam. Modern repo can also be precarious however. In market repo transactions, collateral valuations, haircuts, transaction size, and even market participation are private business decisions. In addition, most repos have an overnight tenor, meaning that terms are adjusted continuously. Repo liquidity that is readily available today may be harder to come by tomorrow, or simply unavailable. The functioning of repo markets has become a source of policy concern as these markets have expanded.

A major question facing the Federal Reserve, as well as other central banks, is what their role should be in this vital monetary sector. For U.S. dollar repo markets, participants include regulated commercial banks and primary Treasury securities dealers, but also many hedge funds, money market and other mutual funds, pension funds, broker-dealers, sovereign wealth funds, and other parties over whom the Federal Reserve has little or no regulatory oversight (Baklanova et al. 2019). Lacking such oversight, the

Federal Reserve has been reluctant to directly engage with these markets. The Fed's hand has nevertheless been forced in at least two recent, well-known instances of market disruption.[29]

The first disruption was the 2007–2008 Global Financial Crisis (GFC), when repo finance of privately issued, mortgage-backed debt instruments collapsed (Gorton and Metrick 2012), ultimately leading to the Lehman Brothers' bankruptcy (Copeland, Martin, and Walker 2011), a global crisis (the GFC), and a host of historic Fed emergency actions (Bernanke, Geithner, and Paulson 2019). A less publicized aspect of the GFC was the subsequent contraction of repo activity in all types of assets, including U.S. Treasuries (Copeland and Martin 2021). This deep falloff in repo liquidity was followed by a series of large open market purchases by the Federal Reserve (quantitative easings or QEs), a pattern of "sterilization" not unknown in eighteenth-century Amsterdam (cf. Chapter 7).

A second disruption occurred in March 2020 when pandemic-induced price fluctuations in U.S. Treasury securities put pressure on parties holding large portfolios of repo-leveraged long bonds, raising the specter of fire sales and accompanying Treasury market dysfunction (Schrimpf, Shin, and Sushko 2020; Barth and Kahn 2021). This again led to a sharp contraction of the repo market in U.S. Treasury securities (Kruttli et al. 2021) and massive Fed interventions, in the form of repos and large outright purchases of the least liquid Treasury issues.[30] This initial burst of open market activity was followed by another round of QE, which in total added $5 trillion of Treasury and agency securities to the Fed's balance sheet before it was phased out in March 2022.[31] This sequence of policy moves gave rise to a situation not unlike that experienced in Amsterdam in 1720 (cf. Chapter 6), when a large expansion of a central bank's balance sheet exerted supply-side pressures in markets for desirable

---

[29] Earlier, "near-miss" disruptions in repo markets include the 1982 failures of two bond dealers, Drysdale and Lombard-Wall (Garbade 2006), and the 1998 failure of a hedge fund, Long-Term Capital Management (LTCM; Jorion 2008). Each of these provoked Federal Reserve responses. Following the Drysdale failure, the Fed expanded its securities lending program, and following the Lombard-Wall failure, the Fed asked Congress to strengthen repos' safe-harbor status. The Fed also coordinated a buyout of LTCM by its creditors.

[30] Total Fed security holdings increased by $1.7 trillion over March and April 2020 and repos peaked at $240 billion (Federal Reserve Table H.4.1, *Factors Affecting Reserve Balances*, releases of March 5, March 12, and April 30, 2020). For a breakdown of Fed purchases over this period, see Barth and Kahn (2021).

[31] Federal Reserve Table H.4.1, *Factors Affecting Reserve Balances*, releases of March 5, 2020 and March 3, 2022.

safe assets (then: gold coins; now: certain Treasury securities). Fed responses to this situation have included an expansion of its reverse repo facility (absorbing cash that might otherwise require the use of Treasuries in the repo markets) and lending out securities in its own portfolio (making the most sought-after Treasuries available to private participants).[32] More recently, the Fed has been engaging in gradual sales of securities accumulated during the 2020–2022 QE episode, a policy known as quantitative tightening (QT).[33] This policy also finds an Amsterdam precedent, in the form of the Bank's gradual selloff of reluctantly accumulated gold coins over 1722–1725 (cf. Chapter 6).

Continued worries about the stability of repo markets have generated high-profile calls for more direct involvement by the Federal Reserve (Task Force on Financial Stability 2021; Group of Thirty 2021). Recommended measures include the operation of a Fed standing repo facility accessible by a broad range of counterparties. A concern mentioned in both of these reports is that such a facility might encourage excessive leverage, but both suggest that this downside would be outweighed by the stability benefit.[34] Partly in response to these and similar recommendations, the Fed established two standing repo facilities on July 28, 2021 (Board of Governors of the Federal Reserves System 2021). Eligible collateral at the facilities includes Treasury issues, agency issues, and agency mortgage-backed securities. Access to these facilities is limited. One facility is intended for use by the Fed's usual market counterparties (primary securities dealers) and the other for use by foreign official institutions.[35] The interest rate charged on repos through both facilities is slightly above market repo rates. This pricing reflects the facilities' announced purpose as backstops, should normal repo market financing become disrupted.[36]

---

[32] In financial statements of July 28, 2022, Fed reverse repos were $2.5 trillion and its loans of securities were $38 billion.

[33] Federal Open Market Committee, "Plans for Reducing the Size of the Federal Reserve's Balance Sheet," May 4, 2022.

[34] The Task Force on Financial Stability recommends that if non-bank users are granted access to the facility, they should pay an up-front fee.

[35] The first facility is formally structured as an auction facility with a minimum bid rate set slightly above prevailing market rates. More recently, it has become available to all commercial banks above a size threshold. The Task Force on Financial Stability (2021, 13) has advocated for broader access, including "all significant nonbank Treasury market participants."

[36] As of early 2022, interest in the first standing facility has been limited. Industry observers have attributed this lack of enthusiasm to stigma associated with transacting at above-market rates (Nelson 2022).

This topical policy issue brings us back to the main theme of this book. The experience of the Bank of Amsterdam shows that the integration of managed fiat accounts with standing repo is not a new concept. As discussed in earlier chapters, the Bank operated (in essence) a standing repo facility with a very aggressive design, made possible in part by the Bank's unique safe-harbor privilege. Any Amsterdam merchant of sufficient stature could be a Bank customer, and any Bank customer was eligible to participate in the repo arrangement. Interest rates at the facility were uniformly low. The Bank offered longer-term (six-month) repos and was willing to fully absorb market risks on eligible collateral, leaving execution of the second leg of the repo to the option of the customer. Haircuts on collateral were mostly determined by market forces and not by the Bank.

Market participants liked these generous terms, but operating such a facility was a tricky business, even in the eighteenth century. The Bank's history offers a litany of hard lessons. Overpricing of one category of collateral (gold coins) caused large quantities of this collateral to be dumped at the Bank in intermittent episodes, forcing temporary shutdowns of the private gold market and causing loss of monetary control for the Bank. Failure to adjust the terms of the facility during the Seven Years War led to an uncontrollable influx of collateral, followed by a major financial panic in 1763. Panic conditions then forced an easing of collateral standards for the repo facility. More generally, highly variable use of the facility compelled the Bank to engage in sterilizing operations, at times very substantial, in order to maintain the stability of its balance sheet. When fiscal dominance threatened the Bank in the early 1780s, it saw the best collateral run away from the repo facility, taking the Bank's reputation with it.

The prominent feature of the Bank that has not yet been replicated is the concentration of repo finance in a central-bank standing facility (cf. Chapter 6). To acquire comparable functionality, a future central bank would need to grant broad access to its accounts and facilities. Also, the central bank would need to be in a position to offer repos on more attractive terms than today's well-developed private repo market. This might occur (as it did with the Bank) due to an enhanced legal privilege, a willingness to deal with a wide cross-section of customers and assets, and a strong tolerance for market risk. If these stars were all to align, then one could imagine a New Bank of Amsterdam offering repos for a variety of near-money assets in exchange for account balances used to settle credits originating from around the world.

We doubt the stars will realign in this way because history rarely repeats so thoroughly, but something unexpected will happen. When it does, the relevance of the Bank's history will be a matter for future generations to determine. Our purpose has been to present this history with a modern sensibility that argues that the liquification of disparate safe assets on a centralized ledger, via repos, is not a novel idea nor one likely to disappear. The Bank's history shows that this idea can work, though success is hardly guaranteed.

Glossary

Where appropriate, equivalent Dutch terms are listed in italics. Definitions of modern terms follow official definitions of the Bank for International Settlements (BIS) or the Organisation for Economic Development and Co-operation (OECD).

Term	Dutch	Definition
acceptance	*acceptatie*	formal declaration by a drawee of a bill of exchange that the bill would be honored, as indicated by drawee's signature on the bill
acceptance credit	*acceptcrediet*	finance via drawing and redrawing bills of exchange, especially via a merchant bank as acceptor of the first bill
acceptor	*acceptant*	drawee of a bill of exchange who has accepted the bill
agio	*agio, opgeld*	premium, in particular the percent premium of Bank money over current money
agio market		our name for the daily spot market where current money was exchanged for Bank money
anticipation loans	*anticipatiepenningen*	credits granted by the Bank to the Company, in anticipation of sales of goods in transit from Asia
assayer	*essaijeur*	Bank employee who tested precious metal assets entering the Bank, as well as engaged in bespoke transactions involving precious metal

(*continued*)

(*continued*)

Term	Dutch	Definition
Bank	*Wisselbank*	the Bank of Amsterdam (*Amsterdamsche Wisselbank*)
bank florin	*bankgulden*	unit of account for Bank money
Bank money	*bankgeld*	money held as balances in Bank accounts
beneficiary	*begunstigde*	the party to whom a bill of exchange instructs to pay
brassage	*brassage*	a coin's unit production cost
bill of exchange	*wisselbrief*	an order instrument made by a drawer, instructing a drawee to pay a certain sum to a beneficiary, after a specified interval (usance)
bill-kiting	*wisselruiterij*	speculative cycle of drawing and redrawing
burgomasters	*burgemeesters*	second layer of City officials beneath the City's governing council, with authority over the Bank commissioners
calibration master	*ijkmeester*	an expert charged with testing weights used in monetary exchanges
cashier	*kassier*	a versatile type of proto-banker, involved in deposit banking, giro payments, banknote issue, settlement of current-money bills of exchange, and brokerage of the agio market
cashier's receipt	*kwitantie*	an order instrument issued by a cashier, entitling its bearer to receive the specified sum from the cashier in coin; essentially a banknote
City	*Stad Amsterdam*	the city of Amsterdam and particularly its government
commissioners	*commissarissen*	City officials in charge of Bank operations
coin weight box	*muntgewichtdoos*	specialized set of weights used to weigh coins
Company	*Oostindische Compagnie Amsterdam, Kamer Amsterdam*	the Amsterdam Chamber (division) of the Dutch East India Company
crowns	*kronen*	silver coins imprinted with a crown; see English crown and French crown
cruzados	*crusaden*	Portuguese gold trade coins

Term	Dutch	Definition
cupellation	*cupellatie*	traditional refining process that uses lead to separate out precious metals
current guilder	*courantgulden, kasgulden*	unit of account for money outside the Bank
current money	*courantgeld*	money in various forms held outside the Bank and not payable through the Bank
debase	*verlagen*	to reduce the precious metal content of a coin
debasement	*muntverzwakking*	generic term for debasing coins by various techniques
dollar	*daalder*	generic term for large silver coin, in reference to the German *Thaler*; often applied to Spanish coins
double stiver	*dubbeltje*	a silver coin worth 1/10th of a guilder
doubloons	*Spanse pistolen*	Spanish gold trade coins (*escudos*)
drawee	*betrokkene*	the party who is ordered to pay by a bill of exchange
drawer	*trekker*	the party making out a bill of exchange
drawing and redrawing	*wissel en herwissel, trekken en hertrekken*	financing arrangement involving reciprocal drawing of bills of exchange between merchants in different cities
drittels	*drittels*	German coins with a value of 1/3 *Thaler*
ducats	*dukaten*	term for large-value trade coins, in the Republic commonly applied to Dutch gold ducats; in reference to Venetian *ducato*
ducatoons	*ducatons*	(a) a large silver coin minted from the early seventeenth century in the Southern Netherlands (b) nickname for a later Dutch trade coin, the *zilveren rijder*
duit	*duit*	Dutch copper coin worth 2 pennies or 1/160th of a guilder
(Dutch) East India Company	*Vereenigde Oostindische Compagnie*	chartered company that managed trade between the Dutch Republic and Asia
endorsement	*endossement*	transferal of ownership of an accepted bill of exchange, as indicated by the signature of the party transferring the bill; endorsement implied joint liability

(*continued*)

(*continued*)

Term	Dutch	Definition
English crowns	*Englische kronen*	English silver coins
fallen (coins)	*vervallen*	term describing trade coins sold to the Bank whose receipt had expired without redemption or renewal
fine gold	*fijn goud*	pure gold
fine silver	*fijn zilver*	pure silver
fineness (of metal)	*gehalte*	pure silver or gold as a share of total weight
		Gold measured as pure = 24 karats (*karaten*) = 288 grains (*greinen*)
		Silver measured as pure = 12 pennies (*penningen*) = 288 grains (*greinen*)
florin	*florijn*	= guilder
French crowns	*Franse kronen*	French silver coins (*écus*)
friend	*vriend*	a merchant in another city who could be relied upon to accept one's bills of exchange
General Mint Masters	*Generaalmeesters van de Munt*	an agency of the States General tasked with supervising mints operated by the provinces
giro		a payment system in which funds are initiated by the payor
gold ducat	*gouden dukaat*	the principal gold coin of the Dutch Republic, primarily a trade coin
gold rider	*gouden rijder*	another Dutch gold coin, intended primarily for domestic use
governing council	*vroedschap*	the highest civic authority of the City of Amsterdam and the ultimate authority over the Bank
guilder	*gulden*	(a) the Dutch unit of account, 1 guilder = 20 stivers (*stuivers*) = 320 pennies (*penningen*)
		(b) a silver coin with a face value of one guilder
guinea	*guinee*	English gold coin, from the original African gold source
holder	*houder*	someone in possession of a bill of exchange, either as the beneficiary or having received it via endorsement
lion dollars, lion crowns	*leeuwendaalder*	Dutch large silver coins; by the late seventeenth century, principally a trade coin

Term	Dutch	Definition
local coins	*standpenning*	coins used primarily for domestic rather than international transactions and usually at par
Louis d'ors	*Franse pistolen*	French gold trade coins
mark	*mark*	(a) a unit of weight equal to 246.084 grams in the Dutch Republic or slightly less in Germany 1 mark = 8 ounces (*ons*) = 160 esterlins (*engels*) (b) during this period, a currency unit in northern Germany equal to 1/3 of a *Reichsthaler*
merchant bank	*banquier*	large firms involved in trade, trade finance, sovereign lending, and proprietary investment; typically not deposit funded
Mexican (coins)	*mexicanen*	Spanish dollars minted in Mexico
mint equivalent	*muntequivalent, muntvoet*	nominal value attached by ordinance to a given weight of precious metal, minted into a given coin
mint price	*muntprijs, leverprijs*	nominal value returned by a mint for a given weight of precious metal, minted into a given coin
moneychanger	*wisselaar*	dealer licensed by the City to exchange coins
open market operation		a sale or purchase of an asset by a central bank, in a market open to private parties (OECD)
patagons	*patagons, cruisdaalders*	silver coins minted in the Southern Netherlands, from the Spanish *patacón*
payee		=beneficiary
precious metals dealers	*Hoogduytsche Joden*	specialized firms trading in precious metal assets, typically run by people of German Jewish descent
penny	*penning*	a unit of account equal to 1/16th of a stiver or 1/320th of a guilder (florin)
pillars	*pilaren*	Spanish dollar minted in Peru
prolongation	*prolongatie*	rolling over a receipt, by payment of a sum equal to the redemption fee

(*continued*)

(*continued*)

Term	Dutch	Definition
protest of a bill of exchange	*wisselprotest*	formal notice, for example, by a drawee indicating non-acceptance of a bill, given in the presence of a notary and witnesses
real-time gross settlement (RTGS)		a modern large-value payment system where payments are executed throughout the day; typically these are giro payments
receipt	*recepis*	a bearer instrument entitling its holder to either (a) repurchase trade coins from the Bank at the sale price plus a redemption fee, within a six-month interval, or (b) to roll over (prolong) the option to repurchase for the same fee
receipt facility or receipt window		our term for the Bank's policy of offering to purchase certain trade coins in indefinite quantities, at a fixed price, against receipts; in effect a standing facility
receiver	*ontvanger*	Bank employee who received deposits of coin from customers
relation	*relatie*	=friend
remedy	*remedie*	permissible deviation of a coin's quality, expressed in terms of weight (*gewicht*) and fine content (*gehalte*)
repo, repurchase agreement		financial instrument involving the sale of (financial) assets at a specified price with a commitment to repurchase the same or similar assets at a fixed price on a specified future date (usually at short term) or on a date subject to the discretion of the purchaser (BIS)
repo facility		a standing facility that allows central bank account holders to engage in repo transactions with the central bank
Republic	*Republiek*	the Dutch Republic; formally, the Republic of the Seven United Netherlands or the United Provinces

Term	Dutch	Definition
reverse repo		the other side of a repo transaction
rider	*rijder*	name applied to coins featuring an equestrian figure
rixdollars	*rijksdaalders*	(a) Dutch silver trade coins, literally "imperial dollars," in reference to the Holy Roman Empire; cf. German *Reichsthaler* (b) nickname for a later Dutch trade coin, the *zilveren dukaat*
seigniorage	*sleischat*	gross seigniorage (*marge*) of a coin is the coin's mint equivalent less its mint price; net seigniorage adjusts this for brassage
shillings	*schellingen*	(a) Dutch small silver coins with a nominal value of 6 stivers each (b) a unit of account equal to 1/20th of a Flemish pound
sight (bill)	*zicht*	term for a bill of exchange that is due immediately on presentation to the drawee
silver ducat	*zilveren dukaat*	a silver coin minted in the Dutch Republic from 1659, informally known as the *rijksdaalder*
silver rider	*zilveren rijder*	a silver coin minted in the Dutch Republic from 1659, informally known as the *ducaton*
small change	*kleingeld, payement*	self-descriptive
Spanish dollar		common English name for Spanish *pesos* or *reales de a ocho*, a.k.a. "pieces of eight"
stablecoin		a cryptocurrency that aims to maintain a stable value relative to a specified asset, or a pool or basket of assets
Stadholder	*Stadhouder*	originally, name applied to provincial-level representatives of the Spanish monarchy in the Netherlands; later, applied to heads of state for provinces in the Dutch Republic; ultimately, applied to the head of state for the entire Republic
standing facility		a central bank facility available to counterparties on their own initiative (OECD)

(*continued*)

(*continued*)

Term	Dutch	Definition
States General, Estates General	*Staten Generaal*	governing assembly of the Dutch Republic; similarly, governing assemblies of the Dutch provinces were known as the States of Holland, etc.
stiver	*stuiver*	(a) a unit of account equal to 1/20th of a guilder, or (b) a coin with the same nominal value
three-guilders	*drieguldens*	Dutch silver coins with a face value of three guilders
toleration	*tolerantie*	a putatively temporary adjustment in the legal value of a coin; in practice such adjustments were rarely temporary
Town Hall	*Stadhuis*	physical location of the Bank and the agio market
touchstone	*toetssteen*	rubbing stone used to test fineness of precious metal
trade coin	*handelspenning, negotiepenning*	coin used principally for international transactions and valued according to its fine content and a liquidity premium
usance	*uso*	the customary maturity of a bill of exchange
VOC	*VOC*	Dutch abbreviation for the East India Company
West India Company	*Westindische Compagnie*	chartered company that managed trade between the Dutch Republic and the New World
WIC	*WIC*	abbreviation for the West India Company

Primary Sources

Van Dillen, Johannes Gerard. *Bronnen Tot de Geschiedenis der Wisselbanken: (Amsterdam, Middelburg, Delft, Rotterdam).* The Hague: Martinus Nijhoff, 1925. (A two-volume edited transcription of many primary sources relevant to the Bank of Amsterdam and other early-modern Dutch municipal banks.).

Amsterdam City Archive (ACA, Stadsarchief Amsterdam)

Archief van de Wisselbank (Archive of the Bank of Amsterdam)
Grootboeken (ledgers), 1666 through 1792, 5077/92–609.
Kasboeken van de Specie Kamer (cash books of the coin room), 1711 through 1792, 5077/1355–1419.
Sommatien (master-account summations), 1711–1792, 5077/1338–1349.
Grootboek van de voorraad gouden en zilveren baren (books of gold and silver bars), 1718 through 1740, 5077/1420–1421.
Balance-boecken (balance books), 1653 through 1694, 5077/1298–1323.
Staten van rekening-courant der 'Koperen Casje' (Reckoning of the Copper Room), 1712 through 1819, 5077/1283–1285.
Opneem boekje van de zilveren speciën in het 'klein secreet" en het vertrek van de Wisselbank (book of silver specie in the small chamber and in transit) 1720 through 1726, 5077/1422
Totaalbalans van de boeken 99–172 en speciekamer (total balances of account books and coin room) 1690 through 1728, 5077/1324.

Baker Library, Harvard Business School

Müntz, Johann Heinrich. "Ausführliche Beschreibung von dem Silber- und Kupfer- Schmelz-Werk ... aufgericht zu Muiden bey Amsterdam,

Eigenthümer davon Der Herr B. V. Ephraim, mit accuraten und vollständigen Rissen versehn." Manuscript, 1769–1770.
(Note: This is an electronic copy of a manuscript held at Baker Library, Harvard Business School. Müntz was Swiss, and at Baker this work is catalogued under the French spelling of his name, Jean Henri Müntz.)
A PDF file of the entire manuscript was generously provided by the International Institute of Social History (Internationaal Instituut voor Sociale Geschiedenis), Amsterdam. Baker provided publication-quality images from the manuscript.

Bank of England

Historical balance-sheet data accessed through the Bank of England's website (www.bankofengland.co.uk/statistics/research-datasets, accessed September 17, 2021).

The Bank of England's Consolidated Annual Balance Sheet, 1696 to 2019
Weekly Balance Sheet of the Bank of England, 1844–2006: Version 2
Note: the latter dataset is referenced as:
Huang, H. and Thomas, R. (2016), "The weekly balance sheet of the Bank of England 1844–2006", OBRA dataset, Bank of England.

Castaing's *Course of the Exchange*

A transcription of twice-weekly exchange rates taken from this publication, running from 1698 through 1783, was generously provided by Larry Neal and Anthony Hotson.

Hamburg State Archive (Staatsarchiv Hamburg)

Preis Couranten (price currents), weekly issues from January 1755 through December 1767. Electronic copies generously provided by François Velde.

References

Accominotti, Olivier, Stefano Ugolini, and Delio Lucena-Piquero. "The Origination and Distribution of Money Market Instruments: Sterling Bills of Exchange during the First Globalization." *Economic History Review* 74, no. 4 (November 2021): 892–921.

Aerts, Erik. "The Absence of Public Exchange Banks in Medieval and Early Modern Flanders and Brabant (1400–1800): A Historical Anomaly to Be Explained." *Financial History Review* 18, no. 1 (April 2011): 91–117.

Aerts, Erik, and Eddy van Cauwenberghe. "Organisatie en techniek van de muntfabricage in de Zuidelijke Nederlanden tijdens het Ancien Regime." *Jaarboek van het Europese Genootschap voor Munt- en Penningkunde* (1987): 7–144.

Akerlof, George A. "The Market for 'Lemons': Quality, Uncertainty and the Market Mechanism." *Quarterly Journal of Economics* 84, no. 3 (August 1970): 488–500.

Allen, Robert C., Jean-Pascal Bassino, Debin Ma, Christine Moll-Murata, and Jan Luiten Van Zanden. "Wages, Prices, and Living Standards in China, 1738–1925: In Comparison with Europe, Japan, and India." *Economic History Review* 64, no. 1 (February 2011): 8–38.

Andreades, Andreas M. *History of the Bank of England.* Translated by Christabel Meredith. London: P. S. King & Son, 1909.

Anson, Mike, David Bholat, Miao Kang, and Ryland Thomas. "The Bank of England as Lender of Last Resort: New Historical Evidence from Daily Transactional Data." Bank of England Working Paper no. 691 (November 2017).

Archer, David, and Paul Moser-Boehm. "Central Bank Finances." Bank for International Settlements Paper no. 71 (April 2013).

Attman, Artur. *Dutch Enterprise in the World Bullion Trade: 1550–1800.* Gothenburg: Kungliga Vetenskaps-och Vitterhets-Samhället, 1983.

American Bullion in the European World Trade: 1600–1800. Gothenburg: Kungliga Vetenskaps-och Vitterhets-Samhället, 1986.

Bagehot, Walter. *Lombard Street.* Westport, CT: Hyperion Press, 1979 [1873].

Bagnall, John, David Bounie, Kim P. Huynh, Anneke Kosse, Tobias Schmidt, Scott Schuh, and Helmut Stix. "Consumer Cash Usage: A Cross-Country Comparison with Payment Diary Data." *International Journal of Central Banking* 12, no. 4 (December 2016): 1–61.

Bahrfeldt, Emil. *Brandenburgisch-Preußische Münzstudien.* Berlin: Verlag der Berliner Münzblätter, 1913.

Bajaj, Ayushi. "Accounting for Debasements: Indivisibility or Imperfect Recognition of Money." *Economic Inquiry* 58, no. 1 (January 2020): 374–85.

Baklanova, Viktoria, Cecilia Caglio, Marco Cipriani, and Adam Copeland. "The Use of Collateral in Bilateral Repurchase and Securities Lending Arrangements." *Review of Economic Dynamics* 33 (July 2019): 228–49.

Bank for International Settlements. "Repo Market Functioning." CGFS Papers no. 59 (April 2017).

"US Dollar Funding: An International Perspective." CGFS Papers no. 65 (June 2020).

BIS Annual Economic Report 2020/21, 2021.

Barrett, Ward. "World Bullion Flows, 1450–1800." In *The Rise of Merchant Empires: Long Distance Trade in the Early Modern World, 1350–1750,* edited by James D. Tracy, 224–54. Cambridge: Cambridge University Press, 1990.

Barth, Daniel, and R. Jay Kahn. "Hedge Funds and the Treasury Cash–Futures Disconnect." Office of Financial Research Working Paper no. 21-1 (April 2021).

Bassetto, Marco D., and Thomas J. Sargent. "Shotgun Wedding: Fiscal and Monetary Policy." *Annual Review of Economics* 12: 659–90 (2020).

Baugh, Daniel. *The Global Seven Years War, 1754–1763.* London and New York: Routledge, 2014.

Bazot, Guillaume, Michael D. Bordo, and Eric Monnet. "International Shocks and the Balance Sheet of the Bank of France under the Classical Gold Standard." *Explorations in Economic History* 62 (October 2016): 87–107.

Bazot, Guillaume, Eric Monnet, and Matthias Morys. "Taming the Global Financial Cycle: Central Banks as Shock Absorbers in the First Era of Globalization." *Journal of Economic History* 82, no. 3 (September 2022): 801–39.

Bech, Morten Linneman, and Rodney Garratt. "Central Bank Cryptocurrencies." *BIS Quarterly Review* (September 2017): 55–70.

Bech, Morten Linneman, and Bart Hobijn. "Technology Diffusion within Central Banking: The Case of Real-Time Gross Settlement." *International Journal of Central Banking* 3 (September 2018): 147–81.

Bech, Morten Linneman, Umar Faruqui, Frederik Ougaard, and Cristina Picillo. "Payments Are A-Changin' but Cash Still Rules." *BIS Quarterly Review* (March 2018): 67–80.

Bernanke, Ben S., Timothy F. Geithner, and Henry M. Paulson, Jr. *Firefighting: The Financial Crisis and Its Lessons.* New York: Penguin, 2019.

Beutin, Ludwig. "Die Wirkungen des Siebenjährigen Krieges auf die Volkswirtschaft in Preußen." *Vierteljahrschrift für Sozial- und Wirtschaftsgeschichte* 26, no. 3 (1933): 209–43.

Bignon, Vincent, and Richard Dutu. "Coin Assaying and Commodity Money." *Macroeconomic Dynamics* 21, no. 6 (September 2017): 1305–35.

Bindseil, Ulrich. *Monetary Policy Operations and the Financial System.* Oxford: Oxford University Press, 2014.

Central Banking before 1800: A Rehabilitation. Oxford: Oxford University Press, 2020.

Blanning, Tim. *Frederick the Great: King of Prussia.* New York: Random House, 2016.

Board of Governors of the Federal Reserve System. Statement Regarding Repurchase Agreement Arrangements, July 28, 2021.

Bolt, Jutta, and Jan Luiten van Zanden. "Maddison Style Estimates of the Evolution of the World Economy. A New 2020 Update." Maddison Project Working Paper WP-15 (October 2020).

Bordo, Michael D. "The Bretton Woods International Monetary System: A Historical Overview." In *A Retrospective on the Bretton Woods System: Lessons for International Monetary Reform*, edited by Michael D. Bordo and Barry Eichengreen, 3–109. Chicago: University of Chicago Press, 1993.

Bordo, Michael D., and Harold James. "The European Crisis in the Context of the History of Previous Financial Crises." *Journal of Macroeconomics* 39, part B (July 2014): 275–84.

Bordo, Michael D., and Pierre L. Siklos. "Central Bank Credibility: An Historical and Quantitative Exploration." In *Central Banks at a Crossroads: What Can We Learn from History?*, edited by Michael D. Bordo, Øyvind Eitreim, Marc Flandreau, and Jan F. Qvigstad, 62–144. New York: Cambridge University Press, 2016.

Braudel, Fernand. *Civilization and Capitalism, 15th–18th Century. Volume III: The Perspective of the World.* Translated by Siân Reynolds. New York: Harper & Row, 1984.

Breen, Johan C. "Eene Amsterdamsche Crediet-instelling uit het laatst der achttiende eeuw." *Tijdschrift voor Geschiedenis* 15, no. 2 (1900): 137–55.

Brown, Kendall W. *A History of Mining in Latin America.* Albuquerque: University of New Mexico Press, 2012.

Broz, J. Lawrence, and Richard S. Grossman. "Paying for Privilege: The Political Economy of Bank of England Charters, 1694–1844." *Explorations in Economic History* 41, no. 1 (January 2004): 48–72.

Bruijn, Jacobus R., Femme Gaastra, and Ivo Schöffer. *Dutch-Asiatic Shipping in the 17th and 18th Centuries.* The Hague: Martinus Nijhoff, 1987.

Buiter, Willem. *Central Banks as Fiscal Players: The Drivers of Fiscal and Monetary Space.* New York: Cambridge University Press, 2021.

Buchner, Wilhelm. *Deutsche Ehrenhalle: Die großen Männer des deutschen Volkes in ihren Denkmalen; Mit lebensgeschichtlichen Abrissen.* Darmstadt: Köhler, 1862.

Buist, Marten G. *At spes non fracta: Hope & Co. 1770–1815.* The Hague: Martinus Nijhoff, 1974.

Büsch, Johann Georg. *Versuch einer Geschichte der Hamburgischen Handlung nebst 2 kleineren Schriften verwandten Inhalts.* Hamburg: Benjamin Gottlob Hoffman, 1797.

Calomiris, Charles W., and Stephen H. Haber. *Fragile by Design: The Political Origins of Banking and Scarce Credit.* Princeton: Princeton University Press, 2014.

Calomiris, Charles W., and Charles M. Kahn. "The Role of Demandable Debt in Structuring Optimal Banking Arrangements." *American Economic Review* 81, no. 3 (June 1991): 497–513.

Carlos, Ann and Larry Neal. "Amsterdam and London as Financial Centers in the Eighteenth Century." *Financial History Review* 18, no. 1 (April 2011): 21–46.

Chen, Yao, Nuno Palma, and Felix Ward. "Reconstruction of the Spanish Money Supply, 1492–1810." *Explorations in Economic History* 81 (July 2021).

Choudary, Sangeet Paul. "Why Business Models Fail: Pipes versus Platforms." *Wired* (2013). Accessed January 9, 2020. www.wired.com/insights/2013/10/why-busi ness-models-fail-pipes-vs-platforms/

Clapham, John. *The Bank of England: A History. Volume I: 1694–1797*. New York: Macmillan, 1945a.

The Bank of England: A History. Volume II: 1797–1914. New York: Macmillan, 1945b.

Cipolla, Carl. *Money, Prices, and Civilization in the Mediterranean World, Fifth to Seventeenth Century*. New York: Gordian Press, 1956.

Copeland, Adam, and Antoine Martin. "Repo over the Financial Crisis." Federal Reserve Bank of New York Staff Report no. 996 (December 2021).

Copeland, Adam, Antoine Martin, and Michael Walker. "Repo Runs: Evidence from the Tri-Party Repo Market." Federal Reserve Bank of New York Staff Report no. 506 (July 2011).

Costabile, Lilia, and Eduardo Nappi. The Public Banks of Naples between Financial Innovation and Crisis. In *Financial Innovation and Resilience: A Comparative Perspective on the Public Banks of Naples (1462–1808)*, edited by Lilia Costabile and Larry Neal, 17–54. Basingstoke, Hampshire: Palgrave Macmillan, 2018.

Cuhaj, George. *Standard Catalog of World Coins 1701–1800*, 5th Edition. Iola: Krause Publications, 2010.

Dang, Tri Vi, Gary Gorton, and Bengt Holmström. "The Information View of Financial Crises." National Bureau of Economics Working Paper no. 26074 (July 2019).

Dang, Tri Vi, Gary Gorton, Bengt Holmström, and Guillermo Ordoñez. "Banks as Secret Keepers." *American Economic Review* 107, no. 4 (April 2017): 1005–29.

Dehing, Pit. *Geld in Amsterdam: Wisselbank en wisselkoersen, 1650–1725*. Hilversum: Uitgeverij Verloren, 2012.

Dehing, Pit, and Marjolein 't Hart. "Linking the Fortunes: Currency and Banking, 1550–1800." In *A Financial History of the Netherlands*, edited by Marjolein 't Hart, Joost Jonker, and Jan Luiten van Zanden, 37–63. Cambridge: Cambridge University Press, 1997.

Del Negro, Marco, and Christopher Sims. "When Does a Central Bank's Balance Sheet Require Fiscal Support?" *Journal of Monetary Economics* 73 (July 2015): 1–19.

De Jong, Adriaan M. *Geschiedenis van de Nederlandsche Bank*. Haarlem: Enschede, 1930.

"The Origin and Foundation of the Netherlands Bank." In *History of the Principal Public Banks*, edited by Johannes Gerard van Dillen, 319–34. The Hague: Martinus Nijhoff, 1934.

De Jong-Keesing, and Elisabeth Emmy. *De Economische Crisis van 1763 te Amsterdam*. Amsterdam: N.V. Intern. Uitgevers en h. Mij, 1939.

De Korte, J. P. *De Jaarlijkse Financiële Verantwoording in de Verenigde Oostindische Compagnie*. Leiden: Martinus Nijhoff, 1984.

De Vries, Jan. "Connecting Europe and Asia: A Quantitative Analysis of the Cape-route Trade, 1497–1795." In *Global Connections and Monetary History, 1470–1800*, edited by Dennis Flynn, Arturo Giráldez, and Richard von Glahn, 35–106. London: Ashgate, 2003.

De Vries, Jan, and Ad van der Woude. *The First Modern Economy: Success, Failure, and Perseverance of the Dutch Economy, 1500–1815.* Cambridge: Cambridge University Press, 1997.

De Zwart, Pim, and Jan Luiten van Zanden. *The Origins of Globalization: World Trade in the Making of the Global Economy, 1500–1800.* Cambridge: Cambridge University Press, 2018.

Dickson, Peter George Muir. *The Financial Revolution in England.* London: St. Martin's Press, 1967.

Finance and Government under Maria Theresia, Volume 2: Finance and Credit. Oxford: Clarendon Press, 1987.

Dutu, Richard. "Moneychangers, Private Information and Gresham's Law in Late Medieval Europe." *Revista de Historia Economica* 22, no. 3 (December 2004): 555–71.

Eichengreen, Barry. *Golden Fetters: The Gold Standard and the Great Depression, 1919–1939.* Oxford: Oxford University Press, 1992.

Exorbitant Privilege: The Rise and Fall of the Dollar and the Future of the International Monetary System. New York: Oxford University Press, 2012.

"Banks, Financial Markets, and the Development of International Currencies." In *Financial Innovation and Resilience: A Comparative Perspective on the Public Banks of Naples (1462–1808),* edited by Lilia Costabile and Larry Neal, 313–26. Cham, Switzerland: Palgrave Macmillan, 2018.

Eichengreen, Barry, and Marc Flandreau. "Editors' Introduction." In *The Gold Standard in Theory and History,* Second Edition, edited by Barry Eichengreen and Marc Flandreau, 1–30. London and New York: Routledge, 1997.

Estevadeordal, Antoni, Brian Frantz, and Alan M. Taylor. "The Rise and Fall of World Trade, 1870–1939." *Quarterly Journal of Economics* 118, no. 2 (May 2003): 359–407.

Esteves, Rui and Pilar Nogues-Marco. "Monetary Systems and the Global Balance-of-Payments Adjustment in the Pre-Gold Standard Period, 1700–1870." In *The Cambridge Economic History of the Modern World, Part II: Factors Governing Differential Outcomes in the Global Economy,* edited by Steven Broadberry and Kyoji Fukao, 438–67. Cambridge: Cambridge University Press, 2021.

European Central Bank. *The Monetary Policy of the ECB* (August 2001).

Fantacci, Luca. "The Dual Currency System of Renaissance Europe." *Financial History Review* 15, no. 1 (2008): 55–72.

Felten, Sebastian. *Money in the Dutch Republic.* Cambridge: Cambridge University Press, 2022.

Flandreau, Marc. "Central Bank Cooperation in Historical Perspective: A Sceptical View." *Economic History Review New Series* 50, no. 4 (November 1997): 735–63.

Flandreau, Marc, and Clemens Jobst. "The Empirics of International Currencies: Network Externalities, History and Persistence." *The Economic Journal* 119 (April 2009): 643–64.

Flandreau, Marc, Christophe Galimard, Clemens Jobst, and Pilar Nogués-Marco. "Monetary Geography before the Industrial Revolution." *Cambridge Journal of Regions, Economy and Society* 2, no. 2 (July 2009a): 149–71.

"The Bell Jar: Commercial Interest Rates Between Two Revolutions, 1688–1789." In *The Origin and Development of Financial Markets and Institutions,* edited by

Jeremy Atack and Larry Neal, 161–208. New York: Cambridge University Press, 2009b.

Flandreau, Marc, and Stefano Ugolini. "Bagehot for Beginners: The Making of Lender-of-Last-Resort Operations in the Mid-nineteenth Century." *Economic History Review* 62, no. 2 (May 2012): 580–608.

Flynn, Dennis O., and Arturo Giráldez. "Cycles of Silver: Global Economic Unity through the Mid-Eighteenth Century." *Journal of World History* 13, no. 2 (Fall 2002): 391–427.

"Path Dependence, Time Lags and the Birth of Globalization: A Critique of O'Rourke and Williamson." *European Review of Economic History* 8, no. 1 (April 2004): 81–108.

Fox, David. "The Case of Mixt Monies (1604)." In *Money in the Western Legal Tradition: Middle Ages to Bretton Woods*, edited by David Fox and Wolfgang Ernst, 224–46. Oxford: Oxford University Press, 2016.

Fox, David, François R. Velde, and Wolfgang Ernst. "Monetary History between Law and Economics." In *Money in the Western Legal Tradition: Middle Ages to Bretton Woods*, edited by David Fox and Wolfgang Ernst, 3–17. Oxford: Oxford University Press, 2016.

Fritschy, Wantje. "Three Centuries of Urban and Provincial Public Debt: Amsterdam and Holland." In *Urban Public Debts: Urban Government and the Market for Annuities in Western Europe (14th–18th Centuries)*, edited by Marc Boone, Karel Davids, and Paul Janssens, 75–92. Turnhout: Brepols, 2003.

Public Finance of the Dutch Republic in Comparative Perspective. Leiden and Boston: Brill, 2017.

Fritschy, Wantje, and René van der Voort. "From Fragmentation to Unification: Public Finance, 1700–1914." In *A Financial History of the Netherlands*, edited by Marjolein 't Hart, Joost Jonker, and Jan Luiten van Zanden, 64–93. Cambridge: Cambridge University Press, 1997.

Frost, Jon, Hyun Shin, and Peter Wierts. "An Early Stablecoin? The Bank of Amsterdam and the Governance of Money." Bank for International Settlements Working Paper no. 902 (November 2020).

Fry, Maxwell J. "The Fiscal Abuse of Central Banks." International Monetary Fund Working Paper no. 93/58 (July 1993).

Gaastra, Femme S. "De Verenigde Oost-Indische Compagnie in de zeventiende en achttiende eeuw: de groei van een bedrijf Geld tegen goederen. Een structurele verandering in het Nederlands-Aziatisch handelsverkeer." *Bijdragen en Mededelingen betreffende de Geschiedenis der Nederlanden* 91, aflevering 1 (1976): 249–72.

"The Exports of Precious Metal from Europe to Asia by the Dutch East India Company." In *Precious Metals in the Later Medieval and Early Modern Worlds*, edited by John F. Richards, 447–76. Durham, NC: Carolina Academic Press, 1983.

Gaettens, Richard. *Inflationen: Das Drama der Geldentwertungen vom Altertum bis zur Gegenwart.* Munich: Richard Pflaum, 1955.

Gandal, Neil, and Nathan Sussman. "Asymmetric Information and Commodity Money: Tickling the Tolerance in Medieval France." *Journal of Money, Credit, and Banking* 29, no. 4 (November 1997): 440–57.

Garbade, Kenneth D. "The Evolution of Repo Contracting Conventions in the 1980s." Federal Reserve Bank of New York Economic Policy Review (May 2006): 27–42.

Birth of a Market: The U.S. Treasury Securities Market from the Great War to the Great Depression. Cambridge, MA: MIT Press, 2012.

After the Accord: A History of Federal Reserve Open Market Operations, the US Government Securities Market, and Treasury Debt Management from 1951 to 1979. Cambridge: Cambridge University Press, 2021.

Gelderblom, Oscar. *Cities of Commerce: The Institutional Foundations of International Trade in the Low Countries, 1250-1650.* Princeton: Princeton University Press, 2013.

Gelderblom, Oscar, and Joost Jonker. "Public Finance and Economic Growth: The Case of Holland in the Seventeenth Century." *Journal of Economic History* 71 (March 2011): 1–39.

Gelderblom, Oscar, Joost Jonker, and Clemens Kool. "Direct Finance in the Dutch Golden Age." *Economic History Review* 69, no. 4 (November 2016): 1178–98.

Gillard, Lucien. *La Banque d'Amsterdam et le florin européen au temps de la République Néerlandaise (1610-1820).* Paris: École des hautes-études en sciences sociales, 2004.

Glahn, Richard von. *The Economic History of China: From Antiquity to the Nineteenth Century.* Cambridge, Cambridge University Press, 2016.

Gleeson-White, Jane. *Double Entry: How the Merchants of Venice Created Modern Finance.* New York: Norton, 2011.

Godfrey, Michael. *A Brief Account of the Intended Bank of England.* Randall Taylor: London, 1694.

Gorton, Gary B. *Slapped by the Invisible Hand: The Panic of 2007.* Oxford: Oxford University Press, 2010.

"The History and Economics of Safe Assets." *Annual Review of Economics* 9 (2017): 547–86.

"Private Money Production without Banks." National Bureau of Economic Research Working Paper no. 2663 (January 2020).

Gorton, Gary B., and Andrew Metrick. "Regulating the Shadow Banking System." *Brooking Papers on Economic Activity* (Fall 2010): 261–312.

"Securitized Banking and the Run on Repo." *Journal of Financial Economics* 104, no. 3 (June 2012): 425–51.

Gorton, Gary B., and Ellis W. Tallman. *Fighting Financial Crises: Learning from the Past.* Chicago: University of Chicago Press, 2018.

Goossens, Eymert-Jan. "The Face of the Bank of Amsterdam." In *The Bank of Amsterdam: On the Origins of Central Banking,* edited by Marius van Nieuwkerk, 56–65. Amsterdam: Sonsbeek, 2009.

Gottardi, Piero, Vincent Maurin, and Cyril Monnet. "A Theory of Repurchase Agreements, Collateral Re-use, and Repo Intermediation." *Review of Economic Dynamics* 33 (July 2019): 30–56.

Gourinchas, Pierre-Olivier, Hélène Rey, and Nicolas Govillot. "Exorbitant Privilege and Exorbitant Duty." Mimeo (October 2017).

Graumann, Johann Philipp. *Abdruck von einem Schreiben, die Deutsche und anderer Völcker Münzverfassung und insonderheit die Hochfürstliche Braunschweigische Münze betreffend,* 1749.

Gesammelte Briefe von dem Gelde; von dem Wechsel und dessen Cours; von der Proportion zwischen Gold und Silber; von dem Pari des Geldes und den Münzgesetzen verschiedener Völker; besonders aber von dem Englischen Münzwesen. Berlin: Christian Friedrich Voss, 1762.

Greitens, Jan. "Geldtheorie und -politik in Preußen Mitte des 18. Jahrhunderts." *Jahrbuch für Wirtschaftsgeschichte* 61, no. 1 (June 2020): 217–57.

Group of Thirty. *U.S. Treasury Markets: Steps Toward Increased Liquidity* (July 2021).

Hall, George J., and Thomas J. Sargent. "Debt and Taxes in Eight U.S. Wars and Two Insurrections." In *The Handbook of Historical Economics*, edited by Alberto Bisin and Giovanni Federico, 825–80. London: Academic Press, 2021.

Hamilton, Earl J. *American Treasure and the Price Revolution in Spain 1501–1650.* Cambridge, MA: Harvard University Press, 1934.

Heckscher, Eli F. "The Bank of Sweden in its Connection with the Bank of Amsterdam." In *History of the Principal Public Banks*, edited by Johannes Gerard van Dillen, 161–99. The Hague: Martinus Nijhoff, 1934.

Henderson, W.O. "The Berlin Commercial Crisis of 1763." *Economic History Review, New Series* 15, no. 1 (August 1962): 89–102.

Heyvaert, Edward. De ontwikkeling van de moderne bank- en krediettechniek tijdens de zestiende en zeventiende eeuw in Europa en te Amsterdam in het bijzonder. Ph. D. dissertation, Katholieke Universiteit te Leuven, 1975.

Hills, Sally, Ryland Thomas, and Nicholas Dimsdale. "The UK Recession in Context – What Do Three Centuries of Data Tell Us?" *Bank of England Quarterly Bulletin* 50, no. 4 (December 2010): 277–91.

Hoensch, Jörg K. "Friedrichs II. Währungsmanipulationen im Siebenjährigen Krieg und Ihre Auswirkung auf die Polnische Münzreform von 1765/66." *Jahrbuch für die Geschichte Mittel- und Ostdeutschlands* 22 (1973): 110–75.

Hoffman, Philip T. *Why Did Europe Conquer the World?* Princeton and Oxford: Princeton University Press, 2015.

Horsefield, J. Keith. "The Origins of the Bank Charter Act, 1844." In *Papers in English Monetary History*, edited by Thomas S. Ashton and Richard S. Sayers, 109–31. Oxford: Clarendon, 1953.

Hotson, Anthony. *Respectable Banking: The Search for Stability in London's Money and Credit Markets Since 1695.* Cambridge: Cambridge University Press, 2017.

Howell, Michael J. *Capital Wars: The Rise of Global Liquidity.* London: Palgrave Mscmillan, 2020.

International Capital Market Association. "How Big is the Repo Market?" Accessed September 20, 2021. www.icmagroup.org/Regulatory-Policy-and-Market-Practice/ repo-and-collateral-markets/icma-ercc-publications/frequently-asked-questions-on-repo/4-how-big-is-the-repo-market/

Irigoin, Alejandra. "Global Silver: Bullion or Specie? Supply and Demand in the Making of the Early Modern Global Economy." London School of Economics and Political Science Economic History Working Paper no. 285 (September 2018).

"The New World and the Global Silver Economy, 1500–1800." In *Global Economic History*, edited by Tirthankar Roy and Giorgio Riello, 271–86. London: Bloomsbury Academic, 2019.

"Rise and Demise of the Global Silver Standard." In *Handbook of the History of Money and Currency*, edited by Stefano Battilossi, Youssef Cassis, and Kazuhiko Yago, 383–410. New York: Springer, 2020.

Israel, Jonathan I. *The Dutch Republic and the Hispanic World, 1606–1661*. New York: Oxford University Press, 1982.

Dutch Primacy in World Trade, 1585–1740. Oxford: Clarendon Press, 1989.

The Dutch Republic: Its Rise, Greatness, and Fall 1477–1806. Oxford: Clarendon Press, 1995.

Israel, Jonathan I., and Geoffrey Parker. "Of Providence and Protestant Winds: The Spanish Armada of 1588 and the Dutch Armada of 1688." In *The Anglo-Dutch Moment: Essays on the Glorious Revolution and Its World Impact*, edited by Jonathan I. Israel, 335–64. Cambridge: Cambridge University Press, 1991.

James, Harold. *Making a Modern Central Bank: The Bank of England 1979–2003*. Cambridge: Cambridge University Press, 2020.

Jiang, Zhengyang, Hanno Lustig, Stijn van Nieuwerburgh, and Mindy Z. Xiaolan. "The U.S. Public Debt Valuation Puzzle." National Bureau of Economics Working Paper no. 26583 (December 2019).

Jobst, Clemens, and Hans Kernbauer. *The Quest for Stable Money: Central Banking in Austria, 1816–2016*. Frankfurt: Campus, 2016.

Jobst, Clemens, and Pilar Nogues-Marco. "Commercial Finance in Europe, 1700–1815." In *Handbook of Key Global Financial Markets, Institutions and Infrastructure*, edited by Gerard Caprio, Jr., 95–108. Boston: Elsevier, 2013.

Jobst, Clemens, and Stefano Ugolini. "The Coevolution of Money Markets and Monetary Policy, 1815–2008." In *Central Banks at a Crossroads: What Can We Learn from History?*, edited by Michael D. Bordo, Øyvind Eitreim, Marc Flandreau, and Jan F. Qvigstad, 145–94. New York: Cambridge University Press, 2016.

Jonker, Joost. *Merchants, Bankers, Middlemen: The Amsterdam Money Market during the First Half of the 19th Century*. Amsterdam: Nederlandsch Economisch-Historisch Archief, 1996.

Jonker, Joost and Oscar Gelderblom. "Enter the Ghost: Cashless Payments in the Early Modern Low Countries, 1500–1800." In *Money, Currency and Crisis, in Search of Trust, 2000 BC to AD 2000*, edited by R.J. van der Spek and Bas van Leeuwen, 240–47. London: Routledge, 2018.

Jorion, Philippe. "Risk Management Lessons from Long-Term Capital Management." *European Financial Management* 6, no. 3 (September 2008): 277–300.

Justi, Johann Heinrich Gottlob von. *Die Kunst, das Silber zu Affinieren, oder das mit andern Metallen vermischte Silber wieder fein zu Machen*. Königsberg und Mietau: Johann Jacob Kanter, 1765.

Justine, Alexander. *A General Treatise of Monies and Exchanges*. London: S. & J. Sprint, 1707.

Kahn, Charles M., and William Roberds. "Transferability, Finality, and Debt Settlement." *Journal of Monetary Economics* 55, no. 4 (May 2007): 955–78.

Kernkamp, Gerhard Wilhelm. "Johann Beckmann's dagboek van zijne reis door Nederland in 1762." *Bijdragen en Mededelingen van het Historisch Genootschap* 33 (1912): 311–459.

Keynes, John Maynard. *A Treatise on Money, Volume 2.* London: Macmillan, 1930.

Essays in Persuasion. Hampshire and New York: Palgrave Macmillan, 2010 [1931].

Kleer, Richard. *Money, Politics and Power: Banking and Public Finance in Wartime England, 1694–96.* New York: Routledge, 2017.

Kluge, Bernd. "Für 8 Groschen ist es genug. Friedrich der Große in seinen Münzen und Medaille." *Münzenwoche* (February 2, 2012).

"Für das Überleben des Staates: Die Münzverschlechterungen durch Friedrich den Großen im Siebenjährigen Krieg." *Jahrbuch für die Geschichte Mittel- und Ostdeutschlands* 59, no.1 (2013): 125–43.

Klüh, Ulrich H., and Peter Stella. "Central Bank Financial Strength and Policy Performance: An Econometric Evaluation." International Monetary Fund Working Paper no. 08/176 (July 2008).

Korthals Altes, Willem L. *De Geschiedenis van de Gulden: Van Pond Hollands tot Euro.* Amsterdam: Boom, 2001.

Koser, Reinhold. "Die preußischen Finanzen im Siebenjährigen Kriege." *Forschungen zur Preußischen und Brandenburgischen Geschichte* 13 (2nd half, 1900): 1–47.

Kosmetatos, Paul. *The 1772–73 British Credit Crisis.* Cham: Palgrave Macmillan, 2018.

Koudijs, Peter, and Hans-Joacim Voth. "Leverage and Beliefs: Personal Experience and Risk-Taking in Margin Lending." *American Economic Review* 106, no. 11 (November 2016): 3367–400.

Krishnamurthy, Arvind, and Annette Vissing-Jorgenson. "The Aggregate Demand for Treasury Debt." *Journal of Political Economy* 120, no. 2 (April 2012): 233–67.

Kruttli, Matthias S., Philip J. Monin, Lubomir Petrasek, and Sumudu W. Matagala. "LTCM Redux? Hedge Fund Treasury Trading and Funding Fragility." FEDS Working Paper 2021-038 (June 2021).

Kuroda, Akinobu. "What Is the Complementarity among Monies? An Introductory Note." *Financial History Review* 15, no. 1 (April 2008a): 7–15.

"Concurrent but Non-integrable Currency Circuits: Complementary Relationships among Monies in Modern China and Other Regions." *Financial History Review* 15, no. 1 (April 2008b): 17–36.

Lagos, Ricardo, and Shengxing Zhang. "The Limits of Monetary Economics: On Money as a Latent Medium of Exchange. NBER Working Paper no. 26756 (February 2020).

Lane, Kris. *Potosí: The Silver City That Changed the World.* Oakland: University of California Press, 2019.

Le Moine de L'Espine, Jacques, and Isaac Le Long. De Koophandel van Amsterdam. Rotterdam: Ph. Losel, J.D. Beman, H. Kentlink, J. Bosch, N. Smithof, d'wed. J. Losel en J. Burgvliet, 1763.

Li, Ling-Fan. "The Stop of the Exchequer and the Secondary Market for English Sovereign Debt, 1677–1705." *Journal of Economic History* 79, no. 1 (March 2019): 176–200.

Liesker, R., and Wantje Fritschy. *Gewestelijke financiën ten tijde van de Republiek der Verenigde Nederlanden: Deel IV Holland (1572–1795).* The Hague: Instituut voor Nederlandse Geschiedenis, 2004.

Lowenstein, Roger. *America's Bank: the Epic Struggle to Create the Federal Reserve.* New York: Penguin, 2015.

Lucassen, Jan. "Deep Monetization: The Case of the Netherlands 1200–1940." *Tijdschrift voor Sociale en Economische Geschiedenis* 11, no. 3 (September 2014): 73–121.

Lucassen, Jan, and Matthias van Rossum. "Smokkelloon en zilverstromen: illegale export van edelmetaal via de VOC." *Low Countries Journal of Social and Economic History* 13, no. 1 (March 2016): 99–134.

Macaulay, Thomas Babington. *The History of England from the Accession of James II.* London: Longman, Brown, Green, and Longmans, 1848.

MacLeod, W. Bentley. "Reputations, Relationships, and Contract Enforcement." *Journal of Economic Literature* XLV, no. 3 (September 2007): 595–628.

Magens, Nicholas. *The Universal Merchant: Containing the Rationale of Commerce, In Theory and Practice.* Edited by William Horsley. London: C. Say, 1753.

Matthews, Philip W. *The Bankers' Clearing House: What It Is and What It Does.* London: Sir Isaac Pitman & Sons, 1921.

McCusker, John J. *Money and Exchange in Europe and America, 1600–1775.* Chapel Hill: University of North Carolina Press, 1978.

McCusker, John J., and Cora Gravesteijn. *The Beginnings of Commercial and Financial Journalism.* Amsterdam: Nederlandsch Economisch-Historisch Archief (NEHA), 1979.

Mees, Willem C. *Proeve eener Geschiedenis van het Bankwezen in Nederland gedurende den Tijd der Republiek.* Rotterdam: W. Messcuert, 1838.

Mehrling, Perry. *The New Lombard Street: How the Fed Became the Dealer of Last Resort.* Princeton: Princeton University Press, 2011.

Melon, Jean-François. *Essai Politique sur le Commerce.* Amsterdam: François Changuion, 1754.

Meltzer, Allan H. *A History of the Federal Reserve. Volume I: 1913–1951.* Chicago: University of Chicago Press, 2003.

Michaelis, Dolf. "The Ephraim Family." *The Leo Baeck Institute Year Book* 21, no. 1 (1976): 201–28.

Michie, Ranald. *British Banking.* Oxford: Oxford University Press, 2016.

Morineau, Michel. *Incroyables Gazettes et Fabuleux Métaux.* London: Cambridge University Press, 1985.

Murphy, Antoin. *John Law: Economic Theorist and Policy Maker.* New York and Oxford: Oxford University Press, 1997.

National Monetary Commission. *Publications of the National Monetary Commission, Volume I: Interviews on Banking in Europe.* Washington, DC: Government Printing Office, 1912.

Neal, Larry. *The Rise of Financial Capitalism.* New York: Cambridge University Press, 1990.

I Am Not Master of Events: The Speculations of John Law and Lord Londonderry in the Mississippi and South Sea Bubbles. New Haven: Yale University Press, 2012.

Nederlantsche munt-boek vervatendende de vorrnamste placcaten ende ordonnattien, de munte, ende het munt-wesen betreffende; geemaneert ende uytgegeven in de Vereenighde Nederlandtsche Provintien, sedert den jaere 1586 tot in den loopende jare 1645. Amsterdam: Jan Janssen, 1645.

Nelson, Bill. "Informal Symposium on Monetary Policy, Bank Regulations, and Money Markets." Bank Policy Institute (February 22, 2022).

Niebuhr, Marcus. *Geschichte der Königlichen Bank in Berlin.* Berlin: Verlag der Deckerschen Geheimen Ober-Hofbuchdruckerei, 1854.

Nogues-Marco, Pilar. "The Microeconomics of Bullionism: Arbitrage, Smuggling and Silver Outflows in Spain in the Early 18th Century." Universidad Carlos III de Madrid Working Papers in Economic History, Working Paper 11-05 (June 2011).

"Competing Bimetallic Ratios: Amsterdam, London, and Bullion Arbitrage in Mid-Eighteenth Century." *Journal of Economic History* 73, no. 2 (June 2013): 445–76.

North, Michael. "Bullion Transfer from Western Europe to the Baltic and the Problem of Trade Balances: 1550–1750." In *Precious Metals, Coinage and the Changes of Monetary Structures in Latin-America, Europe and Asia,* edited by Eddy H. G. van Cauwenberghe, 57–63. Leuven: Leuven University Press, 1989.

Officer, Lawrence H. *Between the Dollar-Sterling Gold Points: Exchange Rates, Parity and Market Behavior.* Cambridge: Cambridge University Press, 1996.

O'Brien, Patrick K., and Nuno Palma. "Danger to the Old Lady of Threadneedle Street? The Bank Restriction Act and the Regime Shift to Paper Money, 1797–1821." *European Review of Economic History* 24, no. 2 (May 2020): 390–426.

O'Rourke, Kevin H., and Jeffrey G. Williamson. "When Did Globalization Begin?" *European Review of Economic History* 6, no. 1 (April 2002): 23–50.

Palma, Nuno. "American Precious Metals and Their Consequences for Early Modern Europe." In *Handbook of the History of Money and Currency,* edited by Stefano Battilossi, Youssef Cassis, and Kazuhiko Yago, 363–82. New York: Springer, 2019.

"The Real Effects of Monetary Expansions: Evidence from a Large-Scale Historical Experiment." *Review of Economic Studies* 89 (May 2022): 1593–627.

Palma, Nuno, and André C. Silva. "Spending a Windfall." Centre for Economic Policy Research Discussion Paper no. DP16523 (September 2021).

Pepys, Samuel. *The Diary of Samuel Pepys, Esquire, F.R.S.* London and New York: George Newnes and Charles Scribner's Sons, 1902 [1666].

Petram, Lodewijk. "The Bank, the Exchange, and Amsterdam." In *The Bank of Amsterdam: On the Origins of Central Banking,* edited by Marius van Nieuwkerk, 66–77. Amsterdam: Sonsbeek, 2009.

"The World's First Stock Exchange: How the Amsterdam Market for Dutch East India Company Shares Became a Modern Securities Market, 1602–1700." Ph.D. dissertation, Universiteit van Amsterdam, 2011.

The World's First Stock Exchange. Translated by Lynne Richards. New York: Columbia University Press, 2014.

Placaet ende ordonnantie van mijn heeren die Staten Generael der Vereenighde Nederlanden, soo op den cours van het geldt, als op de politie ende discipline, betreffende de exercitie van de munte ende muntslagh, midtsgaders het stuck van den wissel, wisselaers, scheyders, affineurs . . ., Volume 1. 's Gravenhage: Hillebrant Jacobsz, 1606.

Pol, Arent. "Tot Gerieff van India: Geldexport door de VOC en de Muntproduktie in Nederland, 1720–1740." *Jaarboek voor Munt- en Penningkunde* 72 (1985): 65–133.

Schepen met geld: de handelsmunten van de Verenigde Oostindische Compagnie, 1602–1799. The Hague: SDU, 1989.

Polak, Menno S. *Historiografie en Economie van de "Muntchaos": De Muntproductie van de Republiek (1606–1795).* Amsterdam: Nederlandsch Economisch-Historisch Archief, 1998a.

Historiografie en Economie van de "Muntchaos": De Muntproductie van de Republiek (1606–1795). Deel II: Bijlagen. Amsterdam: Nederlandsch Economisch-Historisch Archief, 1998b.

Posthumus, Nicolaas. *Inquiry into the History of Prices in Holland.* Leiden: E. J. Brill, 1946.

Postlethwayt, Malachy. *The Universal Dictionary of Trade and Commerce, Volume 2.* London: W. Strahan et al, 1774.

Postma, Johannes Menne. *The Dutch in the Atlantic Slave Trade 1600–1815.* Cambridge: Cambridge University Press, 1990.

Pozsar, Zoltan. "Shadow Banking: The Money View." Office of Financial Research Working Paper no. 14-04 (July 2014).

Pozsar, Zoltan, Tobias Adrian, Adam Ashcraft, and Hayley Boesky. "Shadow Banking." Federal Reserve Bank of New York Staff Report no. 458 (July 2010).

Quinn, Stephen. "Gold, Silver, and the Glorious Revolution: Arbitrage between Bills of Exchange and Bullion." *Economic History Review* 49, no. 3 (August 1996): 473–90.

"Goldsmith-Banking: Mutual Acceptances and Inter-Banker Clearing in Restoration London." *Explorations in Economic History* 34, no. 4 (October 1997): 411–32.

Quinn, Stephen, and William Roberds. "An Economic Explanation of the Early Bank of Amsterdam, Debasement, Bills of Exchange and the Emergence of the First Central Bank." In *The Development of Financial Markets and Institutions*, edited by Jeremy Atack and Larry Neal, 32–70. Cambridge: Cambridge University Press, 2009.

"How Amsterdam Got Fiat Money." Federal Reserve Bank of Atlanta Working Paper Series 2010-17 (December 2010).

"How Amsterdam Got Fiat Money." *Journal of Monetary Economics* 66, no. 1 (September 2014): 1–12.

"Responding to a Shadow Banking Crisis: The Lessons of 1763." *Journal of Money, Credit, and Banking* 47, no. 6 (September 2015): 1149–76.

"Death of a Reserve Currency." *International Journal of Central Banking* (December 2016): 63–103.

"A Policy Framework for the Bank of Amsterdam, 1736–1791." *Journal of Economic History* 79 no. 3 (September 2019): 736–72.

Quinn, Stephen, William Roberds, and Charles M. Kahn. "Standing Repo Facilities, Then and Now." Federal Reserve Bank of Atlanta *Policy Hub* 01-20 (January 2020).

Rachel, Hugo, and Paul Wallich. *Berliner Großkaufleute und Kapitalisten. Zweiter Band: Die Zeit des Merkantilismus, 1648–1806.* Expanded edition, J. Schultze, H.C. Wallich, and Gerd Heinrich, eds. Berlin: Walter de Gruyter, 1967.

Redish, Angela. "Evolution of the Gold Standard in England." *Journal of Economic History* 30, no. 4 (December 1990): 789–805.

Bimetallism: An Economic and Historical Analysis. Cambridge: Cambridge University Press 2000.

Redlich, Fritz. "Jewish Enterprise and Prussian Coinage in the Eighteenth Century." *Explorations in Entrepreneurial History* 3, no. 3 (1951): 161–81.

Reinhart, Carmen, and Kenneth Rogoff. *This Time Is Different: Eight Centuries of Financial Folly.* Princeton: Princeton University Press, 2011.

Rhodes, H. *A Description of Holland and the Rest of the United Provinces in General.* London, 1701.

Ricardo, David. *Proposals for an Economical and Secure Currency.* London: John Murray, 1816.

Plan for the Establishment of a National Bank. London: John Murray, 1824.

Richards, Richard D. "The First Fifty Years of the Bank of England (1694–1744)." In *History of the Principal Public Banks*, edited by Johannes Gerard van Dillen, 201–72. The Hague: Martinus Nijhoff, 1934.

Riley James C. *International Government Finance and the Amsterdam Capital Market 1740–1815.* Cambridge: Cambridge University Press, 1980.

Roberds, William, and François R. Velde. "Early Public Banks I: Ledger-Money Banks." In *Money in the Western Legal Tradition: Middle Ages to Bretton Woods*, edited by David Fox and Wolfgang Ernst, 321–58. Oxford: Oxford University Press, 2016a.

"Early Public Banks II: Banks of Issue." In *Money in the Western Legal Tradition: Middle Ages to Bretton Woods*, edited by David Fox and Wolfgang Ernst, 465–88. Oxford: Oxford University Press, 2016b.

"The Descent of Central Banks." In *Central Banks at a Crossroads: What Can We Learn from History?* edited by Michael D. Bordo, Øyvind Eitreim, Marc Flandreau, and Jan F. Qvigstad, 18–61. New York: Cambridge University Press, 2016c.

Rödenbeck, Karl Heinrich Siegfried. *Tagebuch oder Geschichtskalender aus Friedrichs des Großen Regentenleben (1740–1786), Volume I.* Berlin: Plahn'schen Buchhandlung, 1840.

Rolnick, Arthur J., François R. Velde, and Warren E. Weber. "The Debasement Puzzle: An Essay on Medieval Monetary History." *Journal of Economic History* 56, no. 4 (December 1996): 789–808.

Santarosa, Veronica Aoki. "Financing Long-Distance Trade: The Joint Liability Rule and Bills of Exchange in Eighteenth-Century France." *Journal of Economic History* 75, no. 3 (September 2015): 690–719.

Sargent, Thomas J. "Commodity and Token Monies." *The Economic Journal* 129, no. 619 (April 2019): 1457–76.

Sargent, Thomas J., and François R. Velde. *The Big Problem of Small Change.* Princeton: Princeton University Press, 2002.

Sautijn Kluit, Willem P. *De Amsterdamsche Beurs in 1763 en 1773.* Amsterdam: W.H. Zeelt, 1865.

Sayers, Richard S. *Bank of England Operations, 1890–1914.* London: P. S. King & Son, 1936.

The Bank of England, 1891–1944, Volume I. Cambridge: Cambridge University Press, 1976.

Scheffers, Albert A. J. Om de kwaliteit van het geld. Deel I: Tekst. Doctoral Thesis, Leiden University Institute for History, 2013a.

Scheffers, Albert A. J. Om de kwaliteit van het geld. Deel II: Bronnen. Doctoral Thesis, Leiden University Institute for History, 2013b.

Schepkowski, Nina Simone. *Johann Ernst Gotzkowsky: Kunstagent und Gemäldesammler im friderizianischen Berlin.* Berlin: Akademie Verlag, 2009.

Schieder, Theodor. *Friedrich der Große: ein Königtum der Widersprüche*. Frankfurt: Propyläen, 1983.

Schnabel, Isabel, and Hyun Song Shin. "Liquidity and Contagion: The Crisis of 1763." *Journal of the European Economic Association* 2, no. 6 (December 2004): 929–68.

Schnee, Heinrich. *Die Hoffinanz und der moderne Staat. Erster Theil: Die Institution des Hoffaktorentums in Brandenburg-Preußen*. Berlin: Duncker & Humblot, 1955.

Schneider, Jürgen, Oskar Schwarzer, and Petra Schnelzer. *Historische Statistik von Deutschland. Band XII: Statistik der Geld- und Wechselkurse in Deutschland und im Ostseeraum (18. Und 19. Jahrhundert)*. St. Katharinen: Scripta-Mercuratae-Verlag, 1991.

Schneider, Konrad. "Zum Geldhandel in Hamburg während des Siebenjährigen Krieges." *Zeitschrift des Vereins für Hamburgische Geschichte* 69 (1983): 61–82.

"Untersuchungen zur Edelmetallverhüttung und Probierkunst in Hamburg." *Zeitschrift des Vereins für Hamburgische Geschichte* 71 (1985): 1–44.

Schrimpf, Andreas, Hyun Song Shin, and Vladyslav Sushko. "Leverage and Margin Spirals in Fixed Income Markets during the Covid-19 Crisis." Bank for International Settlements, BIS Bulletin no. 2 (April 2020).

Schrötter, Friedrich Freiherr von. *Das Preußische Münzwesen im 18. Jahrhundert, Münzgeschichtlicher Theil, Zweiter Band: Die Begründung des preußischen Münzsystems durch Friedrich den Großen und Grauman, 1740–1755*. Berlin: Paul Parey, 1908.

Das Preußische Münzwesen im 18. Jahrhundert, Münzgeschichtlicher Theil, Dritter Band: Das Geld des Siebenjährigen Krieges und die Münzreform nach dem Frieden, 1755–1765. Berlin: Paul Parey, 1910.

Das Preußische Münzwesen im 18. Jahrhundert, Münzgeschichtlicher Theil, Vierter Band: Die letzten vierzig Jahre, 1765–1806. Berlin: Paul Parey, 1913.

Selgin, George. *Good Money: Birmingham Button Makers, the Royal Mint, and the Beginnings of Modern Coinage*. Institute of Economic Affairs: London, 2008.

Sims, Christopher A. "Fiscal Aspects of Central Bank Independence." In *European Monetary Integration*, edited by Hans-Werner Sinn, Mika Vidgrén, and Marko Köthenberger, 103–16. Cambridge, MA: MIT Press, 2004.

Singh, Manmohan. "Velocity of Pledged Collateral." International Monetary Fund Working Paper no. 256 (November 2011).

Sissoko, Carolyn. "The Legal Foundations of Financial Collapse." *Journal of Financial Economic Policy* 2, no. 1 (April 2010): 5–34.

"How to Stabilize the Banking System: Lessons from the Pre-1914 London Money Market." *Financial History Review* 23, no.1 (April 2016): 1–20.

Skalweit, August. *Die Getreidehandelspolitik und Kriegsmagazinverwaltung Preußens 1756–1806*. Berlin: Paul Parey, 1931.

Skalweit, Stephan. *Die Berliner Wirtschaftskrise von 1763 und ihre Hintergründe*. Stuttgart-Berlin: W. Kohlhammer, 1937.

Smith, Adam. *An Inquiry into the Nature and Causes of the Wealth of Nations*. Indianapolis: Liberty Fund, 1981 [1776].

Soetbeer, Adolf. *Materialen zur Erläuterung und Beurtheilung der wirthschaftlichen Edelmetallverhältnisse und der Währungsfrage*. Berlin: Puttkammer & Mühlbrecht, 1876.

Stapel, Rombert. "Coin Production in the Low Countries 14th–19th C. (Combined)" International Institute of Social History Data Collection, V 11, 2016. Accessed at https://hdl.handle.net/10622/D5WXZZ.

Stella, Peter. "Do Central Banks Need Capital?" International Monetary Fund Working Paper no. 97/83 (July 1997).

"Central Bank Financial Strength, Transparency, and Policy Credibility." IMF Staff Papers 52, no. 2 (2005): 335–65.

Stern, Selma. *The Court Jew: A Contribution to the History of the Period of Absolutism in Central Europe.* Philadelphia: The Jewish Publication Society of America, 1950.

Der preußische Staat und die Juden, Volume III: Die Zeit Friedrichs des Großen. Tübingen: Mohr, 1971.

Steuart, James. *An Inquiry Into the Principles of Political Economy, Volume II.* London: Millar and Cadell, 1767a.

An Inquiry Into the Principles of Political Economy, Volume III. London: Millar and Cadell, 1767b.

Steur, Jacob J. *Herstel of ondergang: de voorstellen tot redres van de Verenigde Oost-Indische Compagnie 1740-1795.* Utrecht: Hes Uitgevers, 1984.

Szabo, Franz A.J. *The Seven Years War in Europe 1756-1763.* Harlow, England: Pearson Longman, 2008.

Task Force on Financial Stability. "Report." Brookings Institution and Chicago Booth School (June 2021).

Temin, Peter, and Hans-Joachim Voth. *Prometheus Shackled: Goldsmith Banks and England's Financial Revolution after 1700.* Oxford: Oxford University Press, 2013.

't Hart, Marjolein. "The Merits of a Financial Revolution: Public Finance, 1500-1700." In *A Financial History of the Netherlands,* edited by Marjolein 't Hart, Joost Jonker, and Jan Luiten van Zanden, 11–36. Cambridge: Cambridge University Press, 1997.

"Corporate Governance." In *The Bank of Amsterdam: On the Origins of Central Banking,* edited by Marius van Nieuwkerk, 120–31. Amsterdam: Sonsbeek, 2009.

Dutch Wars of Independence: Warfare and Commerce in the Netherlands, 1570-1680. London and New York: Routledge, 2014.

TePaske, John J., and Kendall W. Brown. *A New World of Gold and Silver.* Leiden and Boston: Brill, 2010.

Townsend, Robert M. *Distributed Ledgers: Design and Regulation of Financial Infrastructure and Payment Systems.* Cambridge, MA: The MIT Press, 2020.

Triffin, Robert. "The Myth and Realities of the So-Called Gold Standard." In *The Gold Standard in Theory and History,* Second Edition, edited by Barry Eichengreen and Marc Flandreau, 140–60. London and New York: Routledge, 1997.

Tucker, Paul. *Unelected Power: The Quest for Legitimacy in Central Banking and the Regulatory State.* Princeton: Princeton University Press, 2018.

Ugolini, Stefano. "The Bank of England as the World Gold Market Maker During the Classical Gold Standard Era 1889-1910." In *The Global Gold Market and the International Monetary System from the Late 19th Century to the Present,* edited by Sandra Bott, 64–87. London: Palgrave Macmillan, 2013.

Ugolini, Stefano. "Liquidity Management and Central Bank Strength: Bank of England Operations Reloaded 1889-1910." Norges Bank Working Paper (2016).

Ugolini, Stefano. *The Evolution of Central Banking: Theory and History.* London: Palgrave Macmillan, 2017.

Uittenbogaard, Roland. "Lending by the Bank of Amsterdam (1609–1802)." In *The Bank of Amsterdam*, edited by Marius van Nieuwkerk, 120–31. Amsterdam: Sonsbeek, 2009.

Evolution of Central Banking? De Nederlandsche Bank 1814–1852. Cham: Springer, 2014.

Van Bochove, Christiaan. *The Economic Consequences of the Dutch: Economic Integration around the North Sea, 1500–1800.* Amsterdam: Aksant, 2008.

"Configuring Financial Markets in Preindustrial Europe." *Journal of Economic History* 73, no. 1 (March 2013): 247–78.

Van Cauwenberghe, Eddy and Rainer Metz. "Geld und Währung in den Südlichen Niederlanden Während der Frühen Neuzeit." In *Münzprägung, Geldumlauf und Wechselkurse*, edited by Eddy van Cauwenberghe and Franz Irsigler, 123–50. Trier: Verlag Trierer Historische Forschungen, 1954.

Van de Laar, Henricus J. M. *Opperbankier en Wetenschapsman: Willem Cornelis Mees.* The Hague: Martinus Nijhoff, 1978.

Van der Beek, Marcel, Aleksandr Brzic, and Arent Pol. "The Coinage of the Dutch Republic." In *The Bank of Amsterdam: On the Origins of Central Banking*, edited by Marius van Nieuwkerk, 38–55. Amsterdam: Sonsbeek, 2009.

Van der Oudermeulen, Cornelis. *Recherches sur le commerce ou idées relatives aux intérêts des différens peuples de l'Europe*, Tome 2, Premiere Partie. Amsterdam: D.J. Changuion, 1791.

Van der Wee, Herman. *The Growth of the Antwerp Market and the European Economy (Fourteenth–Sixteenth Centuries). Volume 2: Interpretation.* The Hague: Martinus Nijhoff, 1963.

The Low Countries in the Modern World. Translated by Lizabeth Fackelman. Aldershot: Ashgate, 1993.

Van Dillen, Johannes Gerard. "Een Boek van Phoonsen over de Amsterdamsche Wisselbank." *Economisch-Historisch Jaarboek* 7 (1921): 1–146.

"De Beurscrisis te Amsterdam in 1763." *Tijdschrift voor Geschiedenis* 37 (1922): 241–53.

Bronnen Tot de Geschiedenis der Wisselbanken: (Amsterdam, Middelburg, Delft, Rotterdam) Eerste Stuk. The Hague: Martinus Nijhoff, 1925a.

Bronnen Tot de Geschiedenis der Wisselbanken: (Amsterdam, Middelburg, Delft, Rotterdam) Tweede Stuk. The Hague: Martinus Nijhoff, 1925b.

"Effectenkoersen aan de Amsterdamsche Beurs 1723–1794." *Economisch-Historisch Jaarboek* 17 (1931): 1–46.

"The Bank of Amsterdam." In *History of the Principal Public Banks*, edited by Johannes Gerard van Dillen, 79–124. The Hague: Martinus Nijhoff, 1934.

"Amsterdam als Wereldmarkt der Edele Metalen in de 17de en 18de Eeuw." In *Zeventien Studiën van Nederlanders*, 235–71. The Hague: Martinus Nijhoff, 1964a.

"Bloeitijd der Amsterdamse Wisselbank 1687–1781." In *Mensen en Achtergronden, Studies uitgegeven ter gelegenheid van de tachtigste jaardag van de schrijver*, edited by Johannes Gerard van Dillen, 385–415. Groningen: J.B. Wolters, 1964b.

"Ondergang van de Amsterdamse Wisselbank 1782–1820." In *Mensen en Achtergronden, Studies uitgegeven ter gelegenheid van de tachtigste jaardag van de schrijver,* edited by Johannes Gerard van Dillen, 417–47. Groningen: J.B. Wolters, 1964c.

"Oprichting en Functie der Amsterdamse Wisselbank in de Zeventiende Eeuw, 1609–1686." In *Mensen en Achtergronden, Studies uitgegeven ter gelegenheid van de tachtigste jaardag van de schrijver,* edited by Johannes Gerard van Dillen, 336–84. Groningen: J.B. Wolters, 1964d.

Van Rijkdom en Regenten: handboek tot de economische en sociale geschiedenis van Nederland tijdens de Republiek. The Hague: Martinus Nijhoff, 1970.

Van Nieuwkerk, Marius, ed. *The Bank of Amsterdam: On the Origins of Central Banking.* Amsterdam: Sonsbeek, 2009.

Van Velden, H. "Het kassiersbedrijf te Amsterdam in de 17^e eeuw." *De Economist* 82, no. 1 (December 1933): 48–68.

Van Zanden, Jan Luiten. "Wages and the Standard of Living in Europe, 1500–1800." *European Review of Economic History* 3, no. 2 (August 1999): 175–97.

n.d. "Prices and Wages and the Cost of Living in the Western Part of the Netherlands, 1450–1800." Accessed January 9, 2020. www.iisg.nl/hpw/brenv .php#biblio

Van Zanden, Jan Luiten, and Bas van Leeuwen. "Persistent but Not Consistent: The Growth of National Income in Holland 1347–1807." *Explorations in Economic History* 49, no. 2 (April 2012): 119–30.

Vehse, Eduard. *Geschichte des preußischen Hofs und Adels und der preußischen Diplomatie.* Hamburg: Hoffmann und Campe, 1851.

Velde, François R. "Government Equity and Money: John Law's System in 1720 France." Federal Reserve Bank of Chicago Working Paper no. 2003-31 (November 2003).

"What's a Penny (or a Nickel) Really Worth?" Chicago Fed Letter, no. 235a (February 2007): 1–4.

"Chronicle of a Deflation Unforetold." *Journal of Political Economy* 117, no. 4 (August 2009): 591–634.

"The Neapolitan Banks in the Context of Early Modern Public Banks." Federal Reserve Bank of Chicago Working Paper no. 2018-05 (March 2018).

Velde, François R., Warren Weber, and Randall Wright. "A Model of Commodity Money with Applications to Gresham's Law and the Debasement Puzzle." *Review of Economic Dynamics* 2, no. 1 (January 1999): 293–323.

Veru, Peter Theodore. "Bonds of Independence: The Dutch Era of American Sovereign Finance, 1782–1794." Ph.D. dissertation, University of Colorado, 2018.

"The French Bonds: The Little-Known Bidding War for France's Holdings in American Debt, 1786–1790." *Financial History Review* 28, no. 2 (August 2021a): 1–22.

"Pieter Stadnitski Sharpens the Axe: A Revolutionary Research Report on American Sovereign Finance, 1787." In *Research in Economic History,* edited by C. Hanes and S. Wolcott, 169–99. Bingley: Emerald Publishing Limited, 2021b.

Volckart, Oliver. "Premodern Debasement: A Messy Affair." In *Handbook of the History of Money and Currency,* edited by Stefano Battilossi, Youssef Cassis, Kazuhiko Yago, 177–98. Singapore: Springer, 2018.

Volz, Gustav Berthold, ed. *Die Werke Friedrichs des Großen in deutscher Übersetzung, Volume 7.* Translation by Eberhard König, Friedrich von Oppeln-Bronikowski, and Willy Rath. Berlin: Reimar Hobbing (1913).

Wandschneider, Kirsten. "Landschaften as Credit Purveyors – The Example of East Prussia." *Journal of Economic History* 75, no. 3 (September 2015): 791–818.

Wetterberg, Gunnar. *Money and Power: From Stockholms Banco 1656 to Sveriges Riksbank Today.* Stockholm: Sveriges Riksbank, 2009.

White, Lawrence H. "Competitive Payments Systems and the Unit of Account." *American Economic Review* 74, no. 4 (September 1984): 699–712.

"The Private Mint in Economics: Evidence from the American Gold Rushes. *Economic History Review* 75, no. 1 (2022): 3–21.

Willemsen, René. "The Activities of the Bank of Amsterdam." In *The Bank of Amsterdam,* edited by Marius van Nieuwkerk, 78–91. Amsterdam: Sonsbeek, 2009.

Wilson, Charles. *Anglo-Dutch Commerce and Finance in the Eighteenth Century.* Cambridge: Cambridge University Press, 1941.

Wójtowicz, Grzegorz. "The Origin and History of Polish Money: Part I." *Bank i Kredyt* 37, nos. 11–12 (2006): 3–11.

Zappey, Wilhelmus M. "Porselein en zilvergeld in Weesp." *Hollandse Studiën* 12 (1982): 167–218.

Index